IMAGINING LAW

On Drucilla Cornell

Edited by

RENÉE J. HEBERLE and BENJAMIN PRYOR

STATE UNIVERSITY OF NEW YORK PRESS

Production, Laurie Searl
Marketing, Michael Campochiaro

Library of Congress Cataloging-in-Publication Data

Imagining law : on Drucilla Cornell / edited by Renée J. Heberle,
Benjamin Prayor.
   p. cm. — (SUNY series in gender theory)
   Includes bibliographical references and index.
   ISBN 978-0-7914-7415-0 (hardcover : alk. paper)   1. Cornell,
Drucilla. 2. Feminist theory. 3. Liberalism. 4. Justice.
   I. Heberle, Renee, 1962–   II. Pryor, Benjamin,
1964–
   HQ1190.I43 2008
   301.092—dc22   2007028521

10 9 8 7 6 5 4 3 2 1

Contents

Renée J. Heberle

Introduction

The authors published in this volume consider Drucilla Cornell's contribution to and impact on the several academic disciplines in which she works. They do so from quite diverse perspectives. To comprehensively address Cornell's contributions in one volume is impossible, given that she is actively writing in and widely read in philosophy, political theory, literary criticism, legal studies, women's studies, and lesbian and gay/queer studies. Further, Cornell takes a significantly undisciplined approach to these "disciplines." She draws upon feminism, psychoanalysis, and such very different philosophical voices as Kant, Lacan, Adorno, and Derrida to argue for traditional demands such as rights, dignity, and equality. The quality of these demands becomes radicalized in her hands. The life we would live if they were realized as she describes them becomes open-ended, perhaps more undisciplined in the best possible sense, and certainly more imaginative. Her writing inspires the thinker, the theorist, the academic to consider the lives that are affected by thought in action and encourages activists to think and rethink the ontological and ethical lineages that structure their discourses and practices.

Cornell is on an intellectual journey that leads her in an uncommon direction toward what we might call "postmodern liberalism." We give it a name reluctantly because naming is too often a device of regulation. Naming the "postmodern" has served primarily to obscure fundamental differences among those identified as such but for whom critics wish to have a convenient label against which to work. Worse, it can draw Cornell's writing into relation with the conventional despite its disruptive force. However, while we do not wish to predict where she will go next or from which resources she will find further inspiration for thinking about justice and human dignity, we do believe that the phrase *postmodern liberalism* captures something about the trajectory of Cornell's thinking and practice.

1

Cornell's thinking moves across a vast range of disciplines and issues, offering the reader complex syntheses and new insight into the salience of theorizing to the quality of lived experience. Within this range, there are several critical themes and concepts developed throughout Cornell's work. The first is the rescue of the ideals and practices of justice from conflation with the law. She takes this on in the *Philosophy of the Limit* (1993) as well as in many essays that follow, most recently in *Defending Ideals* (2004). Cornell engages with positivists—those who believe that positive law exhausts the possibilities of justice—and with critics of positivist legal theory, pointing out the positivist impulses implicit in their own work. Why rescue justice from law? Because justice cannot be realized in a final fashion while laws most certainly can, most notably in the form of punishment and death. Further, the law and legality are not mere instruments of justice for Cornell. Law is ultimately about coercion. This fact, along with the regulatory quality of law, shuts down imaginative responses to how implementation of the law always already potentially produces injustices. However, justice is the aspiration that sustains us in thinking critically about and challenging the laws.

When imagining what feminist justice might look like, Cornell moves us beyond the equality/difference debate in feminism. She takes up this theme with the intent of displacing "gender" and thinking instead about "sex" as the focal point. Gender keeps us trapped in the dualism of seeking equality for already identified men and women and sustains a paradigm wherein women are compared to men. Further, it fails to recognize the fluid and changeable quality of sexed or sexuate being. Cornell wants to shift our attention from gender to sex and, perhaps even more important, to include the discussion of freedom in our legal strategies that address equality. She says:

> Of course the demand to be freed from this measure of gender comparison is made in the name of freedom, not in the name of neutered selves. Indeed, because sexual freedom demands that we be able to recognize the hold that gender forms have upon us, both as confinement and as exclusion, the questions of who we are as sexed creatures must be asked at the beginning of every theory of justice. Further, a concept of right that recognizes this freedom must be tailored to provide space for imagining sexual difference. (*At the Heart of Freedom: Feminism, Sex, and Equality*, 1998, 6, hereafter HF)

In moving beyond the equality/difference debate to discuss such issues as abortion, pornography, sexual harassment, and kinship/family arrangements, Cornell deploys an original concept for understanding the self affected by these questions. We cannot understand Cornell's critique of mainstream and feminist legal theory without describing her conceptualization of the 'imaginary domain.' The imaginary domain is the place of the self in relation. Cornell develops her thinking about the imaginary domain in a book of that title, with a subtitle, *Abortion, Pornography, and Sexual Harassment* (1995, hereafter

ID). She returns to the nature and importance of, and further develops her thinking about, the imaginary domain in *Heart of Freedom*. The imaginary domain is more a set of possibilities than a thing. Conceptually it presupposes several arguments that Cornell takes up in various places in her work: "that a person is not something 'there' . . . but a possibility, an aspiration which, because it is that, can never be fulfilled once and for all" (ID, 5). That sex is a (not "the") definitive aspect of the self. "Sex is so basic to who we are that when we imagine ourselves, sex is always already in the picture. Most of us know that on some level. All of us live as sexed beings" (ID, 6). This notion of sex as basic to who we are leads Cornell to identify us as "sexuate beings" and to claim that sexuate being is not easily subjected to rational scrutiny, assessment, regulation, or construction. This latter argument emerges from Cornell's commitment to a modified Lacanian framework for understanding not only the imaginary domain but also how it is that under current conditions sexuate being is distorted and disciplined under the weight of heterosexist and patriarchal norms. Cornell argues we see ourselves so deeply and profoundly from the inside as always already sexed beings that we cannot easily, if at all, separate ourselves from what she calls our "sexuate self."

Cornell places the right to the development of our sexuate being as central to her conception of justice, suggesting, perhaps controversially, not only the essential importance of our sexedness to our sense of self but also that the capacity of each person to develop an integrated sense of a sexuate self is one of the most important aspects of personhood the law can protect. As her position develops in the *Imaginary Domain* and *Heart of Freedom* through discussions of abortion, pornography, and adoption, among other issues, it is clear that her sense of the terms on which our "sexed self" develops, if left as much alone as possible by the law, is quite open-ended. While abiding by and deploying the harm principle (famously articulated by John Stuart Mill) Cornell clearly wishes to deconstruct the deeply moralistic and normative effects legal interpretation and practices (and some feminist interpretation and practice) have had as they identify and enforce "appropriate" limits to sexuate being. One need only refer to the controversy over gay marriage to see how deeply those moralistic and normative beliefs are held by those who promote them. Cornell's work is an excellent intervention and counter to dominant legal practices regarding sexuality and sexuate being that reflect and enforce those beliefs.

While Cornell has a radical feminist's sensitivity as to the harms done to the feminine sexed identity by patriarchy (thought in Lacanian terms by Cornell) and by apparently neutral legal categories, she takes a very different path, which, drawing heavily upon the liberal tradition dating from Immanuel Kant, places strict constraints on the law. She critiques any reliance on the law that suggests it can or should offer the gift of freedom. Her liberalism shines through as she argues the limits of law in making us "be good," by positively identifying community norms and legislating accordingly. For Cornell, the law is there to prevent harm being done, not to promote the good. It is the subtle differences in Cornell's argument that make all the difference, however, between her liberal legalism and a more mainstream liberal legalism. For example, quoting Kant, Cornell argues, "No one can compel me to be happy in accordance with his conception of the welfare of others, for each may seek his happiness in whatever way he sees fit, so long as he does not *infringe* upon the freedom of others to pursue a similar end which can be reconciled with the freedom of everyone else" (ID, 11). We emphasize "infringe" because Cornell will replace it with the more precise "degrade." As long as we do not degrade the rights of others to pursue their definition of happiness, the law should not intervene. It is the degradation of marginal identities—whether those identities are associated with femininity, homosexuality, the transgendered, or transsexuality, all having to do with sexuate being—that Cornell is most concerned with. She argues that "infringe" throws too wide a net to capture the harms that matter. To degrade is to deny the worthiness of the self in question to pursue sexual happiness.

From her very earliest work it becomes clear that Cornell is centrally concerned with developing a critical philosophy that will transform our present without quite knowing what that transformation might bring in the future. The relationships among the past, present, and future that she addresses in different places in her writings are complex. She is an unabashed idealist, centrally concerned about how we imagine ourselves, not how we "know" ourselves either in terms of our material circumstance or in terms of our capacity for reason. We should in fact take special note, as we think about the place of the ideal in Cornell's work, that the imagination displaces knowledge as the critical moment. Even if we "know" something cannot be fully achieved, for example, a coherent self, our imagining of that self, of that possibility, in the moment is nonetheless critical to the ongoing project of becoming a person. It is this freedom to imagine rather than to know in any final way who we are that Cornell emphasizes. This sustains her argument in light of powerful critiques of essentialism and of identity politics recently put forward in the field of feminist political theory.

We open the volume with a chapter by Roger Berkowitz, which captures Cornell's commitment to imagination, to thinking beyond our selves as limited beings. He places Cornell's faith (always a future-oriented condition) in thinking against Heidegger's settlement with thinking (always a present-oriented condition with a problematic relationship, perhaps a nostalgic one, to the past) and outlines a challenge for critical legal theorists in an era when thinking (theorizing) feels like the last thing upon which anyone should be spending any time. As noted above, Cornell's work challenges those who would conflate law and justice or evacuate the possibility of justice from the law through positivist or avowedly realist/postmodern critique. According to Berkowitz, Cornell thus "rejects the spurious conclusion that the indeterminacy of rules requires the absence of justice. . . . Contra Stanley Fish, Cornell argues that the uncontroversial fact of indeterminacy means that justice can never be reduced to a mechanism of validation" (15 this volume). Berkowitz fleshes out Cornell's critical theory of the imagination. He shows her debt to Kant but also how she moves away from Kant's command theory of law. In her rethinking of freedom, Cornell insists upon the pursuit of a community-in-law not grounded in reason but in a more open-ended sense of imagined possibilities. The philosophy of the limit is ultimately about living within the paradox created by the inherent finitude of being human and the needs of/for community. Law will be part of that, but not the final arbiter of justice. Berkowitz's chapter shows us how Cornell works through these paradoxes inherent in the relations among freedom, community, and law.

If Berkowitz's chapter elaborates and builds upon Cornell's thinking about freedom in relation to law, Adam Thurschwell's "Radical Feminist Liberalism" is a finely tuned exegesis of Cornell's feminism. Thurschwell highlights how Cornell moves from an emphasis on equality, long struggled for by "radical" and "liberal" feminists, to an emphasis on freedom. Freedom is the ends to which equality is the means, after all. In and of itself, equality means little if it is not oriented toward what Cornell identifies as our freedom to imagine and become (perhaps never quite hitting the status of "being") ourselves. Cornell radicalizes liberal notions about the protection of individual liberty with the conceptualization, described above, of the self as guided in its becoming through the imaginary domain. Thurschwell effectively shows how her liberalism proscribes the role of the state in ways many feminists may disagree with, arguing that if freedom is the end we seek, and not "equality" as an end in itself, then the imaginary domain must be allowed the space to range beyond the "normal" until, as mentioned earlier in this introduction, it moves to degrade what is other to it.

The issue of liberal universalism, the universalism of such ideals as equality and individual freedom, is quite current in feminist theory. Karin Van Marle's chapter takes up questions related to liberal universalism through putting Cornell's ideas into dialogue with those of Martha Nussbaum and Iris Marion Young. Her chapter carefully outlines the difference Cornell's and Young's theory makes in imagining/constituting just forms of human relations. She argues that they take particularity and difference into account as central rather than peripheral concerns as feminists think across and attempt to disrupt conventional boundaries that delimit identity. Van Marle takes Cornell's ideas to ground, so to speak, in looking at decisions of the Supreme Court of South Africa about claims of substantive unequal treatment under the law, specifically Section 9 of the South African Constitution, which protects the right to equality. Reviewing two significant cases, she concludes that even the effort to attend to substantive equality fails as the Court continues to place persons in groups prior to examination of their particular context and situation. Whether the Court is placing individual claimants into groups of privileged background or in groups of disadvantaged background (vulnerable and "needy"), this approach will not do justice to the particularity of the selves that come before the Court and ask for the freedom to continue to become who they are. We must somehow break with the habit of universalizing the context of the other, whether that other appears to be of the privileged class or of the disadvantaged. This is not to understand each person coming before the Court as an individual prior to his or her context. It is to see individuals as such *within* their context.

While Thurschwell and Van Marle take up Cornell's postmodern liberalism in an affirmative fashion, J. Bernstein critiques her work with the argument that her thinking about the imaginary domain is incomplete. He wants to bring recognitive theory and an awareness of the embodied status of identity to bear on Cornell's thinking. He says that "what she requires is an account that binds what it is to have a sexual identity *uberhaupt* to the imaginative projection of that identity, and then, further, make that imaginative projection a necessary condition of individuated action." (84 this volume) In other words, to prevent the imaginary domain from being merely mental space, or "imagination" in the traditional sense, Bernstein argues it must be a component of action, of projection, of recognitive relations with otherness. He suggests that Sartre's theory of action "that ties action and imagination together through the projection of a revisable identity that forms the horizon of all one's action," (84 this volume) with Simone de Beauvoir's feminist assertion that there is no "I" without a gender qualification works to supplement Cornell's Lacanian thesis about the self.

Benjamin Pryor also suggests an absence in Cornell's thinking, but a far more present absence than that identified by Bernstein. Pryor wonders at the absence of Nietzsche in Cornell's work, given that the philosophers with whom she engages, Derrida, Irigaray, Heidegger, Levinas, are "Nietzschean" in orientation. He wonders about the significance of this absence and about the implications for her work if Nietzsche were to be made more present. Pryor writes specifically in response to Cornell's well-established commitment to liberal ideals. He acknowledges the radical fashion in which she approaches these ideals but wonders at the quality of the approach itself. As discussed in several of these chapters, for Cornell, values are the limit, not the precondition of the law. Even given the "not there yet" quality of our relationship to ideals that Cornell emphasizes again and again, Pryor suggests hesitation is called for in the presence of the "demand that values and ideals orient our approach, even to questions of law." What does the presence of Nietzsche, a presence only indirectly present in Cornell's actual work, do to the presentation of ideals so central to Cornell's thinking?

While the chapters discussed above consider Cornell's thinking about liberalism and freedom, the next three take up the themes of evil and the possibilities of witnessing. Carolin Emcke's and Sara Murphy's meditations on dignity and the problem of witnessing take up the challenge Cornell issues as to how the force of thinking, of philosophy, is indeed an active, transformative force in the world, even in the light of the most difficult and ambiguous of social relations, those of bearing witness to the suffering of others. Their chapters address the question of whether our "thinking," in this case, Cornell's thinking and writing about her mother's death in her book *Between Women and Generations* (2004, herein BWG), understood by Cornell as an act of witnessing, can make any difference at all. Clearly they believe it can. Emcke, however, challenges Cornell to come to terms with the potential for the total erasure of dignity and to sustain her commitment to bearing witness in spite of that erasure. Murphy suggests that Cornell is indeed engaged in a project of bearing witness to women's dignity throughout this book but that in assuming a dignity prior to the web of relationships she describes each of the women in the book to be caught up in, she obscures the radical potential of her own work.

Emcke asks whether dignity is a kind of capacity to act, to resist in the face of overwhelming odds, the most extreme being ongoing, systematic torture, the end of which the victim cannot see. This is classically represented as the treatment of those interned at Auschwitz but could apply to those currently at Guantanamo Bay or in the prisons of Saudi Arabia and Burma. Cornell argues for human dignity as something only "we" can recognize or acknowledge, "even in the face of the dead piled up as corpses that calls us to witness to the full horror of what we have done to each other" ("Thinking the Future," 4). Nazis typically are a kind of "other" in the imagination of the West. Critical theorists ranging from Adorno to Foucault (indirectly) have shown that "they" are indeed always potentially "us." Cornell suggests as much in calling the Holocaust something "we have done to each other" rather than claiming that we can, through the recognition of dignity as a metaphysical fact, see how horrible "they" are. In a sense this shows the importance of arguing dignity as a metaphysical fact, suggesting that the Nazis would have been capable of acknowledging the dignity of those they identified as "others," making their crimes all the more horrific. However, it begs the question Caroline Emcke raises as to whether dignity is not a metaphysical fact, but can be "seen" only in its denial, in the confrontation with bad treatment, in the moment of resistance, as a transgressive assertion of humanity, which, for example, Cornell's mother implicitly engages in spite of statutory laws against assisted suicide and God's law against suicide generally. This relates to Sara Murphy's questioning of Cornell's assumption that dignity is related to autonomy. Does dignity demand the presence of the other in the act not only of witnessing as argued by Emcke, but also in the very project of subject constitution? Is not the difficulty of witnessing wrapped in our "inescapably heteronomous origins" as always already constituted subjects? If dignity is contextual in the way suggested above, only seen in resistance against historical phenomena, then it is not a metaphysical fact. It is something to be valued and witnessed but is not a predictable point of departure as to setting out rules for human conduct or human relations.

Murphy further articulates the difficulties of doing a genealogy of women's relationships in a culture saturated with symbolic images of male genealogies.

Cornell's story shows that women's lives are lived in relation, but not relations of their own making. The demand to bear witness to these relations is no less urgent. Feminism is about engaging the impossible. That is precisely Cornell's project, as Murphy argues, in this volume, and I would suggest, in the rest of her work as well.

In his meditation on evil, Martin J. Beck Matustík identifies a suspicion at the heart of our affirmation of ideals and at the heart of the imaginary domain. He argues through a reading of Cornell in relation to Adorno (through Kant) and Benjamin that to conceive of the ideal of humanity and the resistance to radical evil it entails is to think evil as the limit of those ideals. The task of critical theory is to mark and to measure the radical limit of ideals in the banality of evil, the reverence for progress, and the cruelty—he names it religious cruelty—at the heart of the desire to inhabit truth. Matustík raises the possibility not only that evil limits ideals in our most devoted and reverent attempt to realize them but also that Cornell's cautious idealism—recalled in other essays as her constant attention to threats to dignity that inhabit law, legal philosophy, and institutions in the context of a recollection of justice—can lead us to recall our humanity even as we acknowledge the possibility of cruelty that is its inheritance. Matustík asks us to judge our "selves" as human in what he seems to think are our most intensely human moments (of despair, zeal, cruelty, reverence, and failure) from a perspective that is at once open and excessive, like the imaginary domain. His chapter appeals to us to admit that the ever-present possibility of failure before the wholly other is there at the limit of ideals and, for the critical theorist, shows us a way out of cruelty.

Our volume concludes with a three pieces related to the question of multiculturalism. The piece by Cornell and Sara Muphy, and that written by Pheng Cheah, are reprinted from a symposium originally published in Philosophy and Social Criticism (2002). The final piece is by Elizabeth Grosz. Grosz takes her thinking from an original response to Cornell and Murphy's piece and weaves it into a discussion of her recent critical work on feminist thinking about evolution/history, or, as it is more commonly discussed, the "nature/culture" divide in feminism. We chose to reprint the first two chapters as they bring the complexly interwoven strands of the theoretical work accomplished by Cornell to bear on a well-worn issue. They show how, as in the case of the equality/difference debate in feminism, her thinking infuses life into this issue by raising new questions about apparently trampled political ground. Grosz's chapter is an excellent end piece for this volume as it exemplifies feminist theory that draws apparently unrelated issues together into an unexpected relation and thus moves theory forward.

Pheng Cheah asks, "If we say that the recognition of authentic cultural identity is 'bad' because it violates human dignity, then we have to ask, what is the nature of humanity 'as such' that it possesses this thing called 'dignity' that should not be violated?" (204, this volume) Like Carolyn Emcke, Cheah asks Cornell, what is the relationship between being human and having dignity? What is this thing called "dignity" that we must have in order to be recognized as fully human by others?

Cheah explores this question by thinking about the quality of the faculty of "imagination," more fully than Cornell does in her work. The quality of this faculty is not, however, where his concern with Cornell and Murphy's chapter lies. His chapter takes up the meaning of the term they use to describe the giving of recognition to others, *affordance*. Who or what will afford the space for the imagination, as it conceives and reconceives the self in a world bereft of theological or naturalized sources of authority? Cheah turns to Heidegger to theorize 'affordance' as self-giving and the imagination as a process of giving that "does not emanate from human consciousness but instead from the irreducible temporalization that makes possible (human) existence" (14). Cheah concludes that Cornell and Murphy's critique of authenticity and subsequent affirmation of a more limited form of multicultural identification is adequate to the historically specific context of constitutional democracies wherein civil society (in the Hegelian sense) is developed and may "afford" such space. However, in other contexts conditioned by global capitalism, this "self-giving" is not so affirmative. Aboriginal persons whose lives in communities have been made possible by their proximity to resources global capitalism now wants may take up forms of artificially authentic identifications that necessarily trap them, subjecting them to governmentality, even as it frees them from what Benedict Anderson described as "malign neglect" as the resources that give them life are plundered by capitalist interests. Such trade-offs are not taken into account in Cornell and Murphy's piece. They must be taken into account if we are to have an adequate accounting of who, what, when, and how affordance of psychic space (as reconceptualized by Cheah) is freeing.

Elizabeth Grosz's chapter brings together discussions of the concept of 'futurity', of 'evolution', and of 'identity politics'. It begins by highlighting an otherwise oblique theme in Cornell's work, that of the relationships among the past, present, and future. Feminists have taken what Grosz identifies as two approaches to the question of the future, one extrapolating directly from present conditions to argue (discover?) the future implicit in them and another creating new worlds, probably utopian, but always other than what is. Grosz suggests that Cornell, following Irigaray, takes another approach to futurity, which suggests the new is sustained within present conditions but unseeable with them. The future is never, thus, predictable, but open-ended. For Cornell it is the concept of the 'imaginary domain' that does the work of holding open the possibility of freedom that is the future. Grosz then offers a gloss on her recent work on the critical potential of thinking about evolution for undermining the tenacity of the now unhelpful nature/culture divide in feminist thought. She goes on to take up Cornell and Murphy's chapter on multiculturalism, critiquing their continued adherence to a paradigm of recognition for thinking about identity and political/social/cultural rights. Ultimately Grosz draws a connection between her understanding of evolution and a Nietzschean understanding of the subject as protean, an effect rather than a cause of activity and forces beyond its control but always ultimately subject to its impact. It is this subject Grosz suggests will be the subject of the "new" world of multicultural justice. Grosz's chapter does work on multiple levels within feminist theory, exemplifying the kind of interdisciplinary approach and the bringing together of unexpected ideas and concepts that has also made Cornell's work so helpful in moving feminism forward.

The chapters in this volume are eclectic in form and substance. They are written by authors from various disciplines. Some are more meditative and suggestive and some more traditionally scholarly in tone. The volume as a whole is a provocation to be "undisciplined" as we seek out the theoretical and intellectual resources that will help us see past a present conditioned by reactionary and regressive politics. They do not pretend to engage all the possibilities Cornell's work opens up but lead us down different paths, pushed by the urgency of the questions provoked by her work.

Inspired by the critical readings published here, Cornell's response to the papers offers the reader further clarification of, but no final conclusions about, her thinking. She elaborates on her thinking about the concept of the imaginary. She expands on the relationship of her theorizing to Kant and Hegel and to Levinas and Heidegger. And, importantly, she defends the somatic quality of the feminine personhood we might imagine beyond the reach of patriarchy. She offers breadth and depth in her response while exploring the significance of symbolic objects as they highlight the urgency of questions raised in her work. Her response provokes thinking about self/other relations, what it is to become a self, and about recollective/collective memory and its relationship to the imagined future.

Cornell clearly understands thinking to be a form of action. I have always had a tangled relationship to my "role" as a thinker/teacher. Cornell's work and avowed commitment to thought as radical practice does not settle anything for me. However, her response, and indeed this volume as a whole are emblematic of the potential radicalism inherent in ongoing, respectful yet determinedly agonistic dialogue among those of us who choose to think beyond what is given and imagine beyond what seems possible.

It is in light of the above that we might mention Cornell's initiation and involvement in the Ubuntu Project in South Africa. She mentions this work briefly in her response at the conclusion of this volume. However, readers may become more familiar with it as described in Cornell's own words by going to www.fehe.org and clicking on Drucilla Cornell. They will find there a preliminary report or reflection on interviews Cornell has conducted and further projects that have stemmed from her visits to South Africa over the past several years.

Roger Berkowitz

Transcendence and Finitude in Drucilla Cornell's *Philosophy of the Limit*

A t the end of my first year of graduate school, I was bored. Faced with the reduction of thinking to politics on the one hand and the perversion of thinking into an indulgent pastime on the other, I was experiencing firsthand the anti-intellectualism that now pervades our elite colleges and universities. Yet, from out of the swamp that is the American academy, two discoveries gave me hope. One was the encounter with the thought of Martin Heidegger through my mentor in Berkeley, Philippe Nonet. The other was the work of Drucilla Cornell.

I had never heard of Cornell when I was assigned *The Philosophy of the Limit* in a seminar in the Berkeley rhetoric department in 1992. What struck me in that book—struck me so hard that I sought out the author and, with her blessing, took a leave of absence from graduate school to journey back across the country to study with her for six months—was its *force of thinking*.

Philosophy and thinking matter for Cornell in the deepest sense of the word: philosophy itself "*does* have practical consequences; the practical consequences are precisely that law cannot *inevitably* shut out its challengers and prevent transformation, at least not on the basis that the law itself demands that it do so" (*Philosophy of the Limit*, 165; hereafter PL). Unlike those who enlist philosophy in political causes, Cornell's politics demands that she engage in the activity of philosophy itself. By continually and rigorously pointing to the impossibility of a closed and actualized knowledge of the good, philosophy makes room for utopian dreams and justice. The force of philosophy is to open a space for living justly.

Her devotion to the forceful importance of the *idea* of justice has led Cornell to be called a dreamer, a utopian, and an idealist. She is unapologetically all three. But what is often forgotten is that Cornell's utopia is founded upon a relentless probing of her fundamental concern: the possible unity of freedom and law—a unity that itself has its ground in the activity of thinking.

11

This chapter situates Cornell's work within a specific tradition of thinking the belonging together of law and freedom. From Kant to Heidegger, the possibility of freedom amidst legal obligation is one of the central questions of political and ethical philosophy. Following both Kant and Heidegger, Cornell thinks freedom as the free embrace of obligation. At the same time, Cornell insists that contemporary thinkers take seriously the radical meaninglessness—the absence of both freedom and obligation—that threatens the modern condition. Suspicious of both Kant's turn to a universal law of reason and Heidegger's free embrace of man's finite legal inheritance, Cornell accepts the increasingly widespread view that all meaning and all law are without ground. What is needed, Cornell argues, is a freely accepted embrace of law within and amidst the recognition of radical nihilism. Her insistence that finite beings can and must live in the paradoxical state of commitment to law in the face of the fact of law's meaninglessness is the ethical center of her work.[1]

Cornell's philosophical inquiries gather their force from her conviction that the force of thinking can and does change the world. The force of thinking, in other words, is an active force that furthers justice. However, to say that the philosophy of the limit is the active force of justice is to locate Cornell's thinking on the plane of ontology. This is to use a language that Cornell frequently does not. Yet, if the philosophy of the limit *is* justice, and if justice is that part of law that must be vigilantly protected in its distinction from law, then the philosophy of the limit is a characterization of the essential way in which the law *is*. Understood as the philosophy of the limit, law *is* the thinking of the absolute (the metaphysical dream of universal justice) from the position of human finitude (the limit). As one crossroads where the absolute and the finite meet in human experience, law is a space of paradox—a space of the necessary encounter of the impossible dream of justice.

Before law and freedom can happen in the space opened by the paradox of justice, justice itself must be freed from its particular manifestations. Cornell will never tire of showing us that no theory of justice can ever actualize justice in the world. Man's finitude, his radical inability to know the absolute and bring it to life, ensures that the communal project of transcendence must always remain an aspiration and thus without end. Law, like thinking, can never come to an end. It is for this reason that Cornell's thinking about law takes as its point of departure—and must do so—her critique of legal positivism in all of its motley modern manifestations.

POSITIVISM

The philosophy of the limit, at once the title of Cornell's first book and her name for ethical philosophy, has many resonances. Overtly, it is the name that she gives to the aspect of deconstruction that carries forward the Kantian critical project. In this respect, the philosophy of the limit is thought from out of the fact of human finitude. More specifically, as a way of thinking about law for a finite being such as man, the philosophy of the limit gives voice to the demand that justice not be reduced to law. "[T]he philosophy of the limit protects the divide between law and justice, and protects justice from being encompassed by whatever convention described as the good of the community" (PL, 118). If the philosophy of the limit means anything, it means the care for the difference between positive law and law as the manifestation of justice.

By simultaneously protecting justice against the encroachment of law while insisting that law recall its connection to justice, the philosophy of the limit offers one of the legal academy's most inspired critiques of positivism. What the dry word *positivism* names is the loss of the beyond. Positivism is the doctrine that asserts that truth and justice are, in the highest instance, determined by reasons; as rational, law is grounded upon either natural or social facts. This means that the common claim that positive law emerges out of the drive for legal certainty is of only secondary importance. The desire for and belief in legal certainty is an outgrowth of a prior positivist understanding of the world—one that locates the source of law in scientifically knowable rational principles.

Positive laws, of course, are nothing new; the distinction between a natural *ratio scripta* and willful positive law is ancient. Yet there are two ways in which the relation between rationalism and positivism can be conceived. First, positive law can be understood as the posited expression of a transcendent and esoteric justice. Second, positive law can be understood as the source of justice. The doctrine of legality, for example, asserts that justice is nothing other than the conformity with law (*Gesetzmäßigkeit*). If written law was traditionally understood as simply a positive expression of a true, just, and yet ineffable idea of the good, the distinctive characteristic of modern positive law is the absolute denial of the knowability and thus the power of the good. In its contemporary form, positive law is a way of knowing law that imagines justice to inhere in the posited law itself. As a social fact, justice is knowable, calculable, and useful. This is what is meant by the victory of positive law.[2]

Cornell's opposition to positivism may seem unremarkable given the fact that positivism has a largely pejorative connotation in American legal theory.[3] It is important to see, however, that nearly all of the legal theorists who understand themselves to be anti-positivist critics of positivism are unwitting positivists. Stanley Fish, Jürgen Habermas, and Ronald Dworkin are Cornell's favored targets. What unites all of these critics of positivism as positivists is their inability and unwillingness to hold open the possibility that justice has ethical force beyond its social and normative instantiation in laws, conventions, and norms.

Ronald Dworkin is perhaps the most surprising name on Cornell's list of positivist legal thinkers. Dworkin has made his reputation as a normative critic of H. L. A. Hart's legal positivism. Normative jurisprudence, however, has a double sense. While *normative* connotes moral or ethical principles, its root sense is normal. As a normalization, norms are regulative in the way that habits and usages form themselves, over time, into rules of normal conduct. For a normative thinker such as Dworkin, law has its source not in reason and not in the good, but in social norms.

Dworkin's normative theory fully accepts the basic positivist orientation that equates law and justice. Law, he argues, flows "from the principles of justice, fairness, and procedural due process that provide the best constructive interpretation of the *community's legal practice*."[4] Hercules, Dworkin's mythical judge, must judge according to a knowable principle of justice that is itself founded upon a norm of community behavior. Justice, in other words, is identified with existing social and legal norms. Insofar as Dworkin conflates justice with the best interpretation of community practices, he blurs the distinction between law and justice.

Similarly, Habermas blurs the distinction between the facticity of legal decisions and the validity of legal norms. Since legitimacy cannot be grounded in metaphysical or religious bonds, Habermas seeks legitimacy in the factical decisions of procedural democracy. As Niklas Luhman has seen, Habermas seems to collapse the distinction between legality and legitimacy in favor of legality so that justice is identified with legitimacy guaranteed by existing legal norms.[5] Similarly, Cornell sees the essence of Habermas's positivism in his belief that "majority rule is analogized to the search for truth by the community, grounded only in rational will-formation."[6] By denying any ideal of justice beyond the activity of legalist discourse, Habermas cannot but subordinate law to the social fact of legitimacy.

What unites Habermas and Dworkin as unwitting positivist critics of positivism is their inability and unwillingness to hold open the possibility that justice has ethical force beyond its ultimately social and normative instantiation in laws, discourse, and norms. Since both Dworkin and Habermas root law in positive social practices, judges and legal actors are required to don rose-colored glasses to guide their legal interpretations.[7] But the question remains: If the principles that guide interpretation are themselves grounded in communal practices and, in the end, a "pre-interpretive consensus,"[8] how are Dworkin's Hercules and Habermas's ideal speech situation to escape the tyranny of actually existing social norms? In the end, Dworkin and Habermas both violate Cornell's first principle: to preserve the difference between existing positive laws and the ideal of justice. For Dworkin and Habermas, law and justice are the same.

The dominance of legal positivism ranges far beyond normative legal theorists such as Dworkin and Habermas and includes as well practitioners of feminist and critical legal studies. Stanley Fish, for example, is named as the representative of the "most recent and sophisticated brand of legal positivism" (PL 158). As does much of contemporary jurisprudence, Fish begins with the claim of indeterminacy. Since there is no transcendental good that can constrain legal interpretation, judges are thrown back on their own best efforts to determine the good. And since these judges are socially constructed players within the system of legal rules and principles, there is no exit from the socio-logically closed system of law. All legal decisions are just that, decisions, from which Fish concludes that justice, like the text of literature, has no meaning-ful existence. "For Fish," Cornell writes, "the identification of law with justice is inevitable" (PL, 144).

Fish and other "indeterminist" legal theorists are so captivated by their joy in pointing out the indeterminacy of rules that they don't bother to ask: why has the long-acknowledged fact of legal indeterminacy suddenly come to be seen as so important? This question is especially pertinent because for thousands of years of legal thinking, the indeterminacy of rules was not con-sidered incompatible with just legal practice. From Plato's Statesman to the twelve tables in Rome to the natural law of Kings, law has resisted the equally ancient desire that it be set into ordered and knowable rules. Rather than in-determinacy itself, the new claim of modern critical legal scholars is simply that the unavoidable openness of law is a sin.[9]

Cornell sees through the false radicalism of the indeterminacy thesis. As a result, she can reject the spurious conclusion that the indeterminacy of rules re-quires the absence of justice (PL, 101). Instead of pointing to the evacuation of justice from an indeterminate law, Cornell argues that the indeterminacy of rules makes manifest that law cannot be reduced to positive law. Since "inter-pretation always takes us beyond the mere appeal to the status quo," law "cannot be reduced to a self-generated and self-validating set of cognitive norms" (PL 102). Fish does see law as just such a self-validating mechanism, a "machine" that "functions to erase the mystical foundations of its own authority" (PL 158). Contra Fish, Cornell argues that the uncontroversial fact of indeterminacy means that justice can never be reduced to a mechanism of validation.

The mistake Fish makes—and here he is hardly distinguishable from Dwor-kin and Habermas—is to forget that the interpretation of law always demands an appeal to justice and the good beyond the law. Interpretative judgments, therefore, demand an attention to the distinction between law and justice. A positivist approach to law, in other words, is as impossible as it is dangerous.

THE ABSOLUTE AND THE COMMUNITY OF JUSTICE

Against positivism, Cornell insists upon the "*aspiration* to the ideal of commu-nity" (PL 40). While it might seem surprising to find Cornell idealizing com-munity, her italicized emphasis on "*aspiration*" and the focus on the "*ideal*" of community radically separates her from advocates of communitarianism. The dream of community is—as an aspiration and an ideal—essentially different from community itself.

In her chapter "The 'Postmodern' Challenge to the Ideal of Commu-nity," Cornell rehearses the abiding danger of community. As the source and ground of the norms underlying normative visions of positive law, claims of community insist upon unity. Catholics, Jews, and Muslims are unified by necessary moral and theological commitments just as Americans, Israelis, and Saudis are unified by necessary legal and moral obligations. By privileging unity, communities set the whole above the individual and "can do violence to difference and particularity" (PL, 39).

Even Hegel, who seeks a "true unity" in which the community and each person accord each other reciprocal recognition, eventually sacrifices individual particularity and difference to the overwhelming identity of thinking. The ultimate priority of logic in Hegel's system is itself grounded in Hegel's commitment to the rationality of the world and its necessary ground in logic as the kind of thinking that offers grounds.[10] Thus Hegel ultimately sacrifices particularity to the universality of reason and logic in a way that enables the political subordination of the individual to the community.[11]

In spite of her deep suspicion of claims to community and unity, Cornell explicitly rejects calls to abandon the dream of community. On the contrary, the possibility of law and justice demands the universality of community. She writes that "law is embedded in ontology, in a shared social reality" (PL, 107). The law, in other words, requires a universal conception of the good that is only possible within a shared communal space. All law and all legal interpretation requires a "projection of a horizon of the good within the *nomos* of any given legal system" (PL, 93). The good, by which is meant justice as that which is not captured in positive law, is the claim of universal justice that, as universal, cannot exist apart from an idealized and communal unity of persons.

It is helpful to compare Cornell's cautious embrace of communalism with Aristotle's own cautious embrace of Plato's communism in the *Politics*. Against the Socratic proposal for the community of women and children in the *Republic*, Aristotle offers a qualified critique of his teacher. While granting that it is best for a community to be as unified as possible,[12] he writes that "if the process of unification advances beyond a certain point, the polis will not be a polis at all; for a polis essentially consists of a multitude of persons, and if its unification is carried beyond a certain point, the polis will be reduced to family and family to individual. . . . So that even if any lawgiver were able to unify the state, he must not do so, for he will destroy it in the process."[13] Confronted with Plato's claim that the best polis is the most unified polis, Aristotle sees that the political unity of a community must allow for difference: "And not only does a city consist of a multitude of men, it consists of men differing in kind."[14] The political community, in other words, must be unified in a way that allows for difference.[15]

What Aristotle makes manifest is that politics demands not simply a *unification* of a multitude, but the unification of a *multitude*. As Cornell writes, borrowing from Martin Heidegger's discussion of the belonging together of man and being: to belong together as a plurality requires that we envision a new way of "belonging together," one that understands *belonging* together differently from "belonging *together*" (PL, 45).[16] Cornell's gloss on Heidegger's emphasis makes clear that what she seeks is a communal unity that does not simply accommodate difference but welcomes and treasures what makes each person unique amidst their sameness.

Cornell's effort to think *belonging* together differently is an attempt to "approach 'diversity in unity'" (PL, 37). As she writes: "The power of communalism as a dream lies in the chance of uncovering or having revealed to us a different way of belonging together, which does not revert to classic individualism and which is also not just the identification of the individual with the community in mass society" (PL, 60). Communalism is thus Cornell's ideal of the shared *belonging* togetherness of a multitude that privileges belonging over togetherness. Such a belonging, however, cannot happen without a sense of the universal and the absolute as the aspirational ideal of communal life. Communalism, therefore, necessarily retains a nonpositivist moment of idealism.

The ideal of communalism, "as an *ideal*, expresses the recognition of the sameness and difference that marks each one of us as an individual and thus as both different and the same" (PL, 60). Only if we are struck by the truth of our sameness as well as our difference is it possible that we can belong together in a way that strives for the actualization of a communal *nomos* while also respecting the meaningful differences that separate us.

Whether such a belonging together is *really* possible (realizable, from the Latin *res*) is, of course, not centrally important for Cornell. As Cornell writes in *At the Heart of Freedom*, "A good definition of *utopian* is that what is possible cannot be known in advance of social transformation."[17] The utopian moment that pervades all of Cornell's writing is neither a policy prescription nor a pie-in-the-sky fantasy. Instead, it is an argument for the centrality of imagination to human thinking.

THE TRANSCENDENTAL IMAGINATION AND THE HUMILITY OF JUSTICE

Beyond the posited world of social fact, the aspirational nature of communal justice means that justice—at least when viewed from one side—exists as an imagined ideal. The ontological claim that justice is an imagined ideal cannot be minimized. Justice, as a call to the beyond of the real, is precisely that imagined ideal that is the condition of the possibility of communal being together. Togetherness, in other words, requires the transcendental imagination of the ideal of justice that unites a multitude into a people.

The specific path that the imaginary ideal takes toward transcendence shifts throughout Cornell's work. In *Philosophy of the Limit*, the ideal is figured alternatively as "the other" that marks the ethical relation (PL 99) and the "Good" as the "Law of the Law," that is the responsibility to the other that calls us to justice (PL, 100). Later, in both *The Imaginary Domain* and *At the Heart of Freedom*, the form of the imaginary ideal is identified as the person.

The person, from the Latin *per-sonare* (literally, in English, "to sound through"), "is that which shines through. For a person to be able to shine through, she must first be able to imagine herself as whole even if she knows that she can never truly succeed in becoming whole."[18] The person, "as aspiration, . . . is a chance or opportunity."[19] The person is a "project that demands space for the renewal of the imagination and the concomitant re-imagining of who one is and who one seeks to become."[20] Only by transcending oneself and going over to one's imagined and ideal persona is the freedom to be oneself possible.

The freedom of finite persons depends upon persons becoming who they are. There is no freedom without the struggle for the ideal persona. To be whole requires that finite persons heed the call of the universal law—that which sounds through themselves—and move beyond themselves to their imagined true and universal selves. The freedom of personhood, in other words, requires transcendence, a moving beyond oneself to an imagined ideal of oneself.

In founding her theory of the subject on the divided self of the transcendental person, Cornell makes clear her debt to Kant. Within Kant's critical philosophy, the fact of human finitude raises the problem: If law is an absolute obligation and yet humanity is finite, how can humans stand under the obligation of law without sacrificing their freedom? Kant's answer, and Cornell's as well, is to insist that legal obligation and subjective freedom are the same, united in the split nature of the person.

For Kant, the proof of the identity of freedom and obligation in the person is most economically accomplished in part 2 of the *Grundlegung zur Metaphysik der Sitten*. The "ground" of the "highest practical principle," Kant writes, is *"die vernünftige Natur existiert als Zweck an sich selbst* (rational being exists as an end in itself)."[21] This oft misunderstood statement depends upon the doubled understanding of a person as both a *rational* being and a rational *being:* the person is at once rational (thinking) and sensible (nature). As a rational being, every person is a split subject, both a natural *being* and a *rational* being. Since the purpose and end of a rational being is to be rational, and since it has its reason in itself as one part of itself, every rational being is an end—that is, rational existence—in itself.

Insofar as man is an end for himself—in other words, man has an obligation to be whom he is—he is also a law for himself. Human autonomy means that "the will is not only set under laws, but is so set under, that it also must be seen as giving-itself-the-law and only thus is it subsumed under the laws (which it can consider itself to be the author of)."[22] The Kantian idea of autonomy as self-lawgiving (*auto-nomos*) means that finite man must freely give himself the universal law as an absolute obligation.

Importantly, autonomous self-legislation is, for Kant, not the source of law; rather, autonomy is a necessary *effect* of man's imagination of his rationality in the transcendental apperception.[23] Only in the imaginary moment of the transcendental apperception does mankind *find* himself to be rational—a finding of his imaginary self that he then sets as a law for himself. From out of the transcendental apperception of my rationality—the fact that "man actually finds in himself a power" of reason that "distinguishes him from all other things"[24]— Kantian man stands in awe of the beauty and power of his potential to be rational and of the possibility of a rational world. This awe (*Achtung*) for the universal law at once is the effect of a "finding" of the universal law and "necessitates" that I, at every moment, set myself under the law and "act out of awe for the law."[25] The nonsensible feeling of awe, in other words, is the moral feeling itself that first makes it possible for man to be open to the law.[26] Only someone in awe of the beauty and rationality of universal law can give himself the moral law as an absolute obligation to obey the law, and—what is the same—to be himself.

Just as Kant embraces the transcendental imagination of an awe-inspiring rational law as the original bridge between our positivist-sensible and our imagined-rational selves, so too does Cornell see the imagination as the bridge between individualism and communalism. The imagination is the faculty through which individuals come to experience themselves as those beings who are, in their nature, transcending—as beings who are at once different from others and simultaneously united in their faculty of transcendence. In the face of human finitude, the transcendental imagination makes possible the "recognition of the connection between sameness and difference that allows us to understand belonging together without some overriding spirit in and through which we are connected" (PL, 60). It is through the power of imagination that finite beings can be turned toward the possibility of encountering and knowing others as both the same and as different.

HUMILITY BEFORE AWE: CORNELL'S RATIONAL CRITIQUE OF REASON

In spite of her deep and avowed Kantianism,[27] Cornell departs from Kant in her understanding of the transcendental imagination. Whereas Kant's rational subject stands in awe of the felt-but-unknown reality of the universal law, Cornell's rational subject bows humbly before the impossibility of knowing an other. In place of Kantian awe before the majesty of law, Cornell offers humility before the other. In the face of ineradicable difference, the ethical subject reacts with "humility" and "humor" (PL, 114–15).[28] While she never makes the change from awe to humility explicit, Cornell's ambivalence toward Kant is inseparable from her ambivalence to the Kantian insistence on awe before the law as the essential transcendental feeling.

In substituting humility for awe, Cornell is clearly influenced by the work of Emmanuel Levinas. She quotes Levinas's characterization of reason itself as the name for the humble relationship of the *belonging* together of the subject with the other: "Reason consists in ensuring the coexistence of these terms [rb: the one and the other], the coherence of the one and the other despite their difference, in the unity of a theme; it ensures the agreement of the different terms without breaking up the present in which the theme is held" (PL, 107).[29] Reason, Cornell argues, must acknowledge its humble incapacity to unify the subject or the community.

While Kant's awe and Cornell's humility share a basic grounding in finitude, Cornell suggests that her emphasis on humility avoids the lingering heteronomy of Kant's "morality of duty" (PL, 99). Kant, she argues, seeks a pure ethic of duty that rises above contamination by what is other. His insistence on the universality of law threatens to overcome the necessary humility in the face of the fact of the other that Cornell argues is essential to the ideal of ethical belonging together. Against her suspicion of Kant's lingering universalism, Cornell writes: "The philosophy of the limit clearly guards the trace of otherness that resists assimilation and reduction to the selfsame. . . . To respect the Other as other and, therefore, as phenomenologically symmetrical to me is to respect the being of the Other. Even a 'transcendental' ethics presupposes respect for the phenomena of the 'being' of the Other" (PL, 84–85). The radical "phenomenological symmetry" of Cornell's ethics refuses Kantian universalism, even in the form of autonomy. Even as Kant's free subject gives himself to the law, he constitutes himself as subject: "The attempt to postulate such an independent, autonomous subject," Cornell writes, is, itself, "unethical" (PL, 99).

The premise for Cornell's suspicion of Kantian reason is that reason, for Cornell, is inevitably limiting and oppressive. Yet Kant's thinking of the transcendental imagination suggests that transcendental reason is, most originally, a spontaneous *power* of reason that cannot be conceptualized or argued over. Kant announces: "Now man finds in himself a power through which he distinguishes himself from all other things—and even from himself insofar as he is affected by objects, and that is *reason*."[30] As a power that man "*finds*" in himself, reason is neither an empirical intuition nor a rule of the understanding. Instead, as a "pure self-activity" (*reine Selbsttätigkeit*), reason stands above both sensibility and understanding.[31] Against both conceptual understanding and empirical sensibility, reason "shows a spontaneity so pure that it goes far beyond anything sensibility can offer: it manifests its highest function in distinguishing the sensible and intelligible worlds from one another and so in marking out limits for understanding itself."[32] As an uncharacterized "third," ("*dieses Dritte*," and not a third *term* as Paton misleadingly renders it),[33] reason is the unknown and unknowable transcendental-imaginary ground of sensibility, understanding, and of all knowledge in general.[34] Nowhere in his critical work does Kant endeavor to name the content of the universal law of reason. On the contrary, reason, like freedom, "is a mere idea" that "can never admit of full comprehension."[35] For Kant, reason is a pure, spontaneous, nonsensible feeling of the transcendental imagination, which, by awakening awe, gives rise to the moral law of obligation that is rendered in the categorical imperative.

Against Kant's grounding of freedom on reason, however, Cornell insists upon separating freedom from reason precisely because the awesome power of reason threatens to overwhelm freedom. "Human freedom," she writes, "is not to be found in the human capacity to act according to the dictates of reason" (PL, 28). While Kant finds our call to reason to be the ultimate freedom—either to act rationally or not—Cornell argues that even the call to reason as law is anathema to the freedom of the ethical subject. The very effect of reason, its awesome causality that commands the person to set himself under the law, "corrupts freedom into obedience" (PL, 31). In her rethinking of freedom, Cornell insists upon the pursuit of community not grounded in reason.

In place of reason that risks imposing a law of command, Cornell seeks to build her free community on sympathetic grounds. Cornell argues that "[h]uman freedom . . . is not to be found in the human capacity to act according to the dictates of reason" (PL, 28). Instead, human freedom comes to work most essentially in relation to a suffering other. She intones (quoting Adorno) that "the need to let suffering speak is the condition of all truth."[36] Only by giving voice to the suffering and the corollary demand to give ear to what suffering says can we prepare ourselves for truth. Truth and justice reimagined are made possible only in the hearing of suffering.

The dream to let suffering speak in the name of truth cannot be separated from Cornell's opposition to positivism. Since "the very materiality of human existence demands a socially realized freedom in which want, in its extreme form, has been eliminated," the "idea of freedom is entwined with the experience of unfreedom" (PL, 32, 33). Suffering disrupts all systemic claims of truth and identity and ensures the "disjuncture between reality and utopia" (PL, 16). Suffering, therefore, manifests the illusory nature of the dreams of both truth and justice.

Even as suffering works to demystify ideals, it also serves as the foundation for new ideals and new truths. To give voice to suffering does not mean that we forsake the futile struggle to be at home in the world (PL 16). Instead, the disruption of the suffering other can "illuminate our state of homelessness [so] that we can begin to glimpse through the cracks and the crevices what it would be to be at home in the world" (PL, 16). Suffering is the gateway to the idealized community of *belonging* together.

The vigor with which Cornell seeks to protect not only the suffering other but also the persona of the subject from any and all conceptualization raises questions, however, about her desire to rethink the "status of reconstruction." Every attempt to exercise reason in the name of justice risks doing injustice through an unethical constitution of the subject. As she writes, quoting Ingeborg Bachmann, in the last line of *The Philosophy of the Limit*: "That's why [justice] is simultaneously both oppressive and near, but in the nearness, we call it injustice" (PL, 183).[37] The paradox of justice is that it must be unceasingly pursued and even so steadfastly avoided.

THE PARADOX OF JUSTICE

In spite of her suspicion of reason, Cornell does not fully reject reason and the conceptual understanding of truth. Instead of the irrationalism favored by many critical theorists, Cornell stakes a claim to reason, albeit reason understood as "a practical faith" (PL 107). To set reason alongside its usual antagonist, faith, may seem to invite contradiction; in Cornell's writing, however, the faith of reason names the infinite and impossible responsibility to see in the other someone with whom I belong together amidst our differences. To live in the paradox of finitude and community, the philosophy of the limit "demands that we think about the status of reconstruction differently. More specifically, it demands that we think through the realization that justice can never be reduced to the conventions of what 'is.' This effort is philosophical precisely insofar as it refuses to replace philosophy with sociology" (PL, 181). What philosophy—as opposed to positivist sociology—requires is the suspicion of all normative claims of social justice and, more importantly, an ever-vigilant readiness to live "in the throes of this paradox" (PL, 134). To "be just with justice" means to resist the urge to know and master justice and to hear the call of justice as "a simple command and an infinite responsibility" (PL, 154).

The embrace of the paradox of transcendence and finitude is what Cornell names "justice." Justice requires the acceptance of the irresolvable conflict: "To be just, is to be in the throes of a paradox" (PL, 134). Instead of seeking to overcome the paradox of finitude and the aspiration for community, Cornell counsels that justice requires that we resist the urge to "deparadoxicalization" (PL, 118). The dream of community compels the creation "of unified meaning through the establishment of generalizable or universalizable standards" (PL, 104). And the law of finitude ensures that, because "the Good can never be simply identified with a state of affairs, . . . we need not fear its oppressive power to obliterate difference" (PL, 104–05). Absent a universalizable and knowable concept of the good, we are left, in the end, with a paradoxical and limited injunction to act with regard to practical reason.

The strength of Cornell's thinking is found in her willingness to live within the paradox of justice. Instead of seeking to resolve the paradox, Cornell has sought to articulate the legal and institutional means that would allow us to endure the tragic inevitability of injustice in the pursuit of justice. First and foremost, living amidst the foreclosed demand for justice requires that each person be free for and capable of practical reason as an aspiration. For Cornell, in other words, the success of the deconstructive and epistemological critique of justice leads to a constructive reimagination of the very nature of justice itself.

FINITUDE, TRANSCENDENCE, AND FREEDOM:
CORNELL AND HEIDEGGER

The insistence on the paradoxical essence of justice emerges from Cornell's fundamental effort to think the belonging together of finite human freedom with transcendent law. Following Kant—especially the Kant of the first edition of the *Critique of Pure Reason*—Cornell argues that rational ideals have their source in the imagination. It is these imaginary ideals that she suggests offer a possibility of judgment that is both free and lawful. The imaginary nature of ideals combined with the acceptance of the paradoxical nature of just yet unjust ideals are, together, thought to ensure that freedom can coexist with lawfulness.

What needs to be questioned, however, in Cornell's turn to imaginary ideals, is her continued faith in the conceptualization of ideas at all, whether rational, empirical, or imaginary. In spite of her insight into the impossibility of objectively true judgments, Cornell continues to speak of ideals of justice. Whether she writes of the ideal of preserving feminine sexual difference or the respecting of human dignity, Cornell insists on the need to name ideals of justice. Communalism, Cornell writes, is an "ideal." Similarly, the persona is an aspiration. In this way, truth, for Cornell as Derrida and all those who offer epistemologically based critiques of the Western canon, is still thematized as something correct, something that can be known, or, even if it cannot be known by finite intellects, is knowable. Truth, in other words, continues to be understood as question of the validity of a proposition—albeit a validity of an ideal that is ultimately foreclosed.

In holding on to the ideal of objectively true judgments in the face of their impossibility, Cornell shuns the Heideggerian move to put the conceptual understanding of truth itself into question. Whereas Heidegger comes to see truth as the happening of the historical (*geschichtlich*) inheritance of a people that is revealed in the striving between concealment and unconcealment that happens in, for example, the work of art, the experience of the thinking, or the founding deed of a polity, Cornell will insist that truths might *really* exist. Even as the philosophy of the limit teaches that truths cannot be finally known, it commits one to the search for truths that are politically and ethically imagined as future aspirations. Against Heidegger, Cornell insists that we not abandon the political and metaphysical struggle to define truth. It is here, in Cornell's confrontation with Heidegger, that her work becomes at once most questionable and most worthy of questioning.

It is worth returning to the Heideggerian account of "*belonging* together" that Cornell cites from Heidegger's essay "Identity and Difference." Instead of thinking "belonging *together* in the customary way," in which the "meaning of belonging is determined by the word together, that is, by its unity," Heidegger suggests that "belonging together can also be thought of as *belonging to-gether*."[38] The shift in emphasis reflects the need to free belonging from the unity of a system. Instead, "the 'together' is now determined by the belonging" (PL, 29).

Insofar as Cornell brings Heidegger's meditation on "belonging together" to the question of "diversity in unity," she transposes Heidegger's thought into a realm foreign to it. For Heidegger is not speaking about the relation between an "I" and an ethical ideal of a "we."[39] There is no thought in Heidegger of how best to constitute a polity or an ideal community. Man, he writes, is never a subject that aims for some object or end.[40] Instead, Heidegger is referring to the relation between man (*Dasein*) and being (*das Sein*) in which man holds himself in the *openness* of being as the being who is called upon by being to do so. Such a belonging together is not to be known as an ideal, Heidegger writes, but must be experienced as one's own: the event or happening of ownness (*das Ereignis*), of the belonging together of man and being as historically given (*geschichtlich*), is, he writes, the "experience of thinking."[41]

That Heidegger speaks of the experience of thinking and not the community of justice is not accidental. Above all, he strives to avoid all thinking of "belonging together" that is governed by political, rational, or technical ends. As will Cornell, Heidegger insists that any attempt to lend normative weight to a theory or understanding of justice violates human finitude and risks foreclosing other possibilities of truth and justice. Attention to human finitude demands that we be aware that every attempt to institute justice carries with it the possibility and even the need for injustice.[42]

In *Being and Time*, finitude is part of the ontological heritage of man as a being who is in time.[43] The finitude of man is not a result of his mortality but is a result of his essential relatedness to beings and to being itself. As *Dasein* ("being there"), man must step out beyond himself into the world. *Dasein*, therefore, is man as the finite being who can and must transcend his finitude in its holding itself open to beings and being.[44] And as a being that steps over into the world, *Dasein*'s transcendence is his freedom: as Hans Ruin has written, "The stepping over—*Überstieg*—toward the world is freedom itself."[45] Insofar as *Dasein* transcends his finitude and opens himself to the world, he holds himself there and frees himself for his fate.

By the mid to late 1930s, Heidegger distances himself from his earlier connection of finitude with transcendence and freedom. In his early understanding of *Dasein* as the being who transcends and opens the possibility for freedom, Heidegger—at least to some degree—remained trapped in the very subjectivist worldview against which he was struggling. Freedom, as Heidegger understands its persistence in the idealist tradition from Kant through Schelling, is the demand that a willing subject grounds its relation to the absolute. Such a grounding is infused with the idea of the activity of a willing subject. Thus, to make freedom a doing of man is to say that man is the ground and the cause of being as well as of beings; in other words, man, as the site of freedom, remains the ground and maker of all things.

Heidegger's early emphasis on transcendence and freedom is, insofar as he imagines freedom to be a property of man, infused by the technical thinking that he identifies as the gravest of dangers. The essence of technique is that all beings are summoned forth (*herausfördert*) for some end and according to some principle. Insofar as things come to be for some end, things lose their natural and customary existence. And insofar as man is a being, man too is summoned forth in such a way that he loses any connection to his original or natural way of being. While we may try to think of the dignity of man, doing so is always today a choice in reaction against the prevalent understanding of all persons as human resources. Indeed, the first glimpse that we today have of the belonging together of man and being is in the experience of the reciprocal summoning forth of beings that is the gift of being that Heidegger sees as the essence of the modern technical world.[46]

It is possible that the reciprocal summoning forth of man and being will address us in such a way as to return us to a more original way of the being together of man and being. Such a leap out of the perils of calculating thought, however, is ever less likely so long as man strives to moderate and control the technical powers that he wields. "As long as the sensibility of the atomic age, earnestly and responsibly, only drives towards the peaceful use of nuclear energy and will only be content with that goal, then thinking goes only half way. Through this half-ness is the technical world only secured and furthered in its metaphysical predominance."[47] What Heidegger insists upon is that the escape from the technical world is not up to us. Our efforts to bridle our technical use of technology will not, in the end, save us from the sway of technology. We must accept that our thinking and our doing happens in a tradition that is given to us.

Freedom, Heidegger insists, is not man's act of grounding himself or giving himself to an ideal and universal law. Instead, freedom is a way of being in which man endures his relation to being as that which is given to him as his fate.[48] Freedom is "*Unbegreiflich*," which means both that it is not graspable by man and that it exceeds all effort at conceptualization.[49] As that which belongs not to man but to being, freedom is the "knowing standing-in" (*Innestehen*) in which man stands in the open as "an historical being" (*ein Geschichtlicher*), one who is "to meet his fate, to endure it and take it into himself and for himself."[50] Against the idealist tradition in which freedom, as the will of a subject, is the site of man's capacity to control and legislate his destiny, Heidegger reconceives freedom as the enduring of fate that frees us to think the future in a way free from all willing and planning.[51]

Precisely here, where Heidegger gestures toward the abandonment of all political struggle and the preparation of oneself for the experience of thinking, Cornell rebels. Against Heidegger, Cornell resists the move to thinking as a flight from will. Whereas Heidegger argues that we must bind ourselves to "existing bonds,"[52] Cornell dreams of a better future. If Heidegger locates the possibility of a new founding in the thoughtful confrontation with the essence of technique, Cornell insists that we not foreclose the possibility of improving or bettering our world. Whereas Heidegger speaks of a leap into a new beginning, Cornell struggles to reimagine what we have. In the face of Heidegger's effort to historicize the destiny of modern man, Cornell fights to save the man of reason and technical calculation, even if, as shown above, she recoils from reason's violence and seeks to reimagine reason along the lines of a practical faith. While Heidegger offers the possibility of letting be of rational metaphysics in the turn towards the work of art, Cornell calls for a confrontation with and a rethinking of reason that heeds the call of the suffering other.

Cornell's response to Heidegger's challenge—for asking is the fitness of thinking—is to insist that we do not have the luxury of asking and waiting. Against Heidegger's valorization of questioning and thinking, Cornell offers the active practice of loving: "If thinking demands we live in anxiety, love demands we accept the relation to tragedy."[53] Faced with the tragedy of suffering and injustice, man must act and struggle and fight to actualize justice. There is, for Cornell, an ethical imperative to act in the name of justice, even in the face of the possibility that all action risks reinstating an ideal of justice that threatens itself to justify injustice.

Here is where Cornell makes the choice that first drew me to her work. Her courage as a thinker is manifest in her willingness to fight for the good as possible and necessary in spite of its necessary impossibility. She embraces a paradoxical possibility, since even the impossibility of the good must itself be a limited concept and not absolute. From her opposition to the war in Iraq and the bombing in Afghanistan, to her engagement with legal questions from abortion to sexual harassment, and her committed feminism, Cornell demands that philosophy enable rather than disable political engagement. In doing so, Cornell consciously runs the risk that speaking and advocating for ideals of justice will have both unexpected and undesirable consequences and, what is more important, contribute to the very forgetfulness of our finitude that the philosophy of the limit strives to recall.

Without mitigating these risks, Cornell acts through her thinking, spurred by her conviction that not acting in the face of injustice is inexcusable. The harder she holds fast to man's finite incapacity to speak or know of absolute truth, the more stubbornly she insists that justice demands the speaking of truth in the face of its impossibility. There is no jumping over the shadow of human finitude, yet the dignity and power of Cornell's thinking is that she knows this and nevertheless refuses to shirk from the jump.[54] Just as Kant, "despite everything, holds fast" to the idea that true knowledge "is grounded in principles" that cannot be known,[55] so too does Cornell insist that justice demands a reconstruction of ideals that, in the end, cannot be defended.

The good must be spoken; that is Cornell's challenge in the face of her truth that the good can never be known.

NOTES

1. Drucilla Cornell. *Philosophy of the Limit* (New York: Routledge, 1992)

2. Correspondence with Davide Panagia and Fredrik Westerlund, two readers of earlier drafts of this chapter, contributed to my own formulation of Cornell's central problematic in this paragraph.

3. I offer a genealogy of the victory of positive law and show how positive law is a corollary of the rise of legal science in my book *The Gift of Science: Leibniz and the Foundation of Modern Law* (Cambridge, MA: Harvard University Press, 2005).

4. Anthony Sebok, *Legal Positivism in American Jurisprudence* (New York: Cambridge University Press, 1998), 2. See also Frederick Schauer, "Positivism as Pariah," in *The Autonomy of Law: Essays in Legal Positivism*, ed. Robert George, 1996.

5. Ronald Dworkin, *Law's Empire* (Cambridge: Harvard University Press, 1986), 225 (emphasis added).

6. Jürgen Habermas, *Between Facts and Norms*, trans. William Rehg (Cambridge: MIT Press, 1998). See also Niklas Luhmann, "Quod Omnes Tangit," in *Habermas on Law and Democracy*, ed. Andrew Arato Michel Rosenfeld (Berkeley: University of California Press, 1998).

7. "Response to Thomas McCarthy: The Political Alliance between Ethical Feminism and Rawls's Kantian Constructivism," in *Constellations*, v. 2 (1995), 204.

8. See generally Dworkin, *Law's Empire*, 225.

9. Id., at pg. 65ff. See Drucilla Cornell, "Institutionalization of Meaning, Recollective Imagination and the Potential for Transformative Legal Interpretation," *University of Pennsylvania Law Review* 136 (1988): 1170.

10. For an excellent account of the impossible efforts to order law throughout history, see Rainer Maria Kiesow, *Das Alphabet des Rechts* (Frankfurt am Main: Verlag, 2004).

11. Martin Heidegger, "Die onto-Theo-Logische Verfassung Der Metaphysik," in *Identity and Difference*, ed. Joan Stanbaugh (Chicago: University of Chicago Press, 1969), 126.

12. See, e.g., the excellent discussion of Hegel's approach to Jewish emancipation in Patchen Markell, *Bound by Recognition* (Princeton: Princeton University Press, 2003), ch. 5.

13. Aristotle, *Politics*, ed. G. P. Goold, trans. H. Rackham, vol. 21 (Cambridge: Harvard University Press, 1998), 1261b16–18.

14. Ibid., 1261a17–24.

15. Ibid., 1261a24.

16. On this point, see the excellent discussion in Jill Frank, *A Democracy of Distinction* (Chicago: University of Chicago Press, 2004), 143ff.

17. See Martin Heidegger, "Der Satz Der Identität," in *Identity and Difference*, ed. Joan Stanbaugh (Chicago: University of Chicago Press, 1969), 92. (emphasis in both Heidegger and Cornell). Heidegger's thinking of the essence of belonging in *Ereignis* brings him, of course, to a much different place than Cornell's use of his distinction. In an important way, however, Heidegger's idea of Ereignis as the event of the open where

being shows itself to man is the necessary condition for the kind of free belonging together that Cornell transposes to the legal and political realms.

18. Drucilla Cornell, *At the Heart of Freedom* (Princeton: Princeton University Press, 1998), 185.

19. Drucilla Cornell, *Imaginary Domain* (New York: Routledge, 1995), 4–5.

20. Ibid., 5.

21. Ibid.

22. Immanuel Kant, *Grundlegung Zur Metaphysik Der Sitten*, ed. Karl Vorländer (Hamburg: Meiner, 1965), 429.

23. Ibid., 431.

24. Ibid.

25. Ibid., 452.

26. Ibid., 400.

27. Martin Heidegger, *Kant Und Das Problem Der Metaphysik* (Frankfurt am Main: Klostermann, 1975), 151.

28. Drucilla Cornell, "Response to Thomas McCarthy: The Political Alliance between Ethical Feminism and Rawls's Kantian Constructivism," *Constellations* 2, no. 2 (1995).

29. Interestingly, Cornell largely ignores her reference to humor in *The Philosophy of the Limit* and in her later work.

30. Citing Emmanuel Levinas, *Otherwise than Being or beyond Essence*, trans. Alphonso Lingis (1991), 165.

31. Kant, *Grundlegung Zur Metaphysik Der Sitten*, 452.

32. Ibid.

33. Ibid.

34. Ibid., 447.

35. See Heidegger, *Kant Und Das Problem Der Metaphysik*, sect. 31.

36. Kant, *Grundlegung Zur Metaphysik Der Sitten*, 459.

37. Cornell sets Adorno's line—"The need to let suffering speak is the condition of all truth"—as the epigraph to her first chapter of *Philosophy of the Limit*.

38. Citing Ingeborg Bachmann's novel *Malina*.

39. Heidegger, "Der Satz Der Identität," 92.

40. See also Martin Heidegger, *Über Den Humanismus* (Frankfurt am Main: Klostermann, 1949), 35–36.

41. Ibid.

42. "Die Einfahrt in den Bereich dieser Übereignung stimmt und be-stimmt erst die Erfahrung des Denkens." Heidegger, "Der Satz Der Identität," 97.

42. Markell, *Bound by Recognition*, 4–5.

44. Martin Heidegger, *Sein Und Zeit* (Tübingen: Verlag, 1993), 329–30.

45. In his 1929 essay, "Vom Wesen des Grundes," Heidegger even suggests that the first part of *Being and Time* is "nothing but a project of the concrete-uncovering of *transcendence*." Martin Heidegger, "Vom Wesen Des Grundes," in *Wegmarken*, (Frankfurt am Main: Klostermann, 1967), 162n.59.

46. Hans Ruin, "The Destiny of Freedom-in Heidegger" (2004), 6–7. Paper presented at the Collegium Phaenomenologicum in Citta di Castello, 2004. Paper on file with author. See Heidegger, "Vom Wesen Des Grundes," 163ff.

47. Heidegger, "Der Satz Der Identität," 103.

48. Ibid., 105.

49. Ruin, "The Destiny of Freedom-in Heidegger," 17.

50. Martin Heidegger, *Schellings Abhandlung Über Das Wesen Der Menschlichen Freiheit* (Tübingen: Verlag, 1995), 195–96.

51. Ibid., 196.

52. Heidegger, "Der Satz Der Identität," 106.

53. Heidegger, *Über Den Humanismus*, 38.

54. Drucilla Cornell, *Transformations: Recollective Imagination and Sexual Difference* (New York: Routledge, 1993), 56.

55. See Martin Heidegger, *Die Frage Nach Dem Ding*, 3rd, durchgesehene Auflage ed. (Tübingen: Verlag, 1987), 118.

56. Ibid., 132.

Adam Thurschwell

Radical Feminist Liberalism

Among the first characteristics of Drucilla Cornell's work that strikes one, from any angle of approach, is its synthetic character. Beginning her writing career with work grounded primarily in the critical theory of the Frankfurt School (an interest that grew out of her lifelong engagement with Hegel), she has progressively taken up and, in one way or another, given her own stamp to deconstruction, Luhmannian systems theory, Lacanian psychoanalysis, and Rawlsian liberalism (to mention only a few). Ecumenicism of this breadth is sometimes the sign of thin thinking. In her case, however, it flows from a sustained engagement with each of her intellectual objects, aimed at coaxing its essence (the usual metaphor of "penetrating analysis" being totally inapt for her style) from whatever vocabulary and tradition in which it happens to lie, in the faith that productive dialogue is possible between radically different, and even opposed, intellectual traditions.

In this chapter I propose to examine one such moment in her thinking in some detail, her jurisprudential work from the late 1990s that attempts to reconcile her radical feminist approach to gender with philosophical liberalism. I focus on this work in part because of its inherent philosophical importance but also because I think it is exemplary of some of Cornell's strengths as a thinker more generally—her faith in the reconciliation of (apparent) opposites, her commitment to philosophy as dialogue, her belief in the importance of philosophical thinking for contemporary practical and doctrinal legal debates, and finally, the transparency of her philosophical process, which is remarkably open and honest in its self-critique and self-revision.

The project that I will examine here began with *The Imaginary Domain*,[1] the book in which Cornell first brought together in a systematic fashion her distinctive approach to feminist and the Kantian tradition of liberal political philosophy. It should be noted that successfully integrating these traditions would be no mean feat, since Cornell's feminism—which she calls "ethical feminism"[2]—is grounded in entirely different, and in significant respects anti-thetical, philosophical traditions, post-Hegelian Continental philosophy, and Lacanian psychoanalysis.[3] The idea of reuniting feminism with liberalism also runs against the tide of thirty years of feminist critiques of liberal political the-ory that have given liberal feminism a bad name in many academic (if not practical political) feminist circles.[4]

Three years after *The Imaginary Domain*, Cornell published another book, *At the Heart of Freedom*,[5] which again took up this project, building on the theoretical model established in the earlier book but also modifying it in sig-nificant ways. The synthesis Cornell achieves in these books might be called—to distinguish it from liberal feminism—"radical feminist liberalism."

In this chapter, I will first sketch the background of Cornell's contribution by briefly discussing the nature of feminism's problematic relationship with liberal philosophy. In the second section I then discuss Cornell's notion of the "imaginary domain" as an integral aspect of personhood—the aspect in which we identify ourselves as sexed beings—that requires protection under a liberal rights regime and show how it resolves the feminist criticisms of conventional liberal theory set out in the first section. In the final section I situate her proj-ect in relation to Kant's and Rawls's versions of liberalism, and, inter alia, ex-plain how her project has evolved between *The Imaginary Domain* and *At the Heart of Freedom*. Although both *The Imaginary Domain* and *At the Heart of Freedom* contain a number of novel practical applications of her ideas to vari-ous areas of the law, at base they constitute a sustained philosophical argu-ment, and my discussion will address them primarily at that level. Overall, I hope to show that she convincingly extends the liberal doctrine of freedom into the realm of sexuality in a way that resolves some of feminism's most stub-born dilemmas, while remaining true to liberalism's core principles, she accom-plishes this without sacrificing feminism's own core concern for difference.

I

Understanding Cornell's project requires an understanding of the relationship between feminism and philosophical liberalism.[6] That relationship is marked by paradox. On one hand, liberalism holds that the innate dignity of the person qua person demands equal treatment of all as a matter of legal, political, and moral right, regardless of the particular characteristics, including gender, that differentiate individuals from each other. At first blush that principle appears in-distinguishable from the feminist demand that the sexual difference between women and men not be used as a justification for legal, political, and social dis-advantages imposed on women. Consistent with this (apparently) shared princi-ple, liberal reformers of the last century were in fact among the first to champion equal rights for women,[7] and the main legal and political advances made by women since that time have generally been justified by reference to the right to equal—which is to say gender-neutral—treatment before the law.[8] *Liberal femi-*

nism is the name usually given to feminists who remain within the traditional liberal paradigm and argue for equal treatment based on its premises.[9]

On the other hand, the liberal alliance with feminism masks deeper difficulties. The notion that, for legal and political purposes, we are all to be treated the same presupposes an abstraction from all of our real differences to achieve a gender-neutral juridical subject. What if, however, some of these real differences really matter to our sense of ourselves as persons? What if, worse yet, the universal subject of liberal right is in fact neither "universal" nor "gender-neutral" but modeled on the (white, European) male? If, as Simone de Beauvoir wrote, "man represents both the positive and the neutral,"[10] then the ostensibly gender-neutral "person" of liberalism will mask a masculinist standard that undermines the law's ability to maintain the equal respect that women are entitled to as persons. As Cornell puts it, "if the paradigmatic person entered into the scales to resolve competing interests, and if the scope of the claims persons can make on society is conceptualized as sex neutral, she (or he) is unconsciously identified as white, straight and masculine" (16). Can women be said to be treated with equal dignity, if, for example, the United States Constitution permits them to be excluded with impunity from spheres of life that are among the most socially respected[11] and discriminated against because of their unique anatomy and role in reproduction?[12] These cases illustrate a fundamental difficulty inherent in the use of a universal and abstract standard of comparison to judge the treatment of individuals who are, in fact, differently situated. So long as the masculine remains the unspoken model of the person, making questions of gender equality (and discrimination) turn on liberalism's formal conception of personhood renders philosophically and legally irrelevant the real sexual differences that are integral to women's own personhood.[13]

The critique of liberalism's ostensibly gender-neutral person has taken many forms. Some radical feminists (preeminently Catharine MacKinnon) analyze the genderless "person" of liberalism as an ideological cover for a patriarchal system of sexual domination that denies women "personhood" in any meaningful sense.[14] So-called difference or cultural feminists argue that women's differences (in particular, those connected to their role in reproduction) are fundamental, and underwrite approaches to law and right that cannot be subsumed under the universalist umbrella of the liberal "person."[15] Other theorists, more sympathetic to the liberal paradigm, have attempted to integrate sexual difference into the liberal conception of the person.[16] What these (and other)[17] approaches share is the suspicion that the abstract universalism of liberal political and legal theory denies, denigrates, or represses some characteristic of women that is integral to their personhood (or, in Catharine MacKinnon's argument, obscures their subordinated status).[18]

Apart from the problem of formal equality, feminists have identified a problem with the subject matter of liberal political philosophy, the problem of the public/private dichotomy. The liberal doctrine that persons are to be given maximum freedom and equal treatment requires a specification of freedom *from what* and equal treatment *by whom*. In its original form liberalism's answer to both questions was the state: the early liberal philosophers' primary concern was reconciling the coercive power of the sovereign with the maximum autonomy of the individual. Thus from its beginnings liberalism has concerned itself with the legitimate regulation of the *public* rights of the individual, viewing the private ordering of persons' lives as the sphere that must be protected by those rights rather than regulated by them. While the liberal understanding of what is encompassed within the public sphere has grown over time alongside the growth of the welfare state and public regulation of the economy,[19] that understanding has never included sexual relations or family life.[20] Yet that is precisely the sphere in which the unfair relations of power with which feminism is concerned play themselves out, a concern declared in the feminist credo that "the personal is political."[21] In short, the feminist criticism is that liberalism has wrongly and unjustly consigned sexual difference to the nonphilosophical realm of the contingent, on one hand, and the nonpolitical realm of the private, on the other.

To have identified unfairness in the liberal paradigm, however, does not guarantee that the feminist proponents of difference are able to substitute a new paradigm of right in its place. Three obstacles have stood in the way of such a feminist reconstruction of legal right.

First, having opened the door to the possibility that differences can be as fundamental as similarities, it is difficult for feminists to close their analyses to the other differences that can plausibly claim legal recognition as integral to an individual's experience of herself as a self. These integral differences include (at a minimum) race, class, ethnolinguistic heritage, and sexual orientation. To the extent that these and other differentiating characteristics of individuals attain legally cognizable status, the very category of "woman" breaks up into an endless series of ever more particularized subcategories— Black women, Latinas, lesbians, lesbian Black women, Latina working-class women, and so on—into what one author has aptly called an "anti-essentialist abyss."[22] To take only one example, it can hardly be that the role of sexual difference in lesbians' lives—private, political, social, or economic—is the same as in heterosexual women's lives, yet the ostensibly unitary category of "woman" subsumes this difference in a manner reminiscent of the way the universal term "person" covers over the sexual difference in liberal theory. Similar arguments can be made about the differences among women of different racial and ethnic backgrounds. It is one thing to integrate the special characteristics of "women" into one's theory of equality; it is quite another to attempt simultaneously to account for the different claims to equal valuation of the splintered subgroups that compose the class of all women. It is even more difficult to conceptualize the practical effect (not to mention political acceptability) of multiple *legal* standards of equal treatment that would apply in particular cases depending on whether the claimant was a black woman, a lesbian, and so on.[23] Yet regress into this "anti-essentialist abyss" seems impossible to avoid once recognition of difference, rather than abstract similarity, becomes the leading principle of the legal system.

Second, the attempt to equalize the treatment of women through the legal recognition of sexual difference poses the danger of reifying women's current position within the gender hierarchy.[24] This issue rose to the surface of public debate most prominently in the so-called special treatment/equal treatment controversy over the legitimacy of California's attempt to legislate a special right to four months' unpaid pregnancy leave for female workers. Employers challenged the law under the federal Pregnancy Discrimination Act,[25] claiming that it discriminated among employees on the basis of pregnancy. Some feminists—the "special treatment" advocates—argued that the legislation was a legitimate remedial measure that simply recognized a characteristic distinctively associated with women. Other feminists, however—the "equal treatment" advocates—argued that singling out women for special treatment on the basis of their reproductive function implicitly equated women with that function, symbolically consigning them, in the eyes of the law, to one of the most traditional and limiting feminine stereotypes.[26] The special treatment advocates responded that such a purely formal notion of equality itself consigns women to the position of trying to keep up with men in a race that is stacked against them—what Cornell calls "white-knuckling feminism" (5). The Supreme Court ultimately agreed with the "special treatment" side of the debate without addressing its philosophical implications.[27] The underlying dilemma for feminists, however—how to distinguish between a legal recognition of sexual difference that addresses the unfairness inherent in a facially neutral yet implicitly masculine model of the person on one hand, and a legal recognition of sexual difference that paternalistically puts women back on the pedestal reserved for the "weaker sex" on the other—remains.

Finally, feminists' exposure of the way in which the public/private distinction operates in liberal philosophy to sanction unfair power relations between men and women within the spheres of sexuality and the family creates another dilemma. If the distinction between public and private is purely ideological, then the traditional liberal limitation on the power of the state to intrude on our most intimate choices and relationships becomes difficult to justify. Few are willing to give up that aspect of liberalism, however, as the reactions to Catharine MacKinnon's proposals to regulate pornography attest.[28] Moreover, to the extent that feminist reform of power relations in the private sphere requires the regulation of intimate choices and associations, it is far from clear that the cure will improve on the disease. The assistance of government, once enlisted, will not necessarily turn out to be what feminists expect.[29] That was in fact the Canadian experience after its Supreme Court adopted MacKinnon's approach to pornography—lesbian and gay bookstores were among the first targets of police enforcement.[30] Women's as well as men's autonomy suffers when the state is handed the power to censor, regulate, or even suppress "private" choices and relationships.

This historical and conceptual background haunts any attempt to reconcile feminism's affirmation of sexual difference with liberalism's premise of our innate sameness, that is, the notion that we are all persons with equal inherent dignity demanding equal respect. Liberal principles have historically underwritten women's most significant gains in legal equality; yet, at the same time, the liberal principle of formal equality seems to stand in the way of the full recognition and equal valuation of women's sexual difference that feminism demands. Conversely, incorporating the feminist affirmation of difference into the concept of legal equality appears to make gender comparisons of any kind impossible (since the differing claims of lesbians, black women, and so on must be taken into account), threatens to elevate feminine stereotypes into law, and appears to allow distinctly antiliberal state interference in the most intimate areas of our lives. As I will now try to show, Cornell's specific contribution in this area is to resolve these paradoxes through an extension of the liberal ideal of freedom into the somatic realm.

II

The essential insight central to *At the Heart of Freedom* is that the knot of oppositions in which liberalism and feminism find themselves entwined can be untangled if feminism reorients itself from a focus on equality to a focus on freedom. Cornell has long held that the ultimate goal of feminism should not be to empower women at the expense of men but to liberate all from the oppressive confines of a gender system that in myriad ways restricts what it means to be a "woman" or "man"—that is, a sexed being—in all areas of social, economic and political life.[31] In *At the Heart of Freedom* she found a way to integrate that liberatory ideal into a traditional liberal framework modeled on Kant's moral and political philosophy.

In classical liberal theory, freedom and equality are related but not always consistent values in which freedom is given pride of place—in Kant's formulation, we are equal only insofar as we are to be granted the maximum possible liberty consistent with others' similar liberty.[32] That priority has not sat well with feminists, who have perceived liberal freedom as a mask and an apology for unequal treatment in the spheres of public right and private power. As discussed in the preceding section, if persons qua sexed beings are not similarly situated, then attempts to build a doctrine of equality on the premise of a unitary conception of the free person is doomed to failure. Yet that is precisely the premise with which liberalism begins.

Thus, for Kant, a person's right to equal treatment flows from the fact of reason that we cannot but conceive of ourselves as rational, and therefore free, beings. By "rational" Kant means that we are beings who, in principle at least, are capable of giving ourselves and acting in accordance with ultimate moral ends of our own choice, irrespective of external (or as Kant calls them, "heteronomous") causes.[33] Of course this freedom is "in principle" only, because we are not pure creatures of reason but also empirical creatures with empirical needs, interests, upbringings, and so forth, that also determine our choices of ends. In Kantian terminology, we exist in the realm of "phenomena" (the world of sense data subject to the laws of empirical causation) as well as "noumena" (the nonsensible world of freedom available to us only through reason). Freedom in this sense is not actual but rather what Kant calls an "idea of reason." Nevertheless, regardless of the counterfactual nature of this freedom, because persons (as rational and therefore free beings) are in principle capable of giving themselves their own ends, they are entitled to treatment—and are morally obligated to treat other, similarly rational beings—as ends-in-themselves and never as mere instruments for the achievement of other goals.[34] Kant's social contractarian political philosophy, including his principles of political and social equality, in turn derives from this metaphysical postulate of freedom. Free, rational beings would, Kant says, agree to participate as citizen-subjects under a coercive regime of legal obligation only to the extent that each has an equal right to freedom that does not infringe on the freedom of others, and each has an equal right to coerce others to conform with a general law that restricts the freedom of all equally.[35] Kant thus derives his notion of equality from the prior notion of freedom.

Other liberal theorists have followed this general pattern as well. In John Rawls's *Theory of Justice*, for example, his two principles of justice begin with a protection of liberty that closely follows Kant's—"[E]ach person is to have an equal right to the most extensive basic liberty compatible with a similar liberty for others."[36] Only after the basic freedoms are established are social and economic inequalities addressed in the so-called difference principle and guarantee of equal opportunity for all, with the express proviso that the initial protection of basic liberty is to take precedence over the latter.[37] Rawls' theory, modeling Kant's reliance on the pure rational will independent of all empirical conditioning, justifies these principles on the basis of hypothetical negotiations among hypothetical representatives of society at large who are denied any knowledge of their empirical attributes and stations in life, including their genders (the famous "veil of ignorance").[38]

The problem with these types of liberal theories from a feminist perspective is that the only concept of 'equality' that can be derived from a notion of freedom rooted in the pure rational will abstracted from all phenomenal attributes is a formal notion of equality that, as discussed in the preceding section, seems inevitably to give short shrift to women's (empirical, phenomenal, heteronomous) sexual difference. As a result, much of the feminist critique of Kantian liberalism has focused on a perceived need to undo this abstraction. A number of feminists have argued, for example, that sexual difference should be allowed behind Rawls's "veil of ignorance" as a way of guaranteeing that the specific "standpoint of women"[39] receives equal respect in the construction of the principles of justice.[40]

Cornell shares the feminist concern that sexual difference be respected in any system of justice. She believes, however, that the feminist demand for equality of treatment is a "failed ideal" (3), both because it ensnares feminism in the paradoxes described in the preceding section and because, more fundamentally, feminism's concern should not be with equal treatment for the genders but with freedom from the constraints of gender altogether. By "gender" Cornell means the "'commonsense' view of sexual difference, that human beings come in two 'kinds,' men and women" (6). As the scare quotes around "commonsense" and "kinds" suggest, for Cornell the gender system is neither commonsensical nor natural, but an artificial social-psychological limitation on the otherwise limitless meanings that sexual difference can take on for any given individual, of whatever "gender." The reduction of sexual personality to gender, for Cornell, is a socially and self-imposed truncation on what it means to be human. Thus, a feminism that seeks simply to equalize the gender system's opposing masculine/feminine positions, without challenging the underlying assumptions about sexual identity that underwrite the gender opposition itself, will never escape the system's greatest evil.[41]

More concretely, in *Oncale v. Sundowner Offshore Services*,[42] the Supreme Court held that same-sex harassment may constitute "discrimination because of sex" within the meaning of Title VII of the Civil Rights Act of 1964. Despite holding same-sex harassment to be at least potentially within the scope of the anti-discrimination laws, the Court appeared to remain within the analytic framework that Cornell rejects, by requiring comparative proof that "members of one sex are exposed to disadvantageous terms or conditions of employment to which members of the other sex are not exposed."[43] In other words, gender comparison remains the touchstone of the harassment claim, rather than the view of same-sex harassment as a form of "policing" of gender stereotypes that limits the harassment victim's freedom to express her sexual personality as she chooses.[44] In Cornell's view the great contribution of feminism is the recognition that the gender system's hold on our sexual identities is neither natural nor necessary, and feminism's practical goal should therefore be "sexuate freedom"— the individual's right to determine her own sexual personality outside the constraints of any imposed notions of what it means to be a sexed being.

The inspiration for this ideal of feminism is deeply rooted in her prior engagement with the deconstructive philosophy of Jacques Derrida and psychoanalytic theory of Jacques Lacan.[45] In *At the Heart of Freedom*, however, Cornell demonstrates that this ideal can also be derived from the Kantian-liberal doctrine of freedom.

At the core of this demonstration is Cornell's notion of the "imaginary domain." In *At the Heart of Freedom* she defines the imaginary domain as "the space of the 'as if' in which we imagine who we might be if we made ourselves our own end and claimed ourselves as our own person" (8). More specifically, the imaginary domain is that aspect of our personhood in which we "make ourselves our own end" by imaginatively constituting our corporeal selves as "sexed beings"—as physical, integral, sexually oriented persons. Sexual orientation here denotes something both more specific and more general than heterosexuality or homosexuality. It goes to the most intimate and particular sense one has of oneself as a physical and desiring being, a sense that includes the integration of one's entire personal history, including not only one's sexual preference but all of the other individual characteristics, whether cultural, social, racial or otherwise, that influences one's corporeal self-image (8–11). Cornell calls this self-representation of the body an "imago—a primordial image of how we hang together that each one of us lives out" (6). This imago, or "bodily ego" (35), is fundamental to our sense of ourselves as unified, individual persons, and among its basic attributes is our self-experience as "sexed" beings, whether male, female, hetero-, or homosexual or some combination thereof. The imaginary domain is the social-psychological space we require to develop these imagos in freedom.

Cornell's argument, which is simple, elegant, and, I believe, convincing, is that our imago, and thus our sexuate being, should not be treated as a brute given of our personhood but as something that we are capable, at least in principle, of refashioning according to our own ends—that "we are not fated to be sexed in any particular form" (8). If that is so, however, then the Kantian conception of freedom—which is predicated on rational beings' power to give themselves their own ends—is broad enough to include the imaginary domain within its parameters. As Cornell points out, "the imaginary domain is basic to the freedom of personality; there is nothing more personal to a human being than how she chooses to organize her sexual and familial relationships" (58). Accordingly, "our claim to our person has to include our right to be legally and politically recognized as the legitimate source of meaning and representation of our existence as corporeal, sexuate beings" (8). The form one's sexuate being takes within one's imaginary domain is accordingly entitled to what she calls "equivalent evaluation" (15), in the sense that each form of sexuate being—regardless of its peculiarities and differences from what some might consider the "norm"—is entitled to equal respect.

Cornell's conception of the protected space of the imaginary domain is thus a natural extension of the liberal conception of freedom. According to Kant, each person has the innate right, insofar as they are rational, willing beings, to determine and act on their own ends so long as their ends are consistent with similar freedom for all. As he put it, "[n]o-one can compel me to be happy in accordance with his conception of the welfare of others, for each may seek his happiness in whatever way he sees fit, so long as he does not infringe upon the freedom of others to pursue a similar end which can be reconciled with the freedom of everyone else within a workable general law."[46] In classical liberal theories, those ends are identified with the person's "conscience"—her ultimate goals for her life, her fundamental associations and loyalties, and her philosophical, moral or religious beliefs about her life's meaning.[47] Because conscience constitutes the realm of the person's ultimate ends, protection of this sphere has served as the paradigm for the other liberal rights.[48] Cornell proposes that a liberal rights regime should protect a person's *internal* self-conception—the sexual imago forged in the space of his imaginary domain—to the same extent that it protects his *external* self-conception represented by her conscience (37–38, 200 n.1). Both are intimate spheres of personal choice that are integral to the person's selfhood and autonomy, and a denial of either constitutes a fundamental blow to the innate dignity of the person that liberalism takes as its task to defend.

It is worthwhile pausing at this point to consider an objection to this whole line of argument, that is, that the notion that we are capable of reorienting our sexual, physical sense of ourselves in the same manner that we are deemed able to reorient our moral, religious, and philosophical beliefs is utopian in the extreme. If that is so, then it might appear that legal protection of the freedom of the imaginary domain is futile, if not specious. Cornell herself emphasizes that the bodily ego is formed very early in life and exerts a largely unconscious hold on our thoughts and feelings that is very difficult to change (37). These empirical realities are irrelevant from the perspective of a Kantian-liberal theory, however. Again, Kant's postulate that persons are rational beings capable of autonomously choosing their own ends is merely an idea of reason. We can conceive of this autonomy in principle but can never realize it in fact, because we are not purely rational but empirical creatures with empirical needs, interests, and limitations. It is not what we *are* that is the key to Kant's moral philosophy but what we can conceive of ourselves, at least hypothetically, to be. In this sense the space of the imaginary domain stands on the same moral footing as Kant's autonomous will. It "is the prior place of equivalent evaluation that must be imagined no matter what historical and anthropological researchers tell us is 'true' about women's nature" (15). Thus, like Kant's theory (and Rawls's), Cornell's notion of the imaginary domain is deontological.

Cornell argues, contrary to what other, materialist-oriented feminists have suggested, that feminism benefits from reliance on deontological premises:

> A deontological theory can seem utopian because it insists on the separation between right and reality. But it is just this separation that makes a broad deontology so powerful in feminist theory . . . [because] it shifts the grounds on which critics can challenge feminism as unrealistic: on the level of right, it does not matter whether or not "in reality" women have ever been free or not. . . . The role of the imaginary domain, as of any ideal, is to represent the separation of right from reality, and to maintain the critical edge that delimits the conflation of the two." (185)

Thus, without contesting the feminist critiques that have found hidden masculinist biases in deontological approaches, Cornell nevertheless insists that the two can be separated and the critical leverage provided by deontology thus preserved for feminist use.

Cornell's argument strikes me as a logical, natural, and even necessary extension of the liberal doctrine of freedom to a realm of ends that is no less fundamental to the autonomy and dignity of persons for having been neglected by liberal theorists. What is perhaps less clear is how her conception of somatic freedom serves traditional feminist ends and how it resolves the paradoxes I discussed in the first section. Much of Cornell's work since *The Imaginary Domain* has been devoted to answering these questions through a reconsideration of core feminist concerns such as abortion, pornography, sexual harassment, prostitution and family law through the lens of her reformulated liberalism, and in particular her reformulation of John Rawls's political philosophy in *Political Liberalism*. Key to understanding her analysis of all these areas is her traditionally liberal emphasis on maximum liberty for all rather than equality of treatment between men and women. Cornell's fundamental tenet is that "as *persons,* we [women] be given equal and maximum liberty to determine our sexual lives, including what meaning to give our reproductive capacit[ies]" (67; emphasis added). That is, first, contrary to the feminist objections to the liberal abstract person, Cornell insists that women's rights be derived from the abstract rights of "persons" (38–39). Second, liberty is given pride of place over equality: "If we begin by recognizing women as free persons who can represent their own sexuate being, then the legislation we propose would begin not with an end to gender inequality, but instead with the *realization* of that freedom" (91; emphasis in original).

Cornell can revert to these traditionally liberal motifs without falling back into the dangers of abstraction identified by feminists because protection of the imaginary domain guarantees that the person's sexual difference cannot be used as a marker disentitling the person to equal respect. To see how this would work in practice, consider again the "special treatment"/"equal treatment" debate discussed in the preceding section. As we saw, to the extent that the issue was analyzed in terms of equality, it left feminists with the either/or of treating women like men (the "equal treatment" position)—and thus disadvantaging them in the workplace during the late stages of their pregnancy because only women get pregnant—or appearing to give women "special benefits" that could be construed to demean their equal dignity by implicitly categorizing them as the "weaker sex."[49] The issue appears in an entirely different light, however, when analyzed as a matter of limitations on pregnant women's freedom. In Cornell's terms, the question becomes: Does the pregnancy leave statute violate the sanctity of persons' imaginary domains by imposing upon them a definition or meaning of their sexual difference (in this case, their reproductive capacity)? Or, alternatively, does it respect their fundamental freedom to define their own conceptions of themselves as physical, sexed beings? Analyzed in this way, the permissive nature of the statute (it did not *require* pregnant women to take leaves) and the genuine conflict that some women experience between the physical burdens of the late stages of pregnancy and the demands of work life, make the answer apparent: the statute enhances, rather than restricts, the protection of persons' imaginary domains. Those women who wish to act on their reproductive capacities are permitted to do so without having to sacrifice another of their self-defining characteristics. They are guaranteed the continuing right to participate in employment outside the home.[50] Note that this analysis results in the substantive equality result favored by the "special treatment" advocates, while avoiding the specter of paternalism, because it derives this result from an analysis of the right of a (gender-indeterminate) "abstract person" to her imaginary domain. The somatic freedom guaranteed by protection of the imaginary domain is concrete in the sense that the person's individual conception of her sexual difference is an integral part of that freedom, but it is abstract in the traditional liberal sense of universal applicability.[51]

By protecting sexual difference through a universal, abstract right, Cornell also manages to avoid the infinite regress into the antiessentialist abyss[52] discussed earlier. As she explains, "[t]he demand that each of us have our imaginary domain protected as a matter of moral and legal right does not turn on an appeal to our likeness to other women" (10). Protection of the imaginary domain guarantees freedom to define for one's self the meaning of one's sexuate being regardless of how individual or idiosyncratic that definition might be, and regardless of categories like class, race, or sexual preference. These categories of course remain relevant to the constitution of one's imago in the imaginary domain. Because, however, the protection is couched in terms of freedom rather than equality, the difficult question of comparisons across categories—how to judge the equal treatment of white, working-class women as against white, working-class men, or Black lesbians, and so on—does not arise. All are equally free in that all have an equal right to freedom to represent their sexuate beings as they see fit.

I have suggested how the concept of the imaginary domain allows Cornell to serve the feminist concern with respect for sexual difference from within the liberal paradigm. Cornell's adherence to this paradigm does place her at odds with some feminists, however. She explains, for example, that her "insistence on abstraction is inseparable from the political recognition of the person as the node of choice" (53). This liberal insistence on the autonomy of the person leads her to positions that not all feminists would endorse. For example, she argues against censorship of the production of pornography because she disagrees with Catharine MacKinnon that it is necessarily a mechanism of masculine domination. Rather, she focuses on feminist pornographers for whom pornography is a mode of expressing their sexual freedom.[53] She favors legal intervention in the form of zoning regulations, however, because the pervasive, in-your-face unavoidability of publicly displayed pornography in some large cities is so extreme as to constitute an assault on women's freedom to constitute their own sexual self-images.[54] She is fully aware that women who become prostitutes are often desperate and come from sexually and physically abusive situations. Yet she believes that prostitution is nevertheless a woman's choice of sexual self-representation that the state has no business regulating (45–58). Where personal choice about one's sexual activity is concerned, even the choice to become a porn worker or a prostitute, Cornell consistently believes that the woman's choice must trump the state's paternalistic (alleged) concern for her well-being. "State enforced moralism hinders what we as feminists should seek: the psychic, political, and ethical space for women to represent themselves" (58). In a similar vein, Cornell rejects Susan Moller Okin's suggestion that women's economic dependence—which grows out of the division of labor between the sexes—can be eliminated by providing both partners an equal entitlement to the household income, because she fears that in such a regime "the reach of the state in supervising the family finances is simply too great" (94).

Cornell is aware of the degraded conditions of most (although, she argues, not all) pornography workers and prostitutes, and she shares Okin's concern with women's economic dependence. She nevertheless rejects governmental solutions to these problems, not out of any traditionally liberal belief in the sanctity of the private sphere, but rather from her understanding of the limited role of law in achieving feminist goals. For Cornell the ultimate goal of feminism is freedom for all from the confines of the gender system that dominates our legal, economic, social, cultural, and psychological lives. Freedom in this broad sense is not primarily a legal but an aesthetic concept that demands the opening up of women's (and men's) possibilities of self-representation in all of these spheres. Feminists "demand the widest possible space for expression, precisely because without it, we legitimate foreclosures on what can be said, written, or imagined, and thus undermine and reshelve the project of each of us representing her sexuate being in all its fluidity and incessant opening to new possibilities" (25).

The role of law in this ambitious project is crucial but limited. As constitutional law, law can ensure that the state does not impose, directly or indirectly, any particular conception of gender on citizens and thus infringe on their imaginary domain. As positive legislation, law can seek to extend that freedom into the private sphere by restricting the ability of private parties to impose conceptions of gender on others. With regard to the latter, however, there is an ever-present danger that, under the guise of remedial legislation, the state will reenact some new version of "proper" gender roles. Consistent with the priority she gives individual freedom, Cornell sometimes rejects such remedial legislation (for example, Okin's proposal for a state-enforced division of household income [94]), even where she is in agreement with its goals. The personal is truly political for her: the righting of wrongs done to women in the private sphere demands first and foremost direct political action by women, not paternalistic intervention by the state that risks (as the Canadian experience with censorship illustrates) solutions that are worse than the problems.

Accordingly, Cornell advocates self-organization and collective action by prostitutes and porn workers, not the criminalization of their activities, which only make such collective action impossible (57).[55]

For similar reasons, when "there is an open and public clash between our different representations of our sexuate being"—her example is the ongoing fight between organizers of the St. Patrick's Day Parade in New York who believed that "Irish" and "gay" are mutually exclusive concepts, and the Irish gay and lesbian group that wanted to march in the parade—she believes that "there cannot be any state-ordered solution because such an intervention inevitably involves the state in deciding whose representation of 'Irishness' is better." Rather, she says, "The conflict should be left on the street" (61). Cornell's liberalism thus comes down strongly on the side of traditional liberalism's suspicion of state paternalism, without, however, losing sight of feminism's demand for freedom and equality in the private sphere.

I have suggested that Cornell's extension of the ideal of freedom into the imaginary domain of our somatic and sexual self-conception can be called "radical feminist liberalism." There are two senses in which this term is apt. First, Cornell articulates her own radical conception of feminism—liberation from gender—according to a schema that remains true both to the liberal paradigm and to the feminist critiques of that paradigm. Second, she achieves this synthesis by introducing into the Kantian schema an abstract conception of the body conceived as "ultimate end" and elevating that conception to the same level of dignity that Kant himself afforded the rational will.[56] The hierarchical dichotomy between "mind" and "body" (like that between "culture" and "nature") has long been associated with the gender hierarchy between "man" and "woman."[57] In privileging the purely rational while relegating the body to the realm of the (merely) phenomenal, Kant covertly replicated that traditional hierarchy in one of the foundational acts of philosophical liberalism. By placing somatic/sexual freedom on an equal footing with freedom of the rational will, Cornell's feminist revision disrupts that hierarchy at its source and installs freedom and equality of sexual difference at the heart of liberalism.

Let me now try to situate Cornell's synthesis in the larger context of philosophical liberalism. My thesis is that her feminist reformulation of liberalism is not an aberration from but a continuation of a liberal philosophical tradition that leads from Kant to Rawls. Thus, apart from its consequences for feminist theorizing, Cornell's work affords insight into the project of philosophical liberalism as a whole and the directions it can take in a postmetaphysical age. Situating her work in relationship to Kant and Rawls (and, as I explain below, ultimately to Hegel as well) requires that one go beneath the structural aspects of their theories and examine how each justifies the fundamental liberal premise of subjective freedom. This examination in turn requires a closer look at Cornell's arguments in *The Imaginary Domain* and *At the Heart of Freedom*, which changed significantly between the two books.

In both *The Imaginary Domain* and *At the Heart of Freedom* Cornell argues that Rawls's philosophical liberalism has to be supplemented with recognition and protection of the imaginary domain if women's sexual difference is to be respected.[58] In *The Imaginary Domain*, however, this protection was couched in the language of Rawls's "primary goods." For Rawls, primary goods are those basic, common-denominator resources required by free and equal citizens (represented by those behind the veil of ignorance) to live out rational plans of life: basic rights and liberties, institutional opportunities, wealth and income, and the social bases of self-respect.[59] The primary goods play a key role in his theory, because how they are to be distributed constitutes the content of the principles of justice upon which the representatives behind the veil must decide.

In *The Imaginary Domain*, Cornell linked the protection of the imaginary domain with the primary good of self-respect but not in a manner contemplated by Rawls. Rather than a good necessary for free and equal citizens to carry out their rational life plans, Cornell deemed protection of the imaginary domain to be a necessary precondition of becoming such a "free and equal" person with the moral capacities for justice in the first place[60]—moral capacities that Rawls himself took as a given.[61] As Cornell put it, citizens in Rawls's theory "need the conditions necessary for the equivalent chance of becoming persons" if they are ultimately to engage in social cooperation according to the principles of justice.[62] She called those conditions "minimum conditions of individuation"—those minimal developmental resources required for the development of reflective, moral subjectivity. Her argument in *The Imaginary Domain* was that one aspect of such minimum conditions had to be protection of individuals' freedom to develop and orient themselves as physical, desiring, sexuate beings. Otherwise, Rawls could not guarantee that the freedom, equality, and moral capacity for justice he posited of citizens of the liberal state would extend to all citizens, regardless of their sexuate being.[63]

Cornell later rejected this argument, noting that "[f]or Okin gender is inequality, so what she means by an end to gender is the end of inequality" (94). It is clear, however (as Cornell herself recognizes [194 n.38]), that the same criticism applies to Cornell's own formula in *The Imaginary Domain*. Cornell would surely reject the idea that her notion of the imaginary domain was ever intended to ensure the development of "persons whose psychological and moral development is in all essentials identical,"[64] since protection of the imaginary domain is meant to protect sexual difference and diversity, not impose sameness. Nevertheless, by putting the imaginary domain in the service of producing genuinely "free and equal" representatives behind the veil of ignorance—rather than privileging freedom of sexuate being for its own sake—she was ultimately subordinating the right of sexual difference to the "sameness" of perspective required for effective negotiations behind the veil.

As the preceding section demonstrates, Cornell fundamentally changed her approach in her later work. As she herself explained, in *The Imaginary*

Domain she "still justified the recognition of women's sexual freedom based on their equal citizenship, not simply as an end in itself for a human being."[65] In *At the Heart of Freedom*, by contrast, protection of freedom within the imaginary domain is defended as an ultimate end. Although she still attempts to articulate this freedom in terms that are consistent with Rawls's, this task has become even more difficult than her somewhat strained attempt to equate "minimum conditions of individuation" with a Rawlsian "primary good" in *The Imaginary Domain*. In fact, in *At the Heart of Freedom* it is Kant who comes to the fore, not Rawls.

Thus, while Cornell argued in *The Imaginary Domain* that freedom of the imaginary domain was a condition of Rawlsian citizens *becoming* "free and equal" participants in the hypothetical social contract, in *At the Heart of Freedom* she argues that such freedom *belongs to what it means to be such a "free and equal" being* in the first place. She explains:

> For Rawls, the free person of a freestanding concept of political liberalism is the citizen. Therefore, the political concept of the free person is tailored to these conditions of reciprocity that must exist between citizens if they are to reasonably justify their stances on constitutional essentials to one another. But in Rawls's theory, citizens are already included in the moral community of persons, and thus have to be granted equal maximum liberty. Indeed, this inclusion, granting each person equal citizenship, is crucial to Rawls's elaboration of the symmetry of the original position. (14; notes omitted)

Within this Rawlsian framework, the imaginary domain is "a heuristic device that can help us see . . . what it means for sexed beings to be included in the moral community of persons as an initial matter," an issue that "must be explicitly addressed before principles of distributive justice can be defended by the moral procedure" (15).

This change is more than a nuance, since it shifts the foundation for protection of the imaginary domain from an empirical question—Is such protection really necessary for all individuals to become autonomous and equal moral agents capable of rationally deciding and acting on the requirements of justice?—to a deontological presupposition of the entire Rawlsian procedural approach to establishing the principles of justice.[66] It also, despite the continuing prevalence of Rawlsian terminology, moves her away from Rawls and back towards Kant:

> The kind of freedom feminism demands does ultimately run deeper than Rawls's description: "how citizens think of themselves in a democratic society when questions of political justice arise." True, this freedom is absolutely basic to women's inclusion into the moral community as an initial matter; yet it is irreducible Rawls's conception of the free person because freedom, particularly sexual freedom, is not simply a value to ourselves as

citizens. Thus, the second feminist intervention into Kantian proceduralist conceptions of justice takes us back to Kant's insistence that freedom must be foregrounded in a concept of right because there is nothing more fundamental for a human being. (17)[67]

Or, put even more starkly, "[i]f the subject of [Rawls's] theory of justice is the basic 'structure' of society, the subject of feminism, for purposes of right and legal reform, is first and foremost the free person" (20).[68]

Nevertheless, if her philosophical framework is Kantian, her *justification* for a return to that framework is neither Kantian nor Rawlsian. As Cornell points out, liberal philosophers differ over their justifications for the "politically conceived free person" (19). Kant's justification was expressly metaphysical and derived a priori from the subject's noumenal status as a being with a rational will.[69] Rawls rejects Kant's metaphysical underpinnings by limiting his consideration of the free subject to her role as a citizen within a modern democratic society and therefore derives his "political" conception of freedom from the minimal self-conception necessary for a subject to cooperate as a free and equal citizen of such a society.[70] He finds this minimal self-conception "implicit in the public political culture of a democratic society," and in particular on those "shared ideas and principles" implicit in "[s]ociety's main institutions."[71] Rawls's focus throughout *Political Liberalism* remains resolutely institutional because his project is aimed first and foremost at "specifying *the fair terms of social cooperation* between citizens regarded as free and equal," and not primarily what it means to be "free and equal"[72] in the first instance. This is the reason that "the basic structure of society [and not freedom] is the first subject of justice."[73] Subjective freedom within Rawls's "political conception" of liberalism thus is a derivative and secondary concept.[74]

As explained earlier in this chapter, Cornell intervenes in Rawls's account by calling attention to an additional aspect of what it means to be a "free and equal citizen" of a democratic society, and since Rawls's primary focus is elsewhere (on the institutional arrangements), her notion of the imaginary domain is, or at least could be made to be, consistent with his framework. Moreover, like Rawls, Cornell rejects Kant's metaphysics as a viable ground for her conception of the free and equal citizen and justifies her own deontological premises on the basis of the "tradition of democratic thought"[75] that accompanied the development of the modern democratic state. Her own analysis begins, however, from a different point within that tradition. Rather than departing from the "public political culture" of the existing institutions of constitutional regimes, Cornell begins much earlier and more abstractly, with the "interpretive, historical appeal to the struggle in the bourgeois revolutions against naturalized, stratified differentiations" (19). In other words, she begins with the modern recognition that the subject stands separate from, and philosophically and politically prior to, her social role. It was Hegel who first recognized that the bourgeois revolutions represented the victory of

the free individual of modernity over the caste-bound individual of feudal social systems, and who argued, in Cornell's words, that "the normative significance of this historical change was the political and moral establishment of
the person" as such (197–98 n.50).[76]

Hegel shared with Kant the belief that the freedom of the subject embodied in a scheme of basic rights and liberties was the hallmark of the modern
state. In lieu of Kant's individualistic metaphysics, however, Hegel grounded
this freedom in the historically developed social-ethical mores and self-
understanding of modern bourgeois society. It is Hegel's philosophical-
historical interpretation of the modern person as a subject prior to its social
and economic roles that Cornell relies on in grounding her own philosophy of
sexuate freedom. For Cornell, the free subject of liberalism must be conceived
of as no less prior to and free to change its gender roles than it is prior to and
free to change its social and economic roles.

Her deeper point of contention with Rawls is that the right to the imaginary domain cannot depend on whether citizens of a democratic society, in order to participate in that society's institutions, conceive of themselves as
possessing imaginary domains in need of legal protection. Whether citizens
conceive of themselves in this way is central to Rawls, however, because he derives his abstract conception of the free and equal citizen from an idealized account of the "democratic political culture as marked by reasonable pluralism"[77]
of modern democratic states. The notion that one has a protected right to one's
sexual identity has only begun to surface in our "democratic political culture"
and remains highly controversial, as the recent heated debate over the constitutional status of gay marriage and the passage and subsequent repeal by popular
referendum of various gay rights initiatives demonstrate.[78] More important given
the limited, "political" orientation of Rawls' theory, the notion of such a right
plays almost no role at all in the dominant conception of what it means to participate in the political community as a citizen. Cornell's account, by contrast,
begins directly with an abstract account of the meaning of individual freedom
and only then works out the consequences for the social. This kind of freedom
remains invisible in an account, like Rawls's, that begins with "the basic structure of society" and works its way down to the rights of the citizen through a
consideration of what it means to participate politically in that society. Cornell's
conception of freedom thus runs deeper and more broadly than Rawls's, because
it is ethical—in Hegel's sense of being grounded in the ethos of modern
societies—rather than political in Rawls' limited sense of that term.[79]

To sum up: (1) Cornell's project diverges from Rawls from the vantage point
of its deontological assumptions. Unlike Rawls (but like Kant), Cornell begins
with an abstract conception of the free subject rather than with an abstract conception of the basic institutional structure of society. (2) Cornell agrees with
Rawls in rejecting Kant's dualistic metaphysics, which explained the subject's
freedom on the basis of its noumenal, rational will. She also agrees with Rawls
that the freedom of the "free and equal" subject of liberalism must be justified by

reference to a historical interpretation of the nature of modern democratic societies. (3) She diverges from Rawls, however, in returning directly to an understanding of individual freedom based on the modern subject's liberation from its identification with its political, economic, and social status under feudalism, rather than on Rawls's more circumscribed conception of individual political freedom that is derived from, and limited to, the subject's role as citizen within the basic political institutions of a modern democracy.

Should these philosophical distinctions matter to feminists? I will conclude with two related reasons suggesting that they should, and not only to feminists but to all who share Cornell's commitment to maintaining what remains vital in liberalism while discarding what is dead (or deadly) in it. Feminist philosophers are not the only ones who have criticized liberalism for its indifference to difference. Bernard Yack, for example, takes Kant and Rawls to task for their "unrealistic assumptions about our shared identity" and fears that Kantian liberalism "promotes and reinforces a set of moral dispositions that tends to make us insensitive to the different ways in which various members of our political community conceive of themselves."[80] Yack's objection originates not in feminist concerns but in another strand of the liberal tradition—the skeptical liberalism of Montaigne, Montesquieu, and Mill, "a liberalism that was deeply aware of the distasteful consequences of human pretensions to moral certainty." It is this "pretension to moral certainty"[81] that Yack detects in Kant's metaphysical account of the unitary and abstract nature of the liberal subject, and in Rawls's nonmetaphysical (but equally unrealistic) a priori "conception of democratic public culture."[82] In language reminiscent of feminist critiques, Yack calls for a "continuing readjustment [of the liberal paradigm] as new voices are heard and understood."[83]

At the Heart of Freedom speaks to these skeptical liberal concerns in two respects. First, as I tried to show in the preceding section, Cornell shows how respect for difference can be incorporated into an otherwise traditional Kantian liberal framework that begins with an abstract conception of the freedom of the abstract moral subject. Second, and more important from the skeptical perspective, Cornell's philosophical justification for her conception of freedom leaves that conception open to revision and reinterpretation in ways that Kant's metaphysical and Rawls's political conceptions do not. Cornell's defense of the imaginary domain is expressly tied to a historical interpretation of the meaning of liberal freedom (Hegel's interpretation of modernity as signifying the liberation of the subject from the "naturalized, stratified differentiations" that defined it under feudalism [19–20]). Because Cornell's justification for her conception of freedom is expressly interpretive, both the particular conception of freedom and its historical justification are inherently contestable—not refutable, as an empirical claim or deductive argument would be, but open to reasoned contestation. Rawls's theory is also based on a historical interpretation of sorts. Rawls, however, leaves far less room for argument over the consequences of adopting a conception of the person based on our "democratic political culture,"[84] if only because he focuses so narrowly on the conception implicit in a limited number of specific institutions of our existing democratic societies. Cornell's justification of sexuate freedom, by contrast, returns to the original abstract distinction constitutive of the modern liberal subject as such—the distinction between the subject identified with its social role and the subject independent of its social role.

By returning to the origin for its justification, Cornell's defense of freedom of sexuate being both gains in rhetorical force and opens the door to a productive dialogue over whether the notion of the "bodily ego"—which underwrites the notion of the imaginary domain—should extend similar rights of somatic freedom to other, superficially natural "stratified differentiations" among individuals. For example, one could argue that legal protection of the imaginary domain can and should be extended to persons with physical disabilities, since, like gender, physical disability can be viewed as more a psycho-social-legal construct than a "natural" differentiation between the physically disabled and other persons. Cornell argues that sexuate being can be distinguished from physical disability for purposes of legal protection of the imaginary domain (214–15 n.42), but one can well imagine that her notion could undergo, as Yack puts it, a "continuing readjustment . . . as new voices are heard and understood."[85] Rawls's conception of the person, on the other hand, based as it is on specific moral traits implicit in specific, current institutional arrangements, is dependent on specific claims about current moral-political understandings and thus lacks this flexibility.

This leads to my final point. Cornell's return to the original meaning of liberal freedom provides the key to a certain history of liberalism that includes both Kant and Rawls, in addition to her own theory, and points beyond to the potential for new liberatory liberal doctrines as well—a history of liberalism as the decline in the power of natural fate.

As Kant first articulated it, the liberal doctrine of subjective freedom represents the belief that humans can and should be allowed to choose their own ultimate ends. There are only two constraints on this doctrine—the moral limitation that restricts this freedom to ends consistent with an equal freedom for all and the existential limitation that nature imposes on our acts of will. Because we are human rather than divine, not every goal that we can conceive of can be realized in fact, and in formulating our ends we take these natural limits as the givens with which we begin. The moral limitation gives rise to the liberal doctrine of politics and the legitimate role of the state in enforcing equal maximum freedom for all. The existential limitation, on the other hand, has withered as the natural and social sciences have brought areas of human life once thought beyond our understanding and power to control within the scope of conceivable human ends. The decline in this limitation indexes a progressive history of liberal theory that includes Kant, Rawls, and Cornell's notion of sexuate freedom.

As Hegel recognized, the very idea of the free person of a liberal political order originated with the decline of the feudal social hierarchy, which had embraced a view of personhood that took the individual's social caste and role as her natural fate. Kant believed that this new subjective freedom was strictly limited to the realm of political right. He believed, for example, that freedom was "perfectly consistent with the utmost inequality of the mass in the degree of its possessions, whether these take the form of physical and mental superiority over others, or of fortuitous external property."[86]

We no longer understand, however, as did Kant, a person's accumulation of "external property" as "fortuitous," or as purely a function of the person's (equally fortuitous) "physical or mental superiority." Rather than a result of luck or fate of birth, the contemporary understanding views economic status and wealth accumulation as at least partly a function of conscious social decision making. This understanding is reflected in the fact that the dominant liberal theory of our own time, John Rawls's theory of justice, takes as its "first subject" the "basic structure of society," which includes the legitimate scope of economic freedom and opportunity as well as the basic scheme of political rights. Rawls thus extends the primacy of the human will to an area once thought to be governed by fate.

Cornell's notion of the imaginary domain follows in this same tradition. The idea that gender personality is a natural fact has been subjected to increasing challenge for many years, long before the most recent wave of feminism. Now, as the view of gender as fate has receded, Cornell's notion of the imaginary domain suggests the possibility of expanding the realm of freedom to the intrapersonal, psychosomatic realm of gender constitution. As she puts it, "we are not fated to be sexed in any particular form" (8).

In sum, Cornell has shown that, by returning to the roots of liberalism, radical feminist theses can be placed squarely in the great tradition of liberal philosophy. She has also shown that the liberal affirmation of human freedom is broad enough to demand that the gender system be uprooted at its source. She thus provokes a rethinking of both feminism and liberalism. Hers is a radical feminist liberalism in every sense.

NOTES

1. Drucilla Cornell, *The Imaginary Domain: Abortion, Pornography and Sexual Harassment* (New York: Routledge, 1995).

2. For a concise explanation of the significance of the "ethical" in "ethical feminism," see Drucilla Cornell, "What Is Ethical Feminism?" in Benhabib, Butler, Cornell, and Fraser, *Feminist Contentions* (New York: Routledge, 1995), 78–85.

3. See Cornell, "What is Ethical Feminism?" Drucilla Cornell, *Beyond Accomodation: Ethical Feminism, Deconstruction and the Law* (New York: Routledge, 1991). Indeed, as I have argued elsewhere, to a great extent Cornell's early work defined its

own understanding of law, justice, and ethics through a critique of the Kantian paradigm. See Adam Thurschwell, "On the Threshold of Ethics," *Cardozo Law Review* 15 (1994):1607, 1618–23.

4. See, e.g., Robin West, "Universalism, Liberalism, and the Problem of Gay Marriage," *Florida State University Law Review* 25 (1998):705, 708 ("Does liberal feminism hold, as its many detractors claim, to a false and patriarchal ideal, betraying women, if it aims to do nothing more than increase the number of 'women in suits?'").

5. Drucilla Cornell, *At the Heart of Freedom: Feminism, Sex and Equality* (New Jersey: Princeton University Press, 1998). Further page references will be designated in parentheses in the text.

6. There are of course many forms of liberalism. In the next section I will discuss the liberalism expounded by Kant, because Cornell's project derives its inspiration primarily from Kant's philosophy and because Kant is the chief philosophical forebear of John Rawls, the other leading contemporary philosopher of liberalism that Cornell discusses. See John Rawls, *A Theory of Justice* (Cambridge: Harvard University Press, 1971), 11 & n.4, 12 & n.5, 251–57; John Rawls, "Themes in Kant's Moral Philosophy," in Beiner and Booth, eds., *Kant and Political Philosophy: The Contemporary Legacy* (New Haven: Yale University Press, 1993); John Rawls, *Political Liberalism* (New York: Columbia University Press, 1993). In the following sections I examine more closely the relationships among Kant, Rawls, and Cornell. In this section I am using "philosophical liberalism" more loosely (although fully consistent with Kant) to mean the tradition in political philosophy taken to justify the priority granted to individual rights, freedom and self-governance characteristic of democratic political regimes.

7. See, e.g., John Stuart Mill, "The Subjection of Women," in Mill, *On Liberty and Other Essays*, ed. John Gray (London: Oxford University Press, 1991).

8. For a history of women's political action for equal rights since the suffrage movement, see Mary Becker, "The Sixties Shift to Formal Equality and the Courts: An Argument for Pragmatism and Politics," *William & Mary Law Review* 40 (1998):209, 210–49.

9. See, e.g., Catharine A. Mackinnon, "Difference and Dominance: On Sex Discrimination," in *Feminism Unmodified: Discourses on Life and Law* (Cambridge: Harvard University Press, 1987), 32–33.

10. Simone de Beauvoir, *The Second Sex*, trans. and ed. H. M. Parshley (New York: Vintage Books, 1989), xxi.

11. See *Rostker v. Goldberg*, 453 U.S. 57 (1981) (equal protection not violated by congressional decision to require only men to register for the draft because women were excluded from combat).

12. *Geduldig v. Aiello*, 417 U.S. 484 (1974).

13. See Carol Pateman, *The Sexual Contract* (Stanford: Stanford University Press, 1988), 42. She explains how both Kant and Rawls "subsume feminine beings under the apparently universal, sexually neuter category of the 'individual.'"

14. See Catharine A. Mackinnon, *Toward a Feminist Theory of the State* (Cambridge: Harvard University Press, 1989), 162–64; Catharine A. Mackinnon, *Feminism Unmodified: Discourses on Life and Law.*

15. See, e.g., Robin West, "Jurisprudence and Gender" *University of Chicago Law Review* 55 (1988):1, 14 ("what unifies radical and cultural feminist theory [and what distinguishes both from liberal feminism] is the discovery, or rediscovery, of the importance of women's fundamental material difference from men"). The "difference" school of feminism is often traced to Carol Gilligan's groundbreaking critique of Hans Kohlberg's model of moral development. Carol Gilligan, *In a Different Voice: Psychological Theory and Women's Development* (Cambridge: Harvard Univeristy Press, 1982).

16. See, e.g., Susan Moller Okin, *Justice, Gender, and the Family* (New York: Basic Books, 1989), 107. Okin suggests that John Rawls's *Theory of Justice* be modified by taking into account "the standpoint of women" in its procedure for formulating the principles of justice.

17. Other feminists ground their arguments in Marx's critique of the abstract subject of bourgeois right, uniting feminism with Marxist philosophy and a socialist political agenda. In effect, for these theorists the social-political significance of the sexual difference is explained by and subordinated to the class difference. See, for example, the essays collected in Zillah Eisenstein, ed., *Capitalist Patriarchy and the Case for Socialist Feminism* (New York: Monthly Review Press, 1979).

18. Robin West has asked, "[I]s it really true, as the liberal seems to believe as an article of faith, that the flame of inclusion in a hegemonic community, defined by universally shared human traits, is worth the lost candle of identity or distinctiveness a particular subcommunity or culture may be asked to sacrifice?" Robin West, "Universalism, Liberalism, and the Problem of Gay Marriage" *Florida State University Law Review* 25 (1998):705, 707.

19. Kant held that the "uniform equality of human beings as subjects of the state is . . . perfectly consistent with the utmost inequality of the mass in the degree of its possessions, whether these take the form of physical or mental superiority over others, or of fortuitous external property relations." Hans Reiss, ed., *Kant's Political Writings*, trans. H. B. Nisbet (Cambridge: Cambridge University Press, 1970), 75. In contrast, for John Rawls, the distribution of wealth and economic opportunity constitutes part of the "basic structure of society" that is the subject of a theory of justice. John Rawls, *A Theory of Justice*, 7. I discuss this historical development in the scope of liberal theory further in a later section.

20. See, e.g., Okin, *Justice, Gender, and the Family*, 25–133, examining the traditional exclusion of the family from the "sphere of justice".

21. See, e.g., Catharine A. Mackinnon, *Toward a Feminist Theory of the State*, 190–91. "[P]rivacy doctrine is most at home in the home, the place the women experience the most force, in the family. . . . For women the measure of the intimacy has been the measure of the oppression. . . . This is why feminism has seen the personal as political."

22. See Anne C. Dailey, "Feminism's Return to Liberalism," *Yale Law Journal* 102 (1993):1265, 1271–73. She reviews Katharine T. Bartlett and Rosanne Kennedy, eds., *Feminist Legal Theory: Reading in Law and Gender* (Boulder: Westview, 1991), discussing how feminist rejection of a universal essence of the human leads to an "anti-essentialist abyss" in which the feminist category of "woman" is exploded into endless subcategories; see also, e.g., Kimberlé Crenshaw, "Demarginalizing the Intersection of

Race and Sex: A Black Feminist Critique of Antidiscrimination Doctrine, Feminist Theory, and Antiracist Politics," 1989 *University of Chicago Legal Forum* 139, discussing the overlooked significance of race to feminist legal analysis.

23. One conclusion that could plausibly be drawn from this argument is that feminists should abandon the traditional liberal concept of right entirely. That option is rejected by many of the same critics who have highlighted feminists' failure to take account of the specificity of women of color. See, e.g., Patricia Williams, *The Alchemy of Race and Rights* (Cambridge: Harvard University Press, 1992), 148–165.

24. As Cornell put it in *The Imaginary Domain*, "[t]heoretical appeals to asymmetry as the basis of claims to equality . . . undermine their own appeal by reinscribing themselves in the language of the repudiation of femininity that has informed, throughout history, the denial of women's parity with men." Cornell, *The Imaginary Domain*, 24.

25. Pregnancy Discrimination Act of 1978, 42 U.S.C. § 2000e(k).

26. For a classic statement of the "equal treatment" position, see Wendy Williams, "Equality's Riddle: Pregnancy and the Equal Treatment/Special Treatment Debate," *New York University Review of Law and Social Change* 13 (1985):325.

27. *California Savings & Loan Assoc. v. Guerra*, 479 U.S. 272, 290 (1987), upholding provision because consistent with Title 7's purposes and did "not reflect archaic or stereotypical notions about pregnancy and the abilities of pregnant workers).

28. Compare Catharine MacKinnon, *Only Words* (Cambridge: Harvard University Press, 1996) with Nadine Strossen, "A Feminist Critique of 'The' Feminist Critique of Pornography," *Virginia Law Review* 79 (1993):1099; Carlin Meyer, "Sex, Sin, and Women's Liberation: Against Porn-suppression," *Texas Law Review* 72 (1994):1097.

29. See Strossen, "A Feminist Critique of 'The' Feminist Critique of Pornography," 1143–17 (arguing that censorship will always be used against politically weaker parties, including feminists).

30. *Butler v. The Queen*, 1 S.C.R. 452 (1992); see Strossen, "A Feminist Critique of 'The' Feminist Critique of Pornography," 1099, 1145–47 (describing Canadian experience).

31. Drucilla Cornell, *Beyond Accommodation* (Lanham: Rowman and Littlefield, 1999), 19.

32. See Reiss, ed., *Kant's Political Writings*, 74–75.

33. See Immanuel Kant, *Foundations of the Metaphysics of Morals*, trans. Lewis Beck (New York: MacMillan, 1990), 28. "[A]ll moral concepts have their seat and origin entirely a priori in reason. . . . It is obvious that they cannot be abstracted from any empirical and hence merely contingent cognitions. In the purity of their origin lies their worthiness to serve us as supreme practical principles."

34. Kant, *Foundations of the Metaphysics of Morals*, 56.

35. See Reiss, ed., *Kant's Political Writings* 73–75.

36. Rawls, *A Theory of Justice*, 60.

37. Ibid., 61.

38. Ibid., 136–42.

39. Okin, *Justice, Gender, and the Family,* 107–09. She suggests that the distinctive psychology of women should be included behind the "veil of ignorance" in Rawls's *Theory of Justice;* see also, e.g., Linda R. Hirshman, "Is the Original Position Inherently Male-Superior?" *Columbia Law Review* 94 (1994):1860, 1866–75 (similar critique of Rawls's *Political Liberalism* based on women's physical differences from men).

40. Feminists have argued that, were a specifically feminine voice to be heard among the ostensibly "neutral" (but in reality masculine) representatives behind the veil of ignorance, the individualist slant of Kant's and Rawls's theories and their exclusive focus on justice in the public sphere would be altered, among other changes. Okin, Hirshman, 1875–80.

41. See Cornell, *Beyond Accommodation,* 19, identifying feminism with the critique of "our current system, in which sex is lived within the established 'heterosexual' matrix as a rigid gender identity which creates our separation and identifies us as boys and girls." Cornell cites by way of example the inadequacy of conventional gender discrimination analysis, with its reliance on a formal conception of equality, to address the specific forms of discrimination faced by lesbians and gays in the workplace and elsewhere.

42. *Oncale v. Sundowner Offshore Services,* 118 S.Ct. 998 (1998).

43. Id., at 1002 (quoting *Harris v. Forklift Systems, Inc.,* 510 U.S. 17, 25 (1993) (Ginsburg, J., concurring)).

44. See also Cornell, *The Imaginary Domain,* 170, defining sexual harassment as the "reducing [of] individuals to sexual stereotypes or objectified fantasies of their 'sex.'"

45. See Cornell, *The Philosophy of the Limit* (New York: Routledge, 1992), in which she elaborates her general critique of the limits of any system, including the gender system. The utopian impulse behind Cornell's feminism is well expressed by Jacques Derrida: "[W]hat if we were to approach here . . . the area of a relationship to the other where the code of sexual marks would no longer be discriminating? The relationship would not be a-sexual, far from it, but would be sexual otherwise: beyond the code of binary difference that governs the decorum of all codes, beyond the opposition feminine/ masculine, beyond bisexuality as well, beyond homosexuality and heterosexuality which come to the same thing. As I dream of saving the chance that this question offers I would like to believe in the multiplicity of sexually marked voices. I would like to believe in the masses, this indeterminable number of blended voices, this mobile of non-identified sexual marks whose choreography can carry, divide, multiply the body of each 'individual,' whether he be classified as 'man' or as 'woman' according to the criteria of usage." Jacques Derrida and Christie McDonald, "Interview: Choreographies," in Jacques Derrida, *The Ear of the Other,* ed. Christie McDonald, trans. Peggy Kamuf (Lincoln: University of Nebraska Press, 1988), 163, 184.

46. Reiss, *Kant's Political Writings,* 74.

47. See Rawls, *A Theory of Justice,* 205–211 ("Equal Liberty of Conscience"); Rawls, *Political Liberalism,* 19–20 and citizens' "final ends").

48. Rawls, *A Theory of Justice,* 206.

49. See introduction to this chapter

50. The result would be different if the statute granted maternity (as opposed to pregnancy) leave. By singling out women to receive a child-care benefit that relates

not to their sexual difference as such but to a role that both women and men can play in family life, the state would be sending two messages that denigrate persons' freedom: the message that women *should* play a particular reproductive role based on their sexual difference and the message that men should *not* play this role. Both of these messages hinder persons from defining for themselves the meaning of their sexual difference, be that feminine or masculine, and thus violate the principle of freedom represented by the protection of the imaginary domain.

51. Cornell thus disagrees with Luce Irigaray's attempt to reconcile sexual difference with universality by recognizing sexual difference itself as a universal, one that has, as it were, two faces, one for men and one for women (122; quoting Luce Irigaray, *I Love to You: Sketch of a Possible Felicity in History* trans. Alison Martin, [1994], 51). For Cornell, "the attempt to give rights [to women], thought through gender difference as a universal, denies women the freedom to reimagine their sexual difference" (122), by imposing a state-sanctioned definition on what it means to be a "woman."

52. Anne C. Dailey, "Feminism's Return to Liberalism," *Yale Law Journal* 102 (1993):1265, 1271–73 (reviewing Katharine T. Bartlett and Rosanne Kennedy, eds., *Feminist Legal Theory: Readings in Law and Gender* [Boulder: Westview, 1991]).

53. Cornell, *The Imaginary Domain*, 116–22.

54. Ibid., 147–58.

55. Ibid., 117.

56. Carol Pateman makes a similar point about the "disembodied" aspect of the Kantian person in connection with her argument against the legalization of prostitution but does not develop it as the basis for a reformulated ideal of freedom because of her exclusive focus on the contractual aspects of liberal political theory. Pateman, *The Sexual Contract*, 205–07.

57. See, e.g., Aristotle, *The Politics and the Constitution of Athens*, ed. Stephen Everson, trans. Richard Jowett (Cambridge: Cambridge University Press, 1986), 1254b. "The soul rules the body with a despotical rule, whereas the intellect rules appetites with a constitutional and royal rule. And it is clear that the rule of the soul over the body, and of the mind and the rational element over the passionate, is natural and expedient; whereas the equality of the two or the rule of the inferior is always hurtful. . . . Again, the male is by nature superior, and the female inferior; and the one rules, and the other is ruled." Sherry B. Ortner, "Is Female to Male as Nature Is to Culture?" in *Women, Culture, and Society* 67 (1974):84–85.

58. See Cornell, *The Imaginary Domain*, 8–18, on the feminist alliance with Rawls.

59. Rawls, *Political Liberalism*, 180–82; Rawls, *A Theory of Justice*, 62, 92–93.

60. Cornell, *The Imaginary Domain*, 17–18, 185, 265–66 n.38. It should be noted that Cornell is aware of the uneasiness of the fit with Rawls's own conception of primary goods.

61. Rawls, *Political Liberalism*, 183. "I have assumed throughout, and will continue to assume, that while citizens do not have equal capacities, they do have, at least to the essential minimum degree, the moral, intellectual, and physical capacities that enable them to be fully cooperating members of society over a complete life." See Cornell, *The Imaginary Domain*, 18.

62. Cornell, *The Imaginary Domain*, 18.

63. Ibid., 8–9. Other feminists who are similarly sympathetic to Rawls's liberal framework, and who have also argued that his liberalism could serve feminist ends, have criticized him in similar manner. Susan Moller Okin, for example, has argued both that "[t]here is implicit in Rawls' theory of justice a potential critique of gender-structured social institutions" and that "the abolition of gender seems essential for the fulfillment of Rawls' criterion for political justice." Okin, *Justice, Gender, and the Family*, 105, 104. As to the latter, in an argument that is structurally similar to Cornell's argument in *The Imaginary Domain*, she points out that "if principles of justice are to be unanimously adopted by representative human beings ignorant of their particular characteristics and positions in society, they must be persons whose psychological and moral development is in all essentials identical." Gender, however, exerts such an overarching influence over all aspects of our psychologies and social assumptions that such identical "psychological and moral development" will be a chimera unless and until all the social institutions of gender are demolished. Okin, *Justice, Gender, and the Family*, 107. Okin and others have criticized Rawls's *Political Liberalism* on similar terms, arguing that one of his criteria for the political "stability" of the just liberal society—the development of citizens with an internal sense of justice—cannot be met unless gender inequality is abolished within the family and other private associations. Moller Okin, "*Political Liberalism*, Justice, and Gender," *Ethics* 105 no. 23 (1994):37–39; S.A. Lloyd, "Situating a Feminist Criticism of John Rawls's *Political Liberalism*," *Loyola of Los Angeles Law Review* 28 (1995):1319; see also Susan Miller Okin, "Justice and Gender: An Unfinished Debate," 72 *Fordham Law Review* (2004):1537.

64. Okin, *Justice, Gender, and the Family*, 107.

65. Cornell, *The Imaginary Domain*, 194 n.38.

66. Apart from its greater conceptual clarity, this change has the effect of eliminating other legitimate objections to Cornell's formulation in *The Imaginary Domain*. Because Cornell bases her defense of the imaginary domain on its role in the protection of "minimum conditions of individuation," acceptance of her descriptive argument for those minimum conditions becomes a crucial predicate for acceptance of her argument in favor of the imaginary domain itself. Any description of the minimum conditions required for the development of moral powers and a capacity for social cooperation, however, is doomed to be controversial, to say the least. Cornell's own defense of minimum conditions, which relies on Lacanian psychoanalytic insights, is no exception. See e.g. Heather Keele, Book Note, "Reimagining Equality," *Yale Law Journal* 105 (1996):2303, 2307–08 (reviewing *The Imaginary Domain*, criticizing Cornell's reliance on psychoanalytic theory. Cornell herself recognizes this problem. Cornell, *The Imaginary Domain*, 18: "Minimum conditions of individuation are, admittedly, justified through an appeal to empirical practical reason since they demand some recognition of experience." She cannot avoid it, however, so long as her defense of the imaginary domain rests on arguments about the actual moral development of actual human beings. In *At the Heart of Freedom*, all such arguments from empirical experience are eliminated because freedom of sexuate being is conceived as part of the freedom ascribed to human beings qua human.

67. Quoting Rawls, *Political Liberalism*, 33.

68. See Rawls, *Political Liberalism*, 257 (lecture 7, "The Basic Structure as Subject"): "An essential feature of a contractarian conception of justice is that the basic structure of society is the first subject of justice."

69. See Reiss, *Kant's Political Writings*, 73: "Since every restriction of freedom through the arbitrary will of another party is termed *coercion*, it follows that a civil constitution is a relationship among *free* men who are subject to coercive laws, while they retain their freedom within the general union with their fellows. Such is the requirement of pure reason, which legislates a *priori*, regardless of all empirical ends."

70. Rawls, *Political Liberalism*, 18–19, 29–35 (describing his "political conception of the person").

71. Ibid., 13, 14.

72. Ibid., 3; emphasis added.

73. Ibid., 257.

74. Rawls explains that "[s]ince our account of justice as fairness begins with the idea of that society is to be conceived as a fair system of cooperation over time between generations, *we adopt a conception of the person to go with this idea.*" Rawls, *Political Liberalism*, 18; emphasis added. Whereas Rawls tailors the conception of the person to fit the ideal scheme of social cooperation, Kant derives the scheme of cooperation from the conception of the free person.

75. Rawls, *Political Liberalism*, 18.

76. See generally G. W. F. Hegel, *Hegel's Philosophy of Right*, trans. T. M. Knox (London: Oxford University Press, 1967).

77. Rawls, *Political Liberalism*, xxi.

78. On the issue of these referendums, see *Romer v. Evans*, 517 U.S. 620, 623 (1996).

79. By the same token, her critique of Rawls's conception of the "free and equal citizen" demonstrates that ethical conceptions of the person cannot be avoided in Rawls's ostensibly limited "political" conception of liberalism except at risk of overlooking fundamental rights of personhood.

80. Bernard Yack, "The Problem with Kantian Liberalism," in ed. *Kant and Political Philosophy: The Contemporary Legacy*, Ronald Beiner and William James Booth, 234.

81. Ibid., 240

82. Ibid., 232.

83. Ibid., 238.

84. Rawls, *Political Liberalism*, xxi.

85. Yack, "The Problem with Kantian Liberalism," 238.

86. Reiss, *Kant's Political Writings*, 75.

Karin Van Marle

"The Capabilities Approach," "The Imaginary Domain," and "Asymmetrical Reciprocity": Feminist Perspectives on Equality and Justice

For though the common world is the common meeting ground for all, those who are present have different positions on it, and the location of one can no more coincide with the location of another than the location of two objects
— Hanna Arendt, *The Human Condition*

INTRODUCTION

Feminist theory has traveled a long way since the liberal feminist demand for the right to equality based on the yardstick of neutrality and sameness. One of the most significant shifts from modern and liberal feminist theories to postmodern and critical theories was the switch in focus from a search for abstract universal conceptions of equality and justice to context and the particular. Western feminists, most notably, have come to accept the claim that many feminist theories repeat the harms of patriarchal society by accepting only one view of reality and thereby excluding many women.

Any attempt to describe a feminist conception of justice could be regarded as another act of Western globalization or imperialism. However, many feminists have continued the struggle to find theoretical and practical explanations that include non-Western women, a conception of justice that encompasses all women worldwide. In our reflections on the notion of justice, we should consider whether such a universalizing notion could be applied to feminist concerns with women's "embodiedness" and "embeddedness." Can feminism simultaneously reject the "logic of identity," the "metaphysics of presence," and the "masquerade of femininity," yet still endorse universalist notions of justice?[1]

The aim of this chapter is to consider this search for justice and equality for women in light of our different lives and conditions. It seeks to rethink the possibilities of a feminist perspective on justice and a feminist "community" from and within the demands of difference, respect, dignity, and hope. In so doing it discusses the work of three feminist theorists, Martha Nussbaum, Drucilla Cornell, and Iris Young. I understand all three to strive for a broad framework of universalism in the sense that they are concerned with universal values such as equality, dignity, and justice. However, there are important differences in how they address these concerns. Nussbaum although coming from a Neo-Aristotelian perspective, in her later work accepts what can be called a "liberal notion" of universalism in her defense of universal values and support of international feminism. Cornell stands critical of liberal universalism and relies on the concepts of 'sublimity', 'dignity', and 'women's time' to explain her vision of a new feminist community, and Young posits a heterogeneous public and vibrant city life as alternative to liberal universalism. Together they provide a useful framework within which to contemplate various positions on universalism, difference equality, and justice. It must be noted that Nussbaum in her capabilities approach by no means follows a traditional abstract approach where concrete contexts are negated or ignored and yardsticks of sameness and neutrality followed. However, I argue that Cornell's notion of the imaginary domain and Young's asymmetrical reciprocity go further in showing concern for difference and particularity. I employ this framework here to consider the protection of equality under the South African Constitution and come to argue that the inherent structure of law inevitably leads to a denial of difference and a support for generalisation and universalism based on sameness, even where there is an attempt to recognize difference, for example in the Draft Protocol to the African Charter on Human and People's Rights on the Rights of Women in Africa. I conclude that although law and legal reform will always be more closely allied to Nussbaum's defence of universal values, critical perspectives like those of Cornell and Young should constantly be revisited in order to show the limits of legal reform and suggest something beyond it.

IN DEFENSE OF UNIVERSAL VALUES

Martha Nussbaum is best known for her exploration of Aristotelian philosophy.[2] Her work on "poets as judges" and the "literary imagination" has shown legal scholars how judgment could benefit from philosophical insights.[3] Nussbaum argues that in order to make better judgments, practitioners, particularly judges, need a greater awareness of context. Over the past decade she has focused on women's development, moral theory and justice,[4] and, in her latest work, *Women and Human Development*,[5] extends her approach to the study of what she calls "human capabilities," which she uses as the basis for establishing fundamental political principles for assessing the position of women in developing countries. Noting that women all over the world lack support for these fundamental functions of human life (human capabilities), she argues that this can be explained by understanding women as not being treated as ends in their own right (and therefore deserving of respect) but as mere instruments that serve the ends of others. She observes that as a result women do not have the essential support to live fully human lives.[6]

Thus Nussbaum attempts to formulate an approach to international development that is feminist, philosophical and based on a universalist account of central human functions.[7] She posits basic constitutional principles that protect personal dignity and that can be implemented by all governments, tries to establish their "philosophical underpinning,"[8] and produces a list of "central human capabilities"[9] that can be the object of what she describes as an "overlapping consensus" for people with varying perceptions of the good. Her aim is to develop a normative theory responsive to empirical facts and a form of universalism that remains sensitive to pluralism and cultural difference. In so doing she defends a certain level of abstraction as necessary but also criticises feminist philosophy influenced by postmodern literary theory as being too abstract and of no practical value because, in her own words, it "does not help us see or understand real women's lives better."[10] Nussbaum describes instead a "threshold" level of capabilities that forms the basis for constitutional principles citizens can demand from their governments.[11]

For Nussbaum the human capabilities approach is one that respects each person's struggle for flourishing and treats each person as an end and as a source of agency. It seeks to be simultaneously general and particular by accepting benchmarks and by taking notice of concrete circumstances, and thereby to address the defects of the most prominent approaches in international development work, namely, the focus on GNP, utilitarian approaches, and that which looks at basic resources and their distribution.[12] Her central question concerns what a person is actually able to do and to be,[13] and she presents certain functions central in human life, to be acted out in a truly human way.[14] Thus she narrates the story of two women in India and their struggle to live their lives, observing that despite the particularity of their lives making it difficult for an outsider to understand them "[W]e see efforts common to women in many parts of the world. The body that labours is in a sense the same body all over the world, and its needs for food and nutrition and health care are the same. . . . Similarly, the body that gets beaten is in a sense the same all over the world, concrete though the circumstances of domestic violence are in each society."[15]

Nussbaum maintains that Western philosophy has not focused on the type of choices these women are confronted with and that we should neither underrate nor overate the influence of differences. Instead, we should accept that certain basic aspirations to human flourishing are recognizable across differences of class and context.[16] Although many people are understandably skeptical toward universalism because of its blindness in regard to complexity and particularity, Nussbaum believes that not all universalism suffers from these defects, and in some cases it can account for pluralism and respect difference. She identifies three key elements to arguments raised against a universal framework: culture, diversity, and paternalism.[17] Culture-based arguments maintain that a particular culture may contain powerful norms of female modesty, deference, and so on and that we cannot assume that these are bad norms because to do so would be condescending toward the women who choose to live according to that culture. In response, Nussbaum makes the general point that cultures are dynamic and that such relativist arguments often ignore the fact that in the modern world cultures are not totally insulated from other influences—that they often work with an unrealistic notion of culture that assumes homogeneity where diversity and contestation actually exist.[18] Her view is that a framework of human capabilities does not necessarily contradict the existence of multiple value systems and does not preclude women from leading traditional lives as long as certain economic and political opportunities are in place. She sees it as allowing a great deal of diversity while still setting benchmarks from which to assess values.

The paternalistic viewpoint would be to point out that the notion of general benchmarks shows too little respect for people's freedom as agents. But Nussbaum counters that a commitment to respecting people's choices is not incompatible with the endorsement of universal values and posits a political, rather than comprehensive, liberalism whereby many different conceptions of the good can be pursued so long as they do not harm others.

DREAMING UP SOLIDARITY

Drucilla Cornell articulates an understanding of a justice that could protect all women through the notion of the imaginary domain, a notion she develops through psychoanalytical theory. Her description of what she calls "ethical feminism," which opened feminist discourse to other ways of reflecting on sex, gender, difference, equality, and many other "feminist" concerns, is marked by a nonessentialist starting point and the search for new ways of articulating "the feminine within sexual difference."[19] Her "imaginary domain" denotes the psychic and moral space in which women as "sexed creatures who care deeply about matters of the heart" evaluate and represent who they are.[20] Integral to the concept of imaginary domain is the notion that the person can never be assumed as a given, but is always part of a project of becoming. A person is thus understood as a possibility, an aspiration, and through the development of a psychoanalytical framework, Cornell argues that the freedom to become a person is dependent on minimum conditions of individuation that serve as a prior set of conditions. In other words, the freedom that a person must have to become a person demands the appropriate space for renewing the imagination and for reimagining "who one is and who one seeks to become."[21] Although formal equality is seen as having achieved some gains in this respect, most societies are identified as continuing to impose and reinforce rigid gender identities upon their citizens. So while the imaginary domain demands of a theory of justice that women must be imagined and evaluated as free persons, it also represents the political and ethical basis of the right to self-representation of one's sexuate being.[22] As such, it addresses not only questions of freedom and equality but the question of dignity as well.

This turn to psychoanalysis helps with the protection of dignity because psychoanalytic insight regards dignity as the capability to articulate desire and to make moral evaluations.[23] Cornell wants us to see that "[P]sychoanalysis can help us understand why *the feminine within the imaginary domain* can be infinitely represented, and represented so as to explore the culturally and legally imposed norms of femininity. As I have defined it within the legal sphere, the imaginary domain is the moral and psychic right to represent and articulate the meaning of our desire and our sexuality within the ethical framework of respect for the dignity of all others."[24]

Cornell illustrates the possibility of being prevented from having a free imaginary domain by what she calls "internal tyrants,"[25] and describes the imaginary domain as protecting that moral and psychic space needed to escape them. Focusing on "the feminine within the imaginary domain,"[26] she highlights the subjective aspect of the assumption of sexual identity. Here, however, the feminine does not refer to femininity but to the way in which we might reimagine and redefine women. It affirms the difference of women and how they are represented by the imagination and in language.[27] Cornell argues that feminism is, by definition, multicultural and committed to transnational literacy and that the demand that everyone's rights to the imaginary domain must be protected does not repeat the essentialist claim of likeness. She thus makes a feminist intervention in the search for a legitimate decision-making procedure that requires an initial universalization. This feminist intervention poses the question of how to deal with the fact that human beings are sexed and therefore "ontologically dissimilar."[28]

In addressing this question Cornell demands recognition of the moral space necessary for equivalent evaluation of our sexual difference as free and equal persons.[29] This demand for the imaginary domain must be met prior to the formulation of a broader egalitarian or social justice theory.[30] Cornell notes that some feminists have tried to find a place in reality where women were fully equal with men, but to no avail,[31] that the imaginary domain reflects a utopian moment in its demand for focus on what ought to be, and that liberalism, by focusing only on what is and by rejecting the utopian moment, negates the imaginary domain. A strong feature of her antiessentialist approach is the belief that any theoretical appeal to likenesses denies the full significance of differences: "The feminism I advocate, necessarily demands equality for women as free persons, but does not seek to make law the main vehicle for restructuring the current meaning of our sexual difference. Indeed, such a law would fall foul of the equal protection of the imaginary domain, since it would make the state and not the individual the source of the representation of her sexuate being."[32]

At an international level the imaginary domain has important implications for women in the context of globalization or the "new imperialism."[33] By accepting women's right to dignity and the demand for the imaginary domain, women's "intrinsic worth" can be recognized instead of just subscribing to the typical Western imperialist notion of value or reform that embraces the idea of progress. In "The art of witnessing and the community of the ought to be,[34] Cornell turns to Spivak's chapter on history in A Critique of Postcolonial Reason, where Spivak argues that the subaltern in history has either been absent/silent or misrepresented. The subaltern is not a figure in the traditional sense because she is a "trace," and her story exists only as a "subliminal and discontinuous emergence." Spivak seeks to stand witness to the stories of two women, the one, the rani of Sirmur,[35] the other, a distant family member,[36] and retells them with the ethical purpose of preserving their pathos and dignity and exposing how female subjectivity is affected when enacted in a manner traditionally seen as pitiful. Cornell describes Spivak as "restaging ideological battlegrounds so that the might have been of woman's agency can be returned to the picture,"[37] and interprets Spivak's "feminist inspired historical project" through a reading of Kant's notion of aesthetic judgment.[38] According to Cornell, Spivak seeks a particular kind of community best understood as Kant's *sensus communis aestheticus*, wherein community is understood by way of aesthetic judgment that we are before a sublime or beautiful object or person. Spivak is calling on us to judge loss and fundamental misinterpretation as sublime.[39]

According to Cornell, however, two mistakes are commonly made about the quality of aesthetic judgment. One is to limit Kant's analysis of aesthetic judgment to any particular field. The other is to reduce our emotive response to the sublime as something so purely subjective that it belies judgment.[40] Cornell defines aesthetic judgment as "a specific form of judgment provoked by feeling but that is not simply overwhelmed by it,"[41] and she is critical of interpreters of Kant who reject the subjectivism and reduce the *sensus communis aestheticus* to conventions of an existing community. She explains that a communication of aesthetic judgment is possible in Kant, not because someone shares the existing aesthetic standards of a particular community but because we can imagine that others would join in if we all adopted an "enlarged mentality." The *sensus communis aestheticus* in Kant thus points toward an "ought to be" of a shared community, and the enlarged mentality to which Kant refers does not refer to a given community but to the idea of humanity. So when we judge an object as sublime we include the "should" of the universal, which is inseparable from an idealized humanity. The *sensus communis* thus demands a particular kind of public sense. Yet it is not that which we normally think of as a community. It is an imagined community where all the possible viewpoints of others are imagined.[42]

"COMMUNITY" AS A HETEROGENEOUS PUBLIC
AND "ASSYMETRICAL RECIPROCITY"

Iris Young's concern with justice focuses on how appeals to equality and democracy can be developed and broadened and highlights problems of positivism and reductionism in political theory. Positivism she understands as the
attitude of assuming institutional structures as a given instead of normatively
evaluating them. Reductionism is modern political theory's tendency to reduce political subjects to a unity and to value commonness or sameness over
specificity and difference. Young notes how theories of justice often conflate
moral reflection with scientific knowledge (empirical research) by claiming
universalism, comprehensiveness, and necessity and argues that reflective discourse about justice should not be cast in terms of knowledge, that is, creating
the knower as initiator and master of the known.[43] It is her description of critical theory that can assist us in our search for equality, justice and a feminist
community:

> [C]ritical theory is a normative reflection that is historically and socially
> contextualized. Critical theory rejects as illusory the effort to construct a
> universal normative system insulated from a particular society. Normative
> reflection must begin from historically specific circumstances because there
> is nothing but what is, the given, the situated interest in justice, from which
> to start. Reflecting from within a particular social context, good normative
> theorizing cannot avoid social and political description and planning. . . . So-
> cial description and explanation must be critical, that is, aim to evaluate the
> given in normative terms. . . . Each social reality presents its own un-realized
> possibilities, experienced as lacks and desires. Norms and ideals arise from
> the yearning that is an expression of freedom; it does not have to be this
> way, it could be otherwise. Imagination is the faculty of transforming the ex-
> perience of what is into a projection of what could be, the faculty that frees
> thought to form ideals and norms.[44]

Drawing on various writers[45] and their critiques, Young confronts unify-
ing discourses and concepts such as 'impartiality,' the 'general good', and 'community,' as well as Western paradigms of distributive justice. She sees the
reification, individualism, and pattern orientation assumed by these paradigms
as obscuring issues of domination and oppression and the scope of justice to go
beyond distributive issues to be coextensive with the political. 'Politics' in this
sense becomes a wider concept than is usually understood and reflects on all
aspects of institutional organization, public action, social practices and habits,
and cultural meanings.[46] Young criticizes Western societies for depoliticizing
the process of public policy formation, arguing for democratic decision-making
processes and public discussion.[47]

Central to her argument is the idea that a denial of difference contri-
butes to oppression and her support for a politics that recognizes rather than

represses difference. She points out that the ideal of impartiality, that which suggests that all moral situations should be treated by following the same rules, is present in most theories of justice and that this ideal denies difference between subjects. Moreover, by claiming to provide a standpoint all subjects can adopt and by presenting a unified and universal moral point of view, it thereby creates a dichotomy between reason and feeling. Young refers to the subject as a "heterogeneous process" and argues that because subjects are never fully present, they can never make themselves transparent and wholly present to one another, and accordingly, it is impossible for us to understand them. In opposing the ideal of impartiality, Young posits the notion of a heterogeneous public and city life. However, her criticism of Western liberalism does not lead to an acceptance of community because the ideal of community is also seen as suppressing difference and as excluding. Her alternative, "city life" embodies four virtues that represent heterogeneity rather than unity. They are social differentiation without exclusion, variety, eroticism, and publicity.[48]

Young criticizes the notion of moral respect as a relation of symmetry between self and other and supports a notion of asymmetrical reciprocity.[49] She accordingly criticizes a communicative theory of moral respect that subscribes to the idea of "imaginatively" taking the other's position. Her concern with respect leads her to Luce Irigaray's notion of the value of "wonder" in ethical relations and Emmanuel Levinas's critique of the philosophical tendency to reduce the communicative relation between ethical subjects to a common measure or comparability. Symmetrical reciprocity that entails that each of us should take the perspective of all others in making moral judgments has at least three flaws: it obscures difference; it is based on the supposed possibility of reversing positions; and it is politically suspect.[50] By acknowledging the asymmetrical reciprocity between subjects, we accept that while there may be many similarities and points of contact between subjects, each position and perspective transcends the others and goes beyond their possibility to share or imagine. Young describes the ethical relation of asymmetric reciprocity as a "gift": "the trust to communicate cannot await the other person's promise to reciprocate."[51] The perspectives of subjects are asymmetrical in two ways: in temporality and in position. Each person has her own temporality in the sense that she brings to a situation in her own particular history that cannot be adopted by another person. Each social position is structured by the configuration of relationships among positions, and positions cannot be taken from one context and substituted by another. Trying to take the standpoint of another could be misleading and could have unethical and unjust consequences, but Young does not believe that the impossibility of knowing the other or taking her position should prevent us from making moral judgments, from being concerned about justice, or from being concerned with the other—understanding across difference being both possible and necessary. However, to recognize the asymmetry of subjects we do need a different account of what understanding is and what makes it possible. In contrast to the general belief that in order to understand, we need things in common, we should rather focus on the differences. Young explains that

> the ethical relation of asymmetrical reciprocity looks like this. We meet and communicate. We mutually recognize one another, and aim to understand one another. Each is open to such understanding by recognizing our asymmetry. A condition of our communication is that we acknowledge difference, interval, that others drag behind them shadows and histories, scars and traces that do not become present in our communication. Thus we each must be open to learning about the other person's perspective, since we cannot take the other person's standpoint and imagine that perspective as our own. This implies that we have the moral humility to acknowledge that even though there may be much I do understand about the other person's perspective through her communication to me and through the constructions we have made common between us, *there is also always a remainder,* much that I do not understand about the other person's experience and perspective.[52]

Young's suggestion of an ideal of city life as a vision of social relations affirming difference without exclusion could provide a model for a feminist concept of equality and justice. Her normative ideal represents an alternative to the ideal of both community and liberal individualism. Under "city life" Young understands a form of social relations she defines as the "being together of strangers."[53] This reflects the paradox of being together and being separate, being bound and unbound simultaneously, of being one but not the same. Although some common problems and interests exist, there are no shared final ends a universalist approach would want: "Because city life is a being together of strangers, diverse and overlapping neighbors, social justice cannot issue from the institution of an enlightenment universal public."[54]

SOUTH AFRICAN EQUALITY JURISPRUDENCE

Most, if not all, law and legal reform are reflections of universal thought processes based on notions of sameness and symmetrical reciprocity rather than on an open-ended acceptance of difference and asymmetrical reciprocity. One reason for this is that the law and legal reform are directed at a general level—in the case of the protection of women, women are regarded as representing a certain group or community of individuals. I wish to argue that law and legal reform, even though they have (and must have) formalist and institutional restrictions, can nevertheless benefit from feminist deliberations on heterogeneity and difference. Law and legal reform should approach women by recognizing difference and by acknowledging that it is impossible to know all and therefore fully to cater for difference and diversity.

The "community" of women that the law aims to address can usefully be seen in light of Young's city life, sharing some common problems and interests but having no shared final ends, mutual identification, or reciprocity. We see attempts in the South African protection of equality to expand formal universal models of law and legal reform. However, when we approach these attempts through the views of Cornell and Young, the true colors of a philosophy of the "metaphysics of presence" shine through.

Section 9 of the Constitution of South Africa[55] protects the right to equality. It is generally accepted that this section should be understood as not only protecting formal equality but also substantive equality.[56] In other words, a court will accept that in some instances individuals must be treated differently in order to protect their right to equality. An approach based on substantive equality takes the concrete circumstances of an individual into account in contrast to a formal abstract approach based on sameness.

In *President of the Republic of South Africa and Another v. Hugo*[57] the facts were as follows: Hugo was imprisoned at a time when the former president, Nelson Mandela (in the Presidential Act 17 of 1994), pardoned certain categories of prisoners. One of these categories was all women in prison on May 10, 1994, who were single mothers to children under the age of twelve years. Hugo, a widower and the father of a son under the age of twelve, applied for an order declaring the presidential act unconstitutional on the grounds that it discriminated unfairly against him on the basis of gender. The majority in the Constitutional Court held that there *was* discrimination against Hugo, but that it was *not* unfair. Justice Goldstone argued that the court followed a substantive approach to equality by focusing on the differences between the genders. The court accepted that the president acted in good faith and did not intend to discriminate unfairly and had in mind the benefit of children. The court phrased its approach to equality as follows:

> We need . . . to develop a concept of unfair discrimination which recognizes that although a society which affords each human being equal treatment on the basis of equal worth and freedom is our goal, we cannot achieve that goal by insisting upon identical treatment in all circumstances before that goal is achieved. Each case, therefore, will require a careful and thorough understanding of the impact of the discriminatory action upon the particular people concerned to determine whether its overall impact is one which furthers the constitutional goal of equality or not. A classification that is unfair in one context may not necessarily be unfair in a different context.[58]

Justice O'Regan, concurring in *Hugo*, argued that the presidential pardon did not discriminate unfairly against Hugo, primarily because he, as a man, was not a member of a group that had previously suffered from discrimination. She pointed out that, even though it would be better in the long run for equality if the responsibilities of child rearing were shared fairly between fathers and mothers, the reality at present and in the near future is that mothers bear primary child-rearing responsibility. In this light the pardon benefited a particular group of women in a material way, despite its reliance on what might be a harmful stereotype.

A question to consider is whether this decision truly protected and enhanced equality. To my mind the court affirmed unfair discrimination against Hugo and other single fathers with children under the age of twelve as well as against children under twelve who were in the precarious position of having only a father as single parent. Further, the court's decision negatively affected the dignity and respect of women by affirming the harmful stereotype and generalization that only women are to be considered the primary caregivers of children. To reiterate: the court's approach of substantive equality, which aims to represent a way of regarding difference, by taking a "universal"/ general or stereotyped view of reality as its starting point, harmed the dignity of and respect for women and men.

Justice Kriegler, in a dissenting judgment, argued that Hugo had suffered unfair discrimination. According to him, the relevant section of the presidential pardon was inconsistent with the prohibition against gender or sex discrimination, and, because it had not been shown to be fair, it was invalid. In his view the notion relied upon by the president—namely, that women are to be regarded as the primary caregivers of young children—is a root cause of women's inequality. He said that one of the ways in which one accords equal dignity and respect to persons is by seeking to protect the basic choices they make about their own identities. Reliance on the generalization that women are the primary caregivers is harmful in its tendency to cramp and stunt the efforts of both men and women to form their identities freely. Another aspect Kriegler mentioned is that no data had been presented stating how many male prisoners would have been released if the pardon treated the sexes equally. He focused on the fact that the president relied on an "inherently objectionable generalization" for the benefit of a particular group of women prisoners. Kriegler argued that there was no suggestion in the presidential act of compensation for wrongs of the past or an attempt to make good for past discrimination against women. The primary justification provided for the president's proclamation was the "interest of children." He identified two criteria that must be satisfied for a generalization such as that relied upon in the pardon to be vindicated. There must be a strong indication that the advantages flowing from the perpetuation of a stereotype compensate for "obvious and profoundly troubling disadvantages"; the context would have to be one in which discriminatory benefits were apposite. In terms of the first criterion, he argued that women as a group do not benefit by the perpetuation of the stereotype, and in terms of the second he noted that the fact that women suffered discrimination generally does not mean that they suffered discrimination in the penal context. He concluded by arguing that on occasion sex/gender distinctions can and should be made, but such distinction must be shown not to discriminate unfairly or must be justifiable under the limitations clause.

It was a year later, in *Harksen v. Lane*,[59] that the court formulated the "test" that must be followed in order to determine unfair discrimination. Yet a close look at the court's decision shows how, even given a presumably substantive and transformative aim, the protection of equality can nevertheless result in unjust consequences.

The court in *Harksen* set the test out as follows: Where someone relies on the equality section to attack a legislative provision or executive conduct on the ground that it differentiates between people or categories of people, in such a way as to create *unequal* treatment or *unfair* discrimination, the first question is whether the provision indeed *differentiates* between people or categories of people. If the court finds such differentiation, the next step is to see if there is a *rational connection* between the differentiation in question and a legitimate governmental purpose. If the rational connection is proved, the differentiation does not amount to a breach of the guarantee of equality before the law. However, if there is no rational connection between the differentiation and a legitimate government purpose, the provision in question *violates* this guarantee. The court will then proceed to the limitations clause, to see if the violation may nevertheless be justified. Even when there is a rational connection, the court will turn to the prohibition of unfair discrimination to determine whether, despite the rational connection, the differentiation nonetheless amounts to *unfair discrimination*. To determine whether differentiation amounts to unfair discrimination a two-stage analysis is followed. First, it must be determined whether the differentiation amounts to discrimination and, if it does, whether it amounts to unfair discrimination. The constitution provides for two categories of discrimination. The first is differentiation on one of the grounds specified in the equality section. The second is differentiation on a ground not specified but analogous to such grounds. The Harksen court decided that discrimination on an unspecified but analogous ground is differentiation based on attributes or characteristics that have the potential to impair the fundamental dignity of persons as human beings, or to affect them adversely in a comparably serious manner. If the discrimination is on a specified ground, unfairness will be presumed, but if it is on an unspecified ground, unfairness will have to be established by the complainant. In order to determine whether discrimination is unfair the following factors should be considered: (a) the position of the complainants in society and whether they have suffered in the past from patterns of disadvantage (the court added that this should be taken into consideration, whether the discrimination in the case is on a specified ground or not); (b) the nature of the provision or power and the purpose achieved by it; (c) any other relevant factors. If the discrimination is held to be unfair one will proceed to the final leg of inquiry as to whether the measure can be justified in terms of the general limitations clause.[60]

In the *Harksen* case the assets of the applicant's husband had been sequestrated. In terms of certain provisions of the Insolvency Act 24 of 1936, the applicant's separate estate had, upon sequestration of that of her husband, automatically vested in the Master of the Supreme Court. The purpose of these provisions was to prevent an insolvent spouse from "hiding" assets from creditors in the estate of her or his solvent spouse in anticipation of sequestration. The applicant could claim the release of her property once it had been determined that she was not in fact holding it for her husband.

The applicant challenged these provisions first on the basis that they treated her and others in her position unequally in violation of the guarantee of equality before the law. Second, she alleged that the provisions discriminated unfairly against her and others in her position on the basis of their marital status, because they, as solvent spouses were treated differently from other people who were close associates of insolvent spouses, and so were adversely affected in their human dignity. The majority of the constitutional court held that, as there was a rational connection between the legitimate government purpose of determining whether a solvent spouse's property was indeed hers or his and the impugned provisions, the guarantee of equality before the law was not violated. Further, it held that, although the provisions discriminated against solvent spouses, the discrimination was fair, primarily because solvent spouses were not members of a group that previously suffered from patterns of disadvantage and because the impact of the provision on solvent spouses was thought not to affect their human dignity adversely: their impact amounted to no more than "the kind of inconvenience and burden that any citizen may face when resort to litigation becomes necessary."[61]

Sachs (J.) in a dissenting judgment found that the provisions did in fact discriminate unfairly. He showed how even an approach of substantive equality that seeks to include difference and context can have hegemonic effects. He pointed out how the majority judgment, in its assumption that the impugned provisions of the Insolvency Act did not affect the fundamental dignity of solvent spouses adversely, disregarded the extent to which they reinforced "a stereotypical view of the marriage relationship which . . . is demeaning to both spouses."[62] He argued that the section in the Insolvency Act worked from the assumption that there is only one business mind at work in a marriage and, in this way, enforced an understanding that spouses do not exist as free and equal persons within the marriage union but lose their individuality and capacity for self-realization.

Another problematic aspect of the current approach to substantive equality is the fact that the constitutional court has collapsed the protection of dignity with the protection of equality. Albertyn and Goldblatt note that "the constitutional court has sought to define equality by placing the value of dignity at the centre of the equality right," adding that "we don't agree with this."[63] Their reason for not agreeing is different from the critique I raise against the notion of substantive equality in this chapter, but their argument pronounces the crux of my disagreement with the notion of substantive equality as developed presently in South African jurisprudence. They support the view that the right to substantive equality should be given a meaning that is independent of the value of dignity and that "disadvantage and difference are core characteristics of substantive equality."[64] They also praise the judgment of constitutional court justice Kate O'Regan for placing the "idea of systemic discrimination and patterns of group based disadvantage (and material interests) at the centre of the equality right."[65] For them, "the replacement of disadvantage with dignity returns us to a liberal and individualized concept of the right. The centrality of disadvantage, vulnerability and harm, and their connotation of groups-based prejudice—the essence of the right—is lost."[66]

I have argued elsewhere against a stance that regards transformative ideals and ideology critique as "liberal" and individual-orientated and assumes that only "material reform" may be representative of "true" transformation.[67] Applying Cornell's concern with dignity to the South African discourse on socioeconomic rights, I have argued that we should take heed not to harm the dignity and respect (and right to the imaginary domain) of individuals by defining and approaching them only as "vulnerable," "most needy," and so on.[68] In raising these arguments, I have not negated the utmost importance of material reform that is focused on disadvantage and vulnerability. However, I am concerned that in our attempts to address substantive, material conditions, we harm and violate by not truly regarding difference and otherness, by assuming symmetrical reciprocity, by being presumptuous about our own abilities to understand context, by placing individuals in groups, and ultimately, by ending up doing the very same thing we wanted to break with, namely, universalizing the experiences and contexts of each other. I do not agree with the constitutional court placing the value of dignity at the center of the right to equality because I want to see the right to dignity given independent meaning(s) from equality. When we protect equality and socioeconomic (and other) rights, we should do it in such a way as not to harm the dignity and respect of those very people whose equality and dignity we are protecting.[69]

END REMARKS

How we look at the difficult question of dealing with differences in feminist discourse and moral theory should be a concern of law and legal reform theory. Nussbaum, Cornell, and Young are interested in justice and equality and how it can be approached to the benefit of women. In their work we can identify two opposing attitudes to universality and the idea of whether one person can ever truly understand and reflect the position of another. Nussbaum, though not insensitive to arguments based on relativity or difference, continues to subscribe to the framework of universal values embodied in most attempts at legal reform. Cornell and Young, however, are arguably more critical of universalism or at least strive to articulate a version thereof that recognizes and takes proper account of difference. In comparing Nussbaum and Cornell we see that both use Kant and Rawls as philosophical underpinnings, and both accept the notion of political liberalism as a useful construct. Both also use narrative to illustrate abstract ideas and are sensitive to context and concrete circumstances. However, Cornell, being a poststructural feminist thinker, employs Kant and Rawls in a different way. She emphasizes Kant's writings on aesthetics and the sublime to help her resist any attempt at defining or enclosing reality. For Cornell freedom comes first, more specifically the freedom to dream and to imagine oneself without being restricted to past and present representations.

Nussbaum's critique of poststructural feminists who tend to make things too abstract reveals a lot about her own desire to describe and represent reality. Although she argues for a philosophical and normative theory and against pure empirical and utilitarian approaches, her setting up of a "central" list of human capabilities weakens her position. Cornell recently noted that she has more sympathy with Sen's approach to human capabilities in that he has never attempted to reduce these capabilities to a list and has always taken freedom as the most important value.[70] For Cornell, capabilities include a subjective aspect that is part of what she calls the right to the imaginary domain. She is critical of reducing capabilities to objective statistics and hierarchies and regards it as being in contrast with Kantian freedom. Young joins Nussbaum in her critique of Western paradigms of distributive justice but follows a model of heterogeneity and city life that indicates a mindset like Cornell's, where equality and justice are thought about rather differently from Nussbaum's defense of universal values as one of diversity and not-yet-ness. Cornell and Young stand for an acceptance of difference and acknowledgment of the impossibility of ever knowing the other and therefore being able to represent the other and her needs. Both subscribe to a notion of self as a continuous process of becoming and reject an understanding of the subject as fully present. Young's references to Unger's "imaginative context of social life" connects with Cornell's work on the imagination. Cornell's "community of the ought to be" and Young's asymmetrical reciprocity and their concern with dignity, respect, and wonder create a framework from where equality and justice for all women can be considered in a less harmful way. However, like Nussbaum, Cornell and Young do not refrain from searching for equality and justice.

For Cornell the other should be addressed as the sublime because this would best ensure a protection of her dignity and respect. She follows the Kantian notion of aesthetic judgment to reflect upon the notion of an "imagined" community or "the community of the ought to be" but rejects readings of Kant that apply aesthetic judgment in a rational manner thereby negating the subjective elements.[71] She stresses instead the fact that the Kantian notion of 'enlarged thought' refers to an "imagined" and not to a real position. Young also criticizes the adoption of the notion of enlarged thought that seems to mean that a person can know what the position of the other means. It is this understanding of enlarged thought that underlies most [legal] attempts to deal with difference and otherness.

International and national legal instruments necessarily follow a universalist approach and it seems that even where sensitivity to difference is shown, generalization and universalization cannot be avoided. Murray notes a range of concerns about the way in which women are treated in international human rights law.[72] And while some authors argue that women's rights should be "mainstreamed" in the general human rights instruments, others argue for specific attention. Murray understands the African Charter on Human and People's Rights (a multilateral human rights treaty between member states of the Organization of African Unity)[73] as being more "holistic" and less based on the opposing dichotomies other international human rights instruments and international law in general display. For example, framing human rights in terms of contrasts between state/individual, war/peace, public/private can result in the neglect of the position and experience of women. Murray argues that the African Commission on Human and People's Rights (the African Commission—the regional body tasked currently with the enforcement of the African Charter) has gone beyond for example the public/private division by recognizing violence against women in the private sphere as well as considering the private aspects of work and the value of work in the home. The separation between civil and political and economic, social, and cultural rights is another reason for the neglect of women. In the African Charter, this division is not reproduced, and the rights are seen as of equal importance. Murray argues that the African Commission has also gone beyond the traditional male perspective in its development of economic, social, and cultural rights.

Other dichotomies that the African Charter seems to disrupt instead of repeat are duties/rights, individual/community, and cultural relativism/universality. Because the African Charter has moved beyond a strict dichotomous approach, it has opened the way for the protection of the rights of women. Murray also sees the Draft Protocol to the African Charter on the Rights of Women in Africa[74] as a "strong indication" of the African Commission's willingness to pay attention to women's rights and suggests that the Draft Protocol should be used as the commission's authoritative interpretation of the charter.[75] For her the African Charter indicates a more holistic approach in the move beyond traditional male dichotomies and is in a better position to address women's rights. An important argument that she makes is that the African Commission's move away from traditional dichotomies can be more indicative of a concern with international law being Western biased than a reflection of a concern with women. She argues that the African Commission, because of Africa's history, reflects a mixture of different influences and can take better account of the other in non-Western and nonmale law. It is interesting to note that although she encourages the break with dichotomies and the embrace of a more holistic approach, she questions whether present international law is indeed "universal" and seeks to find a better universal:

[The African Commission] offers a method by which non-western countries' challenges to international law could enlighten and refocus the principles of international law as they now stand. It can thus challenge whether international human rights law as it is presently formulated is *indeed universal*. The approach of the African [C]ommission has been to move away from these unhelpful dichotomies inherent in human rights law towards a more holistic approach that takes account of a variety of perspectives. In this respect it not only offers the possibility of better protection and recognition of women's rights, but also offers something to the international community as a progressive way in which rights could be interpreted.[76]

Murray asks the international community to take account of the African Commission and to use African material in their discussion and development of human rights law. This is not only because she wants to bring diversity into current international law to address its shortcomings, but it is because of "these unusual aspects of the charter, which are essential to a developing international human rights law that is *truly universal and truly reflective of all persons in the world*."[77] From the perspectives discussed earlier in this chapter the predictable question will not be how we can ever develop such a law and such a position able to be reflective of all the persons in the world but whether we should even try.

The impossibility of knowing the other, of not ever fully comprehending each other's standpoints, should not lead to indifference regarding issues of justice.[78] As Cornell notes, our acknowledgment of not being able to know the other in her or his difference can "all too easily degenerate into indifference."[79] She calls for an embrace of "women's time" that will urge us to slow down and put the brakes on any attempt to value or devalue anyone as victim in need of help. It is the idea of women's time and the notions of asymmetrical reciprocity, heterogeneous city life, and an enlarged thought based on the web of human relations reflecting the plurality of the world that we should follow in our reflections on equality and justice. To protect the freedom and dignity of each other, to approach each other with wonder and respect demands of us to slow down, to contemplate our actions, and to avoid hastily believing in the success of feminist theories, governments, and international law to enhance the position of women: "Perhaps at this sloweddown pace we can witness to the sublimity of what has almost never been seen as sublime—the day-to-day endurance of women who sustain, against all odds, their struggle to change the world. If we have the courage to stay in women's time and to place ourselves under the mandate of respect, we may be able to dream up new possibilities of solidarity not ensnared by our imperialist legacy."[80]

NOTES

An earlier draft of this chapter was delivered at the 2001 Critical Legal Conference, University of Kent. My thanks to Andre van der Walt, Wessel Le Roux, Stewart Motha, and Danie Brand for reading the text and for their valuable comments. My thanks also to the referees and editor of *Feminist Legal Studies* for their helpful comments. Research for this chapter was done during a postdoctoral fellowship at the Research Unit for Legal and Constitutional Interpretation, Faculty of Law, University of Stellenbosch. My gratitude to Lourens du Plessis and all other members of RULCI for their support and kind assistance. A word of thanks to Drucilla Cornell for inspirational discussions during her visit to the University of Stellenbosch in July 2001.

1. Drucilla Cornell, (New York: Routledge, 1991), 105.

2. See, for example, Martha Nussbaum, *The Fragility of Goodness: Luck and Ethics in Greek Tragedy and Philosophy* (Cambridge: Cambridge University Press, 1986), and *Love's Knowledge* (New York: Oxford University Press, 1990).

3. Martha Nussbaum, "The Literary Imagination in Public Life," in *New History* (1991): 887–910; "Poets as Judges," in *The University of Chicago Law Review* 62 (1995): 1477–1519.

4. See Martha Nussbaum and Amartya Sen, *The Quality of Life* (Oxford: Clarendon, 1993); Martha Nussbaum, *Women, Culture and Development: A Study of Human Capabilities* (Oxford: Clarendon, 1995).

5. Martha Nussbaum, *Women and Human Development* (Cambridge: Cambridge University Press, 1999). See also Susan Moller Okin, *Is Multiculturalism Bad for Women?* (Princeton: Princeton University Press, 1999).

6. Nussbaum, *Women and Human Development*, 4.

7. Her work is close to Rawls's political liberalism. See John Rawls, *A Theory of Social Justice* (New York: Oxford University Press, 1971).

8. Nussbaum, *Women and Human Development*, 5.

9. Ibid., 78–80. The list of "central human functional capabilities" includes the following life; bodily health; bodily integrity; senses, imagination, and thought; emotions; practical reason; affiliation; other species; play; control over one's environment.

10. Nussbaum, *Women and Human Development*, 11.

11. Her project converges with the work of Amartya Sen, who describes an approach based on functioning and capability in development economics. For Sen "the notion of capability is to indicate a space within which comparisons of quality of life are most fruitfully made. Instead of asking about people's satisfactions, or how much in the way of resources they are able to command, we ask, about what they are actually able to do or to be." Nussbaum, *Women and Human Development*, 12.

There are points of similarity and divergence between Sen and Nussbaum of which a full elaboration is beyond the scope of this chapter. Points of divergence raised by Nussbaum are the following: Although they agree about the poverty of cultural relativism and the need for universal norms regarding development Sen has never explicitly argued against relativism; Sen does not focus on the Marxian/Aristotelian idea of truly human functioning that is central to Nussbaum and in contrast with Nussbaum Sen has never made a list of the central capabilities. Other points of divergence are their approaches to capabilities and functioning; comprehensive and political liberalism; the distinction between well-being and agency; and the relationship between rights and capabilities and the use of narrative method.

12. Nussbaum, *Women and Human Development*, 59–70.

13. Nussbaum explains: "Taking a stand for political purposes on a working list of functions that would appear to be of central importance in human life, we ask: Is the person capable of this, or not? We ask not only about the person's satisfaction with what she does, but about what she does, and what she is in a position to do (what her opportunities and liberties are). And we ask not just about the resources that are sitting around, but about how those do or do not go to work." Nussbaum, *Women and Human Development*, 71.

14. "The core idea is that of the human being as a dignified free being who shapes his or her own life in cooperation and reciprocity with others, rather than being passively shaped or pushed around by the world in the manner of a 'flock' or 'herd' animal. A life that is really human is one that is shaped throughout by these human powers of practical reason and sociability." Nussbaum, *Women and Human Development*, 72.

15. Ibid., 22–23.

16. Ibid., 31.

17. Ibid., 41–59.

18. Ibid., 48.

19. Drucilla Cornell, "The Doubly-prized World: Myth, Allegory and the Feminine," Cornell Law Review 75 (1990): 644–99; Drucilla Cornell, *Beyond Accommodation* (New York: Routledge, 1991); Drucilla Cornell, *Transformations* (New York: Routledge, 1993).

20. Drucilla Cornell, *At the Heart of Freedom* (Princeton: Princeton University Press, 1998), x.

21. Drucilla Cornell, *The Imaginary Domain: Abortion, Pornography and Sexual Harassment* (New York: Routledge, 1995), 5.

22. Cornell, *At the Heart of Freedom*, 159. The philosophical basis that Cornell uses for the imaginary domain is Rawls's conception of our equal moral worth and Kant's idea of our freedom as moral persons.

23. Drucilla Cornell, *Between Women and Generations. Legacies of Dignity* (New York: Palgrave, 2002), 29.

24. Cornell, *Between Women and Generations*, 29.

25. Ibid., 30.

26. Ibid., 31.

27. "Since we not only assume identities but also live them, this process of acting-out is inevitable. We are the ones who externalise the meaning of gender. How we assume these identities is never something 'out there' that effectively determines what and who we can be as men and women—gay, lesbian, transsexual, straight, or otherwise." Cornell, *Between Women and Generations*, 31.

28. Cornell, *At the Heart of Freedom*, 14.

29. Ibid., 11–14.

30. According to Cornell the failure to recognize the prior moral space in describing a legitimate procedure to determine issues of distributive justice prevented Kantian political philosophy from taking account of sexual difference.

31. Cornell, *At the Heart of Freedom*, 15.

32. Ibid., 14.

33. Gayatri Chakravorty Spivak, *A Critique of Postcolonial Reason: Towards a History of the Vanishing Present* (Cambridge: Harvard University Press, 1999).

34. Cornell, *Between Women and Generations*, 71–94.

35. Spivak wanted to investigate sati and women who practiced sati as ritual mourning. Her aim was to retell the stories of these women who were pitied and sentimentalized by history. In her investigation, she found a rani who threatened to commit sati whose name was never recorded by the British and remains only as the rani of Sirmur. Spivak challenges the "ideological battlegrounds" to change the perception of women who committed sati as victims and return their pathos. These women should also be seen as signifiers and not only as the signified.

36. A distant relative committed suicide as a way of giving notice of a political and ethical dilemma that she was facing. She was a national liberation fighter who was asked to commit a political murder that she could not do. The reason for her suicide was seen by her family as that she had an illicit love affair. Spivak uncovers the actual motivation for her suicide.

37. Cornell, *Between Women and Generations*, 79.

38. Ibid., 81. Cornell also refers to Schiller's interpretation and application of Kant's aesthetic judgment "On the sublime" in W. Hinderer and D. O. Dahlstrom, eds., *Friedrich Schiller: Essays* (New York: Continuum, 1998).

39. Cornell, *Between Women and Generations*, 81–82.

40. Ibid., 82.

41. Ibid., 83.

42. Ibid., 85.

43. Iris Marion Young, *Justice and the Politics of Difference* (Princeton: Princeton University Press, 1990), 4.

44. Ibid., 5.

45. Specifically, Derrida, Lyotard, Foucault, Kristeva, Adorno, and Irigaray.

46. Young, *Justice and the Politics of Difference*, 9.

47. See Young in P. Kasinitz, *Metropolis: Center and Symbol of our Times* (London: Macmillan 1995); see also W. B. Le Roux, "From Acropolis to Metropolis: The New Constitutional Court Building and South African Street Democracy," *South African Public Law* 16 (2001): 139–68.

48. See Young, *Metropolis*; Le Roux, "From Acropolis to Metropolis; See also G. Frug, "The Geography of Community," *Stanford Law Review* 48 (1996): 1047.

49. Iris Marion Young, "Asymmetrical Reciprocity: On Moral Respect, Wonder and Enlarged Thought," *Constellations* 4 (1997): 340.

50. Ibid., 346–50.

51. Ibid., 351.

52. Ibid., 354.

53. Young, *Metropolis*, 264.

54. Ibid., 268.

55. Constitution of the Republic of South Africa, 1996. The section reads as follows:

1. Everyone is equal before the law and has the right to equal protection and benefit of the law.

2. Equality includes the full and equal enjoyment of all rights and freedoms. To promote the achievement of equality, legislative and other measures designed to protect or advance persons, or categories of persons, disadvantaged by unfair discrimination may be taken.

3. The state may not unfairly discriminate directly or indirectly against anyone on one or more grounds, including race, gender, sex, pregnancy, marital status, ethnic or social origin, color, sexual orientation, age, disability, religion, conscience, belief, culture, language and birth.

4. No person may unfairly discriminate directly or indirectly against anyone on one or more grounds in terms of subsection (3). National legislation must be enacted to prevent or prohibit unfair discrimination.

5. Discrimination on one or more of the grounds listed in subsection (3) is unfair unless it is established that the discrimination is fair.

56. C. Albertyn, and J. Kentridge, "Introduction to the Right to Equality in the Interim Constitution," *South African Journal on Human Rights* 10 (1994): 149–78; C. L'Heureux-Dube, "Making a Difference: The Pursuit of Equality and a Compassionate Justice," *South African Journal on Human Rights* 13 (1997): 335–53; C. Albertyn and B. Goldblatt, "Facing the Challenge of Transformation: Difficulties in the Development of an Indigenous Jurisprudence of Equality," *South African Journal on Human Rights* 14 (1998): 248–76.

57. 1997(6) B.C.L.R. 708 (C.C.).

58. 1997(6) B.C.L.R. 708 (C.C.), para. 1.

59. (1997 (11) B.C.L.R. 1489 (C.C.).

60. See A. J. H. Van der Walt and H. Botha, "Coming to Grips with the New Constitutional Order: Critical Comments on *Harksen v. Lane*" *South African Public Law* 13 (1998): 17–41.

61. 1997 (11) B.C.L.R. 1489 (C.C.) paragraph [67] at 1516F.

62. 1997 (11) B.C.L.R. 1489 (C.C.) paragraph [120] at 1533D–E.

63. Albertyn and Goldblatt, "Facing the Challenge of Transformation," 254.

64. Ibid., 256.

65. Ibid., 257–60.

66. Ibid., 258.

67. Karin Van Marle, "'No Last Word': Reflections on the Imaginary Domain, Dignity and Intrinsic Worth," *Stellenbosch Law Review* 13 (2002b): 299–308.

68. "No Last Word: Reflections on the Imaginary Domain, Dignity and Intrinsic Worth," authors's response to Drucilla Cornell, delivered at RULCI Colloquium,

University of Stellenbosch, August 2001, published as Van Marle (2002). See also P. De Vos, "Grootboom: the Right of Access to Housing and Substantive Equality as Contextual Fairness," *South African Journal on Human Rights* 17 (2001): 258–76; T. Ross, "The Rhetoric of Poverty: Their Immorality, Our Helplessness," *Georgetown Law Journal* 79 (1991): 1499–1547; P. Williams, "Alchemical Notes: Reconstructing Ideals from Deconstructed Rights," *Harvard Civil Rights-Civil Liberties Law Review* 22 (1987): 401–33; F. Michelman, "Foreword: On Protecting the Poor through the Fourteenth Amendment," *Harvard Law Review* 83 (1969): 7–59; J. R. Pennock and J. W. Chapman, eds., *Nomos XVIII: Due Process* (New York: University Press, 1979).

69. My concern here is not that when we protect equality and socioeconomic rights of one person or group of persons that we should not harm the dignity of others. The point is that the way in which we address inequality and socioeconomic rights should be a reflection of a regard for dignity and respect. My aim is not to prevent social and institutional transformation or to protect "existing rights" but to approach it with a concern for dignity and respect.

70. During a series of Forum lectures delivered by Cornell at University of Stellenbosch, August 2001.

71. According to Cornell, Hannah Arendt and Jurgen Habermas make this mistake of collapsing the *sensus communis aestheticus* into the *sensus communis logicus*. She refers to A. J. Cascardi, *Consequences of Enlightenment* (New York: Cambridge, 1999), 132–74

72. R. Murray, "A Feminist Perspective on Reform," in *African Human Rights Law Journal* 1 (2001): 205–24.

73. African Charter on Human Rights and Peoples' Rights, opened for signature June 26, 1981, entered into force October 21, 1986, 21 I.L.M. 59.

74. Draft Protocol to the African Charter on Human and People's Rights on the Rights of Women in Africa (the Kigali Protocol) (not yet in force, draft completed September 2000).

75. R. Murray, "A Feminist Perspective on Reform," 206–07.

76. Ibid., 223–224; my emphasis.

77. Ibid., 224.

78. The investigation into difference and the (im)possibility of a feminist community and international concept of justice must continue. A next step for me will be to explore the notion of "reflexive politics." See, e.g., E. A. Christodoulidis, *Law and Reflexive Politics* (Dordrecht: Kluwer, 1998); J. L. Nancy, *Being Singular Plural* (Stanford: Stanford University Press, 2000).

79. Cornell, *Between Women and Generations*, 94.

80. Ibid.

J. M. Bernstein

Sexuate Being: Foundations for a Feminist Legal Philosophy?

THE THREE STRUTS SUPPORTING CORNELL'S LEGAL THEORY

At the heart of Drucilla Cornell's feminist legal philosophy is the bold and demanding claim that what women want is the equivalent chance to transform themselves "into individuated beings who can participate in public and political life as equal citizens" (ID 4),[1] The treatment of each as an equal, and not just equal treatment (HF 60), requires that there be equal protection of the minimum, necessary conditions for individuation, acknowledging, indeed insisting upon the fact, that individuation is a social accomplishment that occurs through time and is never complete. Since, for now and for the foreseeable future, all individuals are "sexed," and hence are sexuate beings with an internalized sexual identity possessing its own distinctive forms of activity, desire, and identifications through which one takes on a sexual persona, then the minimum conditions for individuation must ensure the equal opportunity for individuals to form and reform their sexual identity. As psychoanalysis has taught us, we become individuated selves only through developmental sequences in which we take on a sexual identity that incorporates and sustains a comprehension of gender difference(s); hence the conditions of individuation that enable us to become political subjects in general must incorporate within themselves conditions that enable the sustaining of a sexed identity.

What gives Cornell's egalitarian thesis its normative force is her acceptance of John Rawls's contention that the primary political good, that good that must be satisfied if we are to be the kinds of beings that choose our lives and thereby have goods, is self-respect (ID 8–9). Without self-respect an individual ceases to value her own life, hence her own acts of valuing become idle, and nothing seems worth doing. One cannot have a life worth having without self-respect; hence self-respect is the necessary condition of self-worth for an active individual political subject. With this thesis in place, it follows that the devaluing of female sexuate being, through, for example, publicly treating women as if they might be defined solely by their physical endowments, makes being a woman something for which one might feel shame, hence places the individual so positioned in a degraded position in which she does lack the minimum conditions for sexed individuation.[2] Thus the degradation of female sexuality entails the degradation of the individual possessed of a female identity, denying her standing as an equal political person, immediately revealing thereby that sexual devaluation transgresses the principle of minimum equal liberty.

The great power of Cornell's core thesis is eloquently on display in her analysis of sexual harassment where she argues that what is required for a demonstration of such harassment is neither the establishment of a particular (psychological) harm nor the demonstration that there existed a hostile work environment but "whether or not the workplace and the contested behavior effectively undermined the social bases of self-respect by enforcing stereotypes or projecting fantasies onto the plaintiff as one unworthy of personhood. It would be the standard of equality that would give us the "perspective" from which we should view the behavior" (ID 201). The beauty of this is that while the legal claim issues, appropriately, from the right of the individual to equal treatment, what determines harassment is the *content* of the practices of the workplace (the mechanisms of degrading female sexuality) irrespective of either their intent or actual psychological effects.

Supporting and underwriting Cornell's egalitarian legal philosophy are three complex and weighty theoretical figures: (1) the Rawlsian account of self-respect with its attendant deontological apparatus; (2) the conception of the imaginary domain; and (3) the Lacanian construction of sexuate being and gender difference. While I find the orientation and fundamental gestures of Cornell's egalitarian legal philosophy compelling, I find the three theoretical struts supporting it at best shaky and undertheorized and at worst emphatically inappropriate. And, even if granted, the worry would still arise as to how three such utterly disparate and self-enclosed theoretical constructions are meant to hang together in a philosophically consistent and convincing way. Only Cornell's deftness and lightness of touch prevents the syncretistic character of her foundational theoretical armory from issuing in open combat. Her embrace of Lacanian thought is the most egregious component of her philosophy since, as she knows and warns against (ID 129; HF 143), it figures female sexual being in its constitution as a form of incompleteness in comparison with male sexuality: lacking a penis, which may take on the symbolic proportions of the authority-conferring phallus, women are figured as necessarily and permanently abject. Although, then, Cornell indicates that the effectivity of the Lacanian account is dependent on the conditions of patriarchy in the authorization of the phallus as the place of authority, since she binds herself to his oedipal construction of subjectivity, she leaves herself no space to imagine a nonabjected female identity, or rather, when she does so it occurs in the context of the enablements of the legally protected imaginary domain, which is to say, too late. Before turning to the suggestion of an alternative developmental story, however, let me say a few words about the first two struts of Cornell's philosophy. As things transpire, these words will be providential for the reconstruction of the psychoanalytic foundation.

Against the background of her earlier philosophy, I have always regarded Cornell's espousal of Kantian liberal philosophy as propounded by Rawls and Dworkin as a strategic ploy rather than a deep commitment. If the project is to generate a policy-sensitive, practical alternative to existing sex law, then, whatever its overall theoretical liabilities, if the basic principles governing the extant liberal consensus are sufficient to support the practical recommendations wanted, then it is practically rational to employ them, suitably adjusted, rather than some more arcane and contested theoretical apparatus.[3] That said, if the Nietzsche-Adorno thesis that Kantian deontology is nothing but the misbegotten progeny of the theology of the ascetic ideal with its utter repudiation of our embodied being as integral to our standing as rational persons is accepted, then the theoretical liability of the embrace of deontology must be intolerable for Cornell's thought. More pointedly, as I have shown in detail elsewhere,[4] while Rawls's positioning of self-respect as a primary political good is plausible, he cannot provide a nonquestion-begging *characterization* of self-respect that would allow it to play that role. What is required in order for self-respect to have the role it does in liberal jurisprudence is a demonstration of how our standing for ourselves is *constitutively* dependent on the recognition of others, and thence why self-respect, which is our valuing of ourselves as valuers, provides the *limit condition* in which the difference between inside and outside is normatively constituted.[5] Stated baldly, the conception of self-respect and legal right Cornell needs for her theory is only intelligible if it is reconstructed in wholly recognitive terms, especially if our constitutive vulnerability before the other is to play a systematic role in the theory, as it must, and if our dignity is not to be a posit shot from a deontological canon, but rather conceived with our vulnerability as opposing aspects of the very same recognitive dependency on the other (HF 64). In fact, Cornell's commitments to recognitive theory are there to be seen in both *The Imaginary Domain* (42, 60, etc.) and in *At the Heart of Freedom* (62–64); my point is only that the normative heavy lifting she wants from Rawlsian self-respect and egalitarian deontology demand its reconstruction in recognitive terms.

What is most peculiar about Cornell's deployment of the notion of the imaginary domain is that it is used pervasively but hardly theorized at all. She does want to argue that the protection of the imaginary domain comes under the aegis of one of the conditions necessary for individuation. If the imaginary domain is to play this role, then it cannot be thought of as equivalent to the space of the imagination, the space wherein one imaginatively constructs possibilities and alternatives. Hence, the traditional conception of the imagination as the mental-making present of that which is empirically now absent is idle for Cornell's purposes. What she requires is an account that binds what it is to have a sexual identity *überhaupt* to the imaginative projection of that identity and then, further, make that imaginative projection a necessary condition of individuated action. If a sexual identity is a necessary condition for identity, and the possession of a sexual personae grounded in a sexual imago that is open to transformation and transfiguration is a necessary condition for sexual identity (ID 7, 201), then half the problem is solved. But a revisable sexual imaginary so understood is still perilously close to the traditional notion of the space of the imagination. *Only by making the imaginary domain a component of action can the imaginary be prevented from collapsing into mental space.* Cornell rightly argues that "the right to self-represent one's own sexuate being cannot meaningfully separate speech from action, expression from actualization. Self-representation of one's sexuate being involves not only representing oneself in and through sexual personae but setting forth a life that expresses one's moral and effective orientation in matters of sex and family" (HF 40). Normatively this is fine, but surely it is subtended by a stronger thesis that evolves in light of the conception of sexuate identity, namely, that in whatever action we engage, insofar as we engage in it as a fully individuated self, then in so doing we necessarily *are* self-representing a sexual persona and hence locating ourselves in sexual space. In fine, the claim must be that *all* action is done under the horizon of a projected (imagined) sexual persona; unless this is the case, then the thesis about sexual identity being necessary for individuation and individuation necessary for the action of citizen subjects lapses. This makes the imaginary domain above all a theory of action.

Now, as a matter of philosophical fact, there is only one theory of action that ties action and imagination together through the projection of a revisable identity that forms the horizon of all one's action, namely, that propounded by Sartre in *Being and Nothingness*. Where Cornell must depart from Sartre, and the only places that I can see that she does so clearly and emphatically, is in contending, first, that each and every fundamental project (Sartre's term for the projected identity constituting the horizon of every action, acknowledged or unacknowledged) is sexually contoured, that is, there is no "I am" without a gender qualification, say, "I am a woman" (SS xxi);[6] and, second, that the options for gender specification are always already constituted by a history and context not of the subject's choosing: we do in our actions make and remake our sexual identities, but not under conditions of our own making. As it so happens, these two qualifications are precisely the ones that mark off Simone de Beauvoir's departure from Sartre with one small proviso: Beauvoir construes the historically contextualized space of gender identity to be recognitively constituted, indeed constituted through a rigidified and frozen dialectic of master and slave (SS xxiii–xxvi). Woman's abjection, her constitution as the other of the male identity, is first a historical construct before it can be a positionality in the development of infants into persons. But if these qualifications are right, they make Beauvoir feminism look like just what is needed for Cornell's legal philosophy. I will say more about that thought in conclusion; first, it is to Beauvoir as an alternative to Lacan to which I want to turn.

BEAUVOIR AND LACAN

At first glance, it might seem perverse to be urging Beauvoir's feminist theory in this setting, especially since so much excellent feminist theory has emerged in the aftermath of *The Second Sex*. That said, and strangely, it is only in the last several years that Beauvoir's seminal text has begun to be given the kind of serious philosophical reading it deserves; foremost among these new readings is Nancy Bauer's superb and irreplaceable *Simone de Beauvoir: Philosophy and Feminism*.[7] Further, as I have already begun to indicate, at least something like Beauvoir's contextual existentialism looks like a plausible candidate for providing the basic materials through which the three struts requisite for Cornell's legal philosophy might be harmonized and synthesized.

However, my deepest motivation for urging Beauvoir's case here relates to her relation to Lacan (as well his to her) and the appropriation of Lacanian thought by contemporary feminism. In the opening pages of book 2 of *The Second Sex*, Beauvoir explicitly draws on the resources of Lacan's early account of the mirror stage in his 1938 encyclopedia article *Les Complexes familiaux dans la formation de l'individu* in her psychoanalytic accounting of infant development, an account that involves, at the same time, a psychoanalytic recasting of some of the fundamental categories of Sartre's existential ontology, above all, the notions of anxiety, the look, and the desire to act in bad faith, the temptation to bad faith, to make oneself an in-itself (SS 267–70). Now it should be recalled that in *Les Complexes familiaux*, in opposition to Freud and his own later thought, Lacan provides a fully historicized account of oedipal identity formation that locates its achievements narrowly in the formation of the modern bourgeois family, all the while acknowledging both that the positive dialectic of oedipal identity is fast reaching a point of collapse and that, even in its most progressive aspect, it was always a paternalistic/patriarchal formation, entailing that the present crisis of oedipal identity formation is, at least in part, an inevitable consequence of the historical suppression of the feminine principle.[8] Against this background, the argumentative structure of *The Second Sex* can be recognized as, in part at least, a deepening of Lacan's early thought since Beauvoir's brilliant insight is, in book 1, to provide a historical account of the origins and formation of gender domination that is intrinsically deforming for *both* male and female identity formation, and then, in book 2 to explain how this precise construction of gender difference is reproduced initially in infant development and then throughout all the stages of a woman's life. What distinguishes Beauvoir's account of infant development, however, is that it shows how the *mechanisms* of infant development are sensitive to social and historical contents that are wholly separate from the mechanisms themselves and thus how the structures of child development are necessarily and inevitably conveyors of symbolic contents that are formed in the sociohistorical world of parents; it is precisely this that is not the case in the standard Freudian and Lacanian accounts that center on oedipal identity formation. I would contend that the argumentative structure of *The Second Sex* is methodologically necessary and irreplaceable for feminist thought since only through the consideration hierarchical gender difference as a sociohistorical production that is then reproduced in infant development does it become possible to avoid the abjection of the feminine principle and open up sexuate being to historical transformation. Not only is this argumentative structure appropriate for feminist thought, but it is necessary for psychoanalysis too since, as Beauvoir consistently complains, "psychoanalysis fails to [fully and adequately] explain why woman is the *Other*" (SS 49).

The Second Sex was published in 1949. Lacan's seminars in which he transforms his early historical account of the Oedipus complex into a fully transcendental theory of oedipal identity formation in which female identity becomes forever abject begins a few years later, with his most significant comments on female sexuality occurring in the late fifties and early sixties.[9] Given the smallness and cliquishness of the Parisian intellectual universe, the notoriety of Beauvoir's book, not to speak of *The Second Sex*'s explicit acknowledgment of its debt to him, it is impossible to believe that Lacan was not completely familiar with Beauvoir's feminist thought. In her work, again, Beauvoir makes creative use of Hegel's original recognitive account of self-consciousness in the master/slave dialectic, while, following Sartre, she configures a notion of subjectivity that is forever tempted by a wholly imaginary conception of completeness in defensive response to an anxiety incurred through an ontological lack, an existential emptiness that is irresolvable. Both these theoretical tropes are prominent, indeed focal, in the emergence of Lacan's later theory.[10] Most important, in *The Second Sex* Beauvoir emphatically and unmistakably generates the idea that woman is the wholly other of the male, neutral One: he is the human subject, she the abjected Other. Now, while I do not wish to deny Peter Dews's and Mikkel Borch-Jacobsen's contention that the transcendentalizing gesture of Lacan's later thought is in response to his perception of a crisis in the oedipal construction of subjectivity,[11] that transcendentalizing gesture, I want to urge, must be seen as also an explicit and knowing repudiation of Sartre and an effacement of Beauvoir and the claim of feminine sexuality. Through Beauvoir and consistent with his own early theory, Lacan had to be fully aware of the historical formation of woman as the repudiated Other of male identity and the deep social consequences of that systematic domination. Hence, the abjectness of feminine sexuality in his later theory cannot have been a by-the-way and simple consequence of his affirmation of oedipal identity formation, but most, in part at least, have been a reactive and explicit suppression of the claim of women against patriarchal history: transcendental oedipalization is a defense against both the historical failing of oedipal authority and the site of that failure, the uprising of women against its legitimation of domination. Lacan appropriates Beauvoir's originary insight that woman has been historically constituted as the abject Other of the male One (SS xxiv) and gives it transcendental legitimacy. Hence, Lacan's thought is only intelligible as a systematic and self-conscious repudiation of feminist thought as such. Feminists in embracing Lacan participate in that repudiation, that is, finally, in the effacement of Beauvoir's thought.[12] Is not this reason enough for wishing to contest the role of Lacanian theory in contemporary feminism? Is not it reason enough for wishing that Cornell's acknowledgement of the notion of woman as "the second sex" had been a more full-throated acknowledgment of Beauvoir's thought?[13]

BEAUVOIR: PRODUCING AND REPRODUCING GENDER DIFFERENCE

In chapters 4 and 5 of *The Second Sex*, "The Nomads" and "Early Tillers of the Soil," Beauvoir sets in place the core elements of her historical analysis. In essence her argument depends on noting the difference between male "production" qua transformative work and activity and female "reproduction" of the species, which imprisoned her in "repetition and maternity" (SS 63). Let us say that from the get-go, almost, men help reproduce the species only by breaking from nature/embodiment/natural rhythms, and so on.

> Early man's activity had another dimension that gave it supreme dignity: it was often dangerous. If blood were but a nourishing fluid, it would be valued no higher than milk; but the hunter was no butcher, for in the struggle against wild animals he ran grave risks. The warrior put his life in jeopardy to elevate the prestige of the horde, the clan to which he belonged. And in this he proved dramatically that life is not the supreme value for man, but on the contrary that it should be made to serve ends more important than itself. The worst curse that was laid upon woman was that she should be excluded from these warlike forays. For it is not in *giving life* but in *risking life* that man is raised above the animal, *that is why superiority has been accorded in humanity not to the sex that brings life forth but that which kills*. (SS 63–64; emphasis mine)

One misunderstands Beauvoir entirely unless the ambiguity of the final sentence of the passage, as underlined by the irony of the final clause, is appreciated.[14] The giving life/risking life duality structures much of what is to come.

First, notice how Beauvoir is restructuring the Sartrean conceptions of transcendence and immanence into the duality between risking life/giving life. This gives the Sartrean domain of immanence and facticity a far more weighted symbolic significance (with a futurity of its own, which it does not have in Sartre where immanence is equivalent to facticity as the pastness of every present) and a far more complex ontological ordering since risking life is a *mode* of life. Second, Beauvoir uses this structuring of the relation between man and woman in order to reshape Hegel's master/slave dialectic, which, Beauvoir contends, applies "much better to the relation of man to woman" (SS 64).[15] The slave once risked his life and will through work seek to attain the position of master. Woman is never in this story either a risker of life or a worker shaping the world and gaining her autonomy thereby. Indeed the woman here does not battle with the male or thereby demand recognition. What is stranger is that although we are here in the sight of the master/slave dialectic, it is not yet clear that or why the male demands recognition from the woman. Although the relation of man to woman is structurally analogous to the relation of master and slave in terms of essential/transcendence versus inessential/immanent, there is no active dialectic here, no mutual demands, but a strange structural stasis. Of course, this is part of the point in calling woman the "Other," man's Other without being dialectically other, since if she were fully dialectically other than woman's liberation would have come early, surely earlier than any other project of human liberation.

But there is a second part to this analysis. In setting himself as transcending animality, man makes himself the One, as defined by his nature-transcending self-evaluation and all nature, thereby the other. While originally woman was neither the placeholder of natural otherness nor reducible to it, in the course of civilization it is precisely this that occurred: "Spirit has prevailed over Life, transcendence over immanence, technique over magic, and reason over superstition. The devaluation of woman represents a necessary stage in the history of humanity, for it is not upon her positive value but upon man's weakness that her prestige is founded. In woman are incarnated the disturbing mysteries of nature, and man escapes her hold when he frees himself from nature" (SS 75). Man cannot free himself from nature without devaluing it, dominating it, repudiating its authority. Each of those acts of devaluing, dominating, and repudiating is enacted in his relation to woman, who is nature. But because she is nature, because of her fecundity, she is both feared and venerated, she is the source of life and the bearer of transience and death: she is what when configured by the ascetic ideal must be excised and left behind. Said differently, the configuration of the fecund woman as repudiated nature contains all the attributes and problems of the phallic Mother of psychoanalytic thought, which makes the notion of the phallic Mother a retrospective construction from the perspective of oedipal development, not a psychological fact in infant experience.

The consignment of woman to nature in the context of Beauvoir's Hegelian reconstruction of the relation between transcendence and immanence as a dehydrated master/slave dialectic is what finally explicates the meaning of woman as abjected other. Judith Butler states Beauvoir's thought with typical trenchancy:

> Woman are "Other" according to Beauvoir in so far as they are defined by a masculine perspective that seeks to safeguard its own disembodied status [= risking life] through identifying woman generally with the bodily sphere [= giving life]. Male disembodiment is only possible on the condition that women occupy their bodies as their essential and enslaving identities. . . . By defining women as "Other," men are able through the short-cut of definition to dispose of their bodies, to make themselves other than bodies—a symbol of potential human decay and transience and of limitation generally—and to make their bodies other than themselves . . . The body rendered as Other—repressed or denied, and then projected—reemerges for this "I" as the view of others as essentially body. Hence, women become the Other; they come to embody corporeality itself . . . [Male] disembodiment becomes a way of existing one's body in the mode of denial. And the denial of the body—as in Hegel's dialectic of master and slave—reveals itself as nothing other than the embodiment of denial.[16]

Nothing I know of makes the stakes of male gender domination, also known as oedipal identity formation, more palpable and insistent. The necessity of the feminine is that it enacts for the male his relation to this own embodiment; and further, he needs her as a contrast to his (impossible) transcendence and support for it, to recognize it, to hold it in place *as* transcendence in a recognition that does not threaten its authority.[17] Only recognition by woman, in being conscious 'things', enables men to stabilize their (formally impossible) relation to the world (SB ch. 6).

In broad terms, this is the structure of masculine and feminine that needs to be reproduced in infant development. Beauvoir's account begins in a manner that appears utterly continuous with standard psychoanalytic accountings: with the infant at first immersed in the "bosom of the All" (SS 268) and then, little by little, gaining and suffering separation "more or less brutally from the nourishing body" (ibid.).[18] It is in this moment of separation, the crisis it brings about, that Beauvoir begins transforming the discourse of both existentialism and psychoanalysis. It is worthwhile presenting this passage in full.

> [I]t is about when the separation is accomplished, toward the age of six months, perhaps, that the child begins to show the desire to attract others through acts of mimicry which subsequently, become genuine displays, the desire to seduce others. Certainly this attitude is not established through a reflective choice; but it is not necessary to *intend* a situation for it to *exist*. In an immediate manner, the nursing lives the original drama of every existent, which is the drama of his relation to the Other. It is in anguish that the human being feels his abandonment. Fleeing his liberty, his subjectivity, he would like to lose himself in the bosom of the All: here is the origin of his

cosmic and pantheistic dreams, of his desire to forget, to dream, to be ecstatic, to die. He never succeeds in abolishing his separate ego. At the least
he wants to attain the solidity of the in-itself, the en-soi, to be petrified into
a thing. It is especially when he is fixed by the look of others that he appears
to himself as a being. (SS, 268–69)[19]

According to Beauvoir, the immediate response to the crisis of separation is to
seek to overcome it; since overcoming is not possible through refusion with
the maternal All, then the next best thing is to have one's separation take on
the qualities of a thing, to find a stable, reliable, unchanging, and dependable
relation to the world through having one's place in it have the quality of sheer
facticity. Hence, in the first instance, seeking *recognition* is not seeking affirmation of one's independence, but seeking the full Sartrean look of the other
as what makes my subjectivity (which here is still just abandoned separateness
from the All) an object, an en-soi. Now the mechanism through which this is
to be accomplished, over and again according to Beauvoir, is "mimicry," that
is, mimetic adaptation. So the desire for recognition is enacted through mimesis. Since mimesis is a repetition of the other for the sake of relief from an-
guished separation, then mimetic adaptation is Beauvoir's conception of the
death drive in the service of life. It is the death drive of mimetic adaptation
that gives *to* the gaze of the other the power of the transfixing look. Only in
relation to mimetic desire does the gaze of another become a Sartrean look;
but this desire, the desire of bad faith, is inevitable, and not all negative since,
while desiring to become an in-itself is negative, the meaning of that desire
includes the desire for a dependable, reliable, and constant relation to a world
that is forever beyond our control and power.

It is at this juncture that Beauvoir explicitly takes up the Lacanian mirror
stage and bends it to the requirement of her conception of mimetic adaptation. So the passage above continues:

> In a carnal form, he [the infant] discovers finitude, solitude, abandonment
> in a foreign world. He tries to compensate for this catastrophe by alienating
> his existence in an image whose reality and value others will ground. It ap-
> pears that he begins to affirm his identity at the moment at which he recog-
> nizes his reflection in mirrors—a moment that coincides with weaning. His
> ego blends so well with this reflection that is formed only in being alienated.
> Whether the mirror properly speaking plays a role more or less considerable,
> it is certain that the child begins around six months to mimic his parents
> and to grasp himself in their look as an object. He is already an autonomous
> subject who transcends himself toward the world: but it is only in alienated
> form that he will encounter himself. (SS, 269)[20]

Mimetic adaptation has now been significantly complicated; it involves "genuine displays" that involve the attempt to "seduce" the other; the effort of dis-

play and seduction, via mimicry, involves the projecting of an image that is affirmed by the parent, that is, to enter into mimetic adaptation is to display oneself to others in a manner that receives recognition. What hence receives recognition is the image projected by the mimetic display; this is the encounter of the child with himself in alienation. Beauvoir's difficult thought here is the drama of human existence, the recognitive establishment of independence and dependence, separateness (individuation) and connectedness (social bonding), is propelled by a desire for foreclosure: to be misrecognized as a thing, an en-soi, and not an individuated self.[21] In differential ways, but at the expense of the female and to the advantage of the male, gender complementarity satisfies this desire too well. That satisfaction is, in part, the source of the perpetuation of the gender hierarchy that constitutes the miserable history of our race.

Now, and this is the crux of the matter, gender identity is *originally* constituted through mimetic adaptation. Because this moment is so central to Beauvoir's analysis, let me give it a separate designation: *the mimetic preacquisition of gender identity*. I call this the "preacquisition" of gender identity because it is formed without gender complementarity; equally, it is a preacquisition because as mimetic it contains affective and cognitive elements but is neither fully discursive (it is in part prelinguistic, presymbolic) nor normatively underwritten. Because it is a formation of gender identity, without the epistemological apparatus of 'full,' that is, legitimated awareness of gender difference, which possesses a mechanism all to itself, mimetic adaptation, then this stage can be both temporally prior to the acquisition of gender identity proper (gender complementarity) *and* remain a discrete stratum of identity formation that can be continued and deepened, elaborated and developed, even after gender complementarity has been elaborated. It is this continuation of mimetic adaptation that Lacan's transcendental gesture aims to suppress since, for him, the on-going contamination of the symbolic by the mimetic would, precisely, undermine the authority of the oedipal settlement. Conversely, the thesis of mimetic adaptation and its continuance enables the possibility of recognizing the extent of the repudiation of the mimetic in the transcendentalizing gesture, how that repudiation itself thus transforms the entanglement of the mimetic and the symbolic from a normalizing hierarchy into an unstoppable, if endlessly frustrated dialectic.

The mimetic preacquisition of gender identity explains the continuing role of the death drive (the desire for bad faith) in the psychic economy of the adult, the continuation of the drive to acknowledge and survive unmasterable injury. Part of the beauty of the notion of mimetic adaptation is that it removes the necessity for the epistemological extravagances that are usually ascribed to oedipal identity formation: all the wildly implausible business of the infant noticing the difference between mother and father, of somehow registering that the having or not having of the penis is a big deal in itself and what, somehow, makes the difference between mother and father matter and then somehow figuring out that it does or does not have a penis (all this without having a map or any reason to form one, and yet knowing (!) that this gender business is the big thing) and then connecting all this oedipal epistemic inquiry with the differential mechanisms of desiring one parent and identifying with another. The extraordinary epistemic feats of classification, evaluation, self-ascription, and so on, that the infant is supposed to carry out, to form itself in a manner consonant with the deepest and most mysterious demands of civilization without anything like an articulated symbolic background, has always struck me as simply implausible. Mimetic adaptation fills in the missing background perfectly.

The mimetic preacquisition of gender identity provides a simple and direct explanation for how already constituted gender differences are acquired by the child by being projected onto it by parents. The always affectively charged *behavior* of the parents, which is mimetically adopted by the child, is the deepest and most profound source for the child's idea (image) of gender identity, albeit, again, in the first place an identity without difference or rather without complementarity difference. So, crudely, the little girl "continues to be cajoled, she is allowed to cling to her mother's skirts, her father takes her on his knee and strokes her hair. She wears sweet little dresses, her tears and caprices are viewed indulgently, etc." (SS 270), in brief, she finds confirmation of herself in being a "cute thing," a "little darling," as "cute as a picture." So she mimetically makes herself into an object that is to be cajoled and petted and stroked and beloved in her thinghood. In the meantime, the little boy is "denied even coquetry; his efforts at enticement, his play-acting, are irritating . . . he is urged to be 'a little man' (ibid.). Hence, the little boy achieves recognition, that is the status of an en-soi, *by becoming a for-itself,* that is, by enacting his independence; but his enactment of independence is for all that a self-recognition in alienated form, which is precisely how Beauvoir originally configured male dependence on the feminine.

Now, to be sure, Beauvoir's account is slippery in terms of its temporal location. But it seems plausible to suggest that the mimetic preacquisition of gender identity itself should be located as occurring throughout the entire span of time from separation through to the onset of the oedipal stage. Even the role of the penis as the phallus-to-be can be plugged into the stage of mimetic preacquisition. The connection between his mimetically adopting the role of a for-itself and that authority being, finally, "incarnated in his penis" (SS 271) is mediated by the behavior of the surrounding adults: "He does not spontaneously experience a sense of pride in his little lazy sex, but rather through the attitude of the group around him. Mothers and nurses keep alive the tradition that identifies the phallus and the male idea" (ibid.). Conversely, for the little girl, no attention is paid to her genitals; hence, "in a sense she has no sex organ" (SS 272). But this, here, is not a problem: "She does not experience this absence as a lack; evidently her body is, for her, quite complete; but she finds herself situated in the world differently from the boy; and a constellation of factors can transform this difference, in her eyes, into an inferiority" (ibid.). It is not necessary or possible to here follow though the details of Beauvoir's analysis (for a nuanced and detailed accounting see SB 200–19). Its central thesis is clear: *The mimetic preacquisition of gender identity behaviorally, epistemically, attitudinally, and ontologically (the little girl becoming for herself an in-itself, and the little boy becoming an in-itself by becoming a for-itself) prepare the child for the great events of the oedipal phase,*[22] which indeed can now be seen as casting into a rigidified and formalized social form the accomplishments of the preoedipal phase—but in so doing transforming simple gender difference into a gender complementarity in which the feminine is abjected and the masculine authorized. But if the oedipal achievement of identity formation is but the confirmation of an earlier mimetic work, transforming core gender identity into symbolically legitimated gender complementarity, then it follows, both that the deepest stratum of gender occurs through mimetic adaptation to existing social forms and that the oedipal stage itself receives the bulk of its power to fix those gender identities from elsewhere, which explains the significance of oedipal identity formation, its belatedness, and, hence, its emphatically historical constitution.

I would not want to suggest, even for a moment, that Beauvoir's account is sufficient all by itself; it is not meant to replace a full-blown psychoanalytic account of infant development but to restage and transform any such account, to introduce a different framing vocabulary, and to make possible a thorough-going historicization of the gender content that is at the center of any such account. As it stands, Beauvoir does not provide an analysis of precisely how the accomplishments of the mimetic preacquisition of gender identity are elaborated in the oedipal phase, how symbolic authorization takes place, and hence how normativity is sutured onto its mimetic base. Nor does she fully explicate how the most obvious fact of infant life, the awesome power of the mother, her standing as a powerful agent, is made to tally with the idea of feminine passivity. For that, I think, we will require something like Jessica Benjamin's challenging and compelling "daughter hypothesis," a theory I take to be wholly consonant with Beauvoir; indeed, on the surface, Benjamin's hypothesis looks to be a form of mimetic adaptation.

> Let us say that the male child's repudiation of his own passivity, associated with humiliation at the hands of the mother (she rejects him, leaves him, tantalizes him), sparks the father's fantasy of the daughter's passivity . . . [Following Freud], a repressed feminine passivity lodges behind the male's obsessional use of defensive, aggressive activity. In other words, a certain kind of activity is necessary in order to overcome helplessness, and this kind of defensive activity structures the masculine position. If father-daughter incest represents the most egregious encapsulation of this defense, it is made possible by the generalized complementary relationship between the sexes, in which the daughter functions not merely as the split off embodiment of

the passive object but also the missing maternal container into whom the father discharges and expels unmanageable tension. The dual function of embodying passivity and containing unmanageable projected tension gives
form to femininity; this femininity centers on the daughter, not the mother,
as its defining figure.[23]

I would want to first underline how here, as throughout her writings, Benjamin construes gender difference as a complementary relation of active/passive,
subject/object that exactly parallels Beauvoir's analysis.[24] It further explains
how the dual relationship of fear (of the phallic mother) and veneration (of
the passive feminine) gets worked out by splitting the feminine between
mother and daughter and with that splitting can secure the daughter position
as the permanent site of abjection: so there is the perfected oedipal triangle of
mother, father, and (male) child, and its abject, the daughter. The daughter
hypothesis powerfully and terrifyingly crystallizes the abjectness of the feminine with a lapidary perspicacity. However, what is most exacting about the
daughter hypothesis is that, from a Beauvoirian perspective, it explicates how
the dependency of the active male on the recognition of the woman, the
woman figured as both self-consciousness and thing, a dependency which is
adumbrated in the male child's humiliation at the hands of the mother, finds
relief for itself by displacing the mother by the daughter. What this, then, explains is the *stakes* of the father in the (mimetically anticipatory) posing of the
daughter as passive, as the truly feminine, and as his real complementary
other: he has reasons for that cajoling and petting and stroking, reasons that
become actualized in incest. It further explains why the daughter's mimetic
preacquisition of feminine identity should be oedipally realized in (submis-
sive) love for the father.[25] Hence, just as Beauvoir has it, "we might say that
this sexual form of femininity—object of male desire [i.e., "femininity as absorption, accommodation and receptivity"]—meets the girl at the moment
she needs to separate and offers her a route into the world of men."[26]

BEAUVOIR AND CORNELL

Although I find the feminist disavowal and effacement of Beauvoir dispiriting,
I mean my espousal of Beauvoir here not as an outright criticism of Cornell
but as a gift of sorts: Beauvoir provides just the sort of the methodological relating of the historical to the psychoanalytic that Cornell's hopes for legal reform and a transformative feminist politics presupposes. Indeed, without
something like a Beauvoirian account of mimetic preacquisition of gender
identity I do not see how the idea of the imaginary domain and the sort of existential transformations of gender identity it postulates as anyway continuous
could become culturally established. To see that the connection between the
penis and the phallus is historically contingent is not sufficient to dislodge
gender complementarity if the oedipal phase remains the locus of the estab-

lishment of gender identity; a conception of mimetically acquired gender identity without gender complementarity accomplishes the task.

But there is, I think, an even deeper synergy between Beauvoir feminism and Cornell's legal philosophy. I suggested above that three struts supporting Cornell's legal philosophy, even if acceptable separately, were not obviously compatible: the egalitarian deontology underwriting of Rawlsian self-respect and the transcendental fixation of Lacanian gender theory ill consort with one another, and both appear incompatible with the existential openness and brio of the imaginary domain. At its most exorbitant, the doctrine of the imaginary domain shares with Sartrean freedom an ontological indifference to the conditionality of human experience. The fundamental mechanism for binding that exorbitancy is the same for Beauvoir and Cornell: the necessary precondition of every fundamental project, which would equally be posited along with each fundamental project, must be a gender identity. By itself, however, the broad idea of gender identity is insufficient since unless what now gets articulated in terms of gender complementarity responds to some more pervasive aspect of the human condition than anatomical difference, then either we are stuck with gender complementarity (reducing gender to sex after all), or the necessity that what gender differences stand for becomes a mystery. Beauvoir's articulation of gender complementarity as the social articulation of human relations that occurs with the emergence of a domain of value incommensurable with life as the highest good answers perfectly to that demand. What we now experience in terms of gender complementarity is the duality between giving life and risking life, our imminent animality and our transcendent humanity, our nature-bound vulnerable passivity and our self-transcending capacity for transformation in accordance with ideals. Our passivity and constitutive injurability, which is to say the fact that our self is always a fully embodied self, our ego *always* also a bodily ego, that the integrity of the body is both normative and relational (recognitive), together with all the "feminine" features of absorption, accommodation, and receptivity that are lodged in the position of the daughter, are components of subjectivity as such, and hence will be components of any workable human identity no matter how sexed and gendered. It is this demand that identity work a (chiasmic) relation between embodied immanence and value transcendence (entailing the bodily immanence of value and the value transcendence of embodiment) that binds the activity of the imaginary domain, legitimately making its efforts belong to the necessary conditions of individuation. This makes Beauvoir's historically conditioned psychoanalytic theory not merely compatible with the idea of the imaginary domain, but necessary for its meaning and intelligibility.

At the beginning of this chapter, I gestured toward a passage where Cornell connects the need for legal recognition to human vulnerability. She is there complaining that Dworkin "does not address the vulnerability of individuation, and it is precisely this recognition of vulnerability that I think we need to add to his ethical individualism. . . . The demand for the imaginary domain is made in the name of the recognition of our own vulnerability as well as our dignity" (HF 64). Now one may reasonably ask here: How is it that the protection of the imaginary domain might answer to the demand for recognition of our vulnerability and dignity? If vulnerability refers merely to the fact that identity formation is existentially risky and subject to failure, then it is not clear why it should receive legal protection.

Plainly, only if the imaginary domain is bound to the necessary conditions for individuation in the manner I have described between a demand for protection and the fact of our vulnerability can even the hope of a connection be established. The first step in making the connection would be to state that, because of its mimetic conditions of possibility, all identity formation occurs recognitively; that is, individuation is a mimetic as well as a symbolic achievement, and its mimetic conditions of possibility subtend its symbolic achievement. In Beauvoirian terms then, the thesis is not that we are existentially vulnerable, but rather that we are ontologically vulnerable: in establishing a gender identity we are constitutively dependent on the gaze of the other. In the first instance, the imaginary domain is just the alienated image of the self which the child mimetically projects, it is the space of mimetic adaptation itself. If my hypothesis that the oedipal phase adds gender complementarity and symbolic legitimation to a core gender identity (with "simple" gender difference) is correct, then it follows that the symbolic work of the imaginary domain is properly the continuation of mimetic adaptation which can be efficacious only if recognized.[27] Said differently, to conceive of there being an indefinite dialectical exchange between the mimetic and the symbolic entails conceiving of the symbolic as not a release from the recognitive demands of mimetic adaptation but as its continuation. But if the symbolic is a continuation of these demands, then it too is subject to recognitive constraints. In this light, *the primary political good of self-respect as underwriting the minimum conditions for individuation can now be thought of as precisely the recognition of the imaginary domain itself.* The imaginary domain is the point of exchange where our embodied sexual identity, the projection of that identity in action, and the dependency of that identity on the (mimetic *and* symbolic) recognition of others all meet. Our so-called dignity is not, as Cornell half concedes nothing but the flip-side of our vulnerability. Cornell's sentences on vulnerability can now be given with their true, Beauvoir-modified sense: "Given that we are [embodied] creatures [ontologically] thrown into a world not of our own making [but upon which we are nonetheless ontologically dependent] . . . we can be crushed [by nonrecognition and misrecognition] in our efforts to become [transcendent] persons [whose immanent constitution belongs to their full identity as persons]. We need to explicitly articulate and recognize that individuation is a [necessary and perpetual fundamental] project, and one that needs legal, political, ethical, and moral recognition if it is to be effectively maintained" (HF 64). At its best, the doctrine of the imaginary domain gives perfect shape to what Beauvoir considered the project of our time: to become an "independent woman."

BUTLER

Woman are Other according to Beauvoir in so far as they are defined by a masculine perspective that seeks to safeguard its own disembodied status [= risking life] through identifying woman generally with the bodily sphere [= giving life]. Male disembodiment is only possible on the condition that women occupy their bodies as their essential and enslaving identities. . . . By defining women as Other, men are able through the short-cut of definition to dispose of their bodies, to make themselves other than bodies—a symbol of potential human decay and transience and of limitation generally—and to make their bodies other than themselves. . . . The body rendered as Other—repressed or denied, and then projected—reemerges for this "I" as the view of others as essentially body. Hence, women become the Other; they come to embody corporeality itself . . . [Male] disembodiment becomes a way of existing in one's body in the mode of denial. And the denial of the body—as in Hegel's dialectic of master and slave—reveals itself as nothing other than the embodiment of denial.

BEAUVOIR

Early man's activity had another dimension that gave it supreme dignity: it was often dangerous. If blood were but a nourishing fluid, it would be valued no higher than milk; but the hunter was no butcher, for in the struggle against wild animals he ran grave risks. The warrior put his life in jeopardy to elevate the prestige of the horde, the clan to which he belonged. And in this he proved dramatically that life is not the supreme value for man, but on the contrary that it should be made to serve ends more important than itself. The worst curse that was laid upon woman was that she should be excluded from these warlike forays. For it is not in *giving life* but in *risking life* that man is raised above the animal, *that is why superiority has been accorded in humanity not to the sex that brings life forth but that which kills* (SS 63–64; emphasis mine).

[I]t is about when the separation is accomplished, toward the age of six months, perhaps, that the child begins to show the desire to attract others through acts of mimicry which subsequently become genuine displays, the desire to seduce others. Certainly this attitude is not established through a reflective choice; but it is not necessary to *intend* a situation for it to *exist*. In an immediate manner, the nursing lives the original drama of every existent, which is the drama of his relation to the Other. It is in anguish that the human being feels his abandonment. Fleeing his liberty, his subjectivity, he would like to lose himself in the bosom of the All: here is the origin of his cosmic and pantheistic dreams, of his desire to forget, to dream, to be ecstatic, to die. He never succeeds in abolishing his separate ego. At the least he wants to attain the solidity of the in-itself, the en-soi, to be petrified into a thing. It is especially when he is fixed by the look of others that he appears to himself as a being.

In a carnal form, he [the infant] discovers finitude, solitude, abandonment in a foreign world. He tries to compensate for this catastrophe by alienating his existence in an image whose reality and value others will ground. It appears that he begins to affirm his identity at the moment at which he recognizes his reflection in mirrors—a moment that coincides with weaning. His ego blends so well with this reflection that is formed only in being alienated. Whether the mirror properly speaking plays a role more or less considerable, it is certain that the child begins around six months to mimic his parents and to grasp himself in their look as an object. He is already an autonomous subject who transcends himself toward the world: but it is only in alienated form that he will encounter himself (SS, 268–69).

BENJAMIN

Let us say that the male child's repudiation of his own passivity, associated with humiliation at the hands of the mother (she rejects him, leaves him, tantalizes him) sparks the father's fantasy of the daughter's passivity . . . [Following Freud], a repressed feminine passivity lodges behind the male's obsessional use of defensive, aggressive activity. In other words, a certain kind of activity is necessary in order to overcome helplessness, and this kind of defensive activity structures the masculine position. If father-daughter incest represents the most egregious encapsulation of this defense, it is made possible by the generalized complementary relationship between the sexes, in which the daughter functions not merely as the split off embodiment of the passive object, but also the missing maternal container into whom the father discharges and expels unmanageable tension. The dual function of embodying passivity and containing unmanageable projected tension gives form to femininity; this femininity centers on the daughter, not the mother, as its defining figure.

NOTES

1. References in the text to ID are to Drucilla Cornell, *The Imaginary Domain: Abortion, Pornography, and Sexual Harassment* (New York: Routledge, 1995). References in the text to HF are to Drucilla Cornell, *At the Heart of Freedom: Feminism, Sex, and Equality* (Princeton: Princeton University Press, 1998). Other abbreviations are to SS,

Simone de Beauvoir, *The Second Sex*, trans. H. M. Parshley (New York: Vintage, 1989); SB, Nancy Bauer, *Simone de Beauvoir: Philosophy, and Feminism* (New York: Columbia University Press, 2001).

2. Although I cannot develop the thought here, it is certainly worth noting how fully the normative efficacy of self-respect depends upon its relation to a logic of shame and hence the necessity for there being elaborated a compelling normative account of shame. At least in part, it is because I understand self-respect as bound to the intersubjective space of shame that I suggest later in the chapter that self-respect itself must be restructured recognitively.

3. If nothing else, this is just the sort of theoretical accommodation that the idea of an overlapping consensus enables.

4. "Tragic Republicanism: Self-Respect, Difference, and Violence," in Enrique Rodriguez Larreta, ed., *Ethics of the Future* (Rio de Janeiro: Unesco/ISSC/Educam, 1998), 497–524.

5. Ibid. For a somewhat different recognitive account of self-respect see Axel Honneth, *The Struggle for Recognition: The Moral Grammar of Social Conflicts*, trans. Joel Anderson (Oxford: Polity, 1995), ch. 5.

6. Perhaps the most startling and fecund theoretical gesture of Nancy Bauer's *Simone de Beauvoir* is her making Beauvoir's "I am a woman" the inaugural counterstatement to Descartes' *Cogito ergo sum* (SB ch. 2).

7. Other new works that deserve reading include Eva Lundgrin-Gothlin, *Sex and Existence: Simone de Beauvoir's* The Second Sex, trans. Linda Schenck (Hanover, NH: Wesleyan University Press/University Press of New England, 1996); Toril Moi, *What Is a Woman? And Other Essays* (New York: Oxford University Press, 1999); Margaret Simons, *Beauvoir and* The Second Sex: *Feminism, Race, and the Origins of Existentialism* (Lanham, MD: Rowman and Littlefield, 1999); and Karen Vintges, *Philosophy as Passion: The Thinking of Simone de Beauvoir*, trans. Anne Lavelle (Bloomington: Indiana University Press, 1996).

8. Jacques Lacan, *"Les Complexes familiaux"* (Paris: Navarin, 1984), 110–12. My account of Lacan here closely follows the insightful reading of my former colleague Peter Dews, "The Crisis of Oedipal Identity: The Early Lacan and the Frankfurt School," in his *Limits of Disenchantment: Essays on Contemporary European Philosophy* (London: Verso, 1995), ch. 11. It was Dews who years ago pointed out to me the importance of this early work of Lacan. For another take on it in relation to Lacan's later writings, see Mikkel Borch-Jacobsen, "The Oedipus Problem in Freud and Lacan." *Critical Inquiry* 20, no. 2. (Winter 1994), and his *Lacan: The Absolute Master* (Stanford: Stanford University Press, 1991), ch. 1.

9. See the essays collected in Juliet Mitchell and Jacqueline Rose, eds., *Feminine Sexuality: Jacques Lacan and the école freudienne*, trans. Jacqueline Rose (London: Macmillan, 1982).

10. Of course, Lacan ascribes the conception of lack to Heidegger; but its role and shape in Lacan's thought, the way it is tied to the subject's desiring, the misleading role of an image of completeness (a for-itself that is in-itself), the language of lack itself, all reverberate with Sartrean rather than Heideggerian thought.

11. See the work cited in note 6.

12. Another sign of this repression is the way in which Gayle Rubin's trenchant and powerful 1975 essay "The Traffic in Women: Notes on the 'Political Economy' of Sex," reprinted in Linda Nicholson, ed., *The Second Wave: A Reader in Feminist Theory* (New York: Routledge, 1997), ch. 3, has now all but disappeared from theoretical sight.

13. In ID 63–64, Cornell issues a critique of Beauvoir, complaining that her thought is defined by gender complementarity and that female liberation requires a renunciation of some of the most blatant features of female sexuality, such as pregnancy. These complaints seem crude. If Beauvoir does not possess the robust Buterlian conception of gender plurality, since she considers female homosexuality if anything more rational and intelligible than heterosexual desire (and certainly not a "perversion"), then she does not adhere to gender complementarity as normally understood (e.g., via imperative heterosexuality) (SS 405–11). And Beauvoir repeatedly insists that what are presently the handicaps of female embodiment (menstruation, pregnancy and morning sickness, child-bearing) are all only negative in the historically constituted social world in which we live; a woman's body is only significant in a *situation* (SS, 32–36, 315–16 [in comparison to 28–29], 498, 511 [in comparison with 30], 525, 682). I think two facts conspire to give the impression on which Cornell's critique centers: first, that Beauvoir wrote in a "severe" style, letting the critical meaning of her analysis emerge from the concatenation of her insistent and relentless recitation of the negative features of the situation of women throughout history and in the present world, with the reminder that this is all a revisable situation (one becomes and is not born a woman) and not a destiny. Second, the scant image of female emancipation she provides is autobiographically constrained. There is almost nothing of a utopian banquet in Beauvoir; for her Hegelian realism (philosophy without a transcendent "ought"), the documentation of the transformable, structurally incurred misery of women's lives is the form of hope proper to us.

14. I mean by this that the perception of Beauvoir as unequivocally urging that women become transcendent like men and deny everything that is historically embedded in the feminine needs to be set against her dialectical equalizing of transcendence and immanence (which is what allows her notion of "situation" to displace the exorbitance of Sartrean transcendence), and hence, as implicit in her irony, her implicit depreciation of transcendence when it is isolated from the demands of immanence: the valorization of killing over giving life.

15. I presume her thought is that if the Hegelian master is the risker of life who upholds the value of risk in opposition to the slave, and the slave is constituted by the unwillingness to risk, then Hegelian slavery becomes just a highly mediated route, through work, to mastery—which is essentially Kojève's view. Working on nature, transforming it, is still mastery. Kojéve's Hegel, and perhaps Hegel himself (this was Schelling's thought), views immanence as an ontological drag on transcendence rather than an ingredient in a situation containing immanent and transcendent elements. Because woman is constituted by being positioned as standing for the elements constituting immanence, then she is more than a master-to-be: she truly represents the *necessity* of life for self-consciousness (see *Phenomenology of Spirit*, trans. A. V. Miller (Oxford: Clarendon, 1977), sects. 188–89). Another way of stating the same thought would be to say that Hegel thinks that master and slave do recognize that "life is as essential to it as pure self-consciousness" simply by entering into a recognitive relation with one another, the master/slave relation; this fails to acknowledge the depth of the

way in which nature is the other of self-consciousness, hence will entail the suppression of giving life again, which is just what does happen in Hegel.

16. Judith Butler, "Variations on Sex and Gender: Beauvoir, Wittig, and Foucault," in Seyla Benhabib and Drucilla Cornell, eds., *Feminism as Critique: Essays on the Politics of Gender in Late-Capitalist Societies* (Oxford: Polity, 1987), 133.

17. Needless to say, the gendered duality between (impossible) transcendence and (reductive) immanence is precisely the one that we find in Sartre. Beauvoir's generous defenses of Sartre on subjectivity and embodiment need to be seen in the light of her modifications of his basic scheme.

18. It would behoove Beauvoir's theory to allow that even the moment of primal unity with the mother can be, in part, sustained by what I will call "mimetic adaptation." For this conception of the earliest mother/infant dyad see Jessica Benjamin, *The Bonds of Love* (New York: Pantheon Books, 1988), 26–27. Injecting a moment of dissonance into recognition itself, at least that conception of mutual recognition of which Benjamin has been the pioneer and foremost representative, is one limb of the project that I am here inaugurating.

19. I am using Bauer's translation of this passage, SB 207–08.

20. Bauer's translation, SB 208.

21. As it stands, Beauvoir's conception of the need for recognition as a drive to become an in-itself, thinglike, is too one-sided. There is little doubt that the infant, in learning bodily coordination, is learning mastery of the world and hence learning something of independence. This entails that a component of separateness/individuation is self-affirming. Beauvoir's thesis is that both poles of the separateness/connectedness structure are intrinsically riddled with a degenerative aspect: to find separateness in the recognition that makes that constitutive separateness as "thingly." If this destructive desire is thought of as a routine component of the dialectic of recognition in infancy, then recognition itself becomes more ambiguous, its possibilities of success and failure more radically intertwined. Again, all that is necessary in order to achieve this result is that we acknowledge the anxiety of separation, the need for security, the dominantly mimetic element in recognition, and the aspect of foreclosure (the death drive of mimesis) built into mimetic adaptation. One might say that if recognition contains a mimetic element, then potentially each recognition imbricates a simultaneous misrecognition. In psychoanalytic terms, a complex conception of mimesis would help explain the perdurability of narcissism.

22. Jessica Benjamin, *The Shadow of the Other: Intersubjectivity and Gender in Psychoanalysis* (New York: Routledge, 1998), 60, is apparently postulating something similar, in agreement with R. J. Stoller, namely, that alongside a primary identification with the mother, there occurs "an early recognition of one's own assignation to male or female, which he [Stoller] called core gender identity. The notion of a kinesthetic sensibility, a sense of a body ego based on the way one is treated by others, is one that might be better conceived as nominal gender identity—a child becomes organized by it as it does by a name." The notion of a core gender identity, that is, gender identity without gender difference, seems exactly right, as does the fact that this is learned mimetically, "on the way one is treated by others." If Beauvoir is right about how radically core gender identity prepares for full gender identity, then there is something questionable in Benjamin's thinning this down to something merely "nominal." Will relegating core

gender identity to the nominal not place too much on the oedipal moment itself, thus foreclosing the most obvious arena for gender transformation? Since throughout *The Bonds of Love*, especially chapter 3, Benjamin portrays core gender identity as substantive but fluid, not fixed, then perhaps all she means by "nominal" here is "not transcendentally fixed," with which I of course agree.

23. Benjamin, *The Shadow of the Other* 32.

24. Of course, this is no accident; *The Bonds of Love* itself, 7, explicitly flies under the flag of Beauvoir's conception of woman as the other and the consequent conception of gender complementarity.

25. If I am understanding Benjamin correctly, the daughter's desire for the father and identification with the mother is a (direct) *consequence* of the behavior of the father, what is involved in the daughter mimetically responding to his desire. This means, does it not, that the positioning of the daughter is more legible in the first instance than that of the boy? Conversely, the boy's desire for the mother is going to have to be more mediated since it will be routed through the daughter. Not only does this reverse the standard Freudian picture about the availability of the positions of son and daughter, but it reveals how object love and identificatory love receive their full articulation and differentiation as *modifications* of mimetic adaptation. (For the claim that both identificatory love and object love are emergent forms, see Benjamin, *The Bond of Love*, 106–07, 161–62. For Benjamin, plausibly, the dominant effect the current oedipal arrangement is that it forces a repudiation of identificatory love with the mother—hence the title and guiding theme of her second book: *Like Subjects, Love Objects: Essays on Recognition and Sexual Difference* (New Haven: Yale University Press, 1995). On my account, that repudiation is not primarily the consequence of the mechanisms of development but of the genealogy of gender polarity.) Now it might be complained at this juncture that in making the story so existential, Beauvoir has suppressed the Freudian primacy of the sexual. But this is not quite correct: Beauvoir's account explains why gender identity and object choice *become* the arenas in which the deepest existential dilemmas of subjectivity get played out (since from the outset the infant works through the anxiety of separation in mimetic displays that are sexually contoured). So long as who we are is bound to gender identity and object choice, then our being will indeed be sexuate; but this is to say that while there is a thorough-going entanglement of the existential and the sexual, they are not identical. But is it not just this entanglement without identity that is necessary for Cornell's conception of sexuate being? After all her theory requires that the necessary conditions for individuation (the existential) necessitate a sexual component without the component absorbing the individuation, otherwise the demand for recognition could not be normatively generalized.

26. Benjamin, *The Shadow of the Other*, 57.

27. If this is correct, then there is going to be a far more integral relation between "love" and "right" as forms of recognition than Axel Honneth, *The Struggle for Recognition: The Moral Grammar of Social Conflicts*, chs. 5–6, supposes. To put the point crudely, there is already a cognitive dimension to the recognition accorded to the child in the oedipal stage; and, as every postoedipal child would tell Honneth, something approximate to the demand for self-respect that is legally encoded in our principles of equality is already ethically and morally demanded, and to an extant provided for, throughout the latency period. The imaginary domain is, of course, the linking element.

Benjamin Pryor

"*Faute de Mieux*": Defending Ideals

Cindy Sheehan's protest, as is well known, is motivated by the death of her son in Iraq and will end when, as she puts it, our president can explain to her in plain language the "nobility" of the cause for which we fight our war. If the war is being fought on the basis of ideals that qualify as "noble," then the least one can do is defend those ideals to the ones expected to share them: mothers, fathers, brothers, and citizens. Her protest—the fact of it, if not what she says and the very specific power that she embodies—raises questions that I will explore in the context of Drucilla Cornell's *Defending Ideals* (2004, hereafter DI). What exactly does her insistence that Bush defend his ideals mean? Why is defending ideals such an important task, and why is the call to a defense of ideals experienced with such critical and disruptive force, as itself a gesture of support for terrorism, anti-Americanism, and treason? Or perhaps defending ideals is something we do in the wake of something else. I think it is an important task, and one that speaks to democratic aspirations in a particular way. The title *Defending Ideals*, if I read Drucilla Cornell correctly, must be understood to indicate an ongoing activity, always and in principle incomplete. The title of the book is thus a description of what happens in it: It is a label. Calling to mind Sen's definition of life as a series of interrelated functionings, Cornell's book is an enactment, the performance of a function, a record, journal, or account of skirmishes, tactics, and deployments.

There is a certain ambiguity in the distinction between defending specific ideals—the ideals embodied in international law (DI 26), a normative replacement for the ideal of the modern nation state (DI 35), the ideal of peace (DI 37), *jihad* (DI 52), public reason (DI 53), economic development (DI 63), humanity (DI 72, 80), civility (DI 81), and so on—and defending the *having* of ideals, defending the defending of ideals, defending ideals *as such*. In this vein, Cornell approvingly cites Falk's expectation that the Bush administration formulate "ideals as such" (DI 29); reminds us that ideals are on occasion things, instruments in which we "invest" (DI 38); "ideal" is used as an adjective that describes Sen's approach, and "ideality" becomes an aspect of a theoretical approach (DI 71); in Balibar's notion of civility as an ideal, the "fictive universality" of the norms, national ideals, and moral expressions of the ideal of humanity "carries something beyond itself" (DI 81), and so on. On the one hand, then, we see an appeal to specific, singular (a word to which I will return) values that resonate with and are revived by particular encounters with sites of injustice and well-meaning attempts to reanimate the Kantian imagination in the formation of identity. In this appeal we find a resistance to the hypostatization of ideals and an attraction to the fluidity of identity. In short, we find temporality—in the context of a shared commitment to this and that ideal. On the other hand, there is in this book an appeal to the ideal of ideality, to being "carried beyond," to the metaphor of investment and the accompanying hope that by placing this meager hoard into a transcending instrument of value, life might be improved. The remarks that follow will engage with this ambiguity in order to work out the value of the defense (or "defending") of ideals in Cornell's work. This is not a call to judgment but a specific inquiry into a "value" in the sense of value that is closest to the musical sense: the relative value of a note in relation to a time signature. What is the value of the appeal to ideals in the context of a work in which that appeal might just as easily appear as troubled, exorbitant in a literal sense, or extrarhythmic?

FAUTE DE MIEUX?

The "Third Essay" of the *Genealogy of Morals*, as Nietzsche writes in *Ecce Homo*, offers the answer to the question of "whence the ascetic ideal, the priests' ideal, derives its tremendous power although it is the harmful ideal par excellence, a will to the end, an ideal of decadence." Nietzsche continues: "Answer: not, as people may believe, because God is at work behind the priests, but *faute de mieux*—because it was the only ideal so far, because it had no rival." If we take this as both a warning (it is a harmful ideal in question here) and a charge (it was, after all, the only ideal so far), one might conclude that Nietzsche is not dismissing ideals as such but transforming the conditions in which they are appealed to, accepted, and held steady. How might we experience Cornell's appeal to ideals in the context of a transformation of the conditions of that experience? Does Cornell's appeal resist transformation or undergo it in the name not of higher ideals but of the appeal to justice in its withdrawal?

Drucilla Cornell's philosophy takes its beginnings in part from a powerful appropriation of the work of Jacques Derrida, Jacques Lacan, and other thinkers who call into question and ultimately disturb deeply held ideas about the self, the individual, and the legal subject. In her work, she not only weakens but also works in the absence of a sense of the privilege of the idea of an autonomous will as the sole causal source of moral agency, a subject that forms itself through its consciousness of its own self-representation as a moral being.[1] By showing, through her appropriation of Lacan's psychoanalytic thought, that self-representation of oneself as an agent or moral being—the rudimentary structures of psychical life—is formed in a symbolic field and that that field is ultimately a field of undecideability, Cornell establishes a domain of free self-representation not only as the basis of political life and social intercourse but also as the basis of identity. Cornell uses some of the most powerful and controversial thinkers—antipodal thinkers—in our philosophical tradition to set our thinking of identity, sexuate being, and sexual difference on an entirely new course. Remarkably, in *Defending Ideals* as in other works she pursues this course in communication and sympathy with other philosophers and legal thinkers who are maximally dependent on the very discourse of rights, subjectivity, and individuality that are in question in her work. Cornell's thought in relation to jurisprudence is a powerful intervention into the ascendancy of a certain set of assumptions that guide legal critique and thought, albeit in an idiom shared by what she is also disrupting. Using Lacan, Derrida, Irigaray, and others, Cornell focuses the power of their thought on the reign of the masculine—the phallogocentrism—that undergirds the Western dream of legality and that structures the limits our being and our identity. At the same time, through an appeal to contemporary liberalism, particularly John Rawls, and the insistence on the second sense of "defending ideals" (i.e., the insistence on defending ideals as such, the *having* of ideals), Cornell makes a case for the centrality to critical legal theory of the value of dignity and respect for persons. In a gesture that she recognizes in various places as controversial and unexpected, she turns to a Rawlsian discourse of rights and identity in order to redraw the limits of legal and political thought, limits that are inclusive, that bestow dignity on subjects of the law, and that maximize freedom. The controversial aspect of this appeal is perhaps obvious: she appeals to thinkers who are commonly associated with antienlightenment critique to give an ontological or philosophical account of the conditions for engagement in, for lack of a better term, the Enlightenment. Cornell is acutely aware of the dangers of her many engagements: Using Lacan to undermine essentialist conceptions of identity even though his pessimism about the place of woman is, as he says, unavoidable; using Rawls to sketch a conception of identity and dignity even though her use of Lacan would apparently be in tension with this conception. If more academics had such imagination, we might actually get somewhere.

I note that there is something misleading the picture I have started to sketch, a picture that has Cornell drawing from antienlightenment thinkers as a basis for an articulation of an Enlightenment-style philosophy of rights. It is misleading for a number of reasons: it is partisan in its approach to a complex problem of representation, identity, and law. Derrida and Lacan are not *anti*-Enlightenment thinkers. Indeed, Cornell's work goes a long way to pointing out that they are fully engaged in an Enlightenment ethos of critique, which she identifies with the tracing of limits and of exclusions that are constitutive of identity and subjectivity, of purportedly stable essences. However, it is inaccurate and unhelpful to associate Rawls and others in the liberal tradition with a simplistic essentialist notion of identity and rights, with the view that we can by simply consulting the structure of reason and deducing from it a moral law represent to ourselves our duties and obligations as they flow from some fundamental aspect of our being. Cornell has me convinced, again, that on the one hand, thinkers associated with antienlightenment critique are fully within an enlightenment tradition understood as a turn to self-representation as a starting point for thought, and that on the other hand, Enlightenment thinkers are well aware of the transformative and libratory possibilities that emerge from critical thought.

Yet Cornell's increasingly intense relation to classical liberalism and her repeated insistence on ideals—among them the ideals of dignity, freedom, and equality that she associates with liberalism—prompt me to ask, with some uncertainty about why I ask this: What about Nietzsche? I do not mean only to ask after a philosopher who wrote such great books. We are all free to ignore Nietzsche, Plotinus, Von Humboldt, Thomas Reid, or anyone else for that matter without some archivist reminding us of their absence in our thinking. I mean to ask—and I will justify the question in a moment—what about a Nietzschean impatience reflected the *Genealogy of Morals* and *Ecce Homo*, an impatience with all manifestations of that most wily of characters the ascetic priest and perhaps with the very project of having and defending ideals? What of Nietzsche's sustained and searing indictment—and indictment that goes far beyond a mere "anti-Enlightenment" suspicion and to an utterly different relation with the question of value and purpose in life? Perhaps the most important question is, What of Nietzsche as the "philosopher of the future"? In Nietzsche's writing, the ascetic priest is the one who adopts ideals, who insists on the importance of ideals, and whose thought wants nothing more than a meaning, a foothold, a springboard into a life that is governed by ideals and restraint. The priest is immoderate and unrestrained, of course, in clamoring for ideals and restraint but does not recognize the priest's own immoderation. The priest denies it.

Cornell's work almost never engages with Nietzsche as a philosopher who wrote such great books, and even less frequently with Nietzsche's closest intellectual relatives: Deleuze and especially Foucault. She engages with Nietzsche most often through Derrida's deconstructive reading of Nietzsche's remarks on women in *Spurs* in *Beyond Accommodation* or in name only as the "wrathful" philosopher who brought to vivid life the internal connection between German idealism and slave morality. But there is, I think, a curious turning aside from Nietzschean thought—not as an *oeuvre* but as a "movement" in a sort of Hegelian sense—in the bulk of Cornell's work. If "turning aside" is too strong (for it evokes, at least for me, Heidegger's reading of Kant, who allegedly "shrank back" from his own conclusions about the imagination at the heart of the synthesis of reason—one thing from which Cornell decidedly does not shrink back), perhaps instead of saying "turning aside" I can say a "deemphasis." Another question is whether this deemphasis is a product of disinterest and a purposeful focus on something else or whether it is strategic or at least deliberate.

It is important to note that Nietzsche—or a "Nietzschean" temperament—is a presence in Cornell's work, to be sure. Her questioning stance toward ideals, community, and the construction of sexual difference in liberal political thought at least echoes and perhaps exemplifies what I would call a "Nietzschean disposition" (and resonates with contemporary Nietzschean critiques in Nancy, Deleuze, and others). Of course, Nietzsche is a haunting presence in some of those thinkers with whom she is at odds. Posner, for example, is alleged to be a Nietzschean in his spare time.[2] Most striking is that Nietzsche is a powerful presence in more than name only in Derrida's work. Indeed, Nietzsche's influence in Derrida's thought is strongest at the very point at which Cornell finds Derrida most useful and appealing: when Derrida's philosophy—and thus philosophy proper—becomes a "choreography." Still, Nietzsche's prominence in Derrida's thinking is not reflected in Cornell's work, the way, say, Kant's prominence in Rawls's thought plays a role in Cornell's own thinking. Kant is taken on his own terms (though for very specific, even idiomatic uses), while Nietzsche is never taken on his own terms. In short, then, I wonder whether there is a dimension to Nietzsche's thought that, though important and vital to Cornell's philosophical foundations, does not make its way—because it is not admitted—to the upper floors. Is Nietzsche chained in the basement of Cornell's Utopia? Is Foucault in the basement with him? Are angry Nietzscheanisms like this business about ideals being necessary *faute de mieux* simply unwelcome, or do they cause difficulties for Cornell's program that are unanticipated, even as some of Nietzsche's closest inheritors provide the basis for necessity, as it were, in Cornell's thought? So again, I will pose the question and then work toward an answer: Is this absence important?[3]

It is worth noticing that the Enlightenment ideals of freedom, publicity, dignity, and reason have been, incredibly, actively abandoned in contemporary political discourse. The hallmark separation of church and state and the occupation of public space by the free use of reason rather than by religious dogma no longer occupy a place of privilege in political discourse in the United States. The Enlightenment may be fading in Western Europe as well. Given this erosion of the place of the Enlightenment, we might wonder what the absence of an explicitly Nietzschean strain in Cornell's work *says*?[4] I wonder whether by engaging in a utopian discourse of rights and dignity, as Cornell does (though always in the context of a recognition of the primacy of the imagination for our thinking about identity, which is the recognition that identity is never closed, and that representations of identity are subject to continual slippage by virtue of their symbolic construction), whether we resist the erosion of Enlightenment ideals, but not quite enough? In this regard, the discussion from Nietzsche with which I began places Cornell on difficult ground. Despite the harmfulness of the ascetic ideal as a will to the end and an ideal of decadence, the ascetic ideal retains its power in those discourses that pretend we can abandon the values of the Enlightenment in favor of a stronger transcendent guarantee of the meaningfulness of life. For Nietzsche, the ascetic ideal remains powerful not because there is a lingering "good" (or God) behind the posited ideal, a good that we aspire to in any event. There is nothing "behind" Enlightenment—or any—ideals that can be preserved or rescued through a more disciplined insistence on those ideals. Nietzsche's answer to the question of the "whence" of the ascetic ideal—and hence of ideals as such—leaves him with only *"faute de mieux"*: "because it was the only ideal so far, because it had no rival." Turning to Cornell's work, we might ask, Why commit oneself to Defending Ideals, to which the answer may well be, "Just 'Cause."[5]

NIETZSCHE AT HOME IN THE IMAGINARY DOMAIN

To see how Nietzsche hovers just outside the frame that Cornell places around the appeal to ideals and the defense of ideals, we can look at her early taking up of Derrida in *Beyond Accommodation*, and particularly of Derrida's "deconstructive reading of Lacan" in the chapter "The Feminist Alliance with Deconstruction."[6] The essay concerns Derrida's interruption of Lacan's identification of the feminine as the truth of castration. Lacan, says Derrida, is convinced that he has "grasped the truth of Woman" as represented by the masculine symbolic. As fictional as representations of Woman are, they are "inhabited" by truth according to Lacan, the truth of the economy of sexual difference at which symbolic representations and essential determinations merely attempt to grasp. The signifier circles around and never quite grasps woman, but nevertheless, we can find in that circling the "truth" of woman: lack, castration, passivity.

Cornell shows that Derrida reverses the relation between "truth" and fiction and emphasizes the ethical and political implications of the Lacanian insight. Derrida insists on the play of language and the interruption of the idea that the fictions of feminine identity in our tradition refer to essential characteristics and ontological structures that are always subject to the play of language as we name them and describe their articulations. Derrida says that "the economy of fiction, which enforces sexual difference, makes itself true precisely through its enforcement" (BA, 82). This "enforcement" is textual insofar as it "enforces" the connections among representations of woman, identities and essential characteristics, and singular women. Derrida instead insists on "singularity" as an "untranslatable factor," as finite singularity that interrupts identity and sets in motion a "dance," an unpredictable, differenced, and "virtual" future that is no longer anchored to the order of the symbolic, that recognizes *difference* as accompanying presence.

I wish to note two things about this analysis. First, Cornell points out on a number of occasions that Derridean deconstruction, as opposed to Lacanian analysis, is "inherently" and "irreducibly" ethical. But how are we to understand the "irreducibility" of deconstruction as an ethical gesture in this context? Deconstruction is "irreducibly ethical" because it is ethical and nothing else. Unlike most philosophies, deconstruction does not have a "metaphysics" and an "ethics" followed by a volume of ephemera. And it is "irreducibly ethical" because all ethical claims and discourses, to the extent that they engage in questions of value, agency, right, or the good, are touched by deconstruction so that one cannot *do* ethics without eventually running up against deconstructive critique, against the differencing aspect of language in relation to transcending values. Deconstruction *is* ethics, something on which Derrida often insists: as a response to power that denies its own violence, to language that refuses its own questionability, to political and ethical argumentation that in all of its responsibility appears utterly bereft of responsible assessment of the conditions of live, deconstruction finds that in *disconfirming*, disrupting, destructing those langagues, powers, and forms of reason something else comes to presence. Thus, and this is the other sense in which deconstruction is inherently ethical, ethics as a call to responsibility or responsiveness will always find itself caught in a tension that deconstruction most carefully explores.

So deconstruction is ethical, irreducibly so. We discover its ethical force in the displacement and disruption of languages and forms of knowing in Lacan—or in the masculine imagination—that give way to new possibilities, new presences, and unheard of ways of inhabiting our bodies. And not incidentally, we discover its ethical force at precisely that moment when Derrida encounters Nietzsche. The ethical force of deconstruction breaks our ties to phallogocentric discourse right when Derrida is not just inspired by Nietzsche but finds in Nietzsche's texts what Cornell recognizes as a precisely this kind of ethical gesture. Nietzsche's texts contain forces that disrupt their own assertions, that disturb their own conceptuality, and that thus render at least ironic and at most utterly parodic his claims about woman and the truth of woman. In a language that cannot help but reduce woman to an essential identity in a masculine symbolic order, Derrida recognizes that a Nietzschean intensification of countervailing powers and challenges to truth as such provide us with resources that can produce an alternative not just to the future but to the present. The introduction of the ethical force of deconstruction, then, emerges and is inseparable from Derrida's engagement with Nietzsche. At the heart of the powerful critique of Lacan that marks the inception of the imaginary domain, the free futural space in which the dance of sexual difference is performed and identities are encouraged in their reconfiguring, we find not just Derrida, but Derrida's Nietzsche as the inaugurator of an "irreducibly ethical" critique. And thus we entertain Nietzsche's unrecognized—and perhaps unwelcome—presence at an crucial moment in Cornell's text: In his engagement with Nietzsche's text, Derrida shows us how the affirmation of the stereotypes creates a spillage beyond what they have been taken to mean, including by Nietzsche. (BA 85)

Certainly the web of debts is complicated here. Nietzsche cannot be taken "at his word," but at the same time, Nietzsche knows this and writes in the knowledge that his own assertions are subject to overcoming. That Nietzsche's texts famously throw their own assertions into question means that we can read them as undermining their own misogyny. Cornell thus insists on the ethical force of deconstruction, where the ethical force is explicitly and integrally connected to Nietzsche's own "self-overcoming" of ideals. At the moment that deconstruction is intensified and deployed as an ethics, we also find that the specifically ethical value of deconstructive critique is tied to Nietzsche—not only to an analysis of Nietzsche's texts, but to what I have already called a "Nietzschean" movement in which ideals and the life of ideals are, as it were, returned to the earth.

Nietzsche is nowhere to be found in *Defending Ideals*, though there is, as I will show, a different kind of "return to the earth." Indeed, the critical interrogation into ideals as such—into the need for them, their value—falls not to Nietzsche but to Adorno: "Assessing the validity of Adorno's clarion call for a global subject demands, then, that we come to grips with the most searing contemporary critiques of universalism without giving up on the ideal of humanity and its power to halt the systematic destruction of human life" (DI 91). One might reasonably question as an empirical matter whether the ideal of humanity has, in its short life on earth during which many fine arguments and committed people have attempted to sustain and disseminate it, ever exhibited anything like a reliable "power to halt the systematic destruction of human life." Nietzsche recognizes that it has not and argues that therefore defending ideals serves another purpose. In any case, *Defending Ideals*, by maintaining the ambiguity between defending ideals with an emphasis on the verb *defending* as naming an ongoing process and the emphasis on hypostatized ideals, appears to borrow the ethical force of deconstruction in its affinity with Nietzschean critique. More to the point, it repeats the ethical gesture of deconstruction as deconstruction points us to the infinite task of defending ideals (recognizing the impossibility of giving them an adequate representation) in order to pursue another sense of defending ideals that Cornell says, citing Balibar, is a task necessary for the pursuit of liberal politics and for a confidence in progress. This, I believe, is what Nietzsche calls the task of defending ideals *"faute de mieux"*—because we have not managed to think past ideals and to the historical, nonsubjective, nontranscending, singular presencing of "values," always accompanied by countervailing forces and structures. Yet.

FROM DIGNITY TO NIHILISM AND BACK?

Cornell everywhere insists on the complication of the appeal to ideals. Ideals are an "aspiration"—quite literally carried by the breath, the singular exhalation of the one who articulates them. They are appealed to in the context of the ascendancy of the imagination, in the context of a free struggle to become a "person," to construct a singular presence or identity that is, as Lacan would have it, an irruption in the symbolic order, a disturbance of it, rather than an approximation of an identity that is somewhere—but not here—whole, complete, and realized. On one understanding of her project, she actually recapitulates the Nietzschean movement that takes us through the critique of a set of ideals only to return to the *meaning* of those ideals. The *meaning* of ideals is, on this reading, in the imaginative task we engage in when we defend ideals. Still, the emphasis on the tension in the construction of identity and the positing of ideals is precisely where I begin to wonder whether the recapitulation of the Nietzschean movement away from the ascetic ideal in Cornell's work can achieve the kind of freedom that I would call "free spirited," whether at the end of the hard work of criticism we find not an appropriation of anxiety and of temporal mortality, but, in a word, Hegel, in whom Cornell finds the origins of self-consciousness not in techniques of power or in the excessiveness of the will to power in our tradition, but in a relation of recognition with the other.[7] I will address what I think that avoidance does in and for Cornell's texts, and I will try to reconstruct the appeal to Enlightenment ideals and utopian thought in the context of a reawakening of the power of Nietzschean critique in Cornell's thought.

The avoidance of Nietzschean critique as such in Cornell's texts is not tantamount to the avoidance of critique. It constitutes a resistance to a certain movement proper to critique that Nietzsche identifies as a self-overcoming movement characteristic of the will to power. The last two sections of the third essay of Nietzsche's *Genealogy of Morals* raise the question of the value and meaning of the ascetic ideal *today*. That is, Nietzsche explicitly enjoins genealogical critique in a response to the question that is proper to the Enlightenment on Kant's terms: What is the meaning of reason, value, and critique today and for us? Having uncovered in the ascetic ideal a movement that turns all possible ideals against themselves, after finding in the movement of the ascetic ideal as such the possibility of a turning away from its own most compelling productions—values, ourselves, a mistrust of ourselves—Nietzsche finds the meaning of reason, value, and critique in its own will to truth. "All great things," he says, "bring about their own destruction through an act of self-overcoming" (BW 597). Even "Christian truthfulness" concludes this about itself: that it is inevitably guided to the question of the meaning of the will to truth, and the answer to that question is "self-overcoming." Thus the result of the intensification of the ascetic quest for truth behind appearances, for ideals that will provide a thread of stability where ideals are in question is the demise of the ascetic ideal itself. This leaves us, in the end, with the question of the meaning of our being and a range of answers not reducible to a Hegelian resolution of the tension between the will to truth and the withdrawal of any "other" that might give to ideals the resonance of permanence.

What meaning would our whole being possess if it were not this, that in us the will to truth becomes conscious of itself as a problem? Section 27 ends with the possibility that morality will perish or has already perished as the apotheosis of the ascetic ideal. The meaning-giving power of the ascetic ideal turned against its own production—turned against morality, self-denial, and the instantiation of ideals—is in the disturbance of the subject's power of representation as such and leaves us with the possibility of a different kind of willing and a nontranscending place or stance.

In this context, an appeal to ideals—dignity, autonomy, the good—will always run the risk of being *faute de mieux* (EH), and even *faute de mieux par excellence* (GM). That is, the appeal to ideas in the context of a recognition of the self-overcoming power of the will to truth will always run the risk of being at least in alliance with the ascetic ideal and its insistence on some appeal to some values, whatever they are and however *"mieux"* they are. At least there is something there. This appeal to the "at least" is one way of understanding Habermas's or Dworkin's norms and one way of blurring the distinction between law and justice. For in an appeal to ideals in this sense, one understands the appeal to ideals to be inseparable from an observation about what we do or an unavoidable consequence of a shared language or of community. I do not take myself to be saying anything with which Drucilla Cornell would be unsympathetic. She is a fierce critic of the moralists and ascetics who risk justice in the imposition of a definition of justice and who see justice and law as identical, derivable from each other. "Justice," she says, echoing Derrida, "remains beyond our description as the call of the Other." And this constitutes the aporia of justice, namely, that "justice must be singular and yet justice as law always implies a general form" (BA, 113). In short, her appeal to ideals is not just accompanied but is conditioned by a deconstructive critique of the very possibility of mistaking the general forms with which we are given to name the ideals and the singular and withdrawing presence that the ideals themselves are enlisted to protect and enable. But still, this deconstructive critique is in various places used to open a space for the other, to question and decenter the masculine privilege that informs law's vision of women by reminding us of a call, a responsibility that lies beyond law and to which law can never quite do justice. Ultimately the question is whether the criticism that enables the turn to values that Cornell makes carries with it a necessary and dangerous movement that would if pursued carry her discourse away from those values as well, into a constant hesitancy and caution in the presence of a demand that values and ideals orient our approach, even to questions of law. What would happen to Cornell's discourse if the hesitancy rather than ideals constituted the limit of law? Can we engage in a destructive critique that will necessarily involve us in a thought that will weaken the hold of the ascetic ideal—and hence to "ideals" as such—only to return to the values that belong to that ideal?

I understand the destructive, distancing movement that characterizes much of Cornell's earlier works in this context, particularly portions of *Beyond*

Accommodation and *The Imaginary Domain*. That movement strikes me as a kind of journey outward, away from home—from essential determinations of the feminine, from inherited values and discursive formations that are enforced and imposed, from domination—perhaps like the journey of the scholarly honeybee or beast of burden, or at least a deliberate estrangement from the symbolic economy that traps sexual difference. However, I understand the value-positing movement, the insistence that we must have at least this, at least the ideals of—name them—peace, *jihad*, humanity, and so on. But I do not yet understand the turn back from a limit that deconstruction either reaches or at least conveys us toward and to the felt need for ideals. If we do conceive of this as a journey and return, what suffered in our absence? Why not stay at sea? Is the turn and return to values separate from an appeal to the values themselves? Or is it a part of the movement that accompanies the destructive turn? Is the movement of return itself governed by the values that are in question in the thought that generated the distancing move?

Nietzsche and Cornell both refer to a kind of return to earth. But to which earth, and from where? For Nietzsche, the return to the earth is a turn to the body, the nervous system, the digestion. As one looks down, one also recognizes that one "looks from above," at a distance, leaving things undisturbed in their own proper dispersion, "in an abrupt dispossession." What remains to be looked at are forces, identified by Deleuze in his reading of Nietzsche for example as "active" and "reactive" forces. The genealogist is concerned with the historical occurrences of domination, of the specific configurations of individual forces that constitute unities that are never anything more than constellations of forces. But the genealogist is also concerned with the formation of perspective—of the genealogist's capacity to think genealogically—in this reactive formation. Genealogy will always resist the fascination with reactivity that constitutes morality, but it will also resist its own activity, its own shaping power as it gives an account of the formation of its own capacity to think in terms of active and reactive forces.

The Genealogy of Morals is about the reactive triumph in the human world of resentment, bad conscience, and the ascetic ideal. If we, with Nietzsche, imagine that the task of defending ideals is part of this "reactivity," is always in a position of having to reassert its privilege, its necessity, its stand as the bulwark against starvation, degradation, domination, and war, then on these terms, the task of defending ideals is a way of transcending, of decoupling the defending of ideals from their emergence among powers, bodies, nervous systems, practices, and institutional formations that ideals have nothing to do with. Nietzsche and Derrida, among others, return to the earth. That is, Nietzsche travels outward, upward, into the most spiritual reaches and the most scholarly heights, and is drawn again and again to the dark and shifting earth.[8] The return is not understood as a return to representations with which we are forced to dwell and that necessarily structure our thinking and communication. The return is to the struggles—the real and painful struggles of bodies against themselves, other bodies, forces, images, and determinations subject to nondetermination—and the pleasures (let us not forget those) that constitute our singular and finite presence on earth. This contrasts, I think, with a return to "meanings"—the "meanings" of "ideals"—that are understood as structuring the realm of the shared. This is, in a sense, Balibar's "mediation": "Balibar not only defends the importance of ideals, but also recognizes that the justifications, articulations and imaginings of ideals are precisely what mediate them symbolically. His position is thus that political and ethical discourse concerning ideals can occur only at the level of mediation. Hence all the great debates Balibar associates with the tradition of equaliberty: how does one reconcile freedom and equality?" (DI 87). But this "reconciling" and mediating are on genealogical terms themselves bound up with historical and institutional struggles, with bodies, differences, in short, with the earth if, indeed, there is anything like "mediating" going on at all when we justify, articulate, imagine, and defend ideals. If there is no mediation at all, or at least if one might return from the journey undertaken by deconstruction committed to something other than mediation, then perhaps one returns to a different ground, to a ground firm with roots, rhizomes, runners, that begs for a spade. We are left with singular, finite, historical occurrences of ideals that occur in the very gesture that defends, and that withdraw in the course of defending. Again, I think I am in agreement, somewhat, with Balibar and Cornell when I say that mediation is *all there is*. In another context, Jean-Luc Nancy says we do not gain access to anything. We only have access to an access. In the context of a defending of ideals, we need not defend anything. We might instead defend a defending.

On Cornell's terms, values constitute the limit of the law: law does not shape or regulate on the basis of a pregiven identity to which subjects must be held or a measure or ratio to which each individual can be reduced. Law is responsive to the deeply felt and undefinable recognition that difference is constitutive of our being together and to the dream of a life in which each of us can celebrate our differences and make possible the flourishing of variety, difference, plurality. But that recognition is the result of, the product of critical, deconstructive thinking that, if it is to avoid a certain priestly role, must retain its hesitancy and wariness in relation to the redeeming quality of our values and norms. The imaginary domain of law is the free space in which we imagine ourselves "whole," in which we appeal to law—to positive law—in order to protect and respect that which we imagine or the open possibility of becoming in the imaginary domain. At the same time, the imaginary domain is always imaginary—the "wholeness" we imagine is never quite complete and never fully accomplished, a failure that cannot be compensated for by law but is instead the limit of law. So in relation to the fundamental problem of Cornell's work—the limit of the law in relation to the free space of the imaginary domain as constitutive of justice—the questions I am raising lead us to ask in the end whether the withdrawing presence of

Nietzsche in Cornell's texts is in service to a deeper commitment to ideals and whether that commitment is a commitment to liberal values *faute de mieux*, because that is the very least we have got. Or does the recognition of the dangers of ideals so apparent in the philosophers Cornell engages with (Nietzscheans through and through) play a role in the tracing of the limit of law, the limit of the imaginary domain of law, leaving us free to pursue critique and transformation without its being submitted to regulation by a false ideal, an imposed norm, a dream of essential identity? How does the Nietzschean critical movement—the discovery of the will to power and self-overcoming at the heart of our desire for justice—creep into and transform the presentation of the values on which we both must insist and question?

If values have histories, and we cannot evoke them outside of a genealogical context, then the ambiguity with which I began encourages us to think at least two things. First, that defending ideals is a continuous task. Second, that ideals are constituted, shaped, produced in the task of defending them and are therefore less an instrument in which we invest and more like a site around which discursive formations are from time to time oriented. To defend the ideal of "peace" in Iraq, for example, may involve defending not a withdrawal of armed forces (a recipe for disaster and civil war) or a particular political solution (for we might hamfistedly substitute a political solution for an economic or cultural struggle), but a demand that people keep talking, that voices, particularly of women, ethnic minorities, the dispossessed, and the tortured be heard. Defending ideals understood as an ongoing task draws our focus to the historical conditions of that defense and on the possibility of a future in which the task of defending—the ongoing critical task of tracing powers and exclusions— is all we are left with. When Frederick Douglass notes that he has "stolen his own body," he uncovers an insufficiency: stealing is vice and virtue, and no clear moral language can give him a place on legal terrain. But in "pleading the cause" of his brethren, this insufficiency becomes the core of his plea, and one is forced by the insufficiency to trace the formation of a shameful legacy and to create a new sensibility out of this formation.[9] Likewise, we might find that guided by an ideal—call it freedom?—we have created the conditions for a fundamentalist theocracy in Iraq, hostile to our interests, women's interests, and the interests of freedom as such. This means that the ideal as such is in no need of defending but that defending has not stopped and cannot stop.

NOTES

1. Drucilla Cornell, *Just Cause* (Lanham: Rowman-Littlefield, 2000) 5

2. "Nietzsche is perhaps the philosopher who has had the deepest influence on Posner. Posner takes from him a conception of morality (made by humans, not found in the world), a conception of ethics (tenth-hand bromides, clung to by those lacking the courage or imagination to think for themselves), and, most of all, an intellectual

temperament (delighting in muscular language and the power to shock)." *The New Yorker*, December 10, 2001. Posner demonstrates again (he has done it with Foucault too) that one need not read philosophers with much precision or sensitivity to be profoundly influenced by them. It is precisely this kind of extravagant, "muscular, exorbitant" subjectivity that Nietzsche calls into question. (I borrow those adjectives, but I cannot remember their origin).

3. Elizabeth Grosz suggests that the Nietzschean approach to the question of identity and identity formation is relatively unexplored in Cornell's critique of identity and identity politics and that this is because of the dominance of Hegel and the importance of recognition in the account of subject formation. This chapter is an attempt to focus more intensively on the question of the place of Nietzsche in Cornell's work. I hope I have made clear that I do not think merely that Nietzsche would make a valuable supplement to Cornell's arguments, but that Nietzsche is already there, just outside the frame and in part responsible for the framing.

4. See Elizabeth Grosz, "Drucilla Cornell, Identity, and the Evolution of Politics," in Pryor and Heberle, eds., *Imagining Law: Drucilla Cornell* (State University of New York Press, forthcoming). The fact that this marked decline in the strength and meaningfulness of the values of the Enlightenment corresponds to their vociferous reassertion by some intellectuals hostile to what they perceived as a creeping Nietzscheanism is not unimportant here. This perception produced, for example, an angry book by Ferry and Renault, *Why We Are Not Nietzscheans*, followed by a defense of the place of the subject in philosophy.

5. Puns are strictly forbidden in acceptable academic discourse. They are the "lowest form of wit" and never remotely funny. However, Charles Lamb (among others) is enamored with the pun, in part because of its interruptive quality. "It is a pistol let off at the ear; not a feather to tickle the intellect." But Lamb may be too easily led to laughter.

6. Drucilla Cornell, *Beyond Accommodation: Ethical Feminism, Deconstruction and the Law* (New York: Routledge, 1991). References in the text as BA.

7. Again, Elizabeth Grosz emphasizes the magnetism of Hegelian discourse in Cornell's thought, arguably to the exclusion of approaches to history and power that are quite productively engaged by genealogical thought in Nietzsche, Foucault, and some contemporary feminist thinkers.

8. Obviously I am thinking of *Zarathustra* here, which I believe has as much to tell us about defending ideals as the *Genealogy of Morals* does. *Zarathustra* would require careful reading in this context, so I will only mark his presence in these passages.

9. See Lewis Hyde, *The Trickster Makes His World* (New York: North Point, 1999), 209–17, passim. "For a human community to make its world shapely is one thing; to preserve the shape is quite another, especially if, as is always the case, the shape is to some degree arbitrary and if the shaping requires exclusion and the exclusion is hungry." (216–17).

Carolin Emcke

Imagining Loss: Traces of Dignity

The idea of a truth whose manifestation is not glorious or bursting with light, the idea of a truth that manifests itself in its humility. . . . the idea of a persecuted truth—is that not henceforth the only possible modality of transcendence?
—Emmanuel Levinas, *Entre-nous*

INTRODUCTION

Drucilla Cornell's *Between Women and Generations* is an overwhelming book.[1] It is confession, testimony, autobiography, philosophical essay, and probably, therapeutic journey for its author and her readers. It is a breathtakingly honest and fearless work, weaving together the most personal and the theoretical, one informing the other. It is a critical engagement with the fragility of the role of a witness, a role she has promised to enact. It is a journey in which she sounds the burden and the limits of the task of bearing witness to the dignity of an other. And it is a philosophical reflection on the almost forgotten notion of dignity.

Dignity, for Cornell, is an activity, it is a willfulness and an exercise of freedom. Cornell refers to Zora Neale Hurston's character Nanny to define the core of dignity: "You can't beat nobody down so low till you can rob them off their will." Dignity, then, would be a feature of one's will, a sense of moral freedom, an ability or at least a source of resistance against oppression, humiliation, violation. For Nanny—and Cornell—it "is something that we cannot lose" (BWG, xix). No matter how abused, beaten, mistreated you are, dignity remains.

What would that mean? What does it require? Does it require anything at all? Is it dependent on the subject who is subjugated to circumstances that deny her dignity? What is the significance of "dignity"? An inner worth? A particular feature that demands "respect," as Cornell so often suggests? Or is it an activity? An attitude by a subject? Is it then also possible for a subject to *fail* to act with dignity? Is it merely for someone to *recognize* the dignity of another? Where is the *space* for dignity then? Inherent in the subject independent of the situation, dependent on the subject's response to a situation that negates its dignity, or in the space between a subject whose dignity is violated and a significant other, a witness who reconstructs what is absent?

Cornell's book is such a remarkably open and personal work that it seems impossible to debate or even criticize it without transgressing norms of decency and respect for her personal life and her intimate relationships. It would seem like an exploitation of the honesty of the author that allows us to learn so much about dignity and witnessing. My response to Cornell's book therefore is the attempt to offer something in return, a narrative of different voices and speakers, echoing her account, trying to deliver a thick description of the contexts of witnessing. I will approach the question of dignity from the opposite direction: by describing contexts and structures that actually *do* rob people of their will, their moral vision of freedom, their trust in their own sense of subjectivity even, I will seek to reconstruct the variety of responses to such violations. I want to narrate the different modalities of reactions, the shades and colors of the reflection of violence on the faces of those who have to endure it, and thereby hopefully sound the possible meanings of a dignity destroyed and discover the role of the witness. As it turns out, I will search for *spaces of dignity* where it is *absent*. This response will try to sound the topography of violence, despair, and pain negating the very dignity Cornell is claiming.

The authors that I discuss[2] are haunted by and bear witness to an experience that destroyed not only dignity but often even their claim for it. I will then renarrate the role of a witness, of a friend, a stranger who testifies for the person whose dignity has been violated. The witness can only bear witness to traces of a shattered dignity and only in imagining the loss can reconnect the subject to itself.

VISIBILITY IN THE ABSENCE

Death is the sanction for everything a storyteller can tell.
—Walter Benjamin, *The Storyteller:*
Observations on the Works of Nikolai Leskov

Primo Levi writes about the arrival at the barracks in Auschwitz-Monowitz:

> Then for the first time we became aware that our language lacks the words to express this offense, the demolition of a man. . . . It is not possible to sink lower than this; no human condition is more miserable than this. Nothing belongs to us anymore; they have taken away our clothes, our shoes, even our hair. Imagine how a man who is deprived of everyone he loves, and at the same time of his house, his habits, his clothes, in short, of everything he possesses: he will be a hollow man, reduced to suffering and needs, forgetful of dignity and restraint, for he who loses all often easily loses himself.[3]

Levi's "demolition of man" at Auschwitz begins with the description of the slow metamorphosis of an intellectual, a well-educated summa cum laude chemistry graduate from Turin university, with deep attachments to the sound of his language, to the cultural or individual codes and modalities of shame in relation to the body, of someone who is attuned to a certain social space granted to one another among strangers, a person who is a son, a brother, someone with memories of poems, chemical formulas and the light in the mountains of the Piedmont. It is a description of his transformation into a different being: a number engraved into the skin of his arm, dressed in rags, pushed around, yelled at, deprived of his "house and his habits," deindividualized, depersonalized, dissociated from himself. Levi describes, like many other survivors, how the physical decay of man degraded, beaten, humiliated "remodeled" the psychic landscape.

The young arrival Levi in his first days and weeks questions the strange new world around him: still in accordance with his standards of civility and ethics and an unbroken idea of justice, he tries to analyze the logic of the camp, tries to decipher the language of cruelty, seeks to understand the "order of terror"[4]—and fails. In particular the apparent organizational effort of the regime to structure space and time, the "neat" bureaucratic order with signs and explanations everywhere, (mis)lead to the assumption that there was some "reasoning" at the root of this world of destruction. Indeed, the systematic nature of the cruelty at the camps invited a certain hermeneutic illusion: to search for an understanding of actions, behavior, an institution whose amoral, surreal nature the mind resists to understand.

Primo Levi's testimony can be read like a negative "Bildungsroman," a novel of formation of a young apprentice not learning how to find one's place in life but how to find one's place in a system of death and destruction, being "initiated" to the most important lesson: "Ne pas chercher á comprendre!"[5] What Levi seems to suggest is that the experience of being violated in every possible sense, of being displaced, detained, mistreated, the encounter with sheer brutal force, hunger, thirst, dirt, tiredness, with fear and despair in this topography of the senseless, endless suffering is first of all an experience that constitutes a *cognitive threat*. Before it is an existential or a physical confrontation, Auschwitz is an absurdity: it is all too real and yet surreal, impossible to grasp. It scoffs at all common sense, all categories of social or moral expectation and experience.

W. G. Sebald finds a remarkable image for this disorientation in his novel *Austerlitz*: "Next morning, at first light, the Germans did indeed march into Prague in the middle of a heavy snowstorm which seemed to make them appear out of nowhere. When they crossed the bridge and their armored cars were rolling up the Narodní a profound silence fell over the whole city. People turned away, and from that moment they walked more slowly, like somnambulists, as if they no longer knew where they were going."[6] There is a mental resistance to believe, to accept what is happening to you as true. The reality is not only so disturbing because it is so cruel and unjust, but also because it cannot be related to either your past nor your wildest imaginations of what could be possible. For the prisoner there is an epistemological abyss between the pre-Lager life and world and the Lager, which seems impossible to bridge; there is a resistance to give an intelligible account of any linearity, any credible history that could lead to this.[7] "Ne pas chercher á comprendre."

Later, Levi describes the state of mind of someone who was—as Simone Weil wrote—subjected to force that turns a person into *a thing*: "Reduced to suffering and needs, forgetful of dignity and restraint."[8] Unable to focus on anything but his immediate needs, not only at the mind's but at the body's limits,[9] in ultimate urgency to use all remaining sources of energy and skill to survive—"restraint" or other cultural conventions or norms are abandoned, silenced by necessity. In this respect Levi describes how the confrontation with oneself in a context of permanent and structural violence, pain, loss, cold, beatings, and humiliations, destined to die, deprived of help, trust, energy, comfort, how the confrontation with oneself under a regime of murderers, in face of the killings, how the degradation to a fearful, starving animal constitutes a *moral threat*.

The original title of Levi's memoir echoes this theme: *Se questo è un uomo?* (Is this a man?) At first sight, the *questo*, (this) refers to the Nazis, the SS in the camps, the Germans who created Auschwitz. Is this a man, he who is able to deny another human being his dignity? He who can select, beat, kill without reason or shame, who can perform and appreciate Bach's inventions at one moment and shoot defenseless humans the next—is this a man? Who can organize a system of torture and extermination of millions of men and women and children as if it were a normal bureaucratic procedure? What allowed him to act the way he did? What culture, what society, which families could have produced such perpetrators?

But Levi, surprisingly, is not concerned with the perpetrator. He asks an even more disturbing question throughout his book: Is this a man, he who steals food and shoes from his comrades? Who is dominated by his decaying body? Who stops caring about his bunk-mate? Who is robbed off his will? Is this a man who prays aloud to thank God for having survived the selection for the gas chamber—right next to the bunk of a comrade condemned to death on the following day? Is this a man who has stopped dreaming, who has given up thinking about anything else but food, who remains silent when witnessing the torture of others? Is this a man, Levi ultimately asks, who can survive such an experience?

Levi's testimony implicitly seems to reflect on two meanings, forms of dignity (or lack thereof):

1. *Dignity as relational*, dignity that is *invisibly present* in and through the recognition of others, in their behavior towards us, in the treatment we receive by them. It resonates with Cornell, who often refers to the social character of

dignity. It is the relational character that "gives dignity a new urgency."[10] But Cornell assumes that it can be discovered and recognized and in that sense is experienced when it is created or reaffirmed through recognition. I would argue with Levi that relational dignity only becomes *visible as a lack* when it is denied, when it is violated. *Its presence is only painfully felt in its absence.*

Jean Améry, Levi's barrack mate at Auschwitz, writes:

> I must confess that I don't really know exactly what that is: human dignity. One person thinks he loses it when he finds himself in circumstances that make it impossible for him to take a daily bath. Another believes he loses it when he must speak to an official in something other than his native language. . . . I don't know if a person beaten by the police loses human dignity. Yet, I am certain that with the very first blow that descends on him, he loses something we will perhaps temporarily call "trust in the world."[11]
>
> Améry feels uncomfortable about the apparent subjectivity of the notion dignity which includes examples of suffering of uncomparable degrees, natures—but also Améry suggests that dignity is only discovered when it is lost.[12]

2. *Dignity as a personal feature*, realized in and through our actions and behavior *only if and when* the relational dignity is negated as an attempt to reclaim what is denied. It resonates with our usage of the term *dignity*: it almost never appears to refer to decent, ethical behavior in normal circumstances, but only when it is denied.

On the occasion of my eighteenth birthday a friend and mentor of mine wrote a small note for me on a tiny little white card, which she passed over the dinner table almost secretly. It read: "What life is all about? To show dignified behavior under circumstances that suggest the opposite." Her description seems to seize the essence of dignity: It is an unlikely response, it is a *reaction in some asymmetrical relation to what was experienced.* It seems to be a behavior that transcends what is expected, it resists a temptation to give in, give up, to be who the circumstances suggest you are. Whereas Cornell writes that dignity "precedes" the subject, that it cannot be taken away from the person, "because it exists only in principle,"[13] I would claim that dignity is always unlikely; against all odds, it is claimed when it is denounced. It shines only when it is violated. Dignity is only visible against a contrasting background of a humiliating, degrading, desperate situation.

What Levi describes is how he experiences a destroyed dignity in the first sense in Auschwitz because every single rule, attitude, practice, the whole system of the camp, almost every person he encounters violates the humanity of the prisoners. For Levi the essence of this relation in denial of any relation, the core of the impossibility of sociality is crystallized in one scene: Alex, the kapo of Kommando 98, and Levi, walking to the headquarters, cross an area filled with cross-beams and metal frames. Alex walks over and catches hold of a steel cable full of grease. With an exclamation of disgust and nausea the kapo stares at his hand thick with grease, and "without hatred and without sneering,"[14] he wipes his hand on Levi's shoulder, calmly and carefully, both the palm and the back of his hand. For Alex Levi is nothing but a material he could use to clean his hands. In relation to the kapo, Levi is nonexistent. He is denied not only his dignity but also his humanity reduced to nothing but the texture of his rags.

"Without hatred and sneering" seems almost more humiliating than the abuse as such. If Levi could detect hatred as the motive for Alex's dismissive gesture, it would at least indicate that Levi had been recognized as a human, someone not worthy of respect or dignity, but at least worthy of hatred or disgust. But it is the total denial, the complete murder of the other as a person that defines the relation as none. Levi is not an other for Alex. He is absent, just material to rub the grease off one's hands. Levi concludes the anecdote: "He would be amazed, the poor brute Alex, if someone told him that today, on the bases of this action, I judge him and . . . innumerable others like him, big and small, in Auschwitz and everywhere."[15]

The second form of dignity[16] would appear in resistance to the absence of the first. It is this dignity that Cornell refers to when she talks of dignity as an act of "moral freedom." Cornell suggests that one cannot be violated so much that you can "rob people of their will." But Levi over and over again mentions the gravity of the violence endured, the formative character of the system of death and destruction at Auschwitz that actually *does* rob people of their will. He describes the slow disappearance of standards of "good" and "evil" in the daily struggles to survive, the destruction of the sources for resistance, the will for moral freedom. "Intense pain is world destroying";[17] it spreads out, reaches beyond its immediate object, mimes death, and seizes the subject's will. To assume that there would be any energy or spirit left for resistance would be ignorant of the overwhelming force and destructiveness of violence. The traumatic experience of total negation, the annihilation of the victims' existence, the slow destruction of their bodies leaves them in a state of sheer helplessness: the physical decay, as Levi describes it, is accompanied by unstoppable psychic disintegration.

Tadeusz Borowski, in words filled with a bitterness that Levi is incapable of, describes this devastating experience: "In this war, morality, . . . the ideals of freedom, justice and human dignity had all slid off man like rotten rag . . . [T]here is no crime that a man will not commit in order to save himself."[18] Yet, despite Levi's claim that the conditions at the Lager renounce any moral behavior, even though he delineates the impossibility of friendship, solidarity, and generosity under circumstances in which egoism holds the only chance for survival, narrates a counterpoint with outstanding examples of individuals resisting those conditions.[19]

So why does he, nevertheless, claim the impossibility of "dignified behavior" in Auschwitz? Levi writes *against the moralization* of actions that reach beyond the expectable, that transcend the present, that require abilities or strengths, sometimes physical, sometimes emotional, unlikely to remain intact or accessable under those circumstances. Opposition is not always possible. The will to moral freedom does not always remain unharmed by violent realities. The ability to trust one's own rights and powers can be exactly at the core of what a regime of terror seeks to erase. The source for resistance, the faith in a space of freedom, a space of existence can be exactly what is called into question. Not only do regimes of violence beat down and kill bodies, but structural and brutal denial of the individual also implants existential doubt that undermines all possible resistance and, sometimes, the will to live. The gravity of violence often produces a trauma that lives much longer than the actual traumatic experience and that seizes the individual in its tentacles and inhabits a person's ability to envision herself outside, free of the previous limiting, degrading, brutal conditions.

As survival is beyond control, and life or death is left to arbitrariness, coincidence, chance, and—as Levi's account of a selection in which a comrade was, mistakenly, in *his* place sent to the gas chamber proves—error, so are subversion, opposition, small gestures of moral freedom due to chance. They are beyond any law or norm of responsibility, since response-ability is, indeed, an ability to respond not available or accessible to everyone.[20] "Survival without any renunciation without any part of one's own moral world, Levi writes, "was conceded only to very few superior individuals."[21]

So let us look at unlikely responses, at individuals who managed to cope with the reality, and who discovered, against all odds, sources and spaces for resistance. Their example will be narrated without any claim or judgment about those who were not so fortunate. But their stories might help us understand the conditions preparing the ground for what Cornell calls "dignity."

UNLIKELY RESPONSES

Nevertheless.

> —Jürgen Habermas, in a questionaire by the German
> weekly *Die Zeit* asking for his favorite words

What do we mean when we call someone's behavior "dignified"? It relates to a person's response to her environment or others who negate what she is nevertheless claiming. What is it that allows individuals to act in disharmony with what is expected? What are their sources for resisting behaving like a victim despite ongoing victimization? Are they cut out from reality, unaffected by the misrecognition, violence, humiliating circumstances that limit their freedom, shadow their lives, injure them? How can they remain other than absolutely harmed by such threatening conditions? Where do they find the resources, the energy for action or speech despite existential hunger and illness?

In his contemplations of a survivor on "Auschwitz and its realities" Jean Améry writes about such "superior individuals": "I did not want to be with my believing comrades, but I would have wished to be like them: unshakable, calm, strong. What I felt to comprehend at that time still appears to me as a certainty: whoever is, in the broadest sense, a believing person, whether his belief be metaphysical or bound to concrete reality, transcends himself. He is not the captive of his individuality; rather, he is part of a spiritual continuity that is interrupted nowhere, not even in Auschwitz."[22] Améry envies his comrades' religious or political faith, because it provides a framework, a vision of another reality. Individuals who believe in a different order can "double" their existence and therefore cope better with the degrading and destructive environment. Since there is another parallel or promised reality intact, unharmed by the penetration of violence, injustice, or illness, these persons or at least their trust in the other or inner world can remain "unshaken." Since the concrete world surrounding them is not the only reality they accept, they do not disintegrate completely once that world is falling apart, once they are dissociated, displaced. Whereas with the first blow, as Améry says, one loses the trust in the world, in being home, in belonging, individuals with a metaphysical faith do not lose that sense of home. Rooted also in and oriented toward a world apart they do not lose the only system, context of reference, and value for them. It does not mean that they would not get injured, of course. People with metaphysical belief also get harmed, but their entire world does not disintegrate.

There are also nonmetaphysical foundations for humans reclaiming their humanity in extreme situations. Violence and terror do not always succeed in penetrating, dissolving a person. Disciplinary or formative power sometimes fails to shape and destroy its objects. There are all kinds of properties and abilities that account for different rebellious responses regarding the extreme, and there are all kinds of acts and speech acts, movements, and words that can be considered "dignified." Sometimes it is not grand gestures of bravery, not dramatic actions, examples of superior skill or courage. Sometimes signs or attitudes of subversion go almost unnoticed, casually, as if effortless. Sometimes they are nurtured by longing for a good, for a small joy. Sometimes they are incited by love and affection for a child, a mother, a friend, a compatriot. Sometimes the energy needed to act with dignity, to shovel space for difference or dissent, is activated by sheer hatred. Hatred can release enormous resources of will and power and transcend circumstances or weaknesses.

In the unbearable heat of the summer of 1999, I met a Kosovar-Albanian refugee named Emine in the "women's tent" in a lousy, dirty camp in Tirana, Albania. She was forty-six, a former lawyer who had been denied the right to work by the Serbian government about seven years previously and had had no legal job since then. Emine had fled her hometown, Mitrovica, two months earlier. She had friends in Tirana who offered to let her stay with them in their flat, but she refused. She did not want to have the comfort all for herself and rather stayed with all the others in the dirty, hot, snake-infested tents of the camp, facing the heat, the nightmares about the past, and the fears for the future. Half of Emine's family had been missing for two months. She had lost her house, her belongings, her passport, but she smiled when she talked to me. "We have won," she said at a time when the war was still going on. "We have won, already now. We have won because we survived." When I asked her what she meant, she replied that it had been Milosevic's only goal to completely wipe out the entire Albanian population. The fact that there was one, one hundred, maybe thousands left, was not enough, but it was enough to be a proud victor over a racist ideology. "His ideology and his policies wanted *me* dead, but I'm alive. We have won!"

She talked about how she would return to her destroyed house, how she would start a new life: "We will start anew but we will never be the same again. We will never be the same, but we will start to talk with the Serbs again. We have to. We have to have survived for something better than what *they* designed." It was hatred of the Serbian ideology and regime that made her reach out for the former enemies. It was an angry rejection of what they represented that allowed her to embrace the individuals again. It was her anger, her desire to be different than the others thought she would be, that allowed her to try to integrate them.

It is more often details, small deeds, irrelevant and meaningless maybe, under different circumstances, that can be shining examples for others in times of hopelessness. It can be completely useless acts, like the daily attempt to wash oneself at Auschwitz—an effort without success, a sheer waste of energy and warmth. Yet, as Steinlauf, an Hungarian prisoner teaches Levi: "To survive we must force ourselves to save at least the skeleton, the scaffolding, the form of civilization."[23]

What the term *resistance*—which Cornell ties to dignity—falsely suggests is that dignity always has to be some action, aimed at somebody, intended to disturb, oppose. But sometimes it is rather small acts, gestures, not directed against anybody. It can also be almost unconscious habits, rituals, remnants of the past that can be considered dignified, simply because they do not fit, because they do not belong to the present, because they are inappropriate for a victim.

Ruth Klüger tells in her memoir how she recited poetry during her ordeal at the Lager.[24] She was a child when she was deported. She did not have a sense of rebellion attached to the poetry. It was rather that the rhythm of the verses simply kept her going on the marches and during the roll-call, gave her some structure, some "scaffolding of civilization," as Steinlauf called it. It worked as an escape agent out of the desperate present but was also a connection to a world of her own. It literally kept her alive.

What is dignified in this example is not the agent's *willful disobedience* against a repressive system. Rather it seems to be in the act itself, the beauty and tenderness of the language, what denounces the order of terror. The source for the dignified act is not any intentionality, not any moral free-

dom, but rather simply a silent remnant, a reservoir from the past that, originally a luxury, suddenly acquired practical use and proved indispensable.
There is no demonstrative functionality of the deed. There is no symbolic
power attached to this act of dignity. There is no pedagogic meaning for
others profiting from the individual's dignified act. Their acts are nonmetaphysical sources for persons to hold on to some "scaffolding of civilization."
Without refering to another world, a metaphysical belief, these people man-
age to protect small threads connecting them with some feature of who they
were, where they lived, with fragments of former joys, practices, values.
What is rescued by those individuals is a sense of continuity of self and life.

Why can they rescue these abilities despite such a destructive environment? It can be music, poetry, or anything else that was practiced, studied,
performed with such regularity that it has become an almost unconscious
habit, because only if and when so intertwined with the entire person, only
when an almost integral part of the self, can the individual continue to con-
jure these acts, words, gestures under circumstances that have otherwise destroyed all energy and spirit. It has to be possible to perform these deeds, to act
as if they were no action—effortless, almost mindless—to retain a sense of
continuity in a world that disrupted all other connections.

Yet these are all examples of *individuals themselves* able to act, to keep
some inner or outer source of strength, an ability, a reservoir of spirit somehow
undestroyed. Whatever the source for their resistance—whether any metaphysical belief, whether a strong will nurtured by longing or hatred, whether
even a certain madness that protects a person's mind from disintegrating,
whether simply a habit, a skill, an archive of words to offer comfort or only
rhythm for additional stability—these are examples of individuals.[25]

But sometimes people are robbed of their will. They are beaten down completely and do not act willfully anymore. There are no signs of rebellion, no
words or acts of subversion. Their moral freedom is in ruins, remnants of the past
invisible, no traces of human dignity left. The dignity that according to Cornell
"precedes the subject" is shattered with the person.[26] Sometimes it needs another. That is the moment of the witness, the friend, the significant other.

POSSIBILITY OF WITNESSING OR BEARING
THE UNBEARABLE

Unimaginable: a word that doesn't divide, doesn't restrict. The most convenient
word. When you walk around with this word as your shield, this word for empti-
ness, your step becomes better assured, more resolute, your conscience pulls itself
together.

—Robert Antelme, *The Human Race*

"I took him in my arms; I drew my face close to his; I was enveloped in the
fetid, fecal smell of death, which was growing in him like a carnivorous plant

with a poisonous flower, rotting splendidly away."[27] The decaying body in the arms of the witness. Not much dignity, not much humanity left in those words of Jorge Semprun. Nothing demands "respect" in this stinking bundle of rotting flesh. The "body" that Semprun is holding in his arms, struggling with the unrepressible nausea in response to the smell, is Maurice Halbwachs. The scene we are presented here is a student holding his former professor as he lies dying in the barracks of Buchenwald in the spring of 1944. Every Sunday, Semprun sits on the bunk of Halbwachs, witnessing "the black light of death dawning" in his eyes. There is almost nothing left of Halbwachs, no remnants of his past persona, no clothes from his previous existence in Paris, no traces of his former brilliance, of his intellectual life when Semprun studied with him at the Sorbonne. There is no "rational" assessment of his situation, no "coherent" behavior anymore, no symbolic rebellion. Nothing of what Semprun writes about Maurice Halbwachs resembles him in the least. "Death was approaching, veiling (his) eyes, and we shared it like a piece of bread."[28]

But Semprun defies the reality around him; he denounces the materiality in front of him; he ignores what is visible, the smell; he bears witness by not bearing witness to the present; he does not pay respect to the person in his arms. Despite what he sees in reality, he sees his old professor with his former life. Knowing what Halbwachs is not capable of anymore, he treats him as if he were. When Halbwachs cannot speak anymore, Semprun tells him of the spring drawing close. He passes on the latest news of the military developments as if the advancing army could still save the dying man's life. Semprun reminds him of what he had written in his books, the lessons of his teachings. "Dying, he would smile," Semprun says.

Semprun seems to be a witness in both senses of the Latin roots of the term: he is a *testis*, a person who gives a testimony at a trial as someone outside an event but able to give an account of what happened (in this case in relation to Halbwachs because Semprun is not on the threshold between life and death), and a *superstes*, a person who experienced a situation herself, who survived the event (the experience of detention in the Lager).[29]

He is first of all a survivor, in various senses: he survived Buchenwald; he survived Maurice Halbwachs; and he survived all the transformations, disruptions, fragmentations from the prewar realities into the extreme situation of the Lager and then into something altogether different after the war to be able to bear witness. For Halbwachs he represents the only connection not only to his former life, from which he is dissociated, but also the only thread, the only witness to whom he was. In fact, when Semprun recites passages from Halbwachs' lectures in Paris, not only does he renarrate the past and connect his dying professor to his former self, but also by doing so he bears witness in that moment to whom Halbwachs still is. One should also add that what makes this whole scene both unbearably painful and beautiful at the same time is not only that Semprun gives Halbwachs back what the latter cannot reclaim himself anymore: his subjectivity (and his humanity, or what Cornell would call his "dignity") but also that he restages or reenacts in this last moment of Halbwachs the theme of the other's thought.[30]

What is happening in this scene? What kind of witnessing happens here? Does Semprun give an adequate account of what he sees, perceives, of what is present? Does he really represent "dignity"?

What unfolds in this moment is not the "representation of the unrepresentable," nor is it the "enlarged mentality" of Kant's *sensus communis aestheticus.* Rather it is, I think, Cornell's imagined representation or art of witnessing. It seems necessary to integrate a few comments on the debate around the doubts of the possibility of witnessing here.

Gayatri Spivak's attempt to reconstruct the figure of the Hindu widow Rani Gulani who committed sati[31] is commonly used in the literature as an example for the crises of representation. Dori Laub, psychoanalyst and one of the interviewers of the survivors of the Fortunoff Video Archive of Holocaust Testimonies, spoke of the Shoah as the "event without witness."[32] Cornell herself writes about her own endeavor: "I was left with the task of representing the significance of what, on the level of imagination, is unrepresentable: death itself. I was called to this precarious task in my mother's last days. This entire book is my response to her naming me as her witness to her moral freedom."[33] Despite of her own claim, Cornell's entire book is evidence of the *possibility* of witnessing, and I want to argue—in her spirit, I assume—that the claim of the indescribability of certain limit experiences, the impossibility of witnessing extreme situations is based on various misunderstandings of what witnessing actually means.[34]

There is one evident sense in which one could describe the Shoah as the "event without witnesses." If "witness" refers to the *superstes*, the "insider"-witness,[35] and there are no survivors—if for example "event" refers to the gas chambers—then clearly there cannot be insider witnesses to the event.[36] There is nobody alive who could bear witness to the experience of being gassed in the gas chambers of Auschwitz. There cannot be a survivor who could bear witness to the event of the widow burning, the sati. Clearly, Cornell's mother cannot bear witness to her own death. But that is an almost banal claim.

There are events that need an other, an observer, a second witness to testify. But does that constitute a crisis of witnessing? Does it pose a threat to the "truth" of the testimony? Even the truth of the gas chambers can be accounted for via descriptions of observers and artifacts. There are stories of secondhand witnessing, Jewish prisoners of the Sonderkommandos who had to shovel the corpses out of the chamber gave detailed descriptions of the bodies' figurations, giving evidence of the torment and agony of the victims' last minutes. There is the collective memory by almost all survivors of the unforgettable odor of burned flesh that covered the Lager. There are records of Degussa, the company who produced Zyklon B. And if that were not enough, there are probably geological-chemical proofs in the soil of the territory of the death camps.

If "truth" is understood as the *complete* accumulation of all the details, facts of an event, of all sentiments, thoughts, impressions, feelings of an experience, then, certainly, there is no witness to account for the "truth" of the gas chambers, or the Shoah. But then there is never any "truth" to any event or in any speech act. *What* is it that can be witnessed?[37] What is it that the witness has to see, perceive, understand, and then give an account of? Since she cannot possibly collect all facts, details of a historic event; since she cannot possibly trace the entire genesis, since it is impossible to rephrase all of the exact words, all thoughts of an other; since it is in the process of quoting, repeating somebody else's narrative there can always be some misrepresentation, some failure; since pain and suffering fractures, destroys, shatters people's ability to sound intelligible, credible, how can witnessing still be possible?

Whereas witnessing is assumed to refer to observing a situation and giving an accurate account of what is happening or has happened, the ethics of witnessing—as in the example of Semprun and Halbwachs—does not consist of a passive witnessing, but as Cornell calls it an "active imagination" of what is not present, a reverse reconstruction of the genealogy of the present pain, "anomaly," the decaying body, the ethics of witnessing here consists of imagining what is lost[38]—by mourning. Jankel Wiernik wrote in his "Year in Treblinka" how he learned to imagine each living person as a future dead body. How he measured someone's weight, and how he imagined who would carry him to the grave.[39]

From my own experience I would say somehow the opposite applied: in regions of wars, at the massacre sites, one could imagine the tall or short, old or young corpses as fathers and sons, looking at the burned bundle of black flesh in the midst of hundreds of books and papers in ashes one could imagine the dead writer's life. Staring at the weathered, rotten clothes poorly covering fragmented bodies, one could imagine their former lives as farmers in the fields.

Not only does witnessing require an adequate account of what is visible, but it is a hermeneutical challenge, an archeological search among the ruins, the wreckage of artifacts, words, wounds, marks, silences, and tears. It echoes the structure of an account, a gesture. It has to read equally the linearity and circularity of a narrative, the disrupted as the continuous story of calm and upset victims or survivors. It has to imagine the traces of a past. Witnessing for an other requires a double transcendence. It needs an other who is able to bridge the cognitive and the moral gap (that Levi talks about) in which she is positioned. It asks a person to ignore the cognitive dissonance between the inner connection of the relationship in a dialogical exchange and the context of death and destruction surrounding the conversation. The witness has to be able to overcome the sense of absurdity (as in Semprun's talking on a bunk of

Buchenwald to a dying man about lectures on Bergson), the reality of a not-anymore, and act, or listen, or tell *nevertheless*.

Psychoanalyst Dori Laub writes in the context of interpreting a woman survivor's testimony: "In this case, as in many others, the imperative to tell the story of the Holocaust is inhabited by the impossibility of telling and, therefore, silence about the truth commonly prevails."[40] What is the impossibility of telling? It seems reasonable to claim that it is to some extent impossible to *explain* Auschwitz, to explain the "why" of something so counterintuitive, countermoral, counterhuman. Laub suggests that the *gravity of the horror* is difficult to narrate. The event is so painful, so tormenting to the soul, so abominable, so beyond our common experience and knowledge that its size and (amoral) density are difficult to communicate.

Jorge Semprun admits to struggling with the task yet criticizes all claims about the impossibility of witnessing as mere red-herring.

> I start to doubt the possibility of telling the story. Not that what we lived through is indiscribable, which is something else entirely (that won't be hard to understand), something that does not concern the form of a possible account, but its substance. Not its articulation, but its density. . . . You can always say everything. The "ineffable" you hear so much is only an alibi. Or a sign of laziness. You can always say everything: language consists of everything. You can speak of the most desperate love, the most terrible cruelty.[41]

Semprun rehabilitates language as a means of transportation, offering necessary tools for expressing, describing, bearing witness to such an event. Semprun also denounces attempts to load the event with so much, to "sacralize" it so that it becomes, allegedly, undescribable: "You can tell all about this experience," he writes. "You merely have to think about it."[42]

The argument about crises of witnessing extreme situations is often supported by the impact certain experiences and perceptions have not only on the survivor but also on the secondary witness. "It was inconceivable that any historical insider could remove herself sufficiently from the contaminating power of the event so as to remain fully lucid, unaffected witness, that is, to be sufficiently detached from the inside, so as to stay entirely outside of the trapping roles. . . . No observer could remain untainted, that is, maintain integrity."[43] The witness, even the outside witness, gets harmed, infected, contaminated, tainted, sometimes even injured and traumatized. The witness, depending on the variety of contexts of witnessing (whether very far from the original scene and only listening to somebody else's experience retroactively, or indeed witnessing another person being attacked, hurt, or detained is affected.[44] If the witness joins the world of the victim she is not completely outside anymore. Sometimes she is drawn in, pulled in, pushed in, and sometimes she joins voluntarily. Sometimes there is no choice. Sometimes it is actions, circumstances that bring the observer in proximity to the survivor, victim, narrator. Sometimes it is only the conscious or less conscious psychic structure of listening, imagining, and understanding.

But is the witness' "unaffectedness" really a precondition for her "integrity"? Does it really affect an outsider's ability to remain "lucid"? How much detachment is needed?

It seems what is needed is a balance between empathy and critical distance for both parties: victim/survivor and the outsider witness. Witnessing that pays tribute to the social work of restoring, of offering something to the victims, also includes a readiness to be injured:[45] for the witness risks to reliving painful traumatic events, not being heard, being misunderstood, misrepresented, ignored, cared for in one moment and then abandoned again;[46] the witness risks false overidentification, misunderstanding the other and failing in the task, risks getting harmed, disturbed, disoriented by the account. The witness eventually faces *the threat of getting lost on the way of translation* among different individuals, experiences, worlds, cultures.[47] Yet, this is ethically the only possible way to bear witness: to be ready to get harmed.

The possibility of witnessing consists of demarking its abysses and its limits. It has to sound the depths of silences, the ruins of the past; it has to listen carefully and then slowly interpret what is spoken and what remains unspoken; it has to imagine what was taken, destroyed, lost. But the witness has to respect what the narrative cannot reconstruct. When witnessing relies on an other, an observer, a messenger whose testimony also depends on his individual abilities, talents to perceive, listen, understand, and narrate, when witnessing signifies *active* imagination, then one has to acknowledge the *risk* in the process of interpretation and translation through an other. This recognition of the subjectivity and selectivity of his account does not equate a free ride to change, adapt, and completely invent the narrative. Of course, the witness has to at least try to adequately represent, to bear witness to an other's experiences, account, words.

The fact that the testimony of a witness has, as Geoffrey Hartman calls it, an "inevitable rhetoric component"[48] does not necessarily undermine its credibility.[49] Rarely is it only *one* individual who bears witness for an event or an other. A testimony is seldom placed within a complete vacuum. Rather it is situated in a larger context of testimonies from other witnesses or/and images, maps, postcards, stamps, clothes, artifacts that ground, correct, or fill in the testimony. If the accounts of two witnesses differ not only in tone but also in details, due to different abilities to perceive or understand, does that immediately call their authority into question?[50] Or does it only indicate that there are different perspectives on an event?

But this subjectivity, this perspective, is on both sides of the relation between witness and an other for whom she has to bear witness. Often the observer has to call into question what she sees or hears: sometimes the intelligible account she is listening to is incredible, or allegedly unintelligible though credible. Furthermore, the witness always has to question his or her own culturally biased understanding of what is considered incredible. Cornell reminds us: "Respect for dignity requires us to reflect about how we are positioned in this dialogue."[51]

Nevertheless, when giving an account of horrific experiences, of social suffering, when tormented by the despair and pain immanent in both the original event and its narration, the witness who tells remains with a feeling of inadequacy. There is a sense of void, of emptiness, a despair distinct from the despair in the original situation. It has to do with the feeling of the senselessness of the storytelling. The gravity of the experience, the long lastingness of the trauma or the scar, the impossibility of reconciliation seems to call into question the meaning of the interaction, the purpose of the storytelling. This is not because the historic event would be incomprehensible, or because the meaning of the experience would be inexpressible, but because the communication about such experiences seems so limited. The lack of any dynamic, of any horizon, the insecurity about what such witnessing could *open* is disconcerting. There is no adequate response to such narratives left, it seems, no expectations attached to giving the account. Maybe the melancholic paradox of witnessing is that the experience itself calls into question what its purpose could be, but nevertheless the witness remains haunted by the urge to try to give an account.[52]

To claim the impossibility of witnessing, though, would be an abandonment of those whose dignity has been destroyed. It would also be a negation of the responsibility for the other.[53] To concede the complexity of the hermeneutics of witnessing,[54] to understand the other as different, to respect the differences in experience, and to know the imperfection and subjectivity of our bearing witness to an other nevertheless does not free us of our responsibility to try to bear witness. The idea of witnessing should be reformulated as disconnected from the impossible task of adequately representing or fully returning dignity. The meaning of dignity only unfolds when dignity is already negated, when people find themselves in contexts that violate their understanding of dignity. Witnessing for those who are unable to voice their own claim for dignity should not promise what it cannot offer. It is not about bearing witness to dignity but about bearing witness to its denial.

Representing the violence, the suffering is the only form of recognizing what was taken away from the other. It does not restore the victim's dignity. It cannot compensate, but in imagining the loss of the other, the witness can at least offer a recognition of the other's humanity and thereby *welcome* her again. Witnessing does not offer closure. It cannot simply return dignity like a stolen pair of shoes. Witnessing cannot offer the false promise of easy reconciliation. Witnessing cannot offer to bear witness to dignity.

It only offers painful mourning of what was lost. It resembles the kind of pain one feels when rubbing ice-cold, numb feet. It hurts. But it announces the prospect of a return to life.

NOTES

Many thanks to Amelie Rorty whose generosity as a friend was as crucial to this chapter as her precision as an intellectual thinker.

1. Drucilla Cornell, *Legacies of Dignity: Between Woman and Generations* (New York: Palgrave, 2002).

2. There is hardly any other literature that so struggles with and highlights the importance of the notion of dignity as the testimonies of survivors of the Holocaust. In each of the memoirs, essays, reflections of numerous authors, whether written immediately upon their return from their ordeal in the Lager or decades later, the survivors discuss the experience of the denial of dignity. This chapter tries to reconstruct a particular understanding of dignity by narrating a context that violates dignity and the claim for it. Nevertheless, this reference to the Holocaust testimonies in an essay on dignity in general does not seek to level this unique historic context, experience, case by comparing it with others. It is impossible to equate the suffering in completely different examples. There is no implicit relativization of the Shoah intended here. Certainly, an individual fate like the illness of Cornell's mother, which originally initiated her essay on dignity, does not relate to the brutality and violence of a regime of terror such as the concentration camps. Scope, density, intentionality and harm do not compare.

3. Primo Levi, *Survival in Auschwitz* (New York: Summit Books 1986), 26–27.

4. Wolfgang Sofsky, *The Order of Terror* (Princeton: Princeton University Press, 1996).

5. Levi, *Survival in Auschwitz*, 140.

6. W. G. Sebald, *Austerlitz* (New York: Random House, 2001), 171.

7. Clearly, there *was* a history leading to the death camps. They did not just suddenly appear out of nowhere, but the experience inside the KZ was nevertheless incredible to the new prisoners: they were searching rules where there were none, logic where it was denied, a moral grammar of *some* kind where language seemed senseless. Sebald's narrative in the quoted passage suggests a similar idea with the metaphor of the snowstorm that made the Germans appear "as if out of nowhere."

8. Simone Weil, *The Iliad or the Poem of Force*, trans. Mary McCarthy, Politics Pamphlet No. 9 (Wallingford, PA: Pendle Hill, 1956).

9. The title of Jean Améry's testimony. Jean Améry, *At the Mind's Limits: Contemplations by a Survivor on Auschwitz and Its Realities* (Bloomington: Indiana University Press, 1980).

10. Cornell, *Between Women and Generations*, 60.

11. Améry, *At the Mind's Limits*, 27–28.

12. "In the case of dignity there isn't even a code of dignity. But we recognize dignity by the way we react to humiliation." Avishai Margalit, *The Ethics of Memory* (Harvard University Press, 2002), 115.

13. Cornell, *Between Women and Generations*, 66.

14. Levi, *Survival in Auschwitz*, 107.

15. Ibid., 107–08.

16. This is actually the *only* form, since the other is only a painful acknowledgment of it being misrecognized, denied.

17. Elaine Scarry, *The Body in Pain* (New York: Oxford University Press, 1985), 29.

18. Tadeusz Borowski, *This Way for the Gas, Ladies and Gentlemen* (New York: Penguin, 1976), 168.

19. Tzvetan Todorov wrote an entire book on such examples of "moral life in the concentration camps." Tzvetan Todorov, *Facing the Extreme* (New York: Henry Holt, 1996).

20. Compare Giorgio Agamben, *Remnants of Auschwitz, the Witness and the Archive* (New York: Zone Books, 2002) 21.

21. Levi, *Survival in Auschwitz*, 92.

22. Améry, *At the Mind's Limits*, 14.

23. Levi, *Survival in Auschwitz*, 41.

24. Klüger, *Still Alive* (New York: The Feminist Press, 2003).

25. Cornell herself argues that the interpretation of dignity needs to be freed of its "rationalistic and individualistic roots," and she offers a psychoanalytically informed version that argues that "our freedom is always social and relational."

26. Cornell, *Between Women and Generations*, 60.

27. Jorge Semprun, *Literature or Life* (New York: Viking, 1997), 42.

28. Ibid., 17.

29. See also Agamben, *Remnants of Auschwitz*, 17.

30. One should recall that he was the French philosopher, sociologist, Durkheimian, psychologist whose work was dedicated to the understanding of the social construction, the collective framework of *memory*. See Maurice Halbwachs, *On Collective Memory* (Chicago/London: University of Chicago Press 1992).

31. Gayatri Spivak, *A Critique of Postcolonial Reason: Toward a History of the Vanishing Present* (Cambridge: Harvard University Press, 1999.

32. Dori Laub, "An Event without Witness," in Shoshana Felman and Dori Laub, *Testimony. Crises of Witnessing in Literature, Psychoanalyses, and History* (New York Routledge 1992), 75–93.

33. Cornell, *Between Women and Generations*, 87.

34. See also Dominick LaCapra's critical engagement with what he calls the "sacralization" of the Holocaust, in "Holocaust Testimonies," in *Writing History, Writing Trauma* (Baltimore: Johns Hopkins University Press, 2000), 93.

35. The terminology of "insider" and "outsider" witnesses is deceptive since an "observer" need not necessarily be an "outsider," and the "bystanders" are as much "insiders" within the same time-space zone as the "survivors" but clearly not belonging to the group of the "victims" and therefore "outsiders." So there are some unsolvable problems about all of these terms.

36. There is another possibility that the witnesses to a particular experience are so traumatized that they are unable to testify to their own experience: the Muselman is commonly described as such a haunted figure, but even the Muselman sometimes has a voice of his own. Agamben, *Remnants of Auschwitz*.

37. A historic event, as Susan Sontag rightfully points out, needs to be perceived by others abroad as abnormal, as specific, as something "worth" noting, writing about,

witnessing: "For a war to break out of its immediate constituency and become a subject of international attention, it must be regarded as something of an exception." Susan Sontag, *Regarding the Pain of Others* (New York: Picador, 2003), 37.

38. About the distinction between "absense" and "loss," see Dominick LaCapra, "Trauma, Absence, Loss," in *Writing History, Writing Trauma* 43–86.

39. Jankiel Wiernik, *Year in Treblinka* (New York: American Representation of the Jewish Workers Union of Poland, 1944).

40. Laub, "Event without Witness," in *Testimony*, 79.

41. Semprun, *Literature or Life*, 13–14.

42. Ibid., 14.

43. Laub, "Event without Witness," in *Testimony*, 81.

44. "Victims, grieving relatives, consumers of news—all have their own nearness or distance from war." Sontag, *Regarding the Pain of Others*, 61.

45. In a public debate in Paris—that was documented in the Argentinian newspaper *Página 12*—Jorge Semprun pointed out that there is also a particular timing for witnessing, one that is not always under control of those who want to give testimony. Witnessing depends on the dialectic of being ready to bear witness and having a community who is ready to listen. "Hay un tiempo que no depende ni de la naturaleza del dolor ni de la voluntad de cada uno, sino de algo mucho más objetivo. Es el tiempo de la posibilidad de ser escuchado. Los que escribieron de inmediato no fueron escuchados. Sólo lo fueron quince o veinte años después, coetáneamente al momento en que aquellos que no habían podido escribir antes, comenzaron a hacerlo. Esta dialéctica entre el tiempo de la memoria y el tiempo de la capacidad de escuchar escapa completamente a la voluntad de los testigos." "La memoria del mundo," *Página 12*, Radar Libros Nr. 314, 9.11.2003, 3.

46. Avishai Margalit points out that the person who has suffered oppression or has been exposed to brutal violence first of all has to have hope again, the hope in a moral community. "What is so heroic in this hope is the fact that people who are subjected to evil regimes intent on destroying the fabric of their moral community easily come to see the regime as invincible and indestructable and stop believing in the very possibility of a moral community." Avishai Margalit, *The Ethics of Memory* (Cambridge/London: Harvard University Press, 2002), 155.

47. See also Marc Nichanian, "Catastrophic Mourning," in David L. Eng and David Kazanjian, *Loss* (Berkeley: University of California Press, 2002) 99–125.

48. Geoffrey Hartman, "The Ethics of Witness." Interview by Ian Balfour and Rebbecca Comay, in *Lost in the Archives* (Toronto: Alphabet City, 2002).

49. Unless one assumes an individualistic and essentialist concept of authenticity.

50. The entire idea of the New Testament, based on different accounts of the apostles, seems to suggest rather the opposite understanding. In particular the differences between Matthew and John (the first being much less visual, much less concerned with the details of his testimony than John, who provides all information about the geography, characters in the story, the weather, and so on) together should support the credibility of the event and not call it into question.

51. Cornell, *Between Women and Generations*, 97.

52. One should recall that witnessing means to "bear" witness. The "bearing" suggests that it is a burden one carries. One has to bear the experience of "regarding the pain of others" as Susan Sontag calls it, the despair, the sadness of the other whose experience one represents, or one's own pain and suffering, and one has to bear the possibility of failing, breaking under the weight of the task. "Zeugnis ablegen" in German echoes another, related idea. It means to "lay down" a testimony, to take something off your shoulders, off your soul, and place it in front of the others. See Susan Sontag, *Regarding the Pain of Others*.

53. Responsibility here in the Levinasian sense as beyond recognition: "To communicate is indeed to open oneself, but the openness is not complete if it is on the watch for recognition. It is complete not in the spectacle of or in the recognition of the other, but in becoming a responsibility for him." Emmanuel Levinas, *Otherwise than Being* (Boston: Kluwer Academic Publishers, 1991), 119.

54. It is a complexity by far exceeding what can be said in this chapter. A longer project needs to elaborate on the conditions and risks of witnessing, who qualifies as a witness, what constitutes an "adequate" account.

Sara Murphy

Mourning and Metonymy:
Bearing Witness between Women and Generations

We must think back through our mothers.
—Virginia Woolf, A Room of One's Own

Il s'agit de lui redonner la vie, á cette mère là, à notre mère en nous, et entre nous.
—Luce Irigaray, Entre Nous

As if the invisible death which the face of the other faces were my affair, as if this death regarded me.
—Emmanuel Levinas "Truth of Disclosure and Truth of Testimony"

INTRODUCTION

Of all modern genres, it is perhaps autobiography that raises the most complex and often dramatic questions of the ethical. Naomi Schor pointed to one aspect of this when she noted that "the ideal autobiography is necessarily, though reluctantly, realistic."[1] Insofar as the autobiographer seeks to depict an authentic self, presumably rendered invisible by the flow of time and the vicissitudes of social life, it makes claims for an abstract, integral, even transcendent, self. This no doubt is the position associated with Rousseau, the writer most often cited as the commencement of the modern tradition of self-writing. Rousseau's "idealism" in this sense stumbles repeatedly up against itself, dissolving into prevarication, rationalization, and justifications. But as he famously asserts to his readers, if he is no better a man than they, at least he is different. Rousseau's self-representation forms at times a pointed critique of commonly held precepts for moral conduct. This makes manifest in one way the ethical import of autobiography. More important, however, there is another way in which his text might serve as indicator—and monitory figure—for the way in which autobiography as a genre might be profitably put into dialogue with concepts of ethical subjectivity.

At the threshold of the *Confessions*, Rousseau tells of his birth, that event that while enabling the autobiographical can in no sense be understood to be encompassed by it. Rousseau, whose mother died in childbirth, puts it this way: "Je coûtai la vie à ma mere."[2] Rousseau and his father are left only with her books, which they read together long after she is gone. *I cost my mother her life.* At the origin of the autobiography, there is an exchange, between birth and death, between the life of the autobiographer and the life of her who bore him. And in this deadly exchange, that merciless substitution, there is a trace of murder. But it is a strange kind of murder, whose agent appears to be nature itself, understood in terms of necessity. At the same time, it is this death of the mother that founds the autobiographical project as narrative. Born through death, Rousseau's anamnesis of the mother is constituted through the books she once read; this reading is figured as a sentimental alliance with the father. A strange chain of substitutions—the son's life for the mother's, books for life—recalls Freud's successfully completed mourning, the process through which one becomes again "free and uninhibited."[3] Of course, readers of Rousseau's *Confessions* might with good reason wonder if that is what indeed happens to its protagonist. But what I want to draw attention to here is the specific structure, explicit in Rousseau, by which that "ideal" subject of autobiography is constituted as such through the mother's death, figurative or historical, or as here, both at once.

The literary genre most overtly devoted to the representation of subjectivity as autonomous has a great deal to tell us about precisely that which its narrative constructions most frequently operate to conceal: a constitution of the subject in heteronomy. If we are to think of the relations of autobiography and the ethical, we not only need to think of an autonomous subject who claims a particular relation to temporality and to his or her actions, intentions and desires. We need to read for what is silenced, foreclosed even, by the very structure of the autobiographical. As Rousseau's text suggests and as the work of Luce Irigaray underlines, what is often silenced in the canonical texts of modern autobiography is the figure of the mother. "Toute notre culture occidentale repose sur le meurtre de la mere."[4] Her death, a symbolic murder, is the enabling condition for the emergence of the autobiographical subject, an entity knowable by its definitive separation from the maternal body. Rousseau is a particularly salient example because his narrative makes explicit the foundational status of the death of the mother. But we can be more specific, I think. The implicit claim for the completed mourning of the mother is what shapes the narrative autobiography, launching its subject into life told forward and time viewed backward from the standpoint of the narrator.

If autobiography entails a certain closing out of alterity, figured as the mother, an enabling refusal of heteronomy, what happens when the would-be autobiographer wants to tell of the death of the mother, acknowledging that death in a language not that of exchanges and substitutions, murders and necessities? What would it be to give the mother back her difference, her place as another who resists comprehension in terms of a terrifying alterity, a disappearing grounds for subject formation, the silenced beginning of a narrative of self?

This is perhaps the question that begs in studies of gender and the autobiographical, a subfield that began with an interest in women writers at a time where there was little information about the lives and experiences of women in either the literary or historical record. Scholars of women's writing have demonstrated that, in addition to formal autobiographies, women have traditionally elaborated self-representations in many forms and genres outside of canonical autobiography: diaries, letters, journals, novels. Discussions of the ethical in women's self-representations have most frequently focused on the way in which many women's writings emphasize their relations to others and in many texts, their roles within family and community as caretakers. This approach has a number of unquestionable merits: situating women historically and socially, it retrieves and revalorizes the frequently devalued and invisible physical and affective labor that has been performed by women; it permits us to understand the generic and historical constraints on the production of certain forms of writing; and it does allow us to begin to pose questions about the constitution of dominant and subordinated forms of selfhood. However, it also risks identifying women as a category with a particular set of roles or particular forms of labor and occluding the differences between and among women, even in the assumption of those roles. In other words, such an approach may conflate the ethical with the political insofar as it redescribes identities conferred by social and political arrangements without necessarily asking into the conditions of the production of such identities.

How then to delineate a practice of autobiography that simultaneously traces and valorizes the forms of female relationship while introducing another element of feminist ethics, one that risks disrupting the genre by bringing to the fore the very conditions that enable it? To do this, we need to pose our questions in a different language, one that allows us to ask not simply what identities are constructed in autobiographical writing but how they are constructed and what kinds of exclusions are necessary to them. This is an argument that can be read in Drucilla Cornell's recent work, *Legacies of Dignity: Between Women and Generations*.[5] Ostensibly, this is a book of mourning, written at the behest of a dying mother and serving in a sense as an epitaph for her. But while an epitaph conventionally signifies a completed mourning, this book replaces that with a form of witnessing that, by definition, refuses Rousseau's classic fantasy that it is the death of the mother that founds an autonomous subjectivity. In this chapter, I want to suggest a reading that claims it not only as a work engaged in this project of disruption—continuous with Cornell's earlier work on feminist ethics—but also one that charts out the conditions and limits of the autobiographical.

Self-representation is in this book demonstrated to be inextricable from an obligation to a mother, who, if she cannot ever be entirely known, is unknowable precisely to the extent that she is a subject, imbricated in the networks of cultural and social legitimation, embodied in flesh always already inscribed with meanings. Here an experiment in the limits of self-representation binds itself to a concept of ethical subjectivity that would be a condition for feminist politics.

COMMITMENT TO A PROMISE

The book has its beginnings in an impossible command: on the day her mother died, Cornell writes, "[S]he left me committed to the promise to write a book, dedicated to her, that would bear witness to the dignity of her death and that her bridge club would understand"(*Legacies*, xvii). If the latter part of the command appears a challenge—especially for readers familiar with Cornell's earlier work—it is the former that has the aura of an impossibility. At the very least it appears cryptic: What is it to witness, not to another's death, but to the dignity of it? In what sense can anyone's death have dignity? This is the question that haunts this book; moreover, the very structure of this sentence indicates an aspect of that haunting. Cornell says she is left "committed to a promise"—not fully making the promise, not quite having made the speech act, which, however illusorily, projects a future in which the promising subject is self-same but committed to the promise, and perhaps in that commitment, committed as well to the impossibility of such a promise's fulfillment.

Cornell's mother, she tells us rather baldly at the opening of the preface, took her own life after a long sequence of illnesses and a prognosis with no hope of recovery. As a legal scholar, Cornell might have been expected to write then about the right to die, but she defuses such expectations early on.[6] This is a book that takes place outside the realm of the juridical, although one might argue that Cornell is mapping out here some of the conditions upon which questions of the right to die might ultimately be adjudicated. If it is not about the juridical right to die, however, this book is in many ways an implicit meditation on the question of death, particularly of the way in which suicide raises those questions. The term Cornell deploys for this is *dignity*, about which I will have more to say later. At the beginning of the text, it appears as a way of removing the suffering, physically dying body from the scene. "She would not want me to tell you much about her suffering or physical decay. . . . So no more will be said about my mother's bodily condition" (*Legacies*, xvii). Yet a paragraph later: "She sought a suicide recipe that would allow her to die intact" (*Legacies*, xviii). Again, in the language of impossibility, the irresolvable paradox at the heart of Cornell's project. Do any of us "die intact?" What would that mean? What kind of thinking about death is required to believe we can die intact?

There are indeed, as the social historian Carolyn Kay Steedman insists in her memoir of her own mother's life and death, different deaths; at one level of analysis, death is gendered, raced, classed.[7] Perhaps these are all ways of thinking of dying "intact," social, political, and economic ways of thinking obsequies, which are after all rites that transform a brute event into meaning for those left behind. In this description, we might say, lies the hope of this book: that it, and not "a suicide recipe," would permit her mother to die intact, would be the "commitment to promise," the funeral rite. In funeral rites, one conceals the body; it can be literally present, in a casket, an urn, but the rite is only effective to the extent that the body is unseen or is rendered unseen through burial. In Cornell's book, her mother's suffering and dying body is repeatedly displaced in favor of the effort to remain faithful to her mother's stated wishes: to "die intact," to have no mention of the specifics of her physical decline. Her mother's presence in the book is itself limited, and where Barbara June Cornell is introduced, later on in the text, she is a voice on the telephone, connecting at the end of her life and at the end of the book, with the daughter to whom she had never really been able to connect.

A reader might wonder whether there is something suspect about this structure. Does it implicate a dominant philosophical gesture of privileging mind over body, transcendence over immanence? If "dignity" is the sign under which Cornell refuses details of the suffering body, then are we to understand dignity in terms of an abstraction, a disembodied self? The answer to this is complex; it drives us into the problematic of representation that is at the heart of Cornell's project. One of the contentions implicitly made is precisely that: the female body, particularly in suffering, in death, resists representation. This would be the kind of representation we most readily associate with autobiographical narrative, with narrative more generally, and with the various forms of realism in art. Thus the staunch refusal granted the mother—"She would not want me to tell you . . . about her suffering and decay"—is implicitly associated with a representational economy that posits the female body alive as always already in a state of decay [the succubus, the witch, the sexualized woman] or dead as intensely beautiful, a figure that functions to sustain masculine subjectivity in the face of the dissolution that is death.[8] The figure of the mother is implicated in all of these typical representations: When she is not idealized (The Virgin Mary, The Eternal Feminine), she is identified with the body in a slide from matrix to matter. The project of bearing witness to the dignity of the mother's death involves negotiating a path that falls into neither of these broad categories, that posits the mother neither in the terms of a disembodied ideal nor as a wordless embodiment at the origin of all things. Instead, Cornell tries to open a space for the mother as desiring subject, while preserving her from the violation of a specular gaze.

Opening this space, however, demands that Cornell find a way in which to position herself, if not as traditional autobiographer, then perhaps as a sort of feminist Ariadne, drawing a thread through a maze of representations of women, death, and desire. "We die," Toni Morrison memorably asserted in her Nobel lecture. "That may be the meaning of life. But we do language; and that may be the measure of our lives."[9] Yet how to do language when the representational constraints are of such particular rigor? How to bear witness to the suffering of body and mind where the economy of representation always threatens to reinscribe that suffering in unwanted terms? How to do language about the death of another, the one event for which we cannot really have language? How to do it, more to the point, about the death of one's mother? While women have frequently been inscribed as culture's privileged mourners, it is most typically men whom they are mourning. Rituals for a woman's death are hard to come by,[10] more so when that death is by suicide, so easy to dismiss in terms that ascribe irrationality, madness to the act. Is it possible to avoid reinserting this into a representational economy such as Rousseau's, which, far from bearing witness to the dignity of another's death, turns on a consolidation of the ego?

These are other ways of talking about the "commitment to promise," that signal of impossibility that opens this book. And it accounts, I want to argue, for the peculiarity of the book's structure. For if this book is written under the sign of impossibility: It is structured according to that impossibility, shifting from the autobiographical to discussions of Lacanian theory, to literary analyses, to a discussion of Gayatri Spivak's recent work on "postcolonial reason" to a long section of excerpts from interviews with the members of a housecleaners' collective, back at the end to the autobiographical. In fact, *Between Women and Generations* could seem to a casual reader like an intergeneric collage, pieces of a variety of different books stitched together.

Yet read closely, each section evokes a different version of a large struggle, a kaleidoscopic view that performs as it represents the question of the feminine, alterity, women's lives and deaths. In the first chapter, a series of autobiographical reflections on the generations of women in her family delineates both her maternal grandmother's vibrancy and determination to pull her own family out of the working class and her own mother's later imprisonment in 1950's bourgeois expectations that was in part a byproduct of her grandmother's success. It is a complicated story of female desire and its suppression—and the legacy of both as it shaped her own life as a child and as a grown woman, a mother herself. Autobiography gives way to psychoanalytic theory in the second chapter, which includes a discussion of the work of the analyst Judith Gurewich's interventions into Lacanian theory; Lacan's reading of the symbolic as anchored through the phallic signifier is reread to open a space for female desire. In the third chapter, Cornell returns to a theme hinted at in the autobiographical section: that of silencing. By this she means not only the sorts of silencing that occur when one agent or institution explicitly suppresses another subordinate one, although this is part of it. She also is referring to the kinds of gaps in the record that occur because of the various forms of forgetting, historical and personal trauma. While she has alluded to these themes as they might have played out in her mother's life, she takes her central example from Spivak's recent work,[11] focusing on Spivak's scholarly and imaginary relationship with a historical figure, the rani of Sirmur, who threatened to commit sati when her husband was imprisoned by the British in nineteenth-century India. In the later chapters of the book, Cornell records her experiences interviewing members of Unity, a Queens, New York, housecleaners' collective, primarily composed of women from Latin America. The chapters are largely the transcripts of the interviews, translated from their original Spanish into English, but with the Spanish transcripts as appendices to the book. At the end of the book, Cornell returns to the autobiographical, beginning with her story of her grandmother's death and turning at last to the final days of her mother's life.

These chapters are linked by a network of themes: relations between women of the same family, between women as peers, between women of different class and racial backgrounds, of different geographical and historical positionings; traumatic forgetting; the effects upon women's relations between and among themselves of a symbolic order in which women are situated as if they were, as Simone de Beauvoir argued,[12] men's other and in which what Cornell once called the "feminine within sexual difference"[13] has literally no place and must be designated as a utopian moment. The focus on feminine legacies, inheritances, remains contests the hegemonic model within a society where, if property inheritances are no longer passed down solely through the male line, informing psychic structures nonetheless insist on the name of the father. As it does so, it also contests the fixing of the feminine in terms of certain specific forms of embodiment or psychical fantasies of Woman.

Legacies lead back to the death of the mother and the issue of "bearing witness to the dignity of her death"—a phrase that takes on new meaning if we think of these loose thematic networks as organized according to the principle of metonymy. What we can begin to see here is that this metonymic organization is associated with a project of mourning. The mother whose death demands witnessing is the mother who is in some way misrepresented by every attempt to know her life. In order to bear witness to her death, there must be found a way to acknowledge her otherness.[14] The privileged mode in which this can be done is through metonymy, the trope of deferral. The chain of metonymies leads to other women, other locations, each in turn resistant to any efforts to name and situate them fully. As for Lacan, desire works along a metonymic chain, never arriving at its ultimate, obscure destination, here mourning works along a metonymic chain, but now specifically articulated with feminine desire, specifically, as Luce Irigaray puts it, "le désir fou, ce rapport à la mere."[15] That desire is for what is lost and cannot be regained, to be sure. But whereas the strict psychoanalytic interpretation of desire reads it as produced through the Oedipus, leaving women's desire notoriously interrogable,

Cornell here posits a mourning desire for a lost mother that turns productive and even transformational.

METONYMIES: FROM MAD DESIRE TO THE OTHER WOMEN

Cornell's opening chapter appears to engage a project of what we might pro-visionally call "maternal genealogy." Yet insofar as she performs an attempt to construct such a thing, her writing constantly calls attention to the pecu-liarity of the enterprise. For, as Margaret Whitford succinctly put it, "There is no maternal genealogy."[16] Western culture is saturated with stories of father/son relations to the extent that to speak of genealogies and legacies them-selves implies that cultural, personal, generational transmission is itself gen-dered masculine. Luce Irigaray has argued that the intergenerational relations between women remain unsymbolized. To the extent that they appear in representation, they figure women trapped in men's stories, the founding and defining stories of Western culture.[17] The masculine symbolic mediates rela-tions between and among women. This is the core of Irigaray's engagement with Lacanian psychoanalysis. If, for Lacan, the choice is entry into the mas-culine symbolic in which the feminine is unsymbolizable, or psychosis, for Irigaray the system is not so entirely closed. Cornell shares in many ways this aspect of Irigaray's project, of introducing through a conception of the imagi-nary, the possibility of a maternal genealogy, even as that possibility remains under current conditions utopian. In the first chapter of her book, Cornell it-erates the relations among three generations of women, claiming a complex and uneven transmission. Through the attention she pays to the dynamics of these relationships over time, she draws often-subtle attention to the diffi-culty and the utopian possibility expressed by the concept of 'maternal genealogy.'

Turning from the preface that traces her project's genesis in her mother's demand, she moves backward in time, retrieving a history of mother-to-daughter transmissions. She tells her grandmother's story of a working-class girl who marries the boss and later, upon his death, becomes the boss herself. She paints a picture of a tough, driven woman, who, having seen the despera-tion and insecurity that poverty brings, wanted to take care of her own family as best she could—and ultimately proceeded to do so in terms that would have been unimaginable for a girl of her background and historical moment. Yet her own daughter, Cornell notes, raised in relative comfort, "never imagined that her own mother's accomplishments were something all women could achieve" (*Legacies*, 21). Why this might be is the question looming over the autobiographical sections of the work, often poignantly. Why would the privi-leged daughter of a powerful mother find it so difficult to see in that mother a role model? Why would she pursue life choices—domesticity, motherhood—that she would later admit were not interesting to her? What stifled her imagination?

The answer that Cornell provides is in effect that her grandmother could not serve her mother as a role model. The very idea implies a certain kind of imitation, but more to the point, the imaginative possibility of such imitation. The world in which her mother came to adulthood did not admit such a possibility; her grandmother would appear a singular figure, a sort of cultural *hapax*. "While Nana never explicitly encouraged or discouraged my mother to follow in her footsteps, and enter into what she called 'the business world,'" "general social pressure" upon upper middle-class girls in the 1950s seemed to rule it out. When her mother voiced a resistance to having children, her husband, Cornell's father, told her to see a psychiatrist. "A sane woman simply did not declare in public—or in private, for that matter—that she did not want children" (*Legacies*, 21). While her grandmother went against family, church, and convention to marry, Cornell notes, her mother years later would succumb to maternal pressure to abandon the man she might have loved in favor of a man her own mother, for all intents and purposes, chose. Cornell charts an analogous set of disjunctions in her own relation to her mother; if the elder Mrs. Cornell was not explicitly afraid her daughter would violate cultural codes of femininity, she was afraid that the young Drucilla would be "weird" (*Legacies*, 22). At the same time, Mrs. Cornell had sought to condition a destiny of some individuality for her daughter, providing her with an unusual name, "to make sure I would never blend in and get lost in the crowd during [sorority] rush" (*Legacies*, 15).

The humorous anecdote of how she got her name in a way sums up the problematic that Cornell writes around in her opening chapter. For it is a problematic that can perhaps only be written around. The daughter must stand out, be noticeable, not get lost, but the place in which she must not get lost is a stereotypically female environment. She can repeat her mother's life, insofar as that life falls within the parameters of a culturally conditioned femininity, insofar as she does not aspire to an individual destiny that would put her at odds with the dominant understandings of "woman." In this sense, Barbara June Cornell, in her daughter's telling, hands down an ironic legacy provided her by her own mother, who did violate the rules in her own life but whose violations were in some ways enabled by precisely the class and historical locations that spurred them on. In the story of the name is also the untold desire of Mrs. Cornell, the "well-leashed" desire, for a destiny that is not like all the girls', a woman's destiny that would be—as women's are not in a patriarchal system—evinced by a name.

What Cornell delineates, writes around, in her musings on the lives of three generations of women is in a sense a maternal genealogy as it can exist. The mother-daughter relation is unsymbolized; it remains outside the symbolic order. That is not to say, as Cornell's narrative indicates, that mothers, grandmothers, daughters do not have any relationship with one another; it is that those relationships as they exist are within a symbolic order that defines and positions women in terms that they have not made for themselves. Thus in a passage entitled "My Grandmother's Silences," Cornell writes that "we either do not know that there is something there for us to talk about, or we feel our experience recedes before the lack of language" (*Legacies*, 13). The stories of her mother and grandmother that Cornell can tell, and of her relationships to them both, are only ever partial, limited. What she knows is a combination of her own experience and imagination. What for instance was at stake in her grandmother's obsessive interest in Eva Peron, particularly the version of the beneficent Evita of myth?[18] Did she see her own story played out large in that of the ambitious lower-class girl who became the first lady of Argentina and sought to help the impoverished through charity, formal and informal? Is this one of the only ways that her granddaughter can get close to her grandmother's subjective experiences, opinions, feelings about her own life—through the refracted image of Evita's myths and her grandmother's preoccupation with them? Was this perhaps the only way her grandmother, born in the 1890s, could get close to her own experiences, emotions, for which she did not have language and to which she perhaps did not have access? And what lay within her own mother's vacillating mix of pride and ambition and fear and resentment, a volatile combination that could cause her to treat her child's loss in a junior tennis match as if it were a violation of international law but also calmly assume that having two of her children give seminars at the University of Chicago in the same week years later was a completely expected and natural testament to what she had always known of her offspring?

Cornell resists subjecting either of these women to a kind of authoritative analysis that would discern motives, clarify personality traits, lock them into a mother/daughter plot that purports to explain the relations between women either in psychotherapeutic terms or in those offered by standard psychoanalytic interpretations of femininity. Instead she turns to the motif of haunting, particularly as it is understood by Nicholas Abraham and Maria Torok. In their well-known essay, "Notes on the Phantom," Torok and Abraham take from their clinical experience to argue that an individual can be possessed by someone else's unconscious.[19] Interestingly enough, their privileged clinical example has to do with a man obsessed with lineage, with family crests and insignia, feudal markers of legitimacy.[20] Cornell rewrites the notion of the phantom to discuss the ways in which a maternal genealogy might be understood where intergenerational relations between women have no symbolic support. They cannot be truly legitimate, since this involves insertion in the symbolic order under the name of the father, but neither can they be illegitimate, since this too implies a relation to the law. How then are they expressed?

If metonymy becomes the privileged trope for this problematic in this book, it is already in play in the opening chapter I have been discussing. A daughter's imaginary friend who bears the same name as her mother's ancient love interest, Evita Peron, the very complexity of the "intact death" that Cornell's mother planned for herself: all these figurations work metonymically to express meanings and relations deferred. But as the book moves forward, in an apparently disjunctive and slightly disorderly way, it comes clear that precisely that effect of the disjunct and disordered derives from the centrality of a conception of metonymy at the heart of the project.

Metonymy, in poetics, is the taking of a part for a whole, a subset of metaphor broadly construed. But perhaps beginning from Roman Jakobson's framing of metonymy and metaphor in terms of opposites that correspond to different operations of the Freudian unconscious,[21] metonymy has taken a slightly different and oftentimes central position in poststructuralist theory. In her early engagements with Derridean deconstruction and legal feminism, Cornell dwelled extensively on the importance of metonymy for the rewriting of Woman: "Metonymy," she writes in *Beyond Accommodation*, "since it is inevitably bound up with contiguity, would show us the context-bound nature of our statements about Woman and thus show us how all such statements involve prejudice and limitation within the context of gender hierarchy. From within this understanding . . . metonymy is favored because it enacts to uncover the structures of power that produce Woman . . . [T]his unmasking is done . . . not in the name of the authentic Woman, or . . . in the name of discourses beyond power."[22] In this, she is clearly reading Derrida.[23] Even more resonant in this passage is her debt to and ongoing dialogue with the work of Luce Irigaray.[24] There can be no "authentic Woman" against which to measure and define women; for Irigaray, as for Cornell, for feminism to install such a figure would simply reiterate the dominant metaphorization that defines women's place in the symbolic order. And that place, as Irigaray reiterates its Freudian scene in *An Ethics of Sexual Difference,* is a battleground, one in which the girl is positioned to turn violently away from her mother, the necessary condition of the assumption of femininity: "The love of self among women, in the feminine, is very hard to establish. Traditionally, it is left in the undifferentiation of the mother/daughter relationship. And this relation has to be given up, Freud tells us, if the woman is to enter into desire for the man/father. A dimension that must be denied in word and act if the good health of the family and the city is to be ensured, Hegel wrote. . . . If we are to be desired and loved by men, we must abandon our mothers, substitute for them, eliminate them in order to be *same.*"[25]

It is the violence of this logic of the same that Cornell's deployment of metonymy as a structuring device contests. At the same time, her use of metonymy here seeks to move away from its close association in Irigaray's work with a morphology of the female body. This logic, which insists on the dominance of metaphor, and which is also tied to a fantasy of eternal reproduction in which each succeeding generation substitutes for the next, not only shapes relations between women in a gender hierarchy, which has as its modern manifestation the nuclear family. It also, as Cornell makes clear, informs the global relations among women, in which some women attain the status of substituting for all women, of having their standard of femininity, of "authentic

Woman"—however implicit this encoding might be—universalized. Meton-ymy, the trope of contiguity, speaks of links and associations while withhold-ing substitution. Insofar as it performs this task, it is here, as it is for Irigaray, the cornerstone of an ethics grounded in its refusal of the violence entailed in an economy of the same.

In *Between Women and Generations*, however, it becomes the central ges-ture of a discourse of self-representation. Metonymy operates to undo an econ-omy of representation that anchors an autonomous subject at its center. In the place of this autonomous subject, the subject of autobiography we might say, a contiguity is posited, between women, between the stories of women's lives. There is no totalizing narrative of Woman that can be told, yet this absence of narrative enables the imagining of bonds between women that cannot rest on a purely morphological identification among them.

For while in the first chapter, Cornell's focus is on her own family, it moves abruptly away from that in the second chapter. There she is writing once again as a feminist theorist, discussing the challenge presented to Laca-nian theory by the clinician Judith Feher-Gurewich. Yet these passages enact the metonymic principle; Gurewich's clinical and theoretical interventions are not simply legible as an argument with Lacanian theory, but rather with the central tenets in Lacan that reiterate the closure of the symbolic order un-der the sign of the phallus. In other words, the argument is not simply with Lacan's notorious conservatism on the subject of women and the feminine, but precisely in the way that this in itself is understandable as descriptive of the system already long in place in the West. Cornell's Gurewich emerges here as a spy in the house of Lacan (*Legacies*, 49–53),[26] highlighting the contin-gency of the formulation of the oedipal in which it is the mother's desire—for the father, for the phallus—that indicates her status as "lacking" and therefore serves as a "signpost" to the father himself. For Cornell, Gurewich's focus on the mother's desire opens up that which is usually a shut, if not foreclosed, question. What does the mother want that is not the child? The answer given by psychoanalysis is most frequently: the father. But in focusing on the moth-er's desire as perhaps ill-defined or at least not for the father, Cornell reads Gurewich as suggesting that possibility that the mother's desire might be best understood as not necessarily directed toward the father. "What the child must find to separate herself from her mother—and yet find her mother again as an actually separate human being who can continue to support her—is a way to symbolize her mother's desire," Cornell glosses Gurewich. "Her moth-er's desire must have a symbolic referent point beyond the child. . . . But there is no structural reason, under Gurewich's interpretation of Lacan, for that ref-erence not to be" nonheterosexual lovers, other activities in the world, in other words, entities not the father figure of oedipal legend (*Legacies*, 52).

This would entail a radical rereading of psychoanalysis. What is involved in this rereading is a foregrounding of the mother's desire as potentially disrup-tive of, and not coherent with, the standard reading of the oedipal structure that grounds the psychoanalytic theory of subjectivity. This is not the place to engage with the broader implications; but for Cornell's text, for her emergent ethics of self-representation, this re-figuration of the mother's desire as something that cannot be contained or stabilized within the nuclear, oedipalized familial structure has two effects I would want to spotlight in terms of our discussion of metonymy. First, it demands a reading backward, onto the familial story that has formed the first chapter. But as it does so, it opens out as many mysteries as it would resolve. The opening stories, of the generations of Kellow and Cornell women, become stories of desires that could not be named or readily contained within the patriarchal plot—and the impact on each daughter of a mother's desire that, while it might not have been for the phallus, was never to find the language in which it could be symbolized. On the level of her text, this conception of the mother's desire reinscribes the driving force of memorialization: to bear witness to the dignity of the mother's death, one might have to know her desire. But if her desire was not for the father, if her desire was not even symbolizable within the available order, except as cryptic demands, her daughter is left wondering: What did you want? More to the point, perhaps, her daughter, assigned to write a book that would bear witness to her mother's death, is left asking: What did you want of me?

On an immediate level, one could propose that the answer to this question is clear: her mother wanted this book written. Moreover, she wanted her daughter, at least, to understand that her decision of suicide was one clearly and lucidly made by a woman in full command of her faculties, able to assess her own condition and make rational choice about it. Yet on a deeper level, the text testifies to the ways in which this answer can only be understood as provisional, that while it is indeed an answer, it is an answer that leads only to further questions about the factors shaping the mother's expression of her desire and her daughter's. The book that is written in response to the mother's demand cannot espouse traditional narrative, which is fueled by a desire for the end, the conclusion, the satisfying tie-up of events. Nor can it quite stick with one topic, for the question is in the end not topic-bound. The question—What did she want?—stolen back from Freud's mouth has only the answers provided through a metonymic linkage of stories and encounters with different women, different desires, in short, through a sustained series of encounters with difference between women, among women. At every moment in which one might believe that the other woman is somehow understood, captured in one's gaze, in one's understanding, such a possibility is removed.

The governing principle of contiguity and the concomitant refusal of substitution not only structures the text, it also frames the autobiographical subject as constituted in terms of a relation and obligation to another. This is the case in Cornell's retelling of Gayatri Spivak's scholarly research into the life of a nineteenth-century Indian *rani*. Spivak's quest is directed by her commitment to bring South Asian women's voices into a larger discourse of global feminism—a long-term scholarly project that has borne fruit for many years in the forms of Spivak's translations of Indian writers and well-known theoretical and political interventions.[27] However, in her *Critique of Post-colonial Reason*, she limns the ways in which the history of empire has silenced permanently many of those voices.[28] Trying to uncover Indian women's relation to the tradition of sati in the nineteenth century, she notes that the practice became so great a political battleground between the British—who depicted "widow-burning" as a central instance of the Indian need for the "civilizing" force of the colonizers—and indigenous familial structures that the voices and motivations of actual women were erased. In her quest for the true story of the *rani* of Sirmur, Spivak comes up virtually emptyhanded, noting that "between patriarchal subject-formation and imperialist object-constitution, it is the place of the free will or agency of the sexed subject as female that is successfully effaced."[29] What Cornell is especially intrigued by in her discussion is Spivak's fidelity to the trace of the *rani*, to the fact that this other woman's story can never be told in its particularity, and that attempts to read her into a larger colonialist narrative, as convincing as they might turn out for some, will always fail. "I pray . . . to be haunted by her slight ghost," Spivak writes of the *rani*, echoing in very different context a sentiment that appears to shape the "commitment to a promise" that motivates Cornell's own writing.

In the later chapters of the book, Cornell struggles to speak Spanish in her interviews with the women's labor collective; the voices of these women are transcribed directly, as they tell their stories of workplace injustice, emigration, and political violence but never without reminding the reader of the frame in which they are situated, a frame determined by class, location, and language. There is no identifying the women of the labor collective with the aristocratic and doomed nineteenth-century *rani*. The contiguity of their stories within Cornell's discourse emphasizes this. At the same time, these two instances bear structural similarities: in each academic feminists go to search for the stories of other women who have been socially, politically, and economically marginalized. In each case, the academic feminist must respond to a demand from the other, a particular, concrete other. As Cornell and Spivak here engage in parallel inquiries, to be entrusted with the other women's stories, they also must acknowledge that they cannot fully reproduce those stories or represent those women.

THE DEMANDS OF DIGNITY

Throughout this book, as must be evident by now, Cornell continues a long-term engagement with psychoanalysis. But as might also be evident, she treats it as a discourse that is privileged only to the extent that it provides a description of a current state of affairs. As her discussion of Gurewich suggests, she does not wish to treat it as a master discourse. In this book, as has been the case in her earlier work, psychoanalysis offers a means through which the conditions for an ethics might be elaborated. At the cornerstone of this ethics, in

Between Women and Generations, lies a conception of dignity. Dignity operates in this text as a signifier for a feminist ethics that would serve to rearticulate the relations between women. But the specific meaning of the term seems to vacillate a great deal in this text, inviting us to wonder not only what precisely it means for Cornell but also what kind of ethics and politics it is helping her to elaborate. In this section, I want to focus attention on its importance in her text, tracing its vicissitudes and suggesting some ways in which Irigaray's engagement with Levinasian ethics might supplement the term.

As I noted earlier, the term makes its first appearance in the command of the dying mother that her daughter should write a book "bearing witness to the dignity of my death." Dignity here appears to be a metonym, a sign of deferral of possibility, paradoxically perhaps a sign for death itself. In Cornell's autobiographical discourse, "the dignity" of her mother's death is associated with a desire to "die intact," expressed by her mother and a way of inscribing Cornell's acquiescence to her mother's wish that her bodily degeneration not be discussed. Thus, dignity is associated with a discursive distancing of bodily suffering from textual representation. As I suggested earlier, however, such a gesture risks a reiteration of precisely the sort of erasure of the embodiment of the female subject that Cornell elsewhere seems to reject. If dignity is a supposition that is granted to the other, precisely at the moment when "intactness," at least insofar as one can understand this in terms of a bodily state, might fail, is there a way of evading the circuits of representation such that the suffering of the body can be conveyed? Dignity seems something that must be recognized precisely to the extent that it can be taken away; it has to do here also with the refusal of a certain spectatorial power that would transform human beings into objects. At the same time, the term seems to invite an abstraction of the person that threatens to occlude the very bodily life and death that inspires Cornell's writing.

The importance of the term is underlined: "The recognition of the dignity of other women is an ethical limit to feminist politics" (*Legacies*, 2). But still, we might ask in what consists this dignity that we are called upon to recognize? Elsewhere Cornell states that dignity is a "law [that] grants the mother her status as an actively desiring subject" (*Legacies*, 56). For Cornell, in a passage that evokes her concept of the "imaginary domain,"[30] it is a supposition that invites us to imagine utopian conditions in clear terms: "[W]hat are the conditions under which actual human beings are given the chance to affirm their dignity, to present and represent themselves as demanding respect for their dignity, and to adhere to the ethical demand placed upon them by the worthiness of others to do likewise?" This passage establishes both the strength and the centrality of the concept of dignity as integral to the category of the human and integral to Cornell's feminist ethics—but also an indicator of its weakness at doing some of the work she wants it to do.

Cornell is deriving her conception of dignity from Kantian moral philosophy, as is hinted in an early gloss on an adage of her grandmother and is made explicit later in the text. "Dignity is an old-fashioned word, used in some religious and philosophical traditions to respect or revere our uniqueness as human beings who can take rational responsibility for their lives or have an inner divinity that gives them infinite worth" (Legacies, 2). Yet these two things—the power to take rational responsibility for one's life, having an inner divinity—are, in the terms of her text, distinct. If Kant could map them onto one another, an argument for subject constitution derived from psychoanalysis cannot. Her conception of dignity, therefore, involves a fairly substantial revision of Kant. It is worth quoting from Kant's *Groundwork for the Metaphysics of Morals* at some length: "A rational being must always regard himself as law-making in a realm of ends made possible by freedom of the will, be it as member or ruler. . . . Reason then relates every maxim of the will, as general law-giving, to every other will and also every action toward oneself, not on account of any other practical motive or any future advantage, but because of the idea of dignity of a rational being which obeys no law but that which he himself gives. . . . [W]hatever is above all price, and therefore has no equivalent, has dignity."[31]

As Cornell acknowledges, and this well-known passage evidences, Kantian moral philosophy relies upon a vision of the individual as rational and autonomous. To the extent that individuals are rational and autonomous, dignity can be adduced; Kant can make claims for the moral law, represented in the terms of the "categorical imperative," among other ways, to the extent that he can suppose the rationality and autonomy of each individual. "Autonomy lies at the root of human and every other rational nature."

What Cornell wants to argue, however, in her appropriation of this moral philosophy for a feminist ethics, is that one can adduce a Kantian dignity where the sort of autonomy envisioned by Kant is precisely lacking and has become theoretically indefensible. "My argument here," she writes, "is that psychoanalysis can help us reshape the ideas of autonomy and freedom, thereby salvaging dignity from a pre-Freudian understanding of desire." Psychoanalysis has indeed taught us that we are to understand ourselves as structurally bound up in the desire of the Other. We are anything but autonomous, in Kant's high-Enlightenment sense. Cornell alludes to the conclusions drawn by Lacan in his seminar on the ethics of psychoanalysis: "The big Other is what we fantasize as lying behind actual social conventions and which we unconsciously invest with the authority to govern us . . . but the ethical goal of psychoanalysis—to help us see that there is no absolute other whose jouissance threatens us—can return our desire to us. . . . In principle, we can claim it as our struggle without being further hindered by outside forces such as patriarchal institutions" (Legacies, 57–58). In principle, the ethical message of Lacanian psychoanalysis is that there may be a measured and attenuated autonomy graspable by the subject, in the revelation that there is no Big Other in relation to which we must situate ourselves, to whom we must endlessly appeal. And if some of the most prominent manifestations of that fantasy of the Big Other are in the institutions of patriarchal society, the project of unmasking them for what they are can and should indeed be claimed as a feminist project. Cornell quotes Castoriadis's reading of Seminar VII: "[Autonomy] is the establishment of another relation between the discourse of the other and the subject's discourse'" (*Legacies*, 58).

Yet while developing claims for the autonomy of the female subject is vital to a feminist project, especially given the models of care and connection that have dominated so much of feminist ethics in the past, the question remains: What has become of Kantian dignity in the process of being Lacanized? Or more precisely, to what extent can Kant's dignity, which relies so intently on a rational, autonomous subject which is in so many ways not the subject of Lacanian psychoanalysis, survive this analysis? In what ways, I want to ask, does Cornell's use of the concept of 'dignity' in her work demand another reading, one that perhaps is able to sustain the ethical commitment to a form of alterity that also suffuses the book, and that Cornell emphasizes in equal measure to that of autonomy? It is precisely this double commitment, this refusal to choose between the autonomous and heteronymous, that characterizes the structure of this book and is in a sense betrayed by her phrasing of "an ethical command placed upon [human beings] by the worthiness of others" (*Legacies*, 58). While the Kantian element of her argument demands that all human beings be seen as worthy of respect, in much of her work, dignity functions catachretically—as a term for a relation to another that seems to figure autonomy as necessarily compromised, by humans' inevitable imbrication in networks of markets and exchange, and finally, by suffering, decrepitude, death. The autonomy that Cornell valorizes here is, in other words, radically deautonomized: we are not autonomous to the extent that we possess rationality, but rather to the extent that we are bound to other human beings in the project of life.

What I would want to suggest here is that especially insofar as Cornell roots her ethics in an act of mourning for a lost mother, it seems that it is Irigaray's complex engagement with Emmanuel Levinas that helps describe the multiple and complex valences of "dignity" in this text and the ways in which the very use of this term at times functions to obscure precisely that which Cornell is advocating. In other words, what she often calls "dignity" here has in some sense to do with autonomy, but it has more to do with a sort of autonomy that would rely for its meaning on a fundamentally heteronomous subjectivity, rather than, as is the case for Kant, reason. If her ethics of self-representation has, as I am arguing, something central to tell us not just about women's autobiography but also about the ethics of autobiography more generally speaking, it is here in the attempts to delineate a heteronomy, a relation to otherness, that might be unleashed by the psychoanalytic dissolution of the subject's thrall to the Big Other.

For this is perhaps an adequate description of the place—or one of the places—from which Irigaray herself begins, both as it were developmentally in the terms of her own intellectual history and in terms of a body of work that launches an engagement with the texts of Western philosophy from the positions of gadfly, romancer, mimetic. Irigaray holds to the Lacanian insight that an "analysis terminable" would involve decathecting the all-powerful Big Other; her commitment to this insight is so complete that it shapes the subversive play of her texts, in which no discourse's claim to mastery can be sustained. Irigaray's "ethics of sexual difference" is inextricable from this project of radically unsettling the Big Other; if, as she claims, "sexual difference is one of the major philosophical issues, if not the issue of our age,"[32] this can be read not simply as claiming that these are the terms in which any possible ethics must be couched, but that such an ethics is inextricable from the ongoing project, simultaneously psychoanalytic and philosophical, of challenging and displacing master discourses that rest implicitly or explicitly on a logic of the same.

And in this, one can perceive the effects that Emmanuel Levinas's writings on ethics have had on Irigaray's thinking. Yet if Levinas's ethics, founded on the priority of the confrontation with an alterity that cannot be subsumed into totality, form an important intertext for Irigaray, the particular space he gives to the feminine and to paternity in his work causes her consternation. For Levinas, sexual difference is not an "issue" in the sense that Irigaray means it; there is no "ethics of sexual difference." Rather, the feminine occupies a particular place within his development of the idea of alterity. "In civilized life there are traces of this relationship with the other. . . . Does the situation exist where the alterity of the other appears in its purity?"[33] For Levinas, it is in the feminine that such "traces" are found. Irigaray is attentive to the complexity of his treatment of the feminine. In his discussion of eros and the feminine in *Time and the Other*, Levinas focuses on sexual difference as "not some specific difference."[34] It is for him multiple, not binary: "Neither is the difference between the sexes the duality of two complementary terms, for two complementary terms presuppose a preexisting whole."[35] It comes to figure difference itself.

But as Irigaray wishes to point out, explicitly in her two essays on Levinas and implicitly elsewhere in her work, the radical implications of this for a feminist analysis are derailed at the point where it becomes clear that for Levinas alterity seems to be, however paradoxically, identified with a conception of the feminine that "withdraws," is characterized by "modesty" and "mystery."[36] While he makes clear that he is not referring solely to the ideal of Woman as represented through the texts of Western literature and culture, for Irigaray the role of this feminine appears at the end of the day simply to enable a male subject to have "those traces of this relationship to the other." Not only is this not a reciprocal difference, but the relationship to the feminine other is posited in the ultimate interest of Levinas' development of a relation between alterity and temporality that is that of a male subject.

In "Questions for Emmanuel Levinas," she points out that in his treatment of the feminine other, Levinas seems to shift between metaphysical and phenomenological language such that it is not ever entirely clear whether his feminine is a force, a presence, an ideal, or an embodied other. Yet when he moves on, displacing the feminine with paternity and the father/son relationship, which is for him the strongest articulation of alterity and temporality, the stakes become clearer. She writes that "although he takes pleasure in caressing, he abandons the feminine other, leaves her to sink . . . in order to return to his responsibilities in the world of men amongst themselves. For him, the feminine does not stand for an other to be respected in her human freedom and human identity. The feminine other is still left without her own specific face. . . . To go beyond the face of metaphysics would mean precisely to leave the woman her face, and even to assist her to discover it and keep it."[37] Thus, she implies here and in the essay "Fecundity of the Caress," that Levinas betrays his own ethical program, precisely by leaving the feminine in the same old philosophical bind.[38] In Irigaray's analysis, the metaphorical status of Levinas's "face-to-face," as rich as it is, evoking an encounter with that which in each one is irreducibly individual and with a regard that cannot turn away, risks a reinscription of a metaphysics that has consistently effaced female embodiment.

Claire Katz has recently pointed out that Irigaray's critique of Levinas is based very greatly on his work in *Time and the Other,* where the category of the ethical as a relation that is by its nature nonreciprocal is explicitly at stake.[39] Katz quite rightly cautions against a conflation of Levinas's understanding of the category of the erotic, where reciprocity is a desired value, and Levinas's conception of the ethical as asymmetrical. For Irigaray, however, the positing of sexual difference in terms of reciprocity is the condition of all ethical subjectivity. While it is true that she does not address in detail Levinas's later work, her analyses of the erotic in Levinas highlights potentialities for a nonreciprocity that would be nonethical embedded already in this earlier writing, precisely at the point where sexual difference is introduced as providing that glimpse of an alterity that is posited as necessarily preontological. Irigaray's critique of Levinas makes clear the stakes of an ethics that would carry forward the radical impulse hinted at in some of his discussions of sexual difference, a difference that is "not some specific difference." Her insistence, however, that the woman be "left her face" and even assisted in discovering and keeping it, suggests the way in which, as Ewa Ziarek has argued, "for Irigaray, the ethics of sexual difference has to enable different trajectories of gendered becomings without forgetting the obligation to the other . . . maintaining neither the rigid separation between freedom and obligation, as is the case in Levinas's work, nor their symmetrical reversibility as is the case in Kant's ethics."[40]

Ziarek reminds us that Irigarayan ethics diverges from Levinas, perhaps in some regards as much as it does from Kant. While Irigaray has learned a good deal from Levinas, she never follows blindly. Her interest is in enquiring what an obligation to the other might be, if it were taken into serious

consideration that Otherness has historically been identified with the feminine, or with Woman. For her, as for Cornell, the symmetrical reversibility
of freedom and obligation in Kantian ethics risks eliding not simply the material conditions of women's lives, but also the psychic impress of femininity
that many women, including Cornell's mother as represented here, experience. Levinasian ethics seems to pose another version of the problem: there
can be no freedom from the imprecation, the demand of the other. In Cornell's description of her mother's life and death, it is precisely the cultural
and psychic demands of others, actual and symbolic, that silenced the possibility of any sort of "gendered becoming." Of her mother, Cornell remarks
that "the moral and psychic space to dream and make sense of one's own
person . . . was closed down to her" (*Legacies*, xx). So closed down was it
that, according to Cornell's account, her mother only at last achieved a
sense of her own freedom and her own person in taking her own life. Mrs.
Cornell's final showdown was with an illness that had intermittently plagued
her all her life. Her aim was to achieve some control over the battle she
could not win, by "distinguish[ing] herself through managing the ritualiza-
tion of the means of her death. She put it simply: 'I will not be taken by
death'" (*Legacies*, 25). Drucilla Cornell's project here can be understood in
terms of protecting a place for this I, this I that claims it will constitute itself in the management of its death, at the exact point of its eradication as
an I. Acknowledging what Cornell throughout her book has termed "dignity" entails a witnessing of that which exceeds positive knowledge, heeding an obligation to a concrete other, but recognizing that precisely in the
very specificity of the other there is that which cannot be represented.

To "witness to the dignity of the mother's death" certainly entails, as
Cornell suggests, a refusal to treat a suicide in the family, especially a woman's suicide, as a dark secret, undoubtedly associated with a stereotypical female madness. Leaving Barbara June Cornell "her face," in Irigaray's sense,
means not only a refusal of both the undifferentiation that is the preoedipal
and the rivalry and substitution that is the fate of femininity under the law
of the father. It is an acknowledgment of the alterity of the mother that exceeds all available social and cultural legitimations and in doing so, marks
out a hope for a future in which expressions of the feminine would find other
means. But Cornell's narrative of this death also implies that in the tragedy
of a suffering woman who can only feel she is expressing herself as a person
in managing the eradication of her own "I," there is also the dimension that
Levinas hopes to indicate in his use of the concept of 'the face.' That is to
say, Cornell limns her own overwhelming encounter with her responsibility
to her mother, to the conditions of her mother's death, a responsibility she
can only begin to fulfill through writing. In both of these cases, dignity
seems a weak term for both the obligation to her mother that Cornell tries
to fulfill and the limited self-assertion and freedom her mother sought to
exercise.

MOURNING, FEMINIST ETHICS AND AUTOBIOGRAPHY:
A CONCLUSION

For Freud, mourning is a nonpathological and finite process, through which the ego, however painfully, withdraws libido bit by bit from the attachments to a loved and lost object. In *Mourning and Melancholia,* Freud wants to make distinction between this process and that which he ascribes to melancholia, in which "there is an identification of the ego with the abandoned object."[41] Unlike mourning, melancholia refuses the closure that in mourning eventually permits the libido to be displaced onto other objects. Melancholia is, for Freud, constituted by an internalization of the lost object, a simultaneous refusal and acknowledgement of otherness. Recent writers, notably Judith Butler,[42] have drawn attention to Freud's discussion of lost objects in *The Ego and the Id,* where his analysis suggests that the distinction between mourning and melancholia is not as readily made. Freud theorizes that the ego "is itself a precipitate of abandoned object-cathexes and that it contains a history of those object-choices."[43] Viewed in this way, the division between mourning and melancholia ceases to be sustainable; furthermore, as Butler argues, melancholia, an interminable mourning, can be understood as entailing the possibility of being productive and creative, particularly in drawing attention to the ways in which we are constituted through the traces others leave in us. "To accept the autonomy of the ego is to forget that trace; and to accept that trace is to embark on a process of mourning that can never be complete, for no final severance could take place without dissolving the ego."[44]

I want to suggest in closing that this is one way we can think of the infinite mourning that shapes the intervals "between women and generations" in Cornell's text and seems inextricable from a conception of "legacies of dignity." Whereas Butler is predominantly concerned with the social dimension of subject constitution, Cornell's story of incomplete mourning turns to others in the world, to the difficult, if not utopian, necessity of engaging them "face to face." Beginning and concluding with the mother's death, the book's interceding chapters enact a metonymic displacement of this loss—or to put it more specifically, of the remains that mark that loss. As each chapter turns the reader's attention to other women and other locations, reimagines the possibilities for feminism and particularly, in the final sections, for a global feminist response to the north/south circulation of female labor, what becomes clear is that Cornell is developing new possibilities for a melancholic subject of feminist autobiography. Distinct from Freud's clinical melancholic, who suffers self-beratement and paralytic withdrawal, this subject of feminist autobiography that is implied by Cornell knows that writing one's life means finding a way to bear witness to the lives of other women. If the notion of 'maternal genealogies' is as yet an impossible one, there is yet an ethical imperative to remain faithful to the traces of silences and losses. Remaining faithful to those traces, Cornell suggests, may mean that a private loss—the loss of a mother, for instance—be transformed into a public witnessing, one of whose other names is a feminism that is grounded in the acknowledgment of other women's alterity and dreams of freedom—but also in our own inescapably heteronomous origins.

NOTES

1. Naomi Schor, *George Sand and Idealism* (New York: Columbia University Press, 1993), 166.

2. Jean-Jacques Rousseau, *Les Confessions. Tome I* (Paris: Garnier Flammarion, 1968), 45.

3. Sigmund Freud, *Mourning and Melancholia*, in *The Standard Edition of the Complete Psychological Works of Sigmund Freud*, volume 19 ed. and trans. James Strachey (New York: Norton, 1954), 253.

4. Luce Irigaray, *Le Corps a Corps avec La Mere* (Ottawa: Les Editions de la Pleine Lune, 1981), 8.

5. Drucilla Cornell, *Legacies of Dignity: Between Women and Generations* (New York: Palgrave, 2002). Henceforth *Legacies*.

6. "But this is not a book about the right to die. There are complex arguments on both sides of the issue. I leave those articles and books to be written by people whose mother did not decide to exercise that right." *Legacies*, xviii.

7. Caroline Kay Steedman, *Landscape for a Good Woman* (New Brunswick: Rutgers University Press, 1991), 141–45.

8. See especially Elizabeth Bronfen's discussion of this structure underlying the representation of the beautiful dead woman in her *Over Her Dead Body* (New York: Routledge, 1994); Margaret Whitford's discussion of this theme in Irigaray's work in her essay "Irigaray, Utopia and the Death Drive," in Carolyn Burke, Naomi Schor, and Margaret Whitford, eds., *Engaging with Irigaray* (New York: Columbia University Press, 1994), 377–400, sums it up rather precisely : "In this scenario, the man's identity seems to depend on attaching death to femininity; he preserves himself against fragmentation by attaching death to femininity. It is always the woman who is fragmented; in the male imaginary, the woman is in bits and pieces; she is debris, shards, scraps . . . or the 1+1+1+ of the male fantasy described by Lacan." Whitford, "Irigaray," 391.

9. Toni Morrison, "Nobel Lecture," December 7, 1993. Nobelprize.org, http://www.nobel.se/literature/laureates/1993/morrison-lecture.html.

10. The figure of Antigone is of particular resonance here, of course, the woman who tends to the funeral rites of her brother, but herself suffocates after being entombed alive. See also Irigaray's comments on women and death in "The Limits of the Transference," in Whitford, ed., *The Irigaray Reader* (Oxford: Blackwell, 1991), 105–19, where she remarks that "women are dispossessed of access to life and to death as affirmative responsibilities." Iragaray, "Limits," 106.

11. Gayatri Chakravorty Spivak, *The Post-Colonial Critic: Toward a History of the Vanishing Present* (Cambridge: Harvard University Press, 1999).

12. Simone de Beauvoir, *Le Deuxieme Sexe* (Paris: Gallimard Jeunesse, 1999).

13. Drucilla Cornell, *Beyond Accomodation* (New York: Routledge, 1991).

14. See Shoshana Felman and Dori Laub, *Testimony* (New York: Routledge, 1992), and Kelly Oliver, *Witnessing beyond Recognition* (Minneapolis: University of Minnesota Press, 2001).

15. Luce Irigaray, *Le Corps a Corps avec La Mere,* 14.

16. Margaret Whitford, *Luce Irigaray: Philosophy in the Feminine* (New York: Routledge, 1991), 75.

17. See in particular Irigaray, *Speculum of the Other Woman* trans. Gillian C. Gill (New York: Columbia University Press, 1985).

18. According to Cornell, her grandmother "saw cynical interpretations of Eva Perón as a sign of class privilege and a denial of the difficulty of escaping the limits of class, especially if you were a woman." *Legacies,* 11.

19. Nicholas Abraham and Maria Torok, "Notes on the Phantom," in *The Shell and the Kernel,* ed, trans., and intro. Nicholas Rand (Chicago: University of Chicago Press, 1994), 171–76.

20. Abraham and Torok, "Notes on the Phantom," 173.

21. Roman Jakobson, "Two Types of Language and Two Types of Aphasic Disturbance," in *Language in Literature* ed., Stephen Rudy and Krystyna Pomorska, (Cambridge: Harvard University Press, 1990).

22. Cornell, *Beyond Accommodation,*" 167.

23. Jacques Derrida, *The Ear of the Other: Otobiography, Transference, Translation,* ed. Christie MacDonald, trans. Peggy Kamuf (Lincoln: University of Nebraska Press, 1985).

24. "For if she says something, it is not, it is already no longer identical with what she means. Moreover, rather, it is contiguous." Luce Irigaray, *This Sex Which Is Not One,* trans. Catherine Porter with Carolyn Burke (New York: Columbia University Press, 1985), 29, passim. Here and elsewhere in her work, Irigaray's deployment and figuration of the body as it is inscribed in psychoanalysis underwrites her championing of metonymy over metaphor. Margaret Whitford glosses this passage and others by noting that "Contiguity, then, is a figure for vertical and horizontal relationships between women, the maternal genealogy, and the relation of sisterhood. . . . It stands for women's sociality . . . the basis for a different form of social organization and a different economy." Whitford, *Luce Irigaray,* 181.

25. Irigaray, *An Ethics of Sexual Difference,* 101–02.

26. Cornell cites several papers by Gurewich, the majority of which had not been published at the time of the publication of *Legacies of Dignity.* But see Judith Feher Gurewich, "The Subversive Value of Symbolic Castration: The Case of Desdemona," *JPCS: The Journal for Psychoanalysis in Culture and Society* 2 (Fall 1997): 61–66, and "The Philanthropy of Perversion," in *Lacan in America,* ed. Jean-Michel Rabaté (New York: Other, 2000), 361–78.

27. See Spivak, *In Other Words* (New York: Routledge, 1988); *The Post-Colonial Critic: Interviews, Strategies, Dialogues,* ed. Sarah Harasym (New York: Routledge, 1990); and *Outside in the Teaching Machine* (New York: Routledge, 1993).

28. Gayatri Chakravorty Spivak, *The Post-Colonial Critic: Toward a History of the Vanishing Present* (Cambridge: Harvard University Press, 1999).

29. Quoted in *Legacies,* 79.

30. In her book *The Imaginary Domain*, Cornell defends a concept of "right" informed by her reading of Rawls' Kantian constructivism. What Cornell terms "the imaginary domain" expands and revises the traditional concept of the 'person,' as it has been understood in law, to include not only "minimum conditions of individuation" and "bodily integrity" but also an incorporation of the psychic components that must of necessity underlie both of these. Broadly put, the question posed to the law—particularly, here, with regard to abortion, pornography, and sexual harassment—then becomes one of the conditions under which the imaginary domain of a given individual or group is protected. While this is a rich and supple way of addressing the inequalities of sex and gender before the law, what I am suggesting here is that within the context of *Legacies of Dignity* it falls short, precisely to the extent perhaps that from the opening of the book, Cornell has made clear that she is writing outside of a juridical context, exploring a realm in which the negotiations of autonomy and freedom are not entirely, if at all, encompassed by legal right. See *The Imaginary Domain: Abortion, Pornography, and Sexual Harassment* (New York: Routledge, 1995).

31. Immanuel Kant, *Groundwork for the Metaphysics of Morals* (New Haven: Yale University Press, 2002), 53.

32. Irigaray, *An Ethics of Sexual Difference*, 5.

33. Emmanuel Levinas, *Time and the Other*, trans. Richard Cohen (Philadelphia: Duquesne University Press, 2001), 85.

34. Ibid., 85.

35. Ibid., 86.

36. Tina Chanter has recently discussed in great detail the role Levinas accords to the feminine, in many ways developing and extending the *in nuce* critique of Irigaray's two short essays; see Chanter, *Time, Death and the Feminine: Levinas with Heidegger* (Stanford: Stanford University Press, 2001).

37. Irigaray, *An Ethics of Sexual Difference*, 183–84.

38. "The Fecundity of the Caress," in *Face to Face with Levinas*, ed. Richard A. Cohen (Albany: State University of New York Press, 1986).

39. Claire Elise Katz, *Levinas, Judaism and the Feminine: The Silent Footsteps of Rebecca* (Indianapolis: Indiana University Press, 2005).

40. Ewa Ziarek, "Toward a Radical Feminine Imaginary: Temporality and Embodiment in Irigaray's Ethics," *Diacritics* 28, no 1 (Spring 1998): 60.

41. Sigmund Freud, *Ego and the Id*, in *The Standard Edition of the Complete Psychological Works of Sigmund Freud*, volume 11, 368.

42. Judith Butler, *The Psychic Life of Power* (Stanford: Stanford University Press, 1997).

43. Sigmund Freud, *Ego and the Id*, 368.

44. Judith Butler, *The Psychic Life of Power*, 196.

Martin J. Beck Matuštík

Progress and Evil

We are in a conflict between good and evil, and America will call evil by its name.

—George W. Bush, June 1, 2002, West Point Commencement

The problem of evil has been for the most part associated with the slew of logical (deductive) and evidential (probabilistic) arguments for or against theism.[1] This literature treats evil as a problem for any coherent theodicy. Is it not then curious that analytic philosophers of religion would accept Dostoyevsky's last novel, *The Brothers Karamazov*[2] (1950), especially chapters on Ivan Karamazov's and the Grand Inquisitor's rebellion, as a literary version of such arguments?[3] The Grand Inquisitor is not an atheist, rather he is someone who has come to divine good and evil in God's place. Ivan is not an atheist either but rather someone in despair. Dostoevsky does not pose the problem of evil as a challenge to God but to human existence and the idea of progress. Kant's horror at radical and even diabolical evil is likewise not driven by rational arguments for or against theism. Human evil challenges our ability to sustain free existence, and this is what makes evil not only banal, in Arendt's later assessment, but also morally radical for Kant and disastrous for Benjamin or demonic, indeed, diabolical for Dostoyevsky and Kierkegaard.

I leave aside analytic debates about evil and theism as largely marginal to the existential issues raised by Kant and Dostoyevsky. Taking up their challenge to human freedom, I will consider first Drucilla Cornell's later work (2002, 2003a, b, c, d, e),[4] in which she confronts Kant's view of radical evil with Adorno's (1998) notion of progress.[5] How can we conceive of the ideal of humanity in a manner that is at once open and critical? Second, I will revisit the Kantian musings on radical evil with Benjamin and appeal to the weak redemptive power of hope granted to the succeeding generations. If Adorno and Cornell are right—that we must resist radical evil without becoming totalitarian in turn—should we leave this requirement

161

to those whose view of original sin as predestination justifies oppression and domination? What does radical evil disclose about the progress of humanity? Third, I will meditate on cruelty: I hold that its very admission not only delivers us to a genre of redemptive critical theory but also confronts the not so banal shadow of any human will wishing to do good and vanquish evil. I want to conclude that human evil should be regarded as at once banal, radical, and diabolical: banal in the do-gooders who tranquilize themselves on the trivial pursuit of the good, radical in distorting human capacity to progress in freedom, and diabolical in its human-all-too-human religious cruelty.

HUMANITY AS RECOLLECTIVE IMAGINATION

Through war, through the taxing and never-ending accumulation of armament, through the want which any state, even in peacetime, must suffer internally, Nature forces them to make at first inadequate and tentative attempts; finally, after devastations, revolutions, and even complete exhaustion, she brings them to that which reason could have told them at the beginning and with far less sad experience, to wit, to step from the lawless conditions of savages into a league of nations.

—Immanuel Kant, *Religion and Rational Theology*

Cornell adopts a positive ideal of humanity from Kant and reads it through Adorno's[6] (1973) negative delimitation of all totality or utopian concepts. Her philosophy of limit critically informs the task of recollective imagination as well as the conceptuality of the imaginary domain wherein we are to face our humanity as our critically open and always reimagined task.[7] If there is progress, it must respect Kant's insistence that ideals remain regulative (not nameable in a metaphysical sense) and Adorno's corrective to all striving for assimilative closure of ideals in identity logic or totality thinking. With Adorno, Cornell considers Kant's notion of radical evil: progress can overcome evil yet without the progressive ideal becoming itself a homogenizing concept or static achievement. What is the promise of progress, she queries with Adorno? Radical evil in sight, progress lies in the margin between cruelty, which holds no relationship to historical idealities, and violence that still contains a relationship to ideals of humanity. In *Defending Ideals* Cornell illustrates this distinction on the first and second Persian Gulf Wars: "Progressive idealists in the global antiwar movement are insisting on the mediation of violence by ideals . . . [against] the cruelty that treats the citizens of Iraq as disposable people." By labeling some groups or individuals as evil, politicians make it possible (1) to dehumanize the enemy through raising the "fear of the evil they" (2), to raise emblems and fetishes so that they can rally people around God and the nation, and (3) to blur the line between violence and cruelty in the cleansing of evil.

In a recent comment in *Hypatia,* Cornell underscores Kant's point with the case of a Palestinian mother whose suicide bomber daughter killed two Israeli civilians: even the terrorist who commits wrongful violence has a human face. Kant's moral tenor is worth emphasizing: evil must be imputed to human will, but never to the core of our humanity. Hence Kant, unlike the politicians who stir passions against evildoers, affirms "depravity" (*Bösartigkeit*) but downplays "malice" (*Bösheit*) of willing. He absolves our self-legislative will (*Wille*), since it always respects the moral law, and locates evil in our free choice (*Willkür*). This move is replayed in Cornell's distinction between violence that still carries its umbilical cord to human ideals and cruelty that appears to have fallen into nonhuman bestiality. Whether or not humans can commit diabolical evil is another question that Cornell, unlike Kant, does not even raise. She wants to "return to the battle over ideals and attack the cruelty" that underwrites all dehumanization of the sources of human evil.

Adorno unmasks our "false reverence for evil with which we deride hope for perfectability of human nature and condemn human civilization."[8] He defends Kant's perpetual peace in order to wrestle the ideals of progress from mere struggle for self-preservation. Cornell harnesses the ideal of humanity to overcome the civilization of cruelty. Here we find ourselves at the heart of her new critical theory. She productively deploys the antinomy between the transhistorical ideal of humanity and concrete historical humans in order to correct for the positivism of a fully rationalized progress and yet retain its ideality as a critical ally against cruelty. This alliance between critical ideals and suspicion becomes possible thanks to what Cornell invokes as "Kant's negative dialectic of unsocial sociability." "Unsocial sociability" comes from Kant's "Idea of Universal History," thesis four.[9] Its characterization as "negative dialectic" marks Cornell's reading of Kant through Adorno: she speaks of evil as radical limit that presents us with the task to reimagine human ideals. A narrow passage between this limit and human ideals-a free play of imagination perhaps— enables progress.

Even if we were a race of devils, she echoes Kant, we might be able to resist the fate of self-destructive dialectic of enlightenment. Precisely because we are primitively "unsocial," we become sociable in order to protect ourselves from nature and each other. Even as a race of devils, humans could come to control what is other than them. Social harmony would emerge through a self-corrective process of learning. We would stop resorting to warfare when nations have completely exhausted their unsociable ways of coexisting. Perpetual peace would issue as if a dystopian utopia. This Kantian view of history allows for social progress within the margins of rationality winning through unsociable discord and even against our weak moral will.

Cornell echoes Kant's mixed assessment of "human beings who have only come together in order to preserve themselves against endless violence and yet cannot seem to avoid being the bullies on the playground."[10] Progress is never something positively normative but is a dialectic of progress and evil. At the

limit of our self-destructiveness, we project the regulative possibility of "a redeemed humanity" that would reconcile self-preservation and ideal sociability.
Formerly excluded groups would find it possible to represent and reconstitute
this ideality. A human ideal, to be normative in a critical sense, cannot be ontologically immanent to what always already is: "Symbolic universality thus
always carries within it a moment of transcendence since it tries to represent
what does not yet exist."[11] Even as unrepresentable metaphysically, humanity
as a multiple ideality can become "deliberately resistant and inconclusive."
The imaginary domain exists by our birthright (human as well as moral and
legal right) as a field of possibility through which we both relate to received
traditions and envision new ways of being in them. The task of the critical
theorist is to raise one's consciousness that alone must engage the imaginary
domain through what it reimagines, performs, and embodies in existence.
Cornell updates "the Kantian lesson" through Adorno's dialectic of enlightenment and radical evil: "We do not deserve to be human and cannot lose our
humanity"; "we need to learn today that a crime against humanity does not
justify further crimes against humanity."[12]

PROGRESS AS DISASTER

> *This storm is what we call progress. The concept of progress must be grounded in
> the idea of catastrophe.*
>   —Walter Benjamin, *Illuminations*

Cornell apprehends evil as a radical limit of the positive ideals of humanity. If
we are not to leave discourse on evil to those who use original sin to justify dividing the human race into essentially good people and subhumans, then we
need to face radical evil as a limit of the received notions of progress. I return
from Adorno to Kant by way of Benjamin.

Adorno worries about those antiprogress arguments that by "the translation of historical desperation into a norm" legitimate domination. The views
such as "radical evil legitimates evil" or "progress from the slingshot to the
megaton bomb may well amount to satanic laughter" reveal the "false reverence" for evil.[13] They falsely revere evil as if it were some object or face to be
destroyed externally. Kant depicts evil as a quality of free will, and Adorno
sticks with Kant: evil must be imputed to a human will that is free to be good
or evil. Evil acts do not disconnect one from human respect for the rational
moral law.[14]

Yet is there not also a false reverence for progress? Adorno concedes this
possibility partially when he invokes the Judaic prohibition of carved idols to
redeemed life. After Auschwitz any genealogy of human progress is implicated
in a dialectic of evil and enlightenment. Echoing Kant, he foreshortens the
triumph of radical evil: "If progress were truly a master of the whole, the concept which bears the marks of its violence, then progress would no longer be

totalitarian. Progress is not a conclusive category. It wants to cut short the triumph of radical evil not to triumph as such itself."[15] The concept of 'progress' remains productive for Adorno as a negatively dialectical "resistance to perpetual danger of relapse." "Progress can begin at any moment," "at all stages" it exists in forms of "resistance."[16]

Adorno rightly worries about predestination inscribed into the conservative reading of original sin. Cornell helpfully emphasizes the productive ideal of humanity. But can we close our eyes to what "radical evil" teaches us about ideals of humanity and progress? I want to intensify the question whether or not one can hold a false reverence for progress, and I name three temporal limits placed by "radical evil" on the ideals of humanity and progress. If these limits affect everyone in every generation, then disregarding them here and now would attest to one's false reverence for the ideal of progress. First, there is evil of past unredeemed suffering. Second, there is the disconsolate present of reason and will. Third, there is a willed dimension of evil—cruelty—that closes off all prospects of a liberated future.

We run into the first limit with Benjamin's rebuttal to Horkheimer's letter from March 16, 1937.[17] Is human history closed or open? If it is closed, then suffering of the victims of history remains unredeemed. The finality of unjust death of those who were murdered is a consequence of a consistent materialist historiography. But does not crude materialism hold a false reverence for both evil and progress? It regards history as a science that investigates determined facts, it envisions progress as another set of facts. There pivots only an external relationship between the two sets. An unredeemed suffering inflicts a qualitative wound on the happiness and progress built on the blood of the dead victims. With a mixture of bad faith and faint smile, a crude materialist imagines to have escaped and now claims that because "the slain are really slain," one must move on. Benjamin offers a theologically materialist corrective to Horkheimer when he invokes anamnestic solidarity (mindful remembrance) that later generations ought to exercise for the sake of unredeemed suffering. In his "Theses on the Philosophy of History," he develops this idea: "The past carries with it a temporal index by which it is referred to redemption. There is a secret agreement between past generations and the present one. Our coming was expected on earth. Like every generation that preceded us, we have been endowed with a weak Messianic power, a power to which the past has a claim. That claim cannot be settled cheaply."[18]

The second limit placed by radical evil on the ideals of humanity and progress arises if we assume our ethical liability as members of later generations for the past injustices and begin to act responsibly in the present. An existential reading of original sin that respects human freedom, notably by Kierkegaard and Karl Jaspers, shows that no collective guilt for the past injuries may be imputed but collective liability can be accepted in the present historical tense by later generations. Responsibility, just as good and evil, is imputed solely to freely acting will. Reason and will become thus doubly disconsolate in the present. First, just as one cannot be collectively guilty by living in a nation that embarks on an unjust war, so also by living within a generation that has assumed liability for the past evils one cannot become responsible *en masse*. Insofar as imputing good and evil to anyone is possible, one stands alone regardless whether one is a member of a generation that regresses or progresses. Neither does one escape the generational failure without any liability (and that is a sober rendition of original sin without a false reverence for evil), nor can one become responsible by simply closing ranks with a progressing generation (that is a sober existential corrective to a false reverence for progress). Second, no historical progress (even anamnestic solidarity) is able to fill the void of the injurious acts of annihilation or guarantee future outcomes of responsibility. This limit is not the same as the crude materialist's closing the book of life and hope on the past. Progress can infuse our responsible acts today, but it can never guarantee the harmonization of human ends in the future. Indeed, enlightened reason and responsible freedom remain doubly disconsolate. A form of atheism is required to stand guard against a false reverence for progress, lest we reimagine and reinvest humanity with religious faith.

The foregoing limitations of the ideals of humanity and progress turn into an aggravated third limit when human cruelty blossoms into flowers of evil. Adorno is right that progress is available to us at any moment in a manner of human resistance. Benjamin is furthermore more right that progression through empty present time is always catastrophic, while progress through the messianic gate of the now-time ("the time of the now," "Messianic time") is available to us "every second of time."[19] Until I face my ability to close off future hope at any moment, no resistance from within or without, no redemption can overcome my willed ignorance. Free will that binds itself in cruel joy of self-destructiveness lives by catastrophic freedom. Cruelty is the disaster of progress for everyone and in every generation.

Kant was frightened to admit the "diabolical" into enlightened reason and will.[20] This admission would demonize the human person beyond human recognition. The strength of Kant's moral sense of radical evil, underscored by Cornell's reading of the ideals of humanity and progress through Adorno's philosophy of the limit, is that they save the human face of the evildoer against the dehumanizing racism. The humanity of the evildoer is also preserved by Arendt's emphasis on the banality of evil, with which she repudiated her earlier view where she conflated Kant's radical moral evil, he affirms, with diabolical evil, he shuns. Evil is banal for Arendt because it is neither diabolical nor radical.[21]

Yet the most pedestrian form of the diabolical will is the cruel human face of the presumed do-gooder. From this nuanced angle banal evil acts can be as much morally radical as also cruel and thus diabolical, yet without becoming thereby nonhuman. The thesis of banality only affirms that a good neighbor next door—and not some demon—can become perpetrator of monstrous deeds.

One does not need to go far to witness the grimace of a religiously bloated good-will that rejoices in carrying out capital punishment, marching the nation to a war on evil, or cleansing one's ethnic neighborhood of those deemed other. For Kant no less than Adorno or Cornell, no triumph over evil can be called just that excludes part of the human race from humanity. Adorno laments writing philosophy and even poetry after Auschwitz, yet he dialectically exorcizes any Jeremiad on progress as disaster. Squaring Kant and Benjamin, Cornell follows Adorno to use the negative limit category itself as a form of resistance.

But facing one's capacity for cruelty at the heart of the desire to inhabit truth and do good requires courage to grasp radical evil as limit of the ideal of humanity and progress. To think of progress as a developmental achievement that can be passed from one generation to the next is just as naive and danger-ous as thinking of sin as some fixed inheritance. Here the progressivists share the existential blind spot with the conservatives, and Adorno is not off the hook in his own argument against the latter. Both harbor an equally false rev-erence for abstract human existence, an abstraction that the *sui generis* thinker of human existence, Kierkegaard, unmasks as radical evil, indeed, the sin of Christendom. Because evil must be resisted in free will, and because cruelty can be resisted only by willing to be onself without despair, no generation can resist or act on behalf of another. This limits further Benjamin's weak messi-anic force and our adoption of collective liability for the past and responsibil-ity for the future generations. In human existence we begin in radical equality—always at the beginning. That realization offers a humble ideal of humanity and progress, but one that can better guard against its own disaster. Knowing one's humanity marks progress on the spot where one is pinned in existing. Progress becomes knowing oneself in a pregnant sense.

I think that progress is falsely revered when, like evil in reverse, it is pro-jected outwardly as evolution of human history in sync with larger designs of nature. We can admire Kant's optimistic pessimism that "unsocial sociability" of the humankind would deliver us, let us say if the planet can stomach a few more wars, to a more workable U.N. Security Council. We can press his thought further that if moral evil must be imputed to free will, and not exter-nally to evildoers who would have to be destroyed, then progress must be im-putable only to free will. We must then grasp the radicalness of radical evil not as a negative limit of the human intellect and will hampering their progress externally but leaving them internally intact. We need to discern in evil a cat-egory that hemorrhages intellect and will inwardly, affecting even progress nurtured by goodwill and negative resistance. In the process of affirming the humanity of evildoers—thus the sheer banality of evil—we must not water down human evil, speaking of it as negative limit, as finitude or fallibilism, merely intellectually inscrutable something, but never as evil. If we are not to vacate the field to the conservatives who invoke God and sin but name evil by national and sectarian names, we must confront radical evil in the sense Kant and early Arendt conjured up and then hushed away, namely, as cruelty chosen for its own sake.[22] Human evil is more than ignorance. Indeed, evil is at once banal, morally radical, and diabolical. Still, only the last sense of evil reveals its willed stupidity (*bêtise*) discussed by Derrida in an important footnote,[23] and an irreverent vision of progress as catastrophe manifested by Benjamin's *Angelus Novus*.

HUMANITY AND CRUELTY

Freedom and fear, justice and cruelty have always been at war, and we know that God is not neutral between them.
—George W. Bush, September 20, 2001, U.S. Congress

Adorno disparaged a false reverence for evil. But is not radical evil itself a species of false reverence for progress? Is not immediate faith in my own goodness not only banal but also naive? When I project this naive faith as the idea of progress, I embark upon a plan for the regime change of the world. Not only must I now correct the world that offends me, but also, I begin to serve tyranny instead of curing it. I become inwardly a retributive judge of creation and rally outwardly others to my last judgment. This judgment becomes the apotheosis and theodicy of the cruel will: Because the Grand Inquisitor presumes to be in God's service, he is all along fortified by his offense at evil and by his belief in his own goodness. Therein lies the banality of his evil deed carried out in the name of the good. He is no longer offended by the philosopher's evidence from evil against the goodness of the world. As he now usurps God, he measures goodness by his own ideal of progress. Therein lies his radical moral evil done to promote progress. Are not humans who name good and evil by their own name the most cruel? Yet only a postsecular, redemptive critical theory is able to ask an even sharper question, the question that must be posed to the religious establishments: Are not Grand Inquisitor's prayers and public invocations of God also the most spiritless cruelty, the horror that even a religiously "tone-deaf" *religiös Unmusikalisch* atheist intuits as the diabolical sense of evil?[24]

My students always find it shocking to read that Frederick Douglass describes his religious masters as more passionately dedicated in their cruelty to slaves than those who "made no pretensions to, or profession of, religion." And as there be no doubt about this, he adds:

> I assert most unhesitatingly, that the religion of the south is a mere covering for the most horrid crimes—a justifier of the most appalling barbarity—a sanctifier of the most hateful frauds—a dark shelter under which the darkest, foulest, grossest, and most internal deeds of slaveholders find the strongest protection. . . . I should regard being a slave of a religious master the greatest calamity that could befall me. For all slaveholders with whom I have ever met, religious slaveholders are the worst. I have ever found them the meanest and basest, the most cruel and cowardly, of all others.[25]

In the appendix to his autobiography, Douglass attacks the "slaveholding religion of this land," all along distinguishing it from "the Christianity of Christ" that he embraces with force that is equal to the attack on Christendom delivered only ten years later by Kierkegaard. Their dual attack on existing Christianity allows us to note that even if God can be viewed as not neutral between justice and cruelty, someone who invokes divine judgment on humanity and who believes in the goodness of such acts and prayers could be a practitioner of the religion of fear and cruelty. Enter radical evil as a species of the false reverence for progress.

What is cruelty? When guilt consciousness over one's finitude or inability to deliver good becomes one's masked despair, when this despairing self latches on to the negativity of its weak will, when this weak self-willing nothing stands in its own shadow all along masking itself as willing to do good in the world and thus to purify itself of its hidden worm of quiet desperation, then cruelty becomes the master of this self willing to be itself in despair. Cruelty to others reaches its most intense modality in the pursuit of high moral and religious ideals of humanity and progress. Indeed, human evil is at once banal or trivial, radical or morally perverse, and diabolical or religiously cruel.

Why does cruelty have anything to do with goodwill or religion? Why is moral and religious zeal the most cruel? The addiction to self that is weak in its willing, yet wills its nothingness (its shadow existence) rather than nothing at all, this addiction in moral and religious crusades becomes the despair of cruelty. This is the self that pontificates about God who is not neutral between justice and cruelty. When this despairing self pledges itself collectively, it will call evil by its fear name and become cruel to those it wants others to fear. In cruelty one seeks to sever another from the ideal of humanity in the name of progress. This despairing self hides from itself by promoting moral good and God's will. Douglass takes no prisoners when he describes the religious sanction of racism and slavery, and he is not afraid to call such human acts for the ideal of humanity "diabolical": "Never was there a clearer case of stealing the livery of the court of heaven to serve the devil in. . . . Here we have religion and robbery the allies of each other—devils dressed in angels' robes, and hell presenting the semblance of paradise."[26]

How does a spiritless albeit religiously inflected cruelty of the do-gooder originate? It begins in my offense that evil exists; it grows in despair about the failure of God who allows evil to exist and the powerlessness of the human race to do good; and this offended despair matures in smugness whereby I embark on the heroic project of vanquishing evil with my own will.

How do we resist cruelty infecting the very ideals of humanity and progress? Adorno's negative notion of progress as resistance, with which Cornell inhabits the imaginary domain of open and critical ideals of humanity, can help us only part of the way: We learn to resist false reverence for evil and false idols of progress. But by secularizing the spiritual dimension of existence, including by banalizing and moralizing evil (and we know now that evil is

diabolical because of its spiritless religious cruelty), we rob ourselves of any resistance to a false reverence for the Grand Inquisitor at the political pulpit.

Cruelty must be grasped as a religious phenomenon: I hold dear my naive
innocence (this is evil's banality); then in offense I elevate immediate faith in
my goodness into a moral idea of progress (this is radical moral evil that wants
the regime change for the world); and at its most intense, in my despairing offence at the state of creation, I become a heroic yet cruel master praying to myself (this is the evil of spiritless religiosity, namely, the diabolical).

Yet who can truly name the 'religious' in this predicament when God, nation, and evil are all invoked in the same breath? When I confront the spiritless
religious cruelty of my will, then my false reverence of progress becomes un-
masked as itself a species of radical evil. I cannot vanquish any evil before giving
up my offense with which I embarked on the regime change of the universe. I
must divest myself of false reverence for my goodwill, a banal and naive belief
that I can do good, vanquish evil, and remake the world in my own heroic image. Perhaps free of offended despair and free of cruelly spiritless religious will
that masks it, I can become a source of compassion and even change.

How do we face limits of humanity? How do we inhabit finitude freed
from an aesthetic self-relation to our becoming human? For Kierkegaard "the
esthetic conception of spiritlessness by no means provides the criterion for
judging what is despair and what is not." "Spirit cannot be defined estheti-
cally." We must distinguish between aesthetic and religious existence in order
to resist the false religious reverence and resist cruelty masked as moral or religious righteousness. Cruelty is an aesthetic relation to self as well as to God
aggravated by moral or religiously empowered despair. Kierkegaard writes
about the despair of Christendom.[27]

How can we exist without despair, that is, in a self-relation free of cruelty?
How do we progress—better: become human—in concrete existence? Insofar
as we try to resist the false (aesthetic) reverence for the religious within the
ideals of humanity, and we must resist in existence, these all become questions
about spiritual transformation as the basis of human ideals and progress. We
are instantly delivered to a genre of redemptive critical theory. Our discovery
of cruelty at the heart of moral and religious zeal secures the ultimate reason
why ideals of humanity and progress must be studied from a postsecular vantage point. The secular take on religion cannot accomplish what Douglass,
Dostoyvesky, and Kierkegaard, among others, can do from within their articulations of what it means to become human in actual existence, that is, confront despairing offense as the radical core of spiritless religious cruelty.

Cruelty that is "altogether secure in the power of despair," because it is either unaware or ignorant or repressed, can parade itself as the will to good.[28]
This will can in despair take joy from capital punishment or holy war on evildoers. The more unconscious one's despair, the greater the outward moral and
religious zeal, and the greater the cruelty inflicted on those we named as evil
in the name of the good. When the cruel will becomes internally consistent,

it acquires "certain strength." And we get what Kierkegaard names "the demonic person."

Kant did not grasp the demonic, or perhaps did not want to, because he placed religion within the bounds of reason alone. One can do that with religion but not with evil that bursts those very bounds. Cruelty is marked both by aesthetic self-relation (the banality of abstract humanity) and a false reverence for the religious (the idolatry of progress). Ultimately the manifestly cruel is what Kant exorcizes as the diabolical will and Kierkegaard calls "demonic defiance." To resist the intensity of despair found in defiance, the first step would be to acknowledge the possibility that I can be cruel but not thereby lose my humanity as Kant and Arendt once thought I would. I can be cruel precisely in my banally goodwill and even my struggle against evil. That is why false reverence for progress is in its despairing offense itself a species of radical evil. Another way of stating the same would be to admit that in the pursuit of the ideals of humanity and progress, I exist before something wholly other than I ever imagined possible in my imaginary domain, that there is a cosmos or spiritual reality that measures my human self and my progress. But then I know that in my pursuit of the ideals of humanity and progress, I could utterly fail that spiritual reality even in my goodwill, and I could in the process inflict cruelty on others. To admit this possibility into our human ideals and progress is a beginning way out of cruelty.

NOTES

1. Daniel Howard-Snyder, ed., *The Evidential Argument from Evil* (Bloomington: Indiana University Press 1996), xi–xx.

2. Fyodor Dostoyevsky, *The Brothers Karamazov*, trans. C. Garnett. (New York: Random House 1950).

3. See Howard-Snyder.

4. Drucilla Cornell, "Adorno: Civilization, Progress, and Beyond," in *Defending Ideals: War, Democracy, and Political Struggles* (New York: Routledge 2004); "Autonomy Re-Imagined," *Journal for the Psychoanalysis of Culture and Society* 8, no. (2003):144–49; "Facing Our Humanity," *Hypatia* 18, no.1, Special Issue on Feminist Philosophy and the Problem of Evil (2003): 170–74; "The New Political Infamy and the Sacrilege of Feminism," *Metaphilosophy* 35 no.3 (2004): 313–29; Drucilla Cornell, and Daniel Morris "When We Sit in the Hands of the World," unpublished.

5. Theodor Adorno, *Critical Models: Interventions and Catchwords*, trans. Henry W. Pickford (New York: Columbia University Press 1998).

6. Theodor W. Adorno, *Negative Dialectics*, trans. E. B. Ashton (New York: Continuum, 1978; 1966).

7. See Drucilla Cornell, *The Philosophy of Limit* (New York and London: Routledge 1992); *Transformations: Recollective Imagination and Sexual Difference* (New York and London: Routledge 1993); and *The Imaginary Domain: Abortion, Pornography, and Sexual Harassment* (New York and London: Routledge 1995).

8. Adorno, *Critical Models*, 153.

9. Immanuel Kant, *On History*, ed. Lewis White Beck (Indianapolis: Bobbs-Merrill, 1963), 15.

10. Cornell, "The New Political Infamy," 34.

11. Ibid., 52.

12 Ibid., 72.

13. Adorno, *Critical Models*, 153.

14. Immanuel Kant, "Religion within the Boundaries of Mere Reason." *Religion and Rational Theology*, trans. and ed. Allen W. Wood and George Di Giovanni (Cambridge: Cambridge University Press, 1996), 55–215. Cited by marginal numbers of the German edition of Kant's works.

15. Adorno, *Critical Models*, 160.

16. Ibid., 150, 160.

17. Benjamin, "N [On the Theory of Knowledge, Theory of Progress]," *The Arcades Project*, trans. Howard Eiland and Kevin McLaughlin (Cambridge: Harvard University Press, 1999), 471, N7a,8

18. Walter Benjamin, *Illuminations: Essays and Reflections*, ed. and intro. Hannah Arendt, trans. Harry Zohn (New York: Shocken Books, 1968), 254.

19. Ibid., 261–64.

20. Kant, "Religion within the Boundaries of Mere Reason," 6:35, 37.

21. Hannah Arendt, *Eichmann in Jerusalem: Report on the Banality of Evil* (New York: Viking; revised and enlarged edition 1964), Arendt, *The Origins of Totalitarianism* (New York: Harcourt, Brace and World 1951).

22. Kant, "Religion within the Boundaries of Mere Reason," 6:44, 35–37.

23. Jacques Derrida, *Spectors of Marx* (New York: Routledge; 1994) 165n31.

24. Jürgen Habermas, "Zum Friedenspreis des deutschen Buchhandels: Eine Dankrede." The speech on faith and knowledge, was delivered October 14, 2001, at Frankfurt's Paulskirche on the occasion of receiving the Peace Award of the German Publishers. Süddeutsche Zeitung, October 15, 2001.

25. Frederick Douglass, *Narrative of the Life of Frederick Douglass* (New York: Penguin Books, 1968[1845]).

26. Ibid., 120–121.

27. Søren Kierkegaard, *The Sickness unto Death*, ed. and trans. Howard V. Hong and Edna H. Hong (Princeton: Princeton University Press, 1980), 45.

28. Ibid., 44.

Drucilla Cornell and Sara Murphy

Antiracism, Multiculturalism, and the Ethics of Identification

INTRODUCTION

Can multiculturalism be understood only as remedial, a bandage on the wounds of history? In the last several years, this has been the predominant understanding. Associated with the language of "recognition," multiculturalism as a stance and as a series of institutional initiatives has been defended as a compensation for the effects of imperialist domination, of which intractable structural racism is the most evident. Multiculturalism, so the argument goes, responds to the demands of minority cultures for recognition, so long denied to them with devastating effects both on a group and on an individual level. In perhaps the most prominent example, school curricula on all levels are being rewritten, the "canon" of texts in the human sciences being reevaluated and taken apart, so that minority cultures and those formerly silenced by imperialist policies can be represented to new generations of students. These initiatives are all well and good; they must be pursued, with all the work of scholarship and pedagogical research that this entails.

Frequently, however, the demand for recognition is articulated with the supposition of the authenticity of minority identity. That is, it seems integrally tied to the substantiation of an already-formed or pregiven identity. In this chapter, we seek to disconnect the claim to "authenticity" of identity from the demand for recognition. Multiculturalism, we argue, must be understood not simply as the acknowledgment of established and literalized identities, but as fundamental to the recognition of the equal dignity of all peoples.

Perhaps the most well-known discussion of recognition and multiculturalism belongs to Charles Taylor. In his essay "The Politics of Recognition,"[1] Taylor defends the rights of minority cultures to the equivalent evaluation of their significance to global history. Taylor argues for what he terms "a starting hypothesis with which we ought to approach the study of other cultures. . . . Indeed, for a sufficiently different culture, the very understanding of what it is to be of worth will be strange and unfamiliar to us" (66–67). The presumption

173

of equal value, for Taylor, is designed to negotiate between "the inauthentic and homogenizing demand for equal worth on the one hand and the self-immurement within ethnocentric standards on the other" (72). Later in this chapter, we will return to a more detailed consideration of Taylor's position, but for the moment it is important for us to draw attention to the way in which Taylor grounds his discussion of cultures and values.

For Taylor, the moral imperative to recognition is associated with a conception of authenticity. Deriving his understanding of the concept from Lionel Trilling's famous book, Taylor notes that in the modern West, authenticity is understood as carrying moral weight precisely insofar as it describes a relation to oneself: "[I]t comes to be something we have to attain if we are to be true and full human beings" (28). Taylor, of course, is not alone in positing something like this authenticity as crucial for a defense of multiculturalism. What we want to suggest here, however, is that while the aspiration to authenticity may indeed be a vital component for some cultural movements and individuals within those movements, it cannot be the linchpin of a demand for recognition.

As Taylor himself points out, and as Trilling did before him, authenticity derives its moral force, whatever that force may be, from the assumption of an already-constituted and stable identity. Recall the often-cited locus of such a conception, the opening moments of Rousseau's *Confessions*.[2] Rousseau's famous proclamation here locates morality in authenticity, insofar as authenticity is understood along the lines of being true to one's own feelings (*"I feel my own heart . . . I am made like no one else I have ever seen"*). Whatever else he may be, Rousseau has, he tells us, a stable identity—warts and all. For our contemporary discussions of multiculturalism, however, the linking of recognition to authenticity such that stability is presumed, implicitly or explicitly, raises some serious questions. Since recognition is understood to be something demanded of the dominant culture, we must be aware that there is the considerable risk that recognition will shade into an adjudication of authenticity. Recognition tied to authenticity implies that it is already-constituted identities that are at stake; in that case, new formations of minority cultures can fall through the cracks. Only the form of the minority culture acknowledged by the dominant culture—institutionally, socially, politically—will receive official status.

To remark, however, that in the contemporary world identities are in flux is not an arch-theoretical observation. New nation-states arise and new cultural minorities within them. Political alliances create new identifications with demands for new representations of those identifications. In Great Britain, for example, many different minorities today take on the conscious identification as "black" in order to make visible a common struggle against marginalization and oppression in this "postcolonial" era. This identification is dialogic; that is, it simultaneously works to resignify an identity degraded by the dominant culture at the same time as it does not purport to represent a homogeneous group with a shared history, language, or culture. *Multiculturalism* comes to seem a rather weak term for the complex relations between uncon-scious identifications, conscious alliances, and strategic affiliations that shape many people's experiences today.

The current discourse of recognition appears to beg the question: From whom? The notion of recognition, of course, finds its principal articulation in the celebrated "lordship and bondage" parable in the *Phenomenology of Mind*. There, the initial source of recognition at least is the lordship or master. How-ever, this marks a stage in the development of the human spirit toward free-dom, a freedom that for Hegel is achieved in the northern democracies. Clearly, minority cultures are not always, or even mostly, addressing their de-mands for recognition to the majority culture—at least if we are to understand recognition as a comprehension of the minority culture's identity. That free-dom that Hegel saw achieved in the Western European democracies has been, after all, often written on the backs of precisely those minority cultures now struggling for their own national identities, cultural voices, and economic sustainability.[3]

Indeed "recognition" understood as a form of tolerance for and even inter-est in minority cultures can easily mask continued cultural hierarchization as-sociated with Eurocentrism. Gayatri Spivak remarks that "the real demand is that when I speak from [the position of a Third World person] I should be lis-tened to seriously; not with that kind of benevolent imperialism . . . which simply says that because I happen to be Indian or whatever. . . . A hundred years ago it was impossible for me to speak, for the precise reason that makes it only too possible for me to speak in certain circles now."[4] What Spivak sees in contemporary intellectual life as a "suspicious reversal" was described in an-other context by Frantz Fanon as "mummification"; the future orientation of the culture as incarnated by its members is ignored in favor of only apparently respectful attention paid to a stilled and silent image, a synecdoche that is for ever split off from the whole living world to which it refers. Fanon saw in this "a determination to objectify, to continue to imprison, to harden"[5] that should resonate only too forcefully with us today, as a commodified "globalism" flies off racks and shelves in the forms of hennaed lamps, sari silk curtains, and satin cheongsams.

Minority cultures do not want the nod of acceptance under the guise of tolerance for what the master sees as their established, stabilized differences. Nor are they necessarily demanding recognition in the sense that they should be received as having a legitimate, legible place in the majority culture. The demand of minority cultures can even be that they remain unreadable.[6] As a demand of right to the state we think this can best be interpreted through the rubric of freedom and the recognition of equal dignity.

Thus our argument replaces "identity politics," even if understood as the recognition of the value of existing "recognizable" cultural minorities. The demand for freedom must be understood as the affordance of the psychic and moral space necessary for groups and individuals to engage with and re-create their multiple identifications. The practice of literature is one place where we can see this work of re-creation, of what Toni Morrison has termed "rememory," quite vividly. In the poetry of Aimé Césaire, for instance, Africa becomes a place of the imagination; for this poet of the *négritude* movement the continent is no longer just a geographical place, nor is it comprehensible as a homeland to return to or a locus of recoverable identity. Instead, Africa becomes an elaborate and complex trope for imagining a future free of oppression.

At the core of our argument, then, is the insistence that all of us must have the potential to shape our identifications recognized by the state such that we—and not the state—are the source of the meaning they have to us, as individuals and as members of groups. The recognition of this freedom is integral to Taylor's elaboration of a new basis for equal dignity.

However, we also must return to an even more primordial conception of equal dignity. Colonization inevitably involves the identification of the colonized as below the boundary of the human, as beast, as animal, as savage. The colonized are other to humanity; humanity then has been substantiated by the figure of the colonizer and with this figure the most shocking forms of brutality. To challenge this figure would be to challenge the meaning that has been given to humanity.

The idea of humanity *as an idea*, Kant reminds us, is contentless.[7] Humanity, indeed, is just one example of the postulation of free creatures with the capacity of shaping their own moral destiny. Our argument is that the demand for multiculturalism is the freedom to struggle for a different humanity, for the possibility of living otherwise than through the cultural hierarchies imposed by colonialism.

In order to grasp fully the dangers of understanding recognition as a demand for the legitimation of an "authentic" minority culture by the majority, we need to carefully explore the relation between culture, identity, and representation, which we will do in what follows through readings of Nathan Glazer and Anthony Appiah on multiculturalism. We need to examine what harm multiculturalism is meant to remedy or whether multiculturalism should be articulated as protection against prior or potential injuries. As should already be evident, we do not defend multiculturalism on that basis. Through a reading of Toni Morrison's novel *Jazz*, we attempt to show that the relationship between freedom and dignity demands a complex rearticulation of our basic racial, ethnic and linguistic identifications including the cultural forms in which they are represented.

WHY MULTICULTURALISM NOW?

Nathan Glazer recently declared that "we are all multiculturalists now." For Glazer, the ethical mandate for us all to be multiculturalists stems from the failure of our society to effectively undermine racism. Given that racism seems to be so intractable, the least "we" can do is to let racialized minorities affirm their own cultures, indeed, retreat into them as places of safety where they can confirm and develop their own representations of what, for example, it means to be "black." For Glazer, our failure to overcome racist treatment of African Americans has effectively undermined his own earlier dream that all of us citizens of the United States would come to see ourselves as one people who, despite our lived diversity in private life, would share enough of a public culture to agree on what was crucial for the education of our children. Although Glazer is aware that African Americans are not the only group that has been racialized, he believes that their treatment and their reaction to it are an exemplary instance of the political and ethical circumstance that has led many minority groups to insist on multiculturalism in the educational curriculum. Multiculturalism is explicitly understood as a response to the harm of racism. We must integrate into "our" curriculum who "they" tell "us" they are and have been.

But for him, this is an unfortunate if a necessary reparative measure, insofar as it is divisive. It is divisive because it is based on the loss of our ability to identify as "Americans"[8] instead of through our differentiated cultural and religious identities. The identification "American," as Glazer understands it, is one that presumes assimilation of the many languages, religions, and cultural identities of its citizens. Glazer both proclaims and mourns the victory of multiculturalism as a compensation for the harm of racism. Would that it all could have gone differently in this country so racism could have been defeated and the good old ideal of assimilation could still be credibly embraced.

ARE CULTURE AND IDENTITY MISTAKENLY CONNECTED?

Glazer assumes that the assertion and acceptance of a minority culture can be the solution to racism. This assumption that culture is a cure for racism is what K. Anthony Appiah rejects. Indeed, he argues that culture cannot be such a cure. We turn now to Appiah because the question he raises about the relationship of culture to racism has to be examined before we can turn to our own alternative justification for multiculturalism other than the one offered by Glazer.

In his recent writing, Appiah has questioned what he sees as the excessive use of the term *culture,* arguing that most of the social identities that make up our diverse society do not actually have independent cultures that need to be represented in school curricula.[9] What is ultimately at stake for Appiah is our freedom to create ourselves and free ourselves from tightly scripted identities. We share his concern with freedom, although, as will be seen, we do not agree with him that we must disconnect culture and identity in order to protect it.

Prior to his attempts to disentangle culture and identity in the name of freedom, Appiah argues that what are frequently coded as "cultural identities" are in fact social ones and cannot be understood as independent cultures. Appiah recognizes that ethnic groups rather than racial groups have at least historically defined their distinctive identity through the members' attribution of cultural uniqueness. But, according to Appiah, even this attribution of cultural uniqueness comes *post facto*; the uniqueness of cultural identity is truly constituted only retroactively, as members seek to maintain their distinctiveness by highlighting cultural attributes as "theirs." A strength of Appiah's insight from our standpoint is that it presents cultural identity as formed through recollective imagination.[10]

We mean by this phrase that even more traditionally conceived assumptions of identity, social as well as cultural, always involve the imagination as they rework the meaning of the past. Although Appiah does not highlight the role of the imagination in the *post facto* attribution of cultural identities, we believe that his emphasis on their constructed and imaginative nature is integral to his desire to disconnect culture from identity so as to promote freedom. If cultural identity is at least in part the result of imaginative agency, then this can show that the individuals and groups who are attributing the culture to themselves as part of its further development are doing so as an exercise of their freedom. Identities formed through recollective imagination have the potential to be held lightly by the individual because they are already formed through an imaginative effort to envision what they are, how they should remain, or instead be reshaped. Still Appiah accords some traditional ethnic groups the kind of identity that could potentially recollect itself through common cultural markers. In modern "America" however, most ethnic groups have lost the distinctive identity that makes such a quest for the reinforcement of a common culture either possible or ethically desirable. Most ethnic groups have lost the potential precisely because they have met the ideal of assimilation that Glazer argues has been available to immigrant and minority groups that have not been racialized.

Appiah uses "Hispanics" as an example. According to Appiah, "Hispanic" culture has thinned out as this ethnic group has been effectively assimilated and has followed the traditional immigrant pattern of the third generation by losing the Spanish language.[11] Appiah's point here is that the assimilation of minority ethnic groups into American society leaves them little motivation to maintain their cultural distinctiveness even if they remain recognizable groups with a social identity. The idea of social identity is expressive of the diluted and relational reality of cultural life of these groups once they are assimilated into the larger American society. The traditional view of culture and identity, at least maintained in the private zone of the family and neighborhood, is gone. For Appiah, ethnic groups have become more like gender identities. Women may be distinct from men, but they do not have a different culture. What these groups are assimilated into is a social and political culture, not a common national culture.

For Appiah this dilution is a good thing because it keeps us from being engulfed by ethnic identity. Liberal multiculturalism would teach us about the diverse social identities which currently make up the population of the U.S.A. This program should be consistent with the liberal emphasis on individual freedom. As Appiah explains, "Nevertheless, contemporary multiculturalists are right in thinking that a decent education will teach children about the various social identities around them. First because each child has to negotiate the creation of his or her individual identity, using these collective identities as one but only one of the resources; second, so that all can be prepared to deal with one another respectfully in a common civic life" (Appiah, "The Multiculturalist Misunderstanding," 34). To this reasonable form of multiculturalism, Appiah contrasts another sort which is not consistent with individual freedom: "but," he writes, "there is another side of multiculturalism that wants to force children to live within separate spheres defined by the common culture of their race, religion, or ethnicity."[12]

Appiah finds one cause of illiberal multiculturalism in nostalgia for ethnic groups that did share a "pervasive culture."[13] Indeed, he also argues that there is no common culture that is "American." There could not be and should not be any such culture. One of the good things about the United States is that it does not try to capture its citizens into a common culture thus taking away from them or at least limiting the field of possible identifications within the spread of social diversity. In one sense then Appiah is insisting that an American liberal curriculum would naturally be multicultural precisely because so many divergent peoples have come to this country and made their histories, traditions, and languages part of this culture, and these have in turn been reshaped by their integration into the United States. In the vaunted homogenization of U. S. society, Appiah sees no loss for ethnic and racial groups who no longer have a culture that marks them as a cultural group distinct from the dominant social and political liberal culture; this is seen instead as the necessary condition for the freeing of the individual. Unlike Glazer, Appiah is also not mourning the decline or lack of a common American culture.

Appiah further argues that there are no racialized cultures, and that more specifically there is no African American culture. For Appiah it is "cultural geneticism"[14] to attribute to the members of any group, simply because of race or nationality, the cultural artifacts that are rightly or wrongly associated with that group. Since for Appiah there is no unique African American culture, in the sense of shared language, values, practices, and meanings, it is necessarily cultural geneticism to argue that African American cultural identity should be taught in the schools as if all African American students could claim Toni Morrison, for example, as of their own culture even if they have not read her.

Appiah's point here is ultimately ethical. He is not just describing what has happened to most ethnic groups in the United States. He is also calling for an understanding of culture as individual cultivation. Culture, for Appiah, is an ideal and indeed, an ideal of character development. Thus, freedom and cultivation come to be tied together; we can focus on what is truly important in life by educating ourselves so that we are not too tightly scripted by unexamined identifications. This reaching for freedom is the first aspect of what Appiah means by cultivation.

To be encompassed by a single culture is to be sunk in either unwelcome or narrowly circumscribed identifications. To understand cultural identity this way is to make it and freedom oppositional poles. His ideal subject, "the cosmopolitan patriot,"[15] is free to reject or absorb whatever cultural artifacts or experiences come his way due to the coincidence of national and linguistic origin. Free to cultivate his subjectivity, Appiah's cosmopolitan ideal is unapologetically grounded in the capacity to refuse any but "recreational" identities that do not tie him down. But the cosmopolitan patriot also has a responsibility to cultivate himself, in the sense of immersing himself in the best of what art has to offer us. This responsibility to educate oneself is the second aspect of what Appiah means by cultivation.

As Appiah explains, "no African-American is entitled to greater concern because he is descended from a people who created jazz or produced Toni Morrison. Culture is not the problem and it is not the solution."[16] Illiberal multiculturalism involves us in pandering to the lazy and undermines our commitment to cultivation, a commitment that should be expressed in the education of the young.

MORRISON ON JAZZ, BLACKNESS, AND THE ETHICS OF IDENTIFICATION

But is Appiah right that culture should be disconnected from identity? Before turning to this question we at least need to consider that Appiah is working with a concept of 'identity' as constituted through both abjection and disavowal. This is why he is so suspicious of heavy-handed identity politics no matter who practices them. Although Appiah's concern is with the freedom of the person, this concept of identity potentially justifies the devaluation of minority cultures and other more graphic violations of them. We need then at least to explore the possibility of other modes of identification including as they do affirmations of cultural identity. To do so, we now turn to the work of Toni Morrison, with particular attention to her novel *Jazz*.[17]

Much of Toni Morrison's work is concerned both formally and thematically with the relations among identity, abjection, disavowal, and violence. Morrison's *Jazz* in particular uses a scene of violence, the murder of a young woman and the disfigurement of her corpse, to trace the intricacy of abjection and identification. What her literary work does that discursive treatments cannot do is offer both a vision of the complexity of the social-historical-cultural identifications and a hope that there are other modes of identification without abjection available.

For Appiah, the fact that one can produce a genealogy of the term *black*, demonstrating the historical and geographical contingency of the term over at least three centuries of Western cultural and political history, leads him to argue not only that African Americans have in effect no culture, but that black identity does not really exist.[18] In fact he raises a question about identification and the kind of status black identity might have; Morrison raises a similar question but answers it rather differently. Throughout *Jazz*, she draws attention to the excessively scripted narratives of identity in which the characters are caught. But, *contra* Appiah, her fiction does not suggest that the constructed quality of identifications (of "blackness," of jazz, of female sexuality) permits them to be dismantled easily and quickly nor that basic identifications are necessarily imprisoning. In order to understand this more clearly, the complexity of the concept of identification Morrison is using needs to be discussed.

In *Jazz* Morrison tells the story of a love triangle in 1920s Harlem that ends in violence. Fifty-something Joe Trace cheats on his wife, Violet, with a "yellow-skinned girl," the teenager Dorcas; ultimately he kills her. Violet breaks in on Dorcas's funeral and cuts the face of the dead girl as she lies in her coffin. Understanding this related pair of incidents is the task of the narrator of the novel—and the reader as well. Though the narrator begins the story with a sniff of certainty—"Sth, I know that woman"—what is thrown into question throughout the novel is what the narrator, as well as characters and reader, can and does actually know.

This larger question is posed through the narrator and characters' engagement with jazz. Knowing jazz not only comes to be a way of engaging with otherness, but, in particular, a way of engaging the otherness inhabiting the self. The one thing the narrator knows at the beginning of *Jazz* is that jazz is "black." The narrator's initial self-certainty comes from an unconscious identification with Dorcas's guardian, Alice Manfred, who has a definite take on "all that jazz" that Joe, Dorcas, and Violet get caught up in. Like the fear-driven Alice, the narrator's stability turns on the naturalized attribution of jazz as black "race music" that is somehow responsible for sexual and social disorder.

> Alice waited this time, in the month of March, for the woman with the knife. The woman people called Violent now because she had tried to kill what lay in the coffin. She had left notes under Alice's door every day beginning in January—a week after the funeral—and Alice Manfred knew the kind of Negro that couple was: the kind she trained Dorcas away from. The embarrassing kind. The husband shot; the wife stabbed. Nothing. Nothing her niece did or tried could equal the violence done to her. And where there was violence wasn't there also vice? Gambling. Cursing. A terrible and nasty closeness. Red dresses. Yellow shoes. And, of course, race music to urge them on. (Morrison, *Jazz*, 57)

This race music, according to Alice Manfred and the narrator who identifies with her, is responsible for the mess Dorcas got herself into. But it is also responsible for or at least in some way directly associated with black people acting out in the streets. "Alice thought the lowdown music (and in Illinois it was worse than here) had something to do with the silent Black women and men marching down Fifth Avenue to advertise their anger over two hundred dead in east St. Louis, two of whom were her sister and brother-in-law, killed in the riots. So many whites killed the papers would not print the number" (57).

Alice Manfred identifies jazz as the problem and seeks to protect her niece Dorcas against it. But this music cannot be contained. It keeps breaking in and breaking out. While her aunt "worries about how to keep the heart ignorant of the hips and the head in charge of both," Dorcas is listening for the clarinet, the piano, the voice of the blues singer. Authorities have told Alice Manfred what to make of this music, that it is not as troubling as she is making it out to be, but she is not reassured:

> She knew from sermons and editorials that it wasn't real music—just colored folks stuff; harmful, certainly; embarrassing, of course; but not real not serious. Yet Alice Manfred swore she heard a complicated anger in it; something hostile that disguised itself as flourish and roaring seduction. But the part she hated most was its appetite. Its longing was its appetite. Its longing for the bash, the slit; a kind of careless hunger for a fight or a red ruby stickpin for a tie—either would do. It faked happiness, faked welcome, but it did not make her feel generous, this juke joint, barrel hooch, tonk house music. It made her hold her hand in her pocket of her apron to keep from smashing it through the glass pane to snatch the world in her fist and squeeze the life out of it for doing what it did and did and did to her and everybody else she knew or knew about. Better to close the windows and the shutters, sweat in the summer heat of a silent Clifton place apartment than to risk a broken window or a yelping that might not know where or how to stop. (59)

What does Alice Manfred hear in this music? What is it that needs so desperately to be shut out, so shut out that she must box herself into a steaming, airless apartment alone in order not to hear it?

The answer is not simple—for what Morrison is attempting to represent is not that jazz itself is a threat to Alice Manfred's person. Rather, Morrison's aim in this novel is to articulate the conditions under which jazz is audible. The music that Alice Manfred hears is bound to representations of "her and everyone she knew about," a series of images of African-American life as angry, appetite-driven, sexualized in the extreme. Jazz is mediated for Alice through news reports from the white press, through "authorities" proclaiming it unimportant, a lesser musical form. Thus, it is for Morrison a trope not only for black culture in 1920s Harlem, but for the way in which that culture comes to be mediated to its own constituents, of which Alice Manfred in all her repression, in all her rage, is one possible representative.

By no accident, then, is Alice Manfred the guardian of young Dorcas, the niece whom she raises under the iron fist of repression and who breaks free to head out to Prohibition-era speakeasys and jazz clubs. The "under the sash" culture of Prohibition Harlem functions as a figure for the conditions under which African American culture can be represented—and in the figure of Alice, we might say can represent itself to itself—in this novel. Dorcas, dressing up and sneaking out at night with her friend Felice, emblematizes all those things that Alice comes to hear in the music; she is the girl of the "flourish and the roaring seduction" under which is rage, the rage that Alice can not bear to recognize inhabiting her too. Everywhere in this novel there are avatars of wild women, armed women, sexualized women, violent women who cut and bite. In her airless apartment, Alice Manfred tries to shut them all out.

There is a feminine persona that comes with this "colored" music; the call of all that wildness that echoes in the music is the stuff of disavowal out of which the narrator draws the character of Alice Manfred. At the center of the narrator's discourse is the ultimate representation of this feminine persona, "Wild," Joe Trace's purported deserting mother. She is the mother who may or may not be his; Joe never finds out with certainty. In this capacity, "Wild" functions in this narrative allegorically as both the site and figure of abjection. A feral woman who lives in a cave near the West Virginia town where Joe grows up, she is described by the narrator as gaining the name "Wild" when she tries to bite a man who has helped her through childbirth. As a quasimythological point of origin "Wild" represents both the feminine personae in their different manifestations across the narrative as well as the impossibility of knowing what is beyond those personae. Like Alice Manfred's idea of jazz, Wild can only be figured insofar as she is outside the conventional frameworks of identification provided by the structures of law and order.

By breaking into the funeral and slashing Dorcas's face, Violet too has exceeded these frameworks of identification; the narrator begins to describe the slashing Violet as "that Violet," while some of the characters refer to her, poststabbing, as "Violent." What is at stake in this central event of the narrative, this bizarre scene of excess, the defacement of a corpse by a Violet who is no longer her regular self? What does "that Violet" see in the dead face of her husband's teenage lover, the inanimate "cream at the top of the milkpail face," framed by hair that probably never needed straightening? This whitened girl is what has shut her out of her own world of sense. Dorcas has to be marked as other, as the one Alice Manfred cannot identify with. In her attempt to draw out 'that Violet' who picks up the knife and cuts Dorcas, the narrator has to confront the ultimate figure of the "savage" Woman, the woman known only as "Wild." Her risk of identification with this most blackened of all women, "Wild," shakes up her story and allows her to begin again, through a reevaluation of the imposed identifications that had blocked her relationship to the characters as other than kinds of "colored" people.

The paradigmatic kind of "coloured person," in this novel is the racialized and sexualized figure of "Wild," the possible illegitimate mother of Joe Trace who lives in a cave in the West Virginia countryside. Toward the end of the novel, the narrator returns to Wild, only now the figure of the feral woman is no longer envisioned as alien and fear-inspiring. Describing Wild's home, a silent cave full of traces of a life lived and a history marked by her complicated engagements with the world around her, the narrator asserts: "I'd love to close myself in the peace left by the woman who lived there and scared everybody. Unseen because she knows better than to be seen. After all, who would see her a playful woman who lived in a rock? Who could without fright? Of her looking eyes looking back? I wouldn't mind why should I? She has seen me and is not afraid of me. She hugs me. Understands me. Has given me her hand. I am touched by her. Released in secret. Now I know" (221). No longer afraid of her "eyes looking back," the narrator asserts a kind of knowledge—but interestingly enough, it is not in terms that replicate exactly the opening of the narrative. The scoffing "I know that woman" of the first page has been replaced by a different kind of knowing at the end. Yet if this is one way of articulating an identification as black, as female, it is certainly not one that follows from a tightly scripted identity. In fact, this knowing with which *Jazz* ends is one that breaks out of the tightly scripted stories of identity that are everywhere put into play in the novel.

Jazz is a daring novel in that it proceeds through the narrator's own acknowledgment of her disavowal of jazz in the elaboration of her original identification with Alice Manfred, a point of view which had already condemned the characters to play out a limited script. By doing so Morrison is seeking to make identification explicit as an operative force in narrative, as it necessarily designates and delineates its character. She is using identification in at least two senses. First, by making explicit the narrator's transformation of perspective, Morrison is emphasizing the ethical force of identification in narrative fiction: Precisely insofar as the characters are culturally marked out so that they can be knowable, they become unknowable/racialized stereotypes. In *Jazz*, then, the very conception of character as clearly designated, continuous, and unified is thrown into question; the time-honored conventions of realist representation are shown to be precisely that, conventions.

Second, Morrison is engaged in working through the identification of jazz as a black cultural form, and this identification in turn sets the cultural parameters in which the authorial perspective can be articulated. In Appiah's terms the narrator's victory in her storytelling is to reach the viewpoint where her characters are not so tightly scripted by what kind of "colored" people they are as disclosed through their relationship to jazz. For instance, the character of Dorcas is represented in terms of a variety of "scripts"—the light-skinned seductress, the wayward teenager, the disobedient daughter, the "jazzy" one. But at the end, it is revealed that she like everyone else in the narrative exceeds the identifications others use to name her. We learn that she in effect let herself bleed to death the night of the shooting for reasons that are never clear. Dorcas, who seemed barely more than a plot device, turns out to have been unfathomable. The narrator manages to unbind her characters from the networks in which racial stereotypes are constituted and suggest what it means to individuate them.

That the musical form jazz is itself both subject to imposed identifications and constantly exceeding them is the deep background against which the novel works. This background is that jazz is black in two senses: first, as a cultural form created by African American people; and second, as associated with African American culture it has been blackened, becoming a metonymic reminder of a whole series of fears and fantasies to the dominant culture. Anyone who hears the music is going to be engaging with their own identifications or disidentifications with the complex meaning and unconscious fantasy with which jazz has been loaded. White readers, African American readers, Latina readers are fated to this process if they are to read the novel. Since the narrator is engaged in those disavowals and identifications, the reader is obligated to engage explicitly with them as well.

The secret is that no one knows in advance what it means to be released from the identifications that lock us into telling prescribed stories of the sexually voracious teenager, the shooting husband, and the knifing woman, particularly when all readers will know in advance that the characters are all identified as black and scripted by a black woman writer. Novel-reading, Morrison's tale reminds us, is a practice closely bound to identification through character; *Jazz* pushes its reader to acknowledge those identifications that bind character to reader with the aim of both releasing the grip of that process and encouraging a recognition of the process itself as it does so.

This is hardly a novel that engages in what have come to be called "identity politics." The narrator does not come simply to attribute positive value to jazz and blackness. There is no simple inversion of Alice Manfred's early terror of jazz music where "just hearing it was like violating the law." The point is not to whitewash black women with knives or to tame jazz. The ethical injunction of *Jazz*, if it can and should be read that way, is the one we as readers share with the narrator. We are called to confront our own racialized identifications in part as an engagement with the response to jazz as black music. But we can only begin to undertake an ethics of identification, which is what the narrator undertakes, if we start with the recognition that jazz is black and that the narrator was at least right about one thing when she spoke through the voice of Alice Manfred: this is a music meant to be taken seriously.

As Morrison has explained again and again, fidelity to black cultural difference drives her work. But this fidelity to cultural difference in turn takes cultural difference in the sense elaborated by Homi Bhabha: "The very possibility of cultural contestation, the ability to shift the ground of knowledges or to engage in the 'war of position' marks the establishment of new forms of meaning, and strategies of identification. Designations of cultural difference interpolate forms of identity which, because of their continual implication in other symbolic systems are always incomplete or open to cultural translation."[19] What it means for jazz to be received culturally as black, the very complexity of that meaning, is what allows Morrison to represent black cultural difference as distinct from the scary forms that her narrator initially gives it, forms that have already reflected its shaping by white authority. When Appiah asserts that there is no African American culture, he is returning us to his ideal of culture as cultivation, as a quasi-Arnoldian repository of "the best that has been known and thought." Morrison is using a broader concept of 'culture,' which makes central the ethics and politics necessarily involved in the development and perpetuation of a cultural identity. Rather than a just mode of acculturation or an array of objects and texts that acculturate subjects in their consumption, for Morrison 'culture' signifies the day-to-day practices of people living among each other in specific communities and institutions and how these practices are experienced.

We will recall that Anthony Appiah has insisted that culture is "not the problem and not the solution" to racism in contemporary U.S. life. But under this broader definition of culture, the elaboration of culture difference and the new strategies and positions it makes possible for identification can be understood as part of both the problem and the solution to racism in two senses. First, racism proceeds in part through the devaluation of the culture of those who are racialized. Jazz itself in some of its initial reception by white listeners showed how racial fantasies loaded down the meaning that was given to that music.[20] In *Playing in the Dark* Morrison describes exposure to the music of Louis Armstrong as the event that drives the autobiographical heroine of Marie Cardinal's novel *Words to Say It* into therapy. Morrison queries: "Would an Edith Piaf concert or a Dvorak composition have had the same effect? Certainly either could have. I was interested, as I had been for a long time, in the way black people ignite critical moments of discovery or change or emphasis in literature not written by them" (Morrison, *Playing in the Dark*, viii). Morrison is clearly addressing the need to render blackness and the actual art of African Americans visible in its conscious engagement and structural involvement with American literature. This insistence on representation is itself a demand for antiracist correctives. The first antiracist corrective consists of what Morrison describes as the "contemplation of this black presence which is central to any understanding of our national literature," which "should not be permitted to hover at the margins of the literary imagination."[21] The second corrective is the development of a theory of literature, and pedagogical approaches coherent with it, for school curricula that would truly value African American literature in its cultural difference. Such a theory would grapple with African American literature "based on its culture, its history, and the artistic means the works employ to negotiate the world it inhabits."[22]

Of course, the advocacy of this program of basic antiracist correctives turns on a central disagreement with Appiah. Morrison not only believes that there is an African American culture; she explicitly identifies her work as part of it. What does it mean for Morrison to identify herself as a black writer? By analyzing the opening lines of several of her novels Morrison seeks to demonstrate what constitutes the art of a black writer: "The points I have tried to illustrate are that my choices of language (speakerly, aural, colloquial), my reliance for full comprehension on codes embedded in black culture, my effort to effect immediate coconspiracy and intimacy (without any distancing, explanatory framework) as well as my (failed) attempt to shape a silence while breaking it are attempts (many unsatisfactory) to transfigure the complexity and wealth of Afro-American culture into a language worthy of that culture" (Morrison, "Unspeakable Things Unspoken," 150). For Morrison, African American culture is inseparable from her own engagement with it. The meaning of a people's culture is constantly being reworked by those who engage it—listen to jazz—and by those artists who identify with it and represent it as what makes up the constitutive basis of their art.

But culture and identity also are connected in another way. Culture is presented not only as artifacts but as the presentation of personae. In *Jazz*, this reidentification with the black feminine persona represented by Wild opens up a different script for the characters because it opens up the narrator to a different story. The articulation and representation of cultural personae both in art and in life are some of the ways we open up possibilities that allow us to free ourselves from the tight scripts we associate with devaluation of ways of being for the human beings that are identified both by themselves and others as belonging to racialized and marginalized groups. Appiah believes that in order to free oneself from too tightly scripted identities one must proceed through the disassociation of identity and culture. We would argue that it is only through the representation of culturally available personae which through this reformulation then shift their meaning, that we struggle toward freedom.

In Morrison's work, the ethics involved in identification is classic in at least two senses: first, how one comes to know oneself is part of a normative quest for self-knowledge; and second, how one can and should identify with that which the dominant culture has abjected is part of the struggle to end the social structures of oppression that mark us all in a thoroughly racialized society. This ethics is not reducible to mourning the loss of either a full individual or group identity, although it must begin there. For both Joe and Violet Trace come to understand their attachment to each other differently by coming to terms with lost love objects and the fantasies of those objects, indeed fantasies of loss itself. This is indeed an ethics, both as a practice of self-responsibility and as an encounter with how we come to articulate who we are through our identifications which take us beyond ourselves as individuals precisely because we can never be completely in control of the social and symbolic meanings of racial and ethnic categories.

Therefore, there is a sense in which we can be called to identify, as we both feel called to do, as white and Anglo because these categories continue not only to represent privilege but to enforce it. To deny that we are part of the privileged group, then, is not only false; it is, more importantly to us, unethical. The fluidity of categories of race and ethnic identity in no way takes away from the social reality that ethically demands that we confront the meanings of our own identifications. To identify as white and Anglo is a "salutary estrangement,"[23] an effort to see how we are seen and the privileges that inhere in being recognized as part of the dominant race, ethnic, and language group. This is not a so-called politically correct gesture toward guilt, but rather an effort to struggle against the rationalizations that are inherent in the denial that privilege brings with it. No one is above race, ethnicity, and linguistic background. No one is simply human.

To argue that you can reshape an identity and that none of us is entirely captured by our identifications indicates the freedom that we have associated with the work of cultural politics—but it does not mean that we are free to be anything we want to be because these categories take on symbolic lives of their own with material consequences. Certain identifications clearly mark out a group that is devalued. Discrimination is a reality and, indeed, had the effect of fixing racial and ethnic categories. Racialization and socially enforced grouping of individuals into an identity are inseparable, as Appiah continually reminds us. The fight against racism and discrimination cannot proceed by denial of categories that have made race so determinative of a person's fate. For some identifications, their meaning is politically and ethically capable of rearticulation. For others, as in the case of whiteness, for example, which paradoxically presents itself so as to erase its particularity, the move is not simply towards rerepresenting whiteness and European heritage, but by particularizing it. By making whiteness appear as an identification, whiteness not only becomes visible, it becomes separable from the idea of humanity that it has come to stand in for in Eurocentrism.

Disavowal that we are all shaped by our identifications has led to the assumption that we are free to choose between identity politics or some other form of politics that resists the appeal to identity. For us, the ethics of identification demands that the person recognize both the political and the ethical significance of the ways in which she articulates her identity as well as the socially enforced meanings that create it. If, for instance, we simply said that being white and Anglo had no meaning to us, we would be denying the hierarchies that inform our social and political world. What is not noted cannot be changed; thus by recognizing that like it or not we are white and Anglo because we are inevitably shaped by how we are seen, we are ethically respecting the need to call attention to the hierarchies as a first step in calling for their change.

The political contest over the meaning of identifications, including how ethnicities and national identities can be reformed so as to respect the differences among the members who take on that identity as their own, takes place within a specific context of both imperialism and racism. This is why, for us, it is more appropriate to think in terms of a struggle over the meanings of identifications rather than in terms of playful relations to our self-representations. To describe oneself as white and Anglo is an ethical and political decision but one that is necessary precisely because of the inegalitarian structures of a racist society. In this sense, we are not in any way advocating that the political insistence upon such identification either reduces us to it, as a descriptive matter, or captures either one of us in all our complexity. Our point is that our freedom to reform our identifications takes place within parameters that we must also be ethically called upon to recognize as we try to articulate who we are.

TWO REPRESENTATIONS OF CULTURAL IDENTITY

When blacks discovered that they had shaped or become a culturally formed race, and that it had specific and revered difference, suddenly they were told there is no such thing as race, biological or cultural, that matters and that genuinely intellectual exchange cannot accommodate it. In trying to understand the relationship between race and culture, I am tempted to throw my hands up. It always seemed to me that the people who invented the hierarchy of 'race' when it was convenient for them ought not to be the ones to explain it away, now that it does not suit their purposes. But there is culture and both gender and race inform and are informed by it. Afro-American culture exists, and though it is clear (and becoming clearer) how it has responded to Western culture, the instances where and means by which it has shaped Western culture are poorly recognized or understood.[24]

Morrison's wry comment draws attention to the limits of current models of thinking about race, culture, and identity. We have suggested that those models are represented on the one hand through the cosmopolitanism argued for by Anthony Appiah and on the other through the mournful accession to multiculturalism discussed by Nathan Glazer. In the current landscape, we find either an injunction to postmodern, postnational identities or a conception of identity that insists upon a rigidly referential relation between individual and cultural. In both cases, the complexity of identifications as they take form and shift in the histories of individuals and cultures is foreclosed. As a musical form, jazz is an apt trope, a beginning point for a rethinking of the relations between culture and identity, since its codes of improvisation—the rhythms and structures of ancient African musics—constantly rework the relations of individual to group and group to cultural legacies.

But if we do rethink it this way, what we come to is not a proclamation on what identities are or should be. Instead, we come to questions about the conditions under which identifications can be developed, constituted, and represented. The language of recognition that has shaped so much of current debate has much to offer in this regard, due to Charles Taylor's rightly influential article. However, we would want to shift the object of that recognition from legitimation of the value of pregiven cultural identities to identities that demand equal dignity on the part of cultural minorities. When the demand is made as a matter of right, we would argue that we should usually turn to the equal dignity of persons, but that does not mean that such a demand should not include group differentiation rights when that is the best articulation of the right at stake.[25] What is at stake here is the acceptance of what Taylor calls "deep diversity," a diversity that will inevitably result if we publicly recognize the freedom of minorities to reconstitute themselves, including to reconstitute the significance of their cultural difference.

Taylor himself seems to favor this emphasis on dignity, although he gives it a particular meaning. For him, equal dignity turns on the potential to shape an identity. Recall that Taylor can be legitimately read as if the struggle for recognition is in effect a struggle for the expression of authentic identity.[26] While Taylor does sometimes write in that language, since for him the injury to human beings is at least related to the authenticity of group identity being undermined by the degradation imposed upon the minority group by the majority culture or group, his central argument need not be connected to any idea of an underlying authentic identity that minority groups are seeking to have recognized. This is because he ultimately rests his argument on an appeal to our shared dignity as persons, understood to be free in a particular way, rather than on an appeal to the recognition of an authentic identity.

For Taylor, and in this we agree with him, this Kantian-inspired idea of dignity turns us back to a potential that human beings have to shape and form an identity. So far in this chapter, we have tried to articulate the complexity of what this freedom might mean as it allows us to shape an ethics of identification in our thoroughly racialized culture. It is not simply the capacity to form an identity that is the basis of our dignity, but our capacity to make ethical sense out of these identities. We would even dare to interpret Frantz Fanon's humanism as a highly specific appeal to dignity. The dignity of the colonized is rooted in the recollective imagination that allows for a people to shape themselves into a movement through which the struggle for a freedom can be articulated. The truth of an identity is found not by testing the authenticity of its claim to existence but by participating in the ethics and politics it makes possible.[27] As Fanon puts it, "universality resides in this decision to recognize and accept the reciprocal relativism of different cultures, once the colonial status is irreversibly excluded" (*Toward the African Revolution: Political Essays*, 44). Universality turns, then, on the recognition of the equal dignity that includes the colonized as part of humanity with "culture." The animalization of the colonized is inseparable, as Fanon constantly reminds us, from the presumption that the colonized are without culture, which is why they purportedly need to be cultivated by the so-called "civilized" white man. This presumption, of course, can only be made true by the violent shattering of the people's culture. For the colonizer, as Fanon states, "The enslavement, in the strictest sense, of the native population is the prime necessity. For this its systems of reference have to be broken. Expropriation, spoilation, raids, objective murder, are matched by the sacking of cultural patterns, are at least a condition of such sacking. The social panorama is destructured; values are flaunted, crushed, emptied" (*Toward the African Revolution: Political Essays*, 33). It is not then, as Appiah would have, that culture is a cure for racism. The point is somewhat more complex than that. Crucial to the brutal oppression of the colonized is the attempt to crush their culture as part of excluding them from the reach of humanity. Its affirmation, then, is part of the resistance against this exclusion. "Reciprocal relativism of different cultures" is impossible without some version of cultural assertion, because it is part of the insistence on equal dignity, an insistence that rejects the universalization of European culture as "culture."

If we are to recognize the equal dignity of persons to shape their identifications into an identity they claim as their own, then we cannot seek to take back with one hand what we give with the other. We cannot with any moral consistency ask that those who identify with a minority group value their identifications so as to be consistent with certain goals or visions of the larger hegemonic society; whether such consistency is articulated as postmodern cosmopolitanism or as a form of identity politics, it ultimately reproduces ethnic and cultural identities as instrumentalized, deployable to meet a wider notion of the good.

The cultural critic Stuart Hall illustrates this point when he discusses the ways in which some black artists in England have defined their project as one of cultural discovery rather than the articulation of a fully developed political positionality. He acknowledges that there have been at least two broadly understood moments in this process, one addressing the politics of representation and another the relations of representation. The first, he explains, defines "cultural identity" in terms of the idea of

> one shared culture, a sort of collective, one true self hiding inside the many other, more superficial or artificially imposed selves which people with a shared history and ancestry hold in common. Within the terms of this definition, our cultural identities reflect the common historical experiences and shared cultural codes which provide us as one people with stable unchanging and continuous frames of reference and meaning beneath the shifting divisions and vicissitudes of our actual history. This oneness underlying all the other, more superficial differences is the truth, the essence of Caribbeanness.[28]

This understanding of cultural identity is one form of recollective imagination that allows people to emerge and claim their shared reformed history. Such a commitment to articulate what might be shared by marginalized and oppressed groups is often an important part of the struggle for cultural identification and the movements that are formed through them. Crucially, the artists in Hall's example address themselves to their communities. Bringing what Hall here calls "the oneness . . . the essence of Caribbeanness" to representation is in part an act of displacing representations of Caribbean people and culture made and circulated in the dominant culture; works that pit themselves against stereotypes and imposed invisibility are not directed, at least primarily, at the dominant culture, since it is precisely the dominant culture's conscription or occultation of the minority culture that this art seeks to fight. Indeed, one misunderstanding of the claims made by minority cultures for their representation is that they are literalized. One aspect of this literalization is the failure to understand the specific use of literary language to evoke the meaning of identity. As Benita Parry has convincingly argued, the literalization of movements, including that of *négritude*, stems from the failure to grapple with it as in part a literary practice, explicitly influenced by surrealism. In many of his poems, Césaire celebrates the defiance involved in his recollection of himself as a *nègre*, a recollection of himself which is clearly also an act of the imagination. To quote Parry:

> This concrete coming to consciousness was realized by Césaire as a poet; and because many of the writings of Négritude are open to some or all of the charges made against it as an ideological tendency, any argument that as a literary practice it performed a textual struggle for self-representation in which the indeterminacy of language ruptured fixed configurations, invented a multivalent blackness, and wrenched "Africa" out of its time-bound naming and into new significations, is most readily made by referring to his over-determined and polysemic poetry. Although made possible, as he concedes, by surrealism, this exceeded the influence of European modes and violated its forms in what Arnold calls a "sophisticated hybridization, corrosion and parody" of western traditions.[29]

What minority cultures must do to represent themselves against such conscription and occultation depends a good deal on the circumstances in which a given cultural group finds itself. For example, Hall points out that *négritude* was a vital political movement for its time and place. Thus, although Hall clearly advocates what he terms "new ethnicities"[30] as a means of representing cultural identity, his insistence on qualifying that advocacy with a discussion of "essentialist" representation demonstrates his ethical caution. Respect must drive the demand for representational space. Otherwise, recognition can only too easily slide into the "benevolent" tolerance that effectively objectifies the native's culture. This kind of "recognition," as Fanon reminds us, does not take into account the values that are actually borne by the people who bring it to life. The "I know them" or "Look at the wonderful artifacts they have produced" stiffens the colonized into the living dead. It also freezes the one who claims this knowledge into a set of rigidified identifications inseparable from racism. As Toni Morrison aptly remarks, "I hate ideological whiteness. I hate it when people come into my presence and become white, either aggressively white or passively so, using this little code saying, 'I like black people' or 'I know one.' It is humiliating for me and should be for them."[31] The antidote to ideological whiteness is the recognition of the equal dignity, the universality of reciprocal relativism of cultures that Fanon calls for.

This ethical demand can begin to show us a different way of thinking about a problem noted by Taylor, who observes that "the demand for equal recognition extends beyond an acknowledgment of the equal value of all humans potentially and comes to include the equal value of what they have made of that potential."[32] If equal dignity means that people are to be recognized as against the state as the source of the meaning of their own identifications, then the ways in which these identifications are worked out in the course of struggle must be respected. We should recognize that this respect for our equal dignity as persons who inevitably represent themselves through their identifications either consciously or unconsciously is crucial to us all. This must inform how we treat cultural difference, including difference within any particular cultural identity. To argue for equal dignity does not mean cultural and social identities are in some sense "out there," as if there were persons separate from identities; it is because such separation is unthinkable that the recognition of the equal dignity of each one of us is crucial.

Thus, the claim for equal dignity need not rely on an individualistic anthropology. We accept Hegel's analysis that human beings are always constituted by the institutional and social relationships that bring them into existence and frame their reality. Freedom for us is always relational freedom. But it is just because freedom is relational that we need respect for our ability to shape our identifications. As Hall points out in his discussion of *négritude*, the claim for pride in oneself as a black man or woman is exactly what dignity sometimes demands.

However, exactly what dignity demands in different contexts cannot be theoretically determined in advance, since it is linked with the recognition of our freedom to shape an identity and to make ethical sense of them. Our equal worth as persons cannot be reduced to a pregiven value horizon, particularly in the sense of what our identifications are to mean for us, because such a reduction would deny that we, as against the state, should be recognized as the source of the value of our identity. It should be clear that this is a normative judgment about how human beings should be treated; it does not claim that human beings are in truth the only source of the value they give to their identities. Obviously our evaluations are deeply influenced by our social worlds of institutional structures and culturally hegemonic viewpoints and evaluations that stamp out how identifications are supposed to work. Hegel recognized that it is precisely the fragility of the freedom of social selves that makes legal and political recognition of freedom so crucial; we agree with Hegel. But we can say that the value of our identifications, including those bearing on our cultural identities, must be left to us since to impose some preestablished value on any particular identity would take away from some their right to represent who they are.[33] This is why we cannot advocate a version of postmodern identity in the interests of a presumed greater good that this construction of identity would produce. In contrast to a model of postmodern identity, Hall's conception of 'new ethnicities' implicitly recognizes the importance of the respect for dignity within the constitution of new ethnic identities and the inevitable contests over representations of identity that come with such recognition.

Underwriting what Hall understands as the new ethnicities approach is a recognition that even the most vital of representations of the "true" Caribbean identity are to some extent necessarily constructions, rememorations of identities that have disappeared in the sandstorms of the history of imperialism. While Appiah, as we have seen, is concerned that assertions of cultural identity necessarily tie people to the past and limit their capacity to develop new identifications, Hall's analysis of "new ethnicities" makes clear that just such assertions of cultural identity can be understood as the refusal of such limitations. Hall writes, "It seems to me that the various practices and discourses of black cultural production we are beginning to see are constructions of just such a new conception of ethnicity; a new cultural politics which engages rather than suppresses difference and which depends in part on the cultural construction of new ethnic identities."[34]

As Hall points out, the very concept of ethnicity is one that will require considerable redefinition, bound up as it has been with conceptions of nationalism, imperialism and racism. British "ethnicity," or national identity, found its moorings in nineteenth-century discourse precisely through the writing of empire; what was English was defined over and against what was French, German, or "uncivilized," belonging to the geographies of imperialist domination. Yet Hall is optimistic: "I think such a project is not only possible; indeed, this decoupling of ethnicity from the violence of the state is implicit in some of the new forms of cultural practice. . . . We are beginning to think about how to represent a noncoercive and more diverse conception of ethnicity, to set against the embattled hegemonic conception of 'Englishness' which under Thatcherism stabilize[d] so much of the dominant political and cultural discourses, and which because it is hegemonic does not represent itself as ethnicity at all."[35] Hall, like Fanon, sees that the true trauma of the experience of colonization was that it was never just a matter of the simple imposition of Western European modes of governmentality; there is therefore no return to a grounded authentic identity, no simple sense of belonging available. Thus Hall insists that "cultural identity . . . is a matter of becoming as well as of being. It belongs to the future as much as to the past. . . . Far from being eternally fixed in some essential past, [it] is subject to the continuous play of history, culture, and power. Far from being grounded in mere recovery of the past, which is waiting to be found and will secure our sense of our selves in eternity, identities are the names we give to the different ways we are positioned by, and position ourselves within the narratives of the past."[36]

The recuperation and constitution of what Hall calls "new ethnicities" then can be understood best as an on-going practice that, while future-oriented, is nevertheless constantly engaged in the working-through of the past. The temporality of this process is exactly why we have named it recollective imagination.

AESTHETIC VALUE AND FAIR JUDGMENT

When we turn our attention to new forms of cultural production that participate in the constitution and representation of such ethnicities, here is where we often see the much-vaunted crises over the "canon" and criteria of aesthetic judgment flare. Both U.S. and British culture have seen such crises in this decade; the examples are numerous. But Hall provides us with one, recalling his debate over aesthetic value and recent films with novelist Salman Rushdie. For Hall, the stakes of the debate bore more on the categories of analysis and judgment Rushdie deployed than on the particularities of the novelist's judgment. "[Rushdie] seemed to me to be addressing [the films] as if from the stable, well-established criteria of a *Guardian* reviewer," Hall explains. The position of upholding hegemonic standards, Hall points out, is not only inadequate as a basis for political criticism; it necessarily "overlooks precisely the signs of innovation and the constraints under which the filmmakers were operating." To refuse to resolve questions of aesthetic value by the use of "canonical cultural categories," Hall notes, is surely not the same as commending the films in question simply because their directors and writers are black. "I think," he writes, "that there is another position, one which locates itself inside a continuous struggle and politics around black representation, but which then is able to open up continuous critical discourse about . . . the forms of representation, the subjects of representation, above all the regimes of representation."[37] While Hall's example is drawn from a debate around film, where issues of access to technologies and distribution render the question of regimes of representation particularly prominent, we think that the larger implications for aesthetic judgment and standards go to other forms of cultural production as well.

What does and can "fair judgment" mean? Charles Taylor has advocated that we adopt a minimalist aesthetic rationality that would begin with two presuppositions. First, all human cultures should be considered to be of value, including of value to the humanity beyond the reach of that culture. The second presupposition is that it is possible for us to achieve what Taylor terms a "fusion of horizons"[38] of cultures and standards of judgment which would affect the way cultures conceive of themselves, their standards and the standards of others. This fusion of horizons would create new forms of judgment. But the very idea of a fusion still implies a more static idea of culture than the one that we believe is necessary. What Hall is calling for is not just a fusion of horizons between British and black cultures.

We want to make an addition to Taylor's call for a minimalist rationality. We are not arguing that a fusion of horizons is inconsistent with or inappropriate to the reform of critical judgment. In fact, we agree with his first presupposition as crucial to the development of fair standards of aesthetic judgment, particularly as they are to be addressed to emerging cultural identities, and consistent with Fanon's understanding of universality once the colonized status is excluded. What need to be added are standards of critical reflection on the regimes of aesthetic judgment themselves. The existence of cultural artifacts, for example, must be reflected upon within the history of imperialism which has provided the cultures of the North with so many of the metaphors through which we have come to understand what constitutes culture.

The ascription of equal value does not undermine entrenched systems of judgment. Simply saying that all cultures are "equal" both homogenizes cultures and in a sense, elides the issue since we are able to proceed as if we did not have to use standards of judgment when we reflected on the conditions under which cultural objects are created and circulated. Still, since human beings are of culture there must be some way to tie together the recognition of equal dignity of persons with fair standards of evaluation of cultures. It is this tie that we understand Taylor's two presuppositions to be making, without collapsing the recognition of our equal worth into a preconceived judgment that all cultures are in fact equal. The whole point is that such a comparison inevitably demands the articulation of standards by which cultures are to be judged and thus compared.

However, the presumption of equal worth due to the demands of equal dignity does not mean that we actually say that culture X is equal to culture Y; it is instead the critical force which has to be pursued in the name of fairness in education. This is not a simple antiracist corrective but a serious engagement and rearticulation with the way in which judgments are made about who we are as creatures who inevitably develop out of cultures and the systematic inequalities that have been imposed on us by racism and imperialism. A crucial aspect of a multiculturalist program then must proceed at this level of abstraction. Multiculturalism insists upon the rethinking of our standards of judgment as well as the engagement with and introduction of students to the many cultures that make up our contemporary societies.

For example, in a multicultural curriculum designed to meet what we mean by fairness students should be exposed not only to different languages but to the history of those languages within our country. Take Spanish to illustrate our point: the United States has the fifth-biggest Spanish-speaking population in the world, so there are obviously practical reasons why US students should study the Spanish language. But the Spanish language itself and its suppression are also an irrevocable part of U.S. cultural and political history. As we all know, large portions of the south-western United States were originally Mexican territory.[39]

There is one sense in which this kind of multiculturalism is the practice of critical education crucial to what Appiah sees as the modern liberal society.

But it is not identical with what he calls "liberal multiculturalism," because it insists on the right to representational space in which minority cultures are shaped and re-formed by the members of a given community. That is why there is a democratic moment in multiculturalism. Maybe with this notion of the right to representational space, we can begin discerning a new relation between the political and the aesthetic in the sense that struggles to articulate and represent new cultural identities can be understood neither as subjected to the transcendent categories of aesthetics that have most often informed aesthetic judgments over the last two hundred years, nor simply as the effects of a politics drained of the explicit recognition of its own aesthetic dimension. This is what we interpret Hall to mean when he insists there must be "another position" on the judgment of cultural productions: it is impossible to comprehend the cultural works that he refers to outside the framework of struggle. There is no detached position for the traditional aesthetic observer.[40] These practices and discourses cannot continue and fulfill their objectives if they do not remain open to a constant metacommentary and critique on their status as representations. Thus, the inextricability of the struggle for new identities with the conditions under which those identities are represented implies an ethics of identification. And this then demands that the way we see the world and judge it be inseparable from how we judge both who we are and where we stand.

NOTES

1. Charles Taylor, "The Politics of Recognition," in Amy Gutmann, ed., *Multiculturalism* (Princeton, NJ: Princeton University Press, 1994).

2. "Je veux montrer à mes semblables un homme dans toute la vérité de sa nature; et cet homme ce sera moi. . . . Moi seul. Je sens mon coeur et je connais les hommes. Je ne suis fait comme aucun de ceux que j'ai vus; j'ose croire n'être fait comme aucun de ceux qui éxistent. Si je ne vaux mieux, au moins je suis autre. Si la nature a bien ou mal fait de briser le moule dans lequel elle m'a jeté, c'est ce dont on ne peut juger qu'après m'avoir lu." Jean-Jacques Rousseau, *Les Confessions*, vol.1 (Paris: Ganier Flammarcòn, 1967), 43.

3. See Georg W. F. Hegel, *Phenomenology of Mind*, trans. J. Baillie (New York: Macmillan, 1931). For a critique of Hegel's *Philosophy of History* for his uncritical acceptance of the colonial imaginary, see Enrique Ducell, "Eurocentrism and Modernity," in *The Post-Modern Debate in Latin America*, ed. John Beverley, Jose Oviedo, and Michael Aronna (Durham: Duke University Press, 1995).

4. Gayatri Chakravorty Spivak, *The Post-Colonial Critic: Interviews, Strategies, Dialogues*, ed. Sarah Harasym (New York: Routledge, 1990), 59–60.

5. Frantz Fanon, "Racism and Culture," in *Toward the African Revolution: Political Essays*, trans. Haakon Chevalier (New York: Grove, 1967), 34.

6. See Ella Shohat and Robert Stam's discussion on the political significance of confounding the colonizer to unreadability in *Unthinking Eurocentrism: Multiculturalism and the Media* (New York: Routledge, 1994), 44.

7. Immanuel Kant, *Groundwork of the Metaphysic of Morals,* trans. H. J. Paton (New York: Harper and Row, 1958), 118–20.

8. We put this word in quotation marks not to be precious but to remark that its sense is not only what is at stake in Glazer's and other recent discussions of cultural identity in North America. The appropriation of the word by citizens of the United States as if it could belong only to them has been challenged fiercely by those who live in South and Latin America, for example.

9. K. Anthony Appiah, "The Multiculturalist Misunderstanding," *The New York Review of Books* 44, no. 15 (October 9, 1997): 30–36.

10. See Drucilla Cornell, *Transformations: Recollective Imagination and Sexual Difference* (New York: Routledge, 1993).

11. Although there is much support in the literature for Appiah's conclusion about "Hispanics," there is also a countertrend. Latinos and Latinas are seeking to maintain the Spanish language through the generations. It should also be noted here that one aspect of this is the use of the terms *Latino* and *Latina* in the place of *Hispanic* in order to signify and affirm the political and ethical aspiration to maintain a cultural identity that includes an affirmation of identification with the Spanish language, while at the same time maintaining a historically blurred distinction between the cultures of the Americas and that of the Iberian peninsula. There are other factors that also seem to be influencing a trend counter to that which Appiah rightfully notes has been true of most groups of Latinos and Latinas. Many Cubans have defined themselves as exiles with the historic mission of returning to Cuba; therefore, they have worked to keep their children bilingual, succeeding in keeping the language alive into the third generation. Other factors influencing the tendency to break with the immigrant pattern of loss of the mother tongue by the third generation are the rise of the South American community and the establishment of nation-states in the Americas which seek to break from the economic dominance of the United States. More immigrants are returning to their homelands as a result or are anticipating it as an eventuality. Some, following recent examples of Mexican Americans, retain dual citizenship where possible. For a detailed discussion of the pattern of Latino/Latina assimilation, see William Bratton and Drucilla Cornell, "Deadweight Costs and the Intrinsic Wrongs of Nativism: Freedom and the Legal Suppression of Spanish," *Cornell Law Review* 84, (no. 3 1999), and Drucilla Cornell, *Just Cause: Freedom, Identity and Rights* (Boston and Lanham, MD: Rowman and Littlefield, 2000). The point that we would like to stress is that economic and political factors shape the ways in which ethnic groups constitute their identifications.

12. Appiah, "The Multiculturalist Misunderstanding," 34.

13. We borrow the term *pervasive culture* from Avishai Margalit and Joseph Raz: "The group has a common character and common culture that encompasses many and varied aspects of life, a culture that defines or marks a variety of forms or styles of life, types of activity, occupations, pursuits and relationships. With national groups we expect to find national cuisines, distinctive architectural styles, a common language, a distinctive literary and artistic tradition, national music, customs and dress, ceremonies, holidays, etc." See "National Self-Determination," in *The Rights of Minority Cultures,* ed. Will Kymlicka (New York: Oxford University Press, 1995), 83. For Margalit and Raz, the existence of a pervasive culture is one of the conditions that should be

met in a case for self-determination. While they are specifically addressing the conditions under which a people can legitimately demand self-determination, we think that their definition describes the kind of ethnic identity Appiah believes to have been either lost or significantly diluted in the United States.

14. Appiah borrows the term *cultural geneticism* from Henry Louis Gates, *Loose Canons* (Oxford and New York: Oxford University Press, 1993). See Appiah, "Race, Culture, Ethnicity: Misunderstood Connections," paper presented to the Program for the Study of Law, Philosophy, and Social Theory, New York University Law School, October 9, 1997.

15. K. Anthony Appiah, "Cosmopolitan Patriots," *Critical Inquiry* 23, no. 3 (Spring 1997): 617–39.

16. Appiah, "The Multiculturalist Misunderstanding," 36.

17. Toni Morrison, *Jazz* (New York and Harmondsworth, Mx: Penguin, 1993), 79. All other references are to this edition and will be inserted in the text.

18. See Appiah, "Race, Culture, and Identity: Misunderstood Connections," esp. 2–24: "We have followed enough of the history of the race concept and said enough about current biological conceptions to answer . . . the question of whether there are any races" (23).

19. Homi Bhabha, *The Location of Culture* (New York: Routledge, 1994), 134.

20. Of course, the story of jazz reception is a notoriously long and complicated one; in fact, the course of the development of many modern musics is unthinkable without it. But as a salient example of the racialized complexity of that reception among musical minds, one can think of Adorno's peculiar position on jazz. See "Perennial Fashion— Jazz" in *Prisms,* trans. Samual and Shierry Weber (Cambridge: MIT Press, 1983), 121–32. See also Juliet Flower McCannell, "Race/War: Race, War, and the Division of Jouissance in Freud and Adorno," *Journal for the Psychoanalysis of Culture and Society* 2, no. 2 (Fall 1997), for an interesting reading of Adorno's trouble with jazz.

21. Toni Morrison, *Playing in the Dark: Whiteness and the Literary Imagination* (Cambridge: Harvard University Press, 1992), 5.

22. Morrison, 'Unspeakable Things Unspoken', in *The Tanner Lectures on Human Values,* Vol. XI (Salt Lake City: University of Utah Press, 1990), p. 134.

23. Shohat and Stam, *Unthinking Eurocentrism,* 359.

24. Morrison, "Unspeakable Things Unspoken," 150.

25. In certain instances, we would even recognize the right of a group to something like linguistic self-defense. Examples are the Quebecois in Canada and Chicanos/as in the southwestern United States. See Bratton and Cornell, "Deadweight Costs and Intrinsic Wrongs."

26. See Appiah's reading of Taylor, "Identity, Authenticity, Survival: Multicultural Societies and Social Reproduction," in Gutmann, ed., *Multiculturalism,* 149–64.

27. See Frantz Fanon, *Black Skin, White Masks* (New York: Grove, 1967). Also see Homi Bhabha's lectures.

28. Stuart Hall, "Cultural Identity and Cinematic Representation," in *Black British Cultural Studies: A Reader* ed. Houston A. Baker Jr., Manthia Diawara, and Ruth H. Lindenborg, (Chicago: University of Chicago Press, 1996), 211.

29. See Benita Parry, "Resistance Theory/Theorizing Resistance," in *Rethinking Fanon: The Continuing Dialogue*, ed. Nigel Gibson (Amherst, NY: Prometheus Books, 1999), 224.

30. Stuart Hall, "New Ethnicities," in *Stuart Hall: Critical Dialogues in Cultural Studies* ed. David Morely and Kuan-Hsing Chen, (New York: Routledge, 1996), 441–49.

31. Acknowledged by Toni Morrison, personal communication, March 1999.

32. Taylor, "The Politics of Recognition," 63–64.

33. Imposition of such preestablished values is also inconsistent with the understanding of the social basis of self-respect as a primary good. See Drucilla Cornell, *The Imaginary Domain* (New York: Routledge, 1995), 10: "It should go without saying that hierarchical gradations of any of us as unworthy of personhood violates the postulation of each one of us as an equal person called for in a democratic and modern legal system."

34. Hall, "New Ethnicities," 443.

35. Ibid., 447. Hall's evocation of the "transparency" effected by the hegemony of British national identity recalls for us Conrad's *Heart of Darkness*, particularly the novella's ambivalent imperialist narrator, Marlow, who famously begins his shipboard story with a glance at the banks of the Thames: "And this, too, has been one of the dark places of the earth."

36. Hall, "New Ethnicities," 448.

37. Ibid.

38. Taylor, "The Politics of Recognition," 66–67.

39. See Bratton and Cornell, "Deadweight Costs," for further discussion of the implications of this on Spanish language rights.

40. Another approach to the problem of the relations of representation and the crisis in traditional conceptions of an aesthetic observer is presented by John Guillory in his excellent *Cultural Capital: The Problem of Literary Canon Formation* (Chicago: University of Chicago Press, 1993). See especially part 3, "Aesthetics," 269–340.

Pheng Cheah

Affordance, or Vulnerable Freedom: A Response to Cornell and Murphy's "Antiracism, Multiculturalism, and the Ethics of Identification"

Imagination is at bottom the relationship with death. The image is death.
—Jacques Derrida, *Of Grammatology*

In the past decade or so, multiculturalism and the politics of minority identity have been issues of heated theoretical-academic debate in the United States, a settler nation founded on chattel slavery and the extermination of native peoples, and other settler nations such as Canada, Australia, and New Zealand that were also founded on the dispossession of aboriginal tribes. Multicultural recognition has also been an urgent topic of public discussion in other formerly imperialist nation-states in the North Atlantic such as France and Germany that are gradually undergoing sociocultural transformation as the result of increasing migration from the so-called Third World. In "Antiracism, Multiculturalism, and the Ethics of Identification," Drucilla Cornell and Sara Murphy have made an important contribution to the U.S. discussion concerning multicultural recognition by cogently raising fundamental philosophical issues about moral dignity and the nature of minority identity.

In sketchy summary, their central argument is that although multiculturalism must be affirmed as a morally necessary perspective and public-institutional ethos, those cultures that are the subjects/objects of ethical recognition ought not to be viewed as pre-given and eternally unchanging authentic identities. Thus, in what I take to be the two most important sentences of their article, Cornell and Murphy write that "our argument replaces 'identity politics,' even if understood as the recognition of the value of existing 'recognizable' cultural minorities. The demand for freedom must be understood as the affordance of the psychic and moral space necessary for groups and individuals to engage with and recreate their multiple identifications".

(175–176 this volume) In these two sentences, Cornell and Murphy not only tangle with Charles Taylor's elaboration of a theory of multicultural recognition and Anthony Appiah's recent critique of the concept of culture, but they also summon up the philosophical legacies of Kant (moral freedom as human dignity) and Hegel (ethical life or *Sittlichkeit* as the broader context or substrate for moral action) in order to revise them via the prism of a psychoanalytical account of identification. In this chapter, I will assess some of the philosophical issues they raise and point to some limits of their intellectual framework by focusing on one word in which all these issues are conveniently braided together: *affordance*.

AUTHENTICITY AND THE ETHICS OF IDENTIFICATION

Cornell and Murphy's critique of the conventional understanding of multiculturalism essentially involves a critique of the theoretical position that human existence, whether we are speaking of it in its totality or in any of its aspects, is of the order of the merely given. Many contemporary affirmations of minority cultures, they suggest, are mistaken because they end up seeing minority cultures in terms of primordial, preformed and pregiven identities. Although Cornell and Murphy concur in the need to hold on to the demand for recognition, they exhort theorists of multicultural recognition to give up the claim to authenticity: "Multiculturalism, we argue, must be understood not simply as the acknowledgment of established and literalized identities, but as fundamental to the recognition of the equal dignity of all peoples" (173). This claim to authenticity, they suggest, has infelicitous effects that stem from the fact that the idea of authenticity contravenes the dignity that coexists with humanity.

In what way is the idea of authenticity inimical to human dignity? To understand the philosophical import of Cornell and Murphy's argument, we need to consider their critique of Charles Taylor. According to their reading of Taylor, "authenticity derives its moral force, whatever that force may be, from the assumption of an already-constituted and stable identity" (174). Such an identity is inimical to human dignity for at least two related reasons: first, as something with the qualities of stance and stability, such an identity would be an eternal essence underlying all its appearances as an existent being. The various manifestations or existences of this essence would therefore be completely determined by it qua underlying substrate, thereby leading to the death of existential freedom.

Second, when the relationship between a collective or minority culture and its individual members is characterized by means of this philosophical schema (as presumably occurs in Taylor's account of multicultural recognition), the collective identity or culture will be regarded as an eternal essence that dictates the behavior of its individual members. The additional danger here is that this collective identity can be reduced to an ideological instrument of the political dominant. Thus, Cornell and Murphy write that "there is considerable risk that recognition will shade into an adjudication of authent icity. . . . [N]ew formations of minority cultures can fall through the cracks. Only the form of the minority acknowledged by the dominant culture—institutionally, socially, politically—will receive official status" (174). Of course, this kind of adjudication of authenticity can serve the oppressive interests both of the majority in society at large and of the majority *within* the minority culture itself. The latter is commonly called "ethno-cultural fundamentalism," and Cornell and Murphy astutely link it to Orientalist museumization and the commodification of the "cultural other."

It should be obvious by now that Cornell and Murphy are playing Kant to Taylor's Hegel. They do not say this explicitly, but what they clearly imply is that Taylor's account of multicultural recognition represents an updating of Hegel's account of the state as ethical substance for contemporary multicultural societies. For Hegel, the state is ethical substance because it is the substrate or medium in which "personal individuality and its particular interests [can] reach their full *development* and gain *recognition of their right* for itself" because "they . . . *pass over* of their own accord into the interest of the universal. . . . and knowingly and willing acknowledge this universal interest even as their own *substantial spirit*, and *actively pursue it* as their *ultimate end*."[1] Cornell and Murphy seem to imply that in his account of multicultural recognition, Taylor reconfigures the Hegelian state qua ethical substance by introducing as an ultimate end the protection of authentic or substantial multicultural identities. Consequently, the state's minority members will find their particular ends fulfilled only by assuming these authentic cultural identities that are susceptible to state monitoring. For Cornell and Murphy, this constitutes a violation of human dignity in the Kantian sense because it fails to respect the sacrosanct ability of human beings as ends-in-themselves to set their own ends: "[A]t the core of our argument . . . is the insistence that all of us must have the potential to shape our identifications recognized by the state such that we—and not the state—are the source of the meaning they have to us, as individuals and as members of groups" (176).

On the other hand, however, in their critique of Anthony Appiah's dismissal of cultural identity, Cornell and Murphy play Hegel to Appiah's liberal interpretation of Kant. Here, they argue that culture is an irreducible part of one's identity as a relationally and socially constituted being, and as a result, cultural identity is crucial to the liberal project of self-cultivation. Unless the importance of cultural identity is acknowledged, they fear that Appiah's concern with the freedom of the individual can lead to the justification of the devaluation of minority cultures.

Cornell and Murphy attempt to reconcile the Kantian and Hegelian strands of their position by resorting to the psychoanalytical concept of 'identification.' They suggest that if we recognize that a sociopolitically imposed cultural identity is a process of identification rather than an authentic and unchanging essence that governs my every action as an existent, then we can affirm that cultural identity and also transform its oppressive meanings by recognizing that we ourselves can be the source of our identifications: "[W]e accept Hegel's analysis that human beings are always constituted by the institutional and social relationships that bring them into existence and frame their reality. Freedom for us is always relational freedom. But it is just because freedom is relational that we need respect for our ability to shape our identifications" (193). This ethics of identification, they suggest informs Toni Morrison's novel *Jazz* and also the anticolonialist humanism of Frantz Fanon.

AFFORDANCE AND IMAGINATION

Because multiculturalism is an urgent ethical and political matter, we often assess any contribution to the topic in terms of its political efficacy or ethical good sense. The political or ethical usefulness of Cornell and Murphy's contribution to the multiculturalism debate is not in question here. But since Cornell and Murphy's argument is primarily a philosophical argument rather than a social policy statement, the issue at stake should be phrased more precisely. If we say that the recognition of authentic cultural identity is "bad" because it violates human dignity, then we have to ask, What is the nature of humanity in its "as such" that it possesses this thing called "dignity" that should not be violated? Or to put this in more positive terms, What gives minority subjects the ability to resist and escape the straightjacket of an imposed authentic cultural identity so that they can claim that this ability is a rightful ability, one that should be recognized and upheld by the contemporary multicultural state because it is theirs by right because to fail to recognize this right would go against the very nature of being human? In other words, What are the ontological presuppositions of their critique of authenticity and the ethics of identification they propose in its place? I want to suggest that we can see some limits of Cornell and Murphy's ethics of identification by examining its ontological basis.

Essentially, Cornell and Murphy's criticism of the notion of authentic minority identity is based on the idea that humanity is in its degree of being or ontological constitution that which exceeds, goes beyond, and transcends the givenness of natural existence. Their argument is, simply put, a critique of the given nature of authenticity. They seek to show that humanity can, to a certain degree, create itself, and in this lies our freedom. Hence, in place of the recognition of authentic identity, they argue that "the demand for freedom must be understood as the *affordance* of the psychic and moral space necessary for groups and individuals to engage with and recreate their multiple identifications" (my emphasis).

Affordance

Cornell's and Murphy's word that seems to be in the middle voice, both active and passive, resonates with the crucial questions of the given and of giving that interests us here. Who or what affords this space of freedom that is ours by right? Who or what gives or can give us our dignity and our freedom so that we can transcend the merely given? The verb *to afford* almost invariably implies modality. It suggests that one is able to afford, that one can do something or is able to spare something, that one is in a position of strength from which one can afford to be generous. Thus, the verb also involves the act of provision, the giving of a gift. For instance, when we say, "This room affords a view of the sea," we are referring to a giving to sight, a giving of access of something to someone, therefore, also a clearing or giving of space between that someone and that something so that it can be accessible.

In their critique of the given, Cornell and Murphy link the act or moment of affordance or giving with the human power of imagination, with a nod to the faculty of *Einbildungskraft* of German idealism. This is why the typecase and primary example of an ethics of identification they adduce comes from literary creation. Contra Taylor, for them the fundamental feature of being human is not the ability to gain self-reflective knowledge of oneself as a preformed core identity but rather the ability to imagine and to recreate oneself through the imagination. Unlike animals, other organic life-forms or inorganic being, a human being is not merely given because its imagination gives it the ability to create and recreate itself throughout its temporal existence. This ability to produce images that deviate from given reality, images that can be used to transform given reality, is what gives to humanity its sense of futurity—the knowledge that it can exceed the present through projection, and also its dignity, the knowledge that it can set its own ends. This is precisely how Cornell and Murphy understand Kant's idea of humanity as the possibility of being otherwise, of deviating from given reality, even if they stress, with a nod to Hegel, that this possibility of being otherwise necessarily occurs within concrete social and political contexts:

> Humanity, indeed, is just one example of the postulation of free creatures with the capacity of shaping their moral destiny. Our argument is that the demand for multiculturalism is the freedom to struggle for a different humanity, for the possibility of living otherwise than through the cultural hierarchies imposed by colonialism. (176)

> [T]his Kantian-inspired idea of dignity turns us back to a potential that human beings have to shape and form an identity . . . it is not simply the capacity to form an identity that is the basis of our dignity, but our capacity to make ethical sense out of these identities. (190)

Through our imagination, we can transcend the given because even if we cannot quite give ourselves out of ourselves, we can at least reframe or remake the conditions through which we are given. In this respect, at least, it can be said that we can assume the source of our own givenness and that we are what we give ourselves.

By making such an argument, Cornell and Murphy are drawing on a rich philosophical theme that links human perfectibility and freedom to the imagination understood as the ability to understand our lives and direct our actions according to the images that we form of ourselves and the external world. This philosopheme of the imagination has a rich history and is, of course, not limited to Kant. In his Second Discourse, for instance, Rousseau suggests that the imagination is what allows human beings to go beyond natural instinct and its immediate satisfaction because it can arouse in us a desire for things that are not available in present existence. "[W]ho fails to see that everything seems to remove from Savage man the temptation as well as the means to cease being savage? His imagination depicts nothing to him; his heart asks nothing of him. . . . His soul, which nothing stirs, yields itself to the sole sentiment of its present existence, with no idea of the future, however near it may be and his projects, as limited as his views, hardly extend to the close of day."[2] The imagination is thus an active principle that breaches the present and gives to us our sense of futurity, thereby allowing us to progress or to develop ourselves beyond the state of nature in a manner otherwise than as dictated by the rule of instinctual impulse.[3] Similarly, Kant writes that "it is a peculiarity of reason that it is able, with the help of the imagination, to invent desires which not only *lack* any corresponding natural impulse, but which are even *at variance* with the latter."[4]

The connection to freedom as the transcendence of the merely given or the realm of natural mechanism lies precisely in this link between the imagination and absence. For the imagination is essentially a capacity for a certain form of independence from present existence insofar as for Kant, it "is the faculty for representing an object even without its presence in intuition."[5] Indeed, Kant goes on to suggest that as opposed to the *reproductive* imagination, which only recalls an empirical intuition that was previously present and therefore is largely passive or receptive, the *productive* imagination, which functions to unite or synthesize the manifold of intuitions into a single sensible form (i.e., a figure or image) for consciousness in general, is transcendental. The productive imagination is characterized by activity and spontaneity because it is the power of representing or exhibiting an object prior to experience.[6] Indeed, this transcendental synthesis of the productive imagination is paradoxically the necessary ground or condition of possibility of any cognition or knowledge of objects since without the a priori image or figure it generates as a mediating term, we cannot match a concept to a set of intuitions.[7] This means that even though the imagination must always rely in the original instance on a sense representation that was given to our sensibility, in its productive capacity, the imagination is not tied to repeating these given intuitions. Indeed, it has to give to these intuitions an a priori form or figure so that we can makes cognitive sense of them. In other words, this transcendental figurative power of the imagination gives us a degree of freedom or determining power over what is given to our senses because it involves an *original shaping or imparting of form* to the manifold of sensible intuition.[8]

This idea of the productive imagination seems to inform Cornell and Murphy's suggestion that cultural identity can be part of the exercise of freedom because it is always assumed through imaginative work and can therefore be reshaped, even though they refer to "recollective imagination": "even more traditionally conceived assumptions of identity, social as well as cultural, always involve the imagination as they rework the meaning of the past. . . . Identities formed through recollective imagination have the potential to be held lightly by the individual because they are already formed through an imaginative effort to envision what they are, how they should remain, or instead be reshaped" (178).

But if our imagination allows us to rework that in ourselves that the historical past gives to us and to determine how we are given in the sociopolitical present, the question of affordance or giving insists itself at a higher level. For who or what gives us this ability to give form to the merely given? In eighteenth- and nineteenth-century philosophy, the question was almost always resolved by resorting either to an onto-theology and/or a teleology of nature, where the imagination is a faculty that an Absolute Being such as God or an inscrutable but purposive nature gives us so that we can be led beyond nature by developing our disposition for perfectibility. Our self-giving would then become a higher order of the given, a second nature. Thus, Kant suggested that "art, when it reaches perfection, once more becomes nature—and this is the ultimate goal of man's moral destiny."[9] In our demagicized world, we can no longer have recourse to such an argument, so the issue of affordance that is at the heart of Cornell and Murphy's chapter remains unresolved.

To reiterate, their cogent critique of the given involves a defense of minority cultural identities as part of the imaginative-formative process by which we can give ourselves from out of ourselves. This ability of self-giving is linked to human dignity, self-determination, and self-creation. Freedom is therefore a space of self-giving that is coextensive with human dignity. Whatever obstructs this process will necessarily have inhuman consequences.

Given their reliance on literature as a paradigmatic case of imaginative work, the question that I have raised about the ontological basis of Cornell and Murphy's critique of the given has something like a relationship to the Davos dispute of March 1929 between Heidegger and Cassirer over the role of imagination in Kant's philosophy. For like Cornell and Murphy, Cassirer had also located human infinity, i.e., human transcendence of the given, in the ability of the imagination to produce ideal or spiritual forms, i.e., the products of art and culture. In response to Heidegger's question, "What path does man have to infinitude?" Cassirer replies:

In no way other than through the medium of form. This is the function of form, that while man changes the form of his Dasein, i.e., while he now must transpose everything in him which is lived experience into some objective shape in which he is objectified in such a way, to be sure, that he does not thereby become radically free from the finitude of the point of departure (for this is still connected to his particular finitude). Rather, while it arises from finitude, it leads finitude out into something new. And that is immanent in-finitude. Man cannot make the leap from his own proper finitude into a re-alistic infinitude. He can and must have, however, the metabasis which leads him from the immediacy of his existence into the region of pure form. And he possesses this infinity solely in this form. . . . The spiritual realm is not a metaphysical spiritual realm; the true spiritual realm is just the spiri-tual world created from himself. That he could create it is the seal of his infinitude.[10]

In his response, Heidegger suggested that the imagination is not grounded in the power to produce forms. As the spontaneous process of transcendental schematism, it is not a power or gift of the soul but is coextensive with the originary finitude of Dasein. In other words, the imagination qua process of giving does not emanate from human consciousness but instead from the irre-ducible temporalization that makes possible (human) existence.

The difference is clearest in the concept of Freedom. I spoke of freeing in the sense that the freeing of the inner transcendence of Dasein is the funda-mental character of philosophizing itself. In so doing, the authentic sense of this freeing is not to be found in becoming free to a certain extent for the forming images of consciousness and for the realm of form. Rather, it is to be found in becoming free for the finitude of Dasein. Just to come into the thrownness of Dasein is to come into the conflict which lies within the es-sence of freedom. *I did not give freedom to myself, although it is through Being-free that I can first be I myself.* (KPM, 181; my emphasis)

What is foregrounded here is precisely freedom as "affordance," not primarily as a capacity we have to generate images and to remake ourselves through these images but a *scene of giving* where "something" is given to us not by some other Absolute Being but because of our original finitude, even if for Hei-degger we achieve a certain freedom in the acknowledgment of this finitude. The important point here is *not* that freedom is illusory and that we are thereby forever condemned to social or political subjugation and domination. My point is that freedom in the ontological sense is much more vulnerable be-cause it is not something we possess that may be given to us by a higher infi-nite being. Freedom is not an inner power that we only need to make real by translating this power into external social reality. It is instead the sheer force of giving that constitutes all possible existence, and, hence, we are affected by "it" in a way that we cannot control.

Indeed, if we return to the philosopheme of the imagination as the power to reshape the ways in which we exist or are given by means of ideal images, then the very ability to reshape our existence in terms of images presupposes our a priori susceptibility to the image in general, that is to say, our a priori susceptibility to an other, to an outside over which we have no control. This is why the imagination has always been linked to death. It is that which gives us an intimation of death. As Rousseau points out in the Second Discourse, the Savage man who imagines nothing does not fear death, "for an animal will never know what it is to die, and the knowledge of death, and of its terrors is one of man's first acquisitions on moving away from the animal condition" (142). But at the same time, it is only through this originary opening up to what is other and outside that we can determine and reshape ourselves in accordance with ideal images. In other words, it is only through this a priori heterodetermination that we can achieve self-determination or freedom. This is what makes freedom *inherently* vulnerable or susceptible to corruption. The imagination is linked to death, but this is also a death that gives life.

Let me end by briefly relating my examination of the ontological basis of Cornell and Murphy's position back to the concrete scenario of multicultural recognition. For Cornell and Murphy, the type of multicultural recognition that can best respect human dignity is the sort that affirms minority cultural identity not as a preformed or given authentic essence but as a set of imaginative identifications. To fail to do this, they imply, is to repeat in a certain way the inhuman gesture of European imperialism because humanity is precisely that which can remake itself: "the identification of the colonized as below the boundary of the human, as beast, as animal, as savage. The colonized are other to humanity; humanity then has been substantiated by the figure of the colonizer and with this figure the most shocking forms of brutality. To challenge this figure would be to challenge the meaning that has been given to humanity" (176). One can see from this that a form of life or being that is merely given is "other than humanity" in the sense that it is subhuman or lesser than human.

In contradistinction, the prior scene of affordance and giving that I am pointing to is also "other than humanity," or inhuman. But it is not by the same token sub-human because the inhuman refers to those forces that constitute and also exceed our ability to remake ourselves that is the fundamental feature of our humanity.

It is always dangerous to historicize the limits of "ontological" presuppositions. But I want to suggest that Cornell and Murphy's critique of authentic multicultural identity is extremely persuasive in the *metropolitan* scene of multicultural migration in the North Atlantic. Their account of the affirmative nature of multicultural identification is plausible precisely because the nation-states of the North Atlantic have constitutional democracies that have developed out of a long history of *Offentlichkeit* and civil society.

But it is important also to remember that the apparent freedom to transcend the given that characterizes multicultural recognition in the North Atlantic also rests on the structures of global capitalism. The constitutive susceptibility to the inhuman or the vulnerable freedom that is the precondition of the transcendence of the given is perhaps best played out concretely by the search for group rights by tribal minorities in the South. These are tribal or aboriginal minorities who are being displaced by state-sanctioned deforestation and mining projects of northern Trans National Corporations. And they can only survive by taking on a legal group identity that is given to them by the state qua ambivalent agent of global capital flows. Such cultural identities afford them a degree of room for maneuver but it also makes them susceptible to state governmentality. As Benedict Anderson writes:

> In most cases their humble wish is simply to be left alone, or to make quiet, slow adaptations to the outside world. But this outside world—not merely the nation-state, but more importantly the great engines of planetary power—will not leave them be. They may sit on valuable mineral or forest resources coveted by the outside; their subsistence agriculture may be regarded as ecologically destructive by international bureaucrats and national planners; demographic pressures may push lowlanders up into their mountain retreats; and they may be unlucky enough to live on sensitive borders between rival nations or rival world blocs. Their very isolation leaves them unacquainted with the ceremonies of private property, the techniques of co-alition politics, and even the organizational methods required for modern self-defense. The irony is that typically they are *not* ethnic groups; to survive they may have to learn to think and act as such. . . . Yet the costs of going ethnic, that is, participating in ethnic majority politics and economics within the nation-state, are not to be underestimated. Often it means becoming Christian (in Siam or Indonesia) or Muslim (in Malaysia). Almost always it means the end of the kind of cultural autonomy and self-contained integrity they once enjoyed. . . . These identities . . . occlude and submerge non-ethnic local identities in the very process of attempting to defend them. Such identities may, under ill-starred circumstances, invite conscious oppression rather than malign neglect, but they also open the way to developing a necessary political and economic bargaining power.[11]

The identification that brings them state recognition traps as it frees, but there is no way out, which is to say that this is also the only way out. In this inhuman scene of affordance that is global capitalism, the image is a relationship to death that gives life.

NOTES

1. G. W. F. Hegel, *Elements of the Philosophy of Right*, trans. H. B. Nisbet, ed. Allen W. Wood (Cambridge: Cambridge University Press, 1991), 282. I have modified to quotation slightly for grammatical purposes.

2. J-J Rousseau, *The Discourses and Other Political Writings*, trans. and ed. Victor Gourevitch (Cambridge: Cambridge University Press, 1997), 142–43.

3. The description of the imagination as active is implied in the Second Discourse but is explicitly formulated in the "Essay on the Origin of Languages" in rela-

tion to the activation of the natural sentiment of pity: "Pity, although natural to man's heart, would remain eternally inactive without imagination to set it in motion. How do we let ourselves be moved to pity? By transporting ourselves outside ourselves; by identifying with the suffering being. . . . He who imagines nothing feels only himself; in the midst of mankind he is alone," 267–68.

4. Immanuel Kant, "Conjectures on the Beginning of Human History," in *Political Writings*, trans. H. B. Nisbet and ed. Hans Reiss (Cambridge: Cambridge University Press, 1991), 223.

5. Immanuel Kant, *Critique of Pure Reason*, trans. and ed. Paul Guyer and Allen W. Wood (Cambridge: Cambridge University Press, 1997), B 151, 256. Hereafter CPR.

6. Note that this does not mean that the productive imagination can do without sensibility. As Kant notes, "in itself the synthesis of the imagination, although exercised *a priori*, is nevertheless always sensible, for it combines the manifold as it appears in intuition, e.g., the shape of a triangle" CPR, A 124, 240. Cf. Kant, *Anthropology from a Pragmatic Point of View*, trans. Mary Gregor (Hague: Nijhoff, 1974), 45: "But imagination is not exactly *creative* because of its inventions; it cannot bring forth a sense representation that was *never* given to the power of sense; we can always trace the material of its ideas. . . . So no matter how great an artist, and even enchantress, imagination may be, it is still not creative, but must get the *material* for its images from the *senses*."

7. See CPR, A 123–24, 240–41: "It is therefore certainly strange, yet from what has been said thus far obvious, that it is only by means of this transcendental function of the imagination that even the affinity of appearances, and with it the association and through the latter finally reproduction in accordance with laws, and consequently experience itself, become possible; for without them no concepts of objects at all would converge into an experience. . . . We therefore have a pure imagination, as a fundamental faculty of the human soul that grounds all cognition *a priori*. By its means we bring into combination the manifold of intuition on the one side and the condition of the necessary unity of apperception on the other. Both extremes, namely sensibility and understanding, must necessarily be connected by means of this transcendental function of the imagination, since otherwise the former would be sure to yield appearances but no objects of an empirical consciousness, hence there would be no experience."

8. See CPR, B 151–52, 256–57: "This *synthesis* of the manifold of sensible intuition, which is possible and necessary *a priori*, can be called *figurative* (*synthesis speciosa*). . . . [I]nsofar as its synthesis is still an exercise of spontaneity, which is determining and not, like sense, merely determinable, and can thus determine the form of sense *a priori* in accordance with the unity of apperception, the imagination is to this extent a faculty for determining the sensibility *a priori*[.]"

9. Kant, "Conjectures on the Beginning of Human History," 228.

10. "Davos Disputation between Ernst Cassirer and Martin Heidegger," reprinted in Heidegger, *Kant and the Problem of Metaphysics*, trans. Richard Taft (Bloomington: Indiana University Press, 1990), 179. Hereafter KPM.

11. Benedict Anderson, "Majorities and Minorities," in *The Spectre of Comparisons: Nationalism, Southeast Asia and the World* (London: Verson, 1998), 329–30.

Elizabeth Grosz

Drucilla Cornell, Identity, and the Evolution of Politics

[W]hat is needful is a new justice! And a new watchword. And new philoso-
phers. The moral earth, too, is round. The moral earth, too, has its antipodes.
The antipodes, too, have the right to exist. There is yet another world to be
discovered—and more than one. Embark, philosophers!
—Nietzsche, The Gay Science

I cannot hope to do justice to Drucilla Cornell's work in its richness and breadth. Her theoretical interests are vast, encompassing, among other terrains, legal studies, feminist theory, cultural and literary studies, political theory, and psychoanalysis. They range from the most abstract heights of the dialectic and the most intricate deconstructive maneuvers, to the most pressing social issues of the present: abortion, pornography, sexual harassment, homophobia, racism, violence, multiculturalism and globalization. With great bravery and foresight, she has been almost singular in forcing social and legal theory to come to grips with the intellectual and political rigor of deconstruction, or, in her terminology, the "philosophy of the limit," and in turn, forcing deconstruction to answer to these pressing empirical questions and concerns. Instead of dealing with all of these questions—or really any of them directly—I want to look instead at an oblique strand that runs through her work, one that touches on many of these concerns without focusing on them directly.

Cornell puts the question of the time and the future, if not at the center of her work, then at least at a strategically off-center position in her writings and in her vision of feminist ethics and politics, in a place where its sheen reflects on and radiates from all the questions she raises. The question of time, of past, present, and future, and their relations to identity, value, and social position, are explicit objects of speculation and reflection in all of her writings, even if they are not her major preoccupations. She is one of the very few feminist theorists to see the future neither as irrelevant nor as directly manipulable, neither as the realization of current wishes or fears (that is, as simply a projection of the present), nor as simply speculative, utopian, impossible. The future—that field to which all of ethics and politics are directed insofar as they are attempts at amelioration of the past and present—is the condition and very mode of present political, ethical, and legal action and effectivity. Cornell has done feminism an immense service by drawing attention, once again, and in a radically different manner, to the dimension of time or duration, and the privilege that any politics or ethics, any position that aims to improve the present, must grant to futurity.

While the question of futurity is one of the essential ingredients of any account of politics or ethics, or for that matter, any account of being, subjectivity, matter, or identity, it is remarkable how few feminists have tackled it directly. I am not thinking here of a vast series of feminist fictional works, especially works in feminist sci-fi, which predict or project a possible future. As interesting and important as these may be, they still do not raise the more philosophically and politically oriented questions about how to view the link between the present and the future, how to produce rather than imagine a future radically different from a given past and present. They produce the future as a picture or projection, an extrapolation or reversal of the present. While Cornell's work is not a detailed and sustained analysis of temporality and duration, nonetheless, it contains hints and clues about a more productive way of understanding futurity and temporality than that usually assumed in feminist, literary, or philosophical theory. This orientation to the question of the yet-to-come, of what is not yet in being, has always attracted me to her work, which, for this reason, among others, is a philosophy of hope, of activity and of agency (agency, though, in a restricted sense, where it can be understood as precisely the capacity to make the future diverge from the patterns and causes of the present rather than an inherent quality of freedom or the availability of unconstrained possibilities). Hers is a politics that envisions the capacity for transformation inherent in any ordered system, the system itself being unable to contain its own becomings and thus open to potentially endless variation.

TIME AND AGAIN

There are generally two broad ways in which time and futurity are commonly conceived in feminist theory. I would describe the first as extrapolative: it commonly involves drawing out the implications and effects of current trends, predictions, the projected movement of present impulses. This mode is more crucial in some areas than in others (e.g., in studies of economic development, in epidemiology, in public policy and planning, and so on). It is interested in developing procedures that extrapolate from present trends, through magnification, intensification, or specialization, into the future. Most attempts to theorize or project equal rights, or to consider economic development (e.g. Iris Marion Young, Martha Nussbaum) exemplify at least elements of this tendency. The second broad trend is considerably less scientific and more imaginative in its approach. It is more closely associated with literature and the arts than with science or politics: I would describe it primarily as utopian. This involves the imaginative production of other worlds, fictional, cinematic, or cybernetic, which dramatically change certain elements of our experience and our understanding of our world. These imaginative projections are the production of what I understand to be utopian visions, visions of ideal or horrifying futures, narratives of fanciful desire.[1]

What is exciting about Cornell's work is that she thinks the question of time and futurity—or rather, the question of becoming—outside these parameters, not in ignorance of these two trends, but working beyond them and in recognition of their limitations, for ironically, neither is a way of politicizing the present by showing an alternative future, outside the orbit of the present, rather than already contained within it. Her project implicitly, and at some moments, explicitly, addresses the question of temporal unfolding, becoming, as its underlying logic: if the feminine is all that our culture in its patriarchal weight defines it to be, if the feminine is reduced to and identified only with a degraded and secondary version of masculinity, then feminism is ethically and politically impelled to ensure that the future does *not* resemble the past and that the feminine "within sexual difference," a future feminine, is different from and quite other than the feminine that is defined by the masculine today and in the past as its counterpart or other. Feminist ethics and politics is inevitably not just propelled toward rectifying the wrongs done to women but to expanding and transforming the horizons available for their self-representations, which in her own terms Cornell describes as the "imaginary domain," not simply the domain of imagination but also the space of virtuality, of what is new and not yet actualized. This "space" of the virtual, which we need also to regard as the *time* of the imaginary domain, the domain of what is to come, is precisely the time of wonder Irigaray speculates may come into being when it is recognized that there are (at least) two sexes, two kinds of experience, two modes of morphology, two kinds of subject.[2] This is the time of the future perfect, the future anterior, the time in which the future can look at this present as its superceded past.

Cornell raises the question of time and futurity in numerous places, from her earlier works, such as *Beyond Accommodation* (1991) and *The Philosophy of the Limit* (1992) to her more recent, *The Imaginary Domain* (1995),[3] and other coauthored works,[4] though only ever fragmentarily and indirectly. The first mention of the question of the "beyond" of the present, the excess left over in the present that enables it to generate a future unforeseen by it occurs, not altogether surprisingly, in one of her first references to Irigaray:

> [T]he "female blossoming that keeps open the future of sexual difference," and at the same time allows us to judge the past as the "silence of female history" in which our suffering was inexpressible, is dependent upon the affirmation of the specificity of the feminine as *difference* beyond the established

system of gender identity (and more generally any pregiven identity). If the feminine is repudiated . . . we will be left in the masculine arena in which the old games of domination are played out. There will only be repetition, no re-evolution to the future. Irigaray is ultimately a thinker of change.[5]

Irigaray is primarily a thinker of change: she addresses what it is to think change, to think differently, in terms that will accommodate not just otherness, but the kind of otherness that is beyond the limit, outside the definition and control of the self-same and the self-identical. This question articulates Cornell's project as much as, and in accordance with Irigaray's and separates them from most other feminist thinkers.[6] Cornell refers to an "unerasable trace of utopianism"[7] (BA, 107) in all ethical and political thought, the ways in which it is crucial that thought (ethics and politics, are always implicated in thought as well, and as much, as in practice) is always a mode of *inadequation* of the real, a mode of inducing a more-than-the-real, which I understand in terms of the virtuality of the real, its latencies, its impetus to something other, and more. Cornell, like Irigaray, is advocating the necessity for there to be an outside to any and every system, a locus of excess, which contains the seeds of something other or beyond the present:

> I am aware how difficult it is to understand this "unerasable" trace of utopianism. But this is why I refer to this moment . . . as endlessly "there." It is not a chronological *moment* to be surpassed, which is why I refer to it as unerasable utopianism. Nor is it a projection of utopia: "this is what it would be like," our dream world. This trace of utopianism, that cannot be wiped out can be summarized as follows. The "subject" is never just the hostage of its surroundings, because these surroundings cannot be consolidated into an unshakable reality that defines us and by so doing necessarily limits possibility to the evolution of what already "is." (BA, 107)[8]

Cornell suggests here, as elsewhere, that the subject is always more than its social constitution, in excess of "ideology," "training," "expectation," an excess that is not just material or spatial but also necessarily temporal. She has recognized, as few others have, that this is the very condition of feminism itself: that beyond highlighting the wrongs done to women, beyond the account of women as the victims of patriarchal oppression, that very oppression also contains within it the virtual conditions of feminism and the openness of a future beyond present constraints.

In her earlier writings, Cornell attributes this position to Derrida and to deconstruction: as Derrida himself has always insisted, deconstruction, as the analysis of *difference*, is the unraveling of presence in the light of the processes of spatialization and temporization that make it possible yet which it covers over.[9] As Cornell claims: "We must look more closely at the play of *différance* as it relates to temporalization and to Derrida's unique conception of the future as the not yet of the never has been. *Différance* can be understood as the 'truth' that 'being' is presented in time, and, therefore, there can be no all-encompassing ontology of the 'here' and "now."[10] The future must be understood not as the preordained or as the constrained. In order for there to be politics and ethics now, in order for there to be history and reflection on the past, the future must be open and uncontained by the past and present, even though it is conditioned by them. This is not simply temporization, the putting of matter and events into a time line or chronology, the construction of a linear history or genealogy, but is rather the abandonment of the force of the present, whether in the givenness of the past or the self-evidence, the actuality, of the present. Which is not, as Cornell and Derrida recognize, an abandonment of responsibility but its most bitter irony: we must act in the present, with the light the past sheds on that present, but we must, by virtue of the difference that inhabits the present, cede any control of our present act to a future that we cannot foresee or understand. This is what dissemination is, the failure of definitive destination, the openness of any thing (whether it be a text, an event, a subject, a particle) to what befalls it, or more precisely, to what will have befallen it. This is the very heart of politics and is the direct implication of Derrida's understanding of iteration. It is a direct consequence of the kinds of antihumanism to which both Cornell and Derrida are committed: we must act but have no direct control over the ramifications of our acts, which makes us, ironically, more rather than less responsible for them.

Politics requires that relations among the past, present, and future be rethought so that the conventions accumulated through the past can be refigured, rearticulated, redone. Politics is the opening up of norms to the subversions that are already virtual within them: "Such a project demands the rethinking of the relationship between the *past*, embodied in the normative conventions which are passed down through legal precedent, and the projection of *future* ideals through which the community seeks to regulate itself."[11]

Cornell understands that without some nonenvisionable future (rather than, as most political theory has it, without a definite or positive plan for improvement), the present could never be as such, and politics could not exist except as some fantasmatic consolation. She tends in some texts to see this in terms of the redemptive possibilities a notion of the future entails. (This redemptive model, I believe, ties her work more closely to what I have described as a utopian feminist position, though she herself may not altogether object to this categorization.)

Once we understand the relationship between myth and allegory in accounts of the feminine, we can also unfold the role of the utopian, or redemptive perspective of the "not yet." This perspective exposes our current system of gender representation as "fallen." Within feminist theory, feminine sexual difference has often stood in as the figure that gives body to redemptive perspectives. How should we hope to become? Where do we find the new economy of desire? . . . Ethical feminism explicitly recognizes the "should be" in representations of the feminine . . . [E]thical feminism rests its claim for . . . intelligibility and coherence . . . not on what women "are" but on the remembrance of the "not yet."[12]

Instead of focusing only on the present, which gives us women, and relations between the sexes only under the order of masculine domination, we need to look more carefully at the *virtuality* laden within the present, its possibilities for being otherwise, in other words, the unactualized latencies in any situation which could be, may have been, instrumental in the generation of the new or the unforeseen. This is the very condition of feminism, or any radical politics, any politics that seeks transformation, what Cornell calls the "not yet," or Irigaray might call "what will have been."

WHAT'S EVOLUTION GOT TO DO WITH IT?

Cornell is one of a few feminists to be actively interested in the philosophy of temporality and in the issues of active becoming it raises. But her understanding of futurity and becoming are closely tied to, and in many ways symptomatic of, a series of other issues she deals with, or attempts to avoid, which mitigate and problematize not only her understanding of futurity but also her conceptions of politics and ethics. I am thinking here primarily of Cornell's resistance to questions of biology, nature, and matter in favor of questions of culture, subjectivity, and desire. She very carefully observes the more conventional dividing lines feminists have drawn between oppositional categories, taking them to the "limit," perhaps, but always accepting that there is in fact a line of demarcation. In particular, the oppositions between nature and culture, and the body and the psyche, still remain aligned in her work. She carefully avoids discussion of the biological, the natural, and the real as if they in some way detract from or mitigate the cultural and political issues at hand.

There are numerous places where Cornell states that her interest is specifically *not* about biology, anatomy, or body parts, not about matter, nature, or the real. She focuses, for example, on sex "not as biological body parts, but as sexuality.[13] She argues that Lacan's work is crucial precisely because it is not the result of biology or the real but in divergence from it: "Lacan helps us to understand why this recognition [of castration] is not the result of biology but of the symbolic order."[14] Lacan is the psychoanalyst of choice because he distinguishes the penis from the phallus, the biological from the symbolic. Indeed, the politics of feminism itself, she wants to believe, is not or should not be directed to biological questions but only to questions of the symbolic, which to some extent at least means *representations* of biology rather than biology itself: "I am using flesh as a metaphor, not as a literal description of the body. . . . Flesh is the metaphor of psychicality that can never be fully articulated. There is no body that is just there."[15]

In this relegation of biology, matter, and the real to a never possible, ever receding background upon which "originary" writing takes place, Cornell joins Judith Butler and an entire tradition of "postmodern," "constructivist," or "performative" feminism in devaluing matter or in transforming it from noun to verb and in the process desubstantializing it. For Cornell, as for Butler, the body itself dissolves, the real always displaces itself by being written on, and matter disappears in the process of mattering, of being valued: "To [find a way to resymbolize feminine sexual difference], we first need an account of how bodies come to matter. As Judith Butler shows us, the word 'matter' has a double meaning. Bodies matter, that is, they materialize and take on reality while also carrying an implicit normative assessment. Bodies matter, in other words, through a process by which they come to have both symbolic and ethical significance".[16]

Following Butler here, Cornell claims a double meaning for matter: materializing, and mattering (i.e., having value). But ironically, both elide matter itself. To understand matter as "materializing" implies a process of putting into materiality that elides or denies that matter is itself what enables materialization (one cannot materialize what is always already material); and matter itself is what enables those valuations that are designated as mattering (mattering is a process of privileging one mode of materiality over another). What slips out, what disappears, is stuff, the real, biology, nature, matter, which are thus relegated either to Kantian noumena or to Lacanian passivity. Butler is concerned with the important question of value: what *counts* as a body, as a subject, as a being, what is included (what "matters") in social categories or what is excluded, abjected, as intolerable (or "does not matter"). But these issues of value and valuation, of mattering, are in fact never independent of or capable of effectivity except insofar as they are lived through bodies, in biologies, in and as the real. The process of mattering cannot be cut off from what matter it is. Cornell follows Butler in claiming that it is the counting, the mattering, of bodies, of anatomies, and of sexual differences that is at stake in feminism, without acknowledging that the very mark of being counted, of mattering, can only be accomplished on and through matter, in this case, biological or organic matter. Matter is both presupposed by and inexplicable for the kinds of culturally and psychically—that is, symbolically—oriented feminist projects undertaken by Cornell and Butler and the entire field of feminist social constructionism. My claim, by contrast, is that if becoming, difference, and iteration are what make the self-identity of the subject and of culture impossible, so too, they immensely complicate and render self-identity problematic in the arena of nature and materiality as well. The biological, the natural, and the material remain active and crucial political ingredients, precisely because they too, and not culture alone, are continually subjected to transformation, to becoming, to unfolding over time. Moreover, ethics would itself dictate that the natural be owed the debt of culture's emergence, insofar as it is precisely the open-ended incompletion of nature itself that induces the cultural as its complexification and supplement. This is not the end or the supercession of the natural but its ever-transforming self-representation. In this sense, culture is the self-image of nature, not, as cultural theory argues, nature is the fantasmatic projection of culture.

It is this refusal to accord the natural, the biological, or the anatomical any role, even that of raw material, in understandings of the cultural, the symbolic, and the subjective that lies behind Cornell's insistent, if sometimes haphazard, division of a culturally conceived futurity, understood as "transformation" from a naturally bound and thus inherently limited futurity, that of "evolution." Although this distinction is made only in passing, it is made frequently enough (although with frustrating brevity) to allow us to believe that it is an ongoing commitment in her work. I believe that it is symptomatic of a common, near pervasive, feminist refusal to attribute becoming to the domain of the natural that ties us firmly back into an unproductive natural/cultural opposition that is particularly crucial for feminist theory to challenge.

For example, Cornell begins *Transformations* (1993, 2) by suggesting a crucial "difference that makes a difference," a difference between "transformation," which she understands as the capacity of a system to "so alter itself that it no longer confirms its identity, but disconfirms it, and through its iterability, generates new meanings which can be further pursued and enhanced by the sociosymbolic practice of the political contestants within its milieu" in other words, the capacity of a system to be contested in the future, to be different from what it is now. This is sharply contrasted with "change reduced to evolution."[17] She articulates this claim elsewhere, in for example, *The Philosophy of the Limit*: "The deconstructibility of law is . . . exactly what allows for the possibility of transformation, not just the evolution of the legal system".[18] It is clear that the one side of this opposition—transformation—is privileged at the expense of the other—evolution. Not only does it become a methodological label for all of Cornell's work, but also it becomes the very title of one of her books: transformation is to culture what evolution is to nature. Or rather, with more complexity, transformation is an openendness of the future, while evolution is construed—or rather, misconstrued—as predelimited, contained, bound to the system and its confirmation.

Cornell tends to identify autogenic or self-replicating systems that exhibit emergence rather than supervening order, erroneously with determined or constrained systems that function within the web of the deterministic causal chains. She tends to see nature itself, though it is rarely spoken of as such, as a self-enclosed system that, while not entirely irrelevant to cultural activity, is nonetheless entirely dispensable for understanding cultural activity. Nature functions in an enclosed net of determinations that necessarily hold the future to the terms that govern the past and the present. It requires description rather than imagination; it is mired in fact rather than in possibilities. Identifying systematicity, the systematicity of natural systems perhaps, with some of the writings of Niklas Luhmann, Cornell relegates any notion of self-enclosure to an impossible quest for presence.

Yet ironically, it is precisely the self-organization of natural systems, and particularly evolutionary systems—that is, biological systems—that perhaps best exemplifies Derridean *différance* in terms of their refusal to be contained as systems within the parameters and constraints that dictate their "normal" regulation. Derrida himself seems to recognize this more readily than Cornell. Evolution offers precisely the openness to contingency and to futurity that Cornell seeks in the legal system. My point here is not to correct Cornell of her misunderstanding of the concept of 'evolution' but to make clear that unless the same generative productivity is granted to the natural and the biological as to the cultural and the symbolic, we will have no understanding either of the impetus or force of the cultural itself, nor will we understand the debt, and the relation of responsibility that the cultural owes to the natural, the psychical owes to the biological, the phallus owes to the penis, the subject owes to materiality. Moreover, we will not have heeded Derrida's own understanding of the inherent seepage of oppositional pairs, the coinfection of each with the other, which is as relevant for the nature/culture opposition as it is for any other oppositional forms. Unless the active, differential force of the biological and the natural is understood, we risk precisely what Cornell warns us against when analyzing the work of Catherine MacKinnon—that is, we reduce the subject entirely to culture, entirely to writing, and in the process efface the very matter of *resistance*, the locus of change and of transformation.

THE TIME OF THE OTHER

Cornell explicitly links the question of otherness, including the relations of sexual difference, to questions of violence and temporality. Justice is tied to the call of the other and the possible honoring of the call, a call that in a sense can never be honored, can never be adequately answered but that the subject must in any case address. This is not the striving for a Kantian ideal but the gesture toward the satisfaction of the most intimate and concrete needs that the most concrete other calls forth from us. Justice is never given in the here and now; justice never exists in full presence but is the horizon of the yet-to-be, the future. Among Cornell's most subtle insights is her understanding, not of the impossibility of the call to justice, but of its temporal suspension. Justice demands, requires what is yet to come.

Cornell quotes Derrida: "There is an *avenir* for justice and there is no justice except to the degree that some event is possible which, as event exceeds calculation, rules, programs, anticipations and so forth. Justice as the experience of absolute alterity is unrepresentable, but it is the chance of the event and the condition of history".[19]

For Cornell as for Derrida, then, justice is tied to what is not yet, what has never been but what can be, and is already being generated from the present, from the impossibility of the self-presence of the present, from the simultaneously impossible and necessary *self-replication*, *iteration*, and *failure* of repetition that generates the new from the latencies or virtualities of the (impossibly) present. This is a key concept in refiguring politics—which has tended to be about "calculations, rules, programs, anticipations"—for it shows the element of the accidental, of chance, of the singularity of events, in short the movement of openendedness or indetermination—"evolution." This is not an evolution in Cornell's sense of constrained, systemically dictated, regulated, ordered, contained change, but precisely the unexpected, the contingent, and the random, open-ended change. The movement of dissemination, as a movement of transformation, is precisely evolutionary becoming: a species' fitness is measured not simply by its success in a given milieu but by its openness to upheavals in milieu its openness to the new and the surprising. Evolution is the movement *beyond* a given situation or determination, the playing out of the excess contained within but undeveloped by its present situation or determination. It is perhaps another name for deconstruction itself.

Cornell's understanding of the complex interplay between law and justice, which is itself a balancing act between convention and precedent, between the concerns of a memorialized past and the interests of a not-yet existent future, between the established interpretations of law and its most extreme innovations, poses precisely this movement of the opening out of being to becoming that Darwin and Bergson understood as evolution. She argues that law cannot be, and never has been, invested in simply applying technical rules in mechanical fashion, and even if it could do so (which seems hardly possible given the ever-increasing subtlety of what counts as crime), this would not be justice: "Law . . . cannot be reduced to a self-generated and self-validating set of *cognitive* norms. Interpretation always takes us beyond a mere appeal to the status quo".[20] Cornell insists that justice is the call to remember and honor a past by making it open into a future that the past alone cannot call forth:

> The Good, as it is interpreted as the yet unrealized potential of the *nomos*, is never simply the mere repetition of conventional norms, because there can be no mere repetition. In this sense, the Good . . . cannot be conceived as the truth of a self-enclosed system which perpetuates itself. The dissemination of convention as a self-enclosed legal system does not leave us with a fundamental lack, but with an opening. . . . As a result, when we appeal 'back' to what has been established, we must *look* forward to what "might be."

> Thus the deconstructive emphasis on the opening of the ethical self-transcendence of any system that exposes the threshold of the "beyond" of the not yet is crucial to a conception of legal interpretation that argues that the "is" of Law can never be completely separated from the elaboration of the "should be" dependent on an appeal to the Good.[21]

The time of the other, the time of Justice, is the time of the future. Not a future that we can imagine from the standpoint of the present, but a future that is contained in but unconstrained by the present as its unactualized virtualities. The "beyond" that is such a crucial element in Cornell's work is neither redemptive nor utopian, though it contains elements of both. It is the very condition of the present, as well as the undoing of self-presence. This mode of self-undoing, of going beyond, is not just the condition of the legal system, or of cultural, political, and ethical relations more generally, but is the very condition of life itself. Life itself is precisely an incessant teaming, an ongoing movement to be more, to be other, to be beyond what is. This is precisely why the model of evolution is no mere metaphor of the social order but is its condition, and moreover, the very condition of ethics, politics, and justice: we are impelled, whether we choose it or not, to move forward, to innovate in the semblance of repetition, to generate the new.

THE FUTURE OF THE SUBJECT

In her more recent writings, Cornell has addressed the question of the fluidity of the subject and its openness to the future through the imaginative identifications available to it that may enable it to bypass the impacts of phallocentrism, racism, and the imperative to a broadly interchangeable uniformity generated by the forces of globalization. This is the focus of her jointly authored chapter with Sara Murphy, "Anti-Racism, Multiculturalism and the Ethics of Identification" (2002, reprinted in this work).

The central argument of the chapter, put crudely and simply, is that the politics of recognition, which the authors identify with seeking the "equal dignity of all peoples" (2002, 2) from the state and its instrumentalities, need not be tied to any authentic or given identity but must also be bestowed on strategic or provisional identities and identifications—not just to those with a clear-cut and recognizable history, language, or geography but those whose identifications are in the process of being formed or changing, which direct themselves to the possibilities the present holds for the future. In short, their aim is to "disconnect the claim to 'authenticity' of identity from the demand for recognition" (2002, 420). Rather than tying recognition to a stable, "authorized," historically structured location or position, the official or recognized minority position, new, incipient "identities," authentic or self-consciously constructed, historically laden or recently acquired, also require the authorization of social recognition. This recognition, at least ideally, should not be a repressive or patronizing tolerance, nor should it be a mode of adjudication of the authenticity and validity of any particular identity; rather, it should affirm "as a demand of right to the state . . . under the rubric of freedom and the recognition of equal dignity" (2002, 422), the universal and reciprocally defining identification of the other as subject. Cornell and Murphy claim that such identities may be produced through those acts of self-cultivation and the cultivation of collective imagination that constitutes cultural life. These identities need not be bound up with bodily, geographical, historical, ethnic, and collective verities, with materialities of various kinds; what is as significant are the modes and specific forms of identification that the subject undertakes.

While the authors affirm the value of self-representation and self-definition in the constitution of one's social (and biological) identity, understood as a process of moving beyond pregiven identities and cultural stereotypes, producing new identities through new identifications and new cultural imaginings, nevertheless, they accept that there are limits to the type and form of identification possible—at least for those in dominant positions, limits that are, ironically, directly connected to the social significance of biological characteristics. Although Cornell, in consistency with her earlier writings, wants to free the subject from the apparent fixity that is contained in and as its biology, nevertheless, she wants to leave open the possibilities of extending biological and other material categories according to the options culturally open to distinct subjects:

> [There] is indeed an ethics, both as a practice of self-responsibility and as an encounter with how we come to articulate who we are through our identifications which take us beyond ourselves as individuals precisely because we can never be completely in control of the social and symbolic meanings of racial and ethnic categories.

> Therefore, there is a sense in which we can be called to identify, as we both feel called to do, as white and Anglo because these categories continue to not only represent privilege but to enforce it. To deny that we are part of the privileged group, then, is not only false; it is, more importantly to us, unethical. The fluidity of categories of race and ethnic identity in no way takes away from the social reality that ethically demands that we confront the meanings of our own identifications. (2002, 435–6)

There are "social realities" which "fluid identifications" must nevertheless acknowledge as an ethical imperative, at least insofar as these social realities constitute one as a member of a socially dominant group. So, although there are, as it were, limits to what one can affirm as one's identity ("like it nor not we are white and Anglo because we are inevitably shaped by how we are seen" there are no such limits on imaginative identifications with racialized, minoritarian cultural phenomena, even if not with minoritarian identities), we are free to "reform our identifications" within parameters, those that "we must also be ethically called upon to recognize as we try to articulate who we are" (2002, 437).[22]

Cornell and Murphy seek a certain kind of identity—no longer a fixed, pregiven, or stereotyped identity but one that the subject has a degree of freedom to reformulate, to reconceive, through imaginative identifications. There are, however, two sets of constraints, two unrecognized limits to these identifications, one coming from without and the other from within the subject. From without, the subject is constrained by the structure of recognition, which requires the acknowledgement of value and worth—even dignity—from the other, or at least the "other," the social order; and from within, the subject is constrained by the history of its own structures of identification and its capacity to have an imaginative breadth in its relations to new identificatory objects.

Clustered together in Cornell and Murphy's argument is a cluster of terms: *recognition/ identification/ subject-formation*. These terms have a long and illustrious history, as the authors acknowledge, which can be marked or dated within a quite powerful philosophical tradition from Hegel's *Phenomenology of Mind* and that structures the phenomenological reflections of Husserl and Heidegger, Kojéve, the existentialists such as Camus, Sartre, and de Beauvoir, through to the Hegelian inflection of psychoanalysis provided by Lacan, and on to the structuralist and poststructuralist versions of feminist, class, and minority identity discourses. The model of a subject produced through identification and recognition seems pervasive in the contemporary discourses of class, race, and gender primarily because these political traditions carry with them an often unacknowledged debt to Hegelianism.[23] Cornell and Murphy's project needs to be located within this framework in which the subject can only become a subject as such through being recognized by another (individual or collective) subject as a subject. This Hegelian "law of desire" informs and underlies most of what today is called "identity politics": identity is not something inherent, given, or internally developed, a property of a self, but is bestowed by an other, and only an other, and thus can also be taken away by an other. Identity is rendered precarious, intangible, elusively under the other's control. The powers and dangers posed by this other, who can bestow or destroy the subject's self-identification, is enormous: there is no subject without another subject with whom to identify and who in turn can threaten the (psychical or physical) annihilation of the subject. Identity comes only as a result of a dual motion of the internalization, an introjection of otherness, and the projection onto the other of some fundamental similarity or identification with the subject. Two beings must encounter each other in their alienness for either to have an identity of its own. Hegel's paradox is that the autonomy and identity of the subject comes only at the cost of the subject's indebtedness to the alien other whom he presumes and makes his counterpart, an other for and of him.

In other words, Cornell and Murphy, as is common in much contemporary feminist, postcolonial, and antiracist theory, have wedded together a Hegelian understanding of the subject's identification/ projection structure of recognition and a psychoanalytically-modeled understanding of the subject as a creature of internalization, the introjective processes of taking in the other's representations of the subject as part of the subject's identity and the corresponding processes of projecting outward its own identificatory needs onto the other. In this indebtedness to Hegelianism, Cornell and Murphy share with Seyla Benhabib, Wendy Brown, Judith Butler, Nancy Fraser, and many—perhaps most—other feminist, queer, and antiracist theorists, a fundamental reliance on the structures of recognition and identification that inscribe the other onto and as the subject and the subject as the other's counterpart.[24]

Pervasive as this tradition of phenomenology has been—and it has been disproportionately influential in accounts of sexed and raced forms of subjectivity from de Beauvoir and Fanon onward—it has become the dominant and almost uncontested discourse of minority cultures by being brought together with a psychoanalytic understanding of the ego and ego ideal as the media through which the subject is "interpellated," constituted, or comes to find itself.[25] This Hegelian strand of Cornell and Murphy's argument, that strand that underlies *all discourses* on identity that require the other's tacit implication in the subject's formation, needs to be counterbalanced with an alternative tradition, one with a considerably shorter history and much less influence on contemporary politics, which can be dated from the Nietzschean rewriting of the Hegelian dialectic as the servile rationalizations of the slave and the herd, rather than as the movement of an enlightening "spirit" to its own self-fruition. Nietzsche offers an entirely alien framework to that posited by the Hegelians, Marxists, and phenomenologists: instead of identity, Nietzsche seeks out forces or wills; instead of dialectical, continuous self-modification, he favors the dramatic and untimely leap into futurity, instead of the becoming of being, he seeks the being of becoming, instead of identity, he seeks a model of action and activity.[26] This redirection of interest from the subject's internal constitution, its psychical interiority inhabited by the specter of the other, is turned inside out in a Nietzschean framework: what marks the subject as such is its capacity to act and be acted upon, to do rather than to be, to act rather than to identify. Where the Hegelian subject remains fundamentally vulnerable to the incursions of the other, to the other's attempted mastery over the subject's own self-definition, the Nietzsche subject, indifferent to the other, acts and, through acting, produces values, interpretations, modes of dealing with the world, and modes of addressing the other without succumbing or giving over power to the other. There is a growing influence of this Nietzschean conception in politics, through the efforts of his reader-theorists such as Foucault, Deleuze, Kofman, Irigaray, and others, but these remain, in spite of their reputations within the humanities, still minority positions within a field that seems dominated by identity politics, the politics of identification with sociocultural categories, conceived outside and beyond bodies and forces in themselves.

What is it that subjects seek? To be recognized? Cornell and Murphy ask the crucial question—the question at the very heart of the Hegelian structure of recognition: to be recognized by whom? From whom do oppressed groups and individuals seek identity through recognition? Hegel's own answer changes and moves with the very structure of the dialectic itself: while two equal self-consciousnesses seek recognition from each other, the dialectic rapidly transforms this apparent or provisional equality into the very structure of lordship and bondage. Now it is the slave who seeks the recognition of the master, and paradoxically, the master has no adequate or equal other to provide recognition for him. Through other permutations and developments of the dialectic, in the end, the subject seeks recognition for itself from the social and political order, seeks to be adequately represented and thus adequately recognized by it by having its place as a unique combination of categories and identifications affirmed socially and politically. Yet Cornell and Murphy are not able to entirely affirm Hegel's understanding: "Clearly, minority cultures are not always, or even mostly, addressing their demands for recognition to the majority culture—at least if we are to understand recognition as a comprehension of the minority culture's identity. That freedom that Hegel saw achieved in the Western European democracies has been, after all, often written on the backs of precisely those minority cultures now struggling for the own national identities, cultural voices and economic sustainability" (2002, 421).

While the authors confirm that it cannot be the "majority culture"—whether conceived as white, middle class, heterosexual, male, Eurocentric, English-speaking—that bestows identity on minoritarian cultures, they remain unclear about why it is a recognition structure that is the remedy for their minoritarian status. If it is not the majoritarian values that attribute an identity to the minority, if, indeed majoritarian interests are vested in the nonrecognition and a noncomprehension, an abjection, or expulsion of "the minority culture's identity," then why is recognition necessary, and what does it confer? Or perhaps this is another way of asking Why are identity and the struggles around identity—rather than, say, around the right to bodily activities and practices—are the rallying cry for politics. Can we reconceive politics without identity? (This is what Cornell and Murphy seek in their chapter.) And if so, why do we still need the residual concept of recognition (as they continue to affirm)?

In place of the desire for recognition as the condition for subjective identity, we need to begin with different working assumptions, which may cover some of the same issues as those conceived by identity politics, without, however, resorting to the language and assumptions governing recognition. In place of the desire for recognition, the emptiness of a solipsistic existence, the annihilation of identity without the other, the relation of desperate dependence on the other for the stability of one's being, we could develop an account of subjectivity, identity, or agency at the mercy of forces, energies, practices, which produce an altogether different understanding of both politics and identity.

Subjects can be conceived as modes of action and passion, a surface catalytic of events that subjects do not control but participate in, which produce what history and thus whatever identity subjects may have. This is precisely what evolutionary theory offers. In place of a phenomenology of identificatory subservience, as entailed by the adoption of Hegelian structures of recognition, the political struggles of subjugated peoples can be regarded as struggles for *practice*, struggles at the level of the pragmatic, struggles around the right to act, do, and make. Oppression cannot simply be resolved into failed, unsuccessful, or unaffirmed identities lagging for want of recognition. A more dynamic and affirming representation is to understand identity in terms of bodily practices: one is what one does, the history of what one has done, and what has been done to one, constitute one's character; and what one can or will do is that which is unpredictable and open. Identity is thus a synthesis of what one has done (and had been done to one) but also a dissipation of patterns and habits in the face of an open future. This identity has little to do with how one represents oneself and everything to do with the processes and actions one engenders and of which one partakes. What we are is determined to a large extent, not by who recognizes us, but by what we do, what we make, what we achieve or accomplish.

It is only if the subject, its identity, desire, and possibilities for becoming is linked to some conception, not only of identification, imagination, projection, but of action, materiality, forces that direct it beyond its control, which position it as a subject with particular characteristics—morphological, genetic, developmental, given, acquired, or emergent—that we can understand the limits of the subject and its modes of transformation into something other and more. Sexual difference, the acquisition of at least two radically different types of subject position according to at least two different morphological structures, racial difference, the acknowledgment of a multiplicity of corporeal and cultural variations are neither constrained to the forms in which we currently know them, nor are they open to self-conscious manipulation, identification, or control by subjects. They are material, evolutionary forces through which we work but that we do not control, that we cannot rise above but that nevertheless direct us towards the possibilities of change. Without an adequate acknowledgment of the material, natural, biological status of bodies (these terms being understood as vectors of change rather than as forms of fixity), we lose the resources to understand how to best harness these forces that invariably direct us to the future; we lose an understanding of our place in the world as beings open to becoming, open to activities, if not identities, of all types.

NOTES

This chapter was originally written for a special session on Drucilla Cornell's writings at the Society for Phenomenology and Existential Philosophy Conference held in Lexington, Kentucky in 1996. It has been considerably modified for this publication.

1. I have attempted to address the problems of utopian visions for feminists, and for theorists of space, in a chapter, "Embodied Utopias," in my book, *Architecture from the Outside: Essays on Virtual and Real Space* (Cambridge: MIT Press, 2001).

2. See Luce Irigaray, *An Ethics of Sexual Difference*, trans. Carolyn Burke and Gillian C. Gill (Ithaca: Cornell University Press, 1993), for her discussion of Cartesian wonder.

3. Drucilla Cornell, *Beyond Accomodation Ethical Feminism, Deconstruction & Law* (New York: Routledge, 1991); Cornell, *Philosophy of the Limit* (New York: Routledge 1992) Cornell, *The Imaginary Domain* (New York: Routledge 1995)

4. Especially, for example, Drucilla Cornell and Sara Murphy, "Anti-Racism, Multiculturalism, and the Ethics of Identification," Philosophy and Social Criticism 28, no. 4 (2002): 419–50 (reprinted in this volume).

5. Cornell, *Beyond Accomodation* (New York: Routledge, 1991), Here adter BA, 9.

6. Cornell's relations with Irigaray seem more complex and ambivalent than her earlier writings attest. For a more explicit and recent representation of her ambivalent relation to Irigaray, see the interview Butler and Cornell (1998) gave on Irigaray's relevance to her and Butler's writings. There are other feminist theorists, however, who, since the early 1990s, have taken up Irigaray's understanding of the interminable and indeterminable struggles of sexual difference, most notably Margaret Whitford, *Luce Irigaray: Philosophy in the Feminine* (London and New York: Routledge, 1991); Kelly Oliver, *Womanizing Nietzsche: Philosophy's Relaton to the "Feminine"* (New York: Routledge 1994); Ellen Mortensen, *The Feminine and Nihilism: Luce Irigaray with Nietzsche and Heidegger* (Olso, Copenhagen, and Stockholm: Scandinavian University Press 1994); Claire Colebrook, "Feminist Philosophy and the Philosophy of Feminism: Irigaray and the History of Western Metaphysics," Hypatia 12, no. 1 (Winter 2001); Lorraine Tamsin, Irigaray and Deleuze: Experiments in Visceral Philosophy (Ithaca: Cornell University Press, 1999); Dorothea E. Olkowski, "The End of Phenomenology: Bergson's Interval in Irigaray" Hypatia 15.3 (2000); and Penelope Deutscher, *A Politics of Impossible Difference: The Later Work of Irigaray* (Ithaca: Cornell University Press, 2002).

7. Derrida is quite explicit about the future directedness of dissemination, of difference, and of deconstruction: "An interval must separate the present from what it is not in order for the present to be itself but this interval that constitutes it as present must, by the same token, divide the present in and of itself, thereby also dividing, along with the present, everything that is thought on the basis of the present, that is, in our metaphysical language, every being, and singularly substance or the subject. In constituting itself, in dividing itself dynamically, this interval is what might be called *spacing*, the becoming-space of time or the becoming-time of space (*temporization*). And it is this constitution of the present, as an "originary" and irreducibly nonsimple . . . synthesis of marks, or traces of retentions and protentions . . . that I propose to call archi-writing, archi-trace, or différance. Which (is) (simultaneously) spacing (and) temporization" Jacques Derrida, "Différance," in *Margins of Philosophy*, trans. Alan Bass (Chicago: University of Chicago Press, 1982), 1–28.

8. This argument is very convincingly developed by Pheng Cheah in his analysis of *Bodies That Matter* and the concept of 'materiality' underlying Butler's conception of materialization. See Pheng Cheah, "Mattering" Diacritics 26, no. 1 (1996): 108–139.

9. It is significant that, while we are free to identify ourselves with any social category we may choose, for the limits of identification are as broad as our imaginations, we are not free to undertake any type of identification whatsoever: our identificatory relations depend not only on who we are and how we see ourselves (our self-definition) but as significantly, who others are and how they see us (their self-identification). To undertake imaginative identifications within a solipsistic vacuum, where I alone dictate who and what I will identify with, without the symbolic confirmation of collective inclusion, is to risk the very notion of identity itself in its psychotic self-elaboration.

10. BA, 108.

11. Cornell, 1992: 23

12. Cornell, 1992: 145

13. Cornell, 1992: 5

14. Cornell, 1992: 137

15. Cornell, 1992: 145

16. Cornell, 1995: 34

17. Cornell, 1992: 2

18. Cornell, 1992: 166

19. Derrida, quoted in Phil of Limit 1992: 112

20. Cornell, 1992: 102

21. Cornell, 1992: 110–111

22. Judith Butler's Hegelianism is most explicit in her earliest writings. Butler, while certainly not a representative of identity politics, nevertheless remains today probably Hegelianism's most active feminist proponent. See Butler, *Subjects of Desire: Hegelian Reflections in Twentieth Century France* (New York: Columbia University Press, 1987), Her understanding of performative production of identity, and the centrality of recognition—or the withholding of recognition—by dominant social groups in the constitution of subject-positions (1990; 1994) is among the most current and powerful reenvisionings of Hegelian dialectics. See also Butler, *Gender Trouble: Feminism and the Subversion of Identity* (New York: Routledge, 1990), and *Bodies That Matter: On the Discursive Limits of "Sex"* (New York: Routledge, 1994).

23. There are also many feminist and queer theorists who work outside and beyond the problematic of recognition. See, for example, the writings of Eve Sedgwick, Luce Irigaray, and Sarah Kofman.

24. This tradition of subject interpellation dates from Althusser's earliest musings on the subject of ideology. See Althusser, *Writings on Psychoanalysis*, trans. Jeffrey Mehlman (New York: Columbia University Press, 1996), and Slavoj Zizek's more recent attempts to revitalize the same problematic. Also consider the use of Althusserian and Lacanian concepts of 'subject constitution' for explaining raced, sexed, and class or ethnic identifications.

25. As pervasive as the Hegelian tradition has been in feminist theory, the Nietzschean tradition has also had its feminist proponents, among them Luce Irigaray (1991; 1993), Claire Colebrook (2001), Ellen Mortensen (1994), and Kelly Oliver (1994).

26. The model of lordship and bondage has been the object of feminist investigation for several decades, ever since it was recognized that Hegel's schema of two "equal" self-consciousnesses could be read in terms of a kind of mythic prehistory of the relations between man and woman, or even between mother and child, that is, a relation between two different subjects that transforms into a relation of unequal subjects, a hypothesis that was certainly not part of Hegel's own understanding. See Angela Davis, "Unfinished Lecture on Liberation—II." in *The Angela Y. Davis Reader*, ed. Joy James (Oxford: Blackwell, 1998), for an early feminist and antiracist reading of Hegel's master/ slave dialectic; see Patricia Jagentowicz Mills, *Feminist Interpretations of G. W. F. Hegel*, (University Park: Pennsylvania State University Press, 1996), for an overview of more recent feminist writings.

Drucilla Cornell

Thinking the Future, Imagining Otherwise

I am grateful to the writers who have offered such appreciative, careful attention to my writing. I have treasured these readings; I am sometimes surprised, sometimes strongly disagree, but I am always learning.[1] While I have thought about each essay, and referred to each, I have often let these writings, collectively, spur me to keep thinking—off on my own as it were.

In truth, however, I never think alone. More than most philosophers I think with other philosophers—especially Levinas, Kant, and Heidegger. I think with them not primarily as they think alone but as they think with and against each other. I take to heart Levinas' quarrel with Heidegger who quarrels with Hegel who quarrels with Kant. For the most part, in the remarks I make now, I will stand with Kant. My position may change, but I will always be taking up my place among these thinkers.

I let philosophical abstractions develop out of my active personal relations and political commitments, as the experience of living ethical commitments is very much a part of working out the logic of the ideas. I do philosophy as a daughter whose mother wanted to die with dignity, as the mother of a young woman who confronts daily the racist attitudes and practices in the United States, as a friend of a friend in despair, as a playwright and lover, as a union organizer, peace activist, canvasser getting out the vote. To paraphrase from Immanuel Kant, "if justice goes out of the world, then human life is not worth living." Perhaps, the entire body of my work has been inspired by my profound and heartfelt agreement with Kant and with the recognition of how fragile the thinking of justice is in these times that have claimed the victory of technocratic policy making as the central task of political theory.

DIGNITY AS AN IDEAL ATTRIBUTE

Several of the chapters in this volume discuss my conceptualization of dignity. I want to make a few general remarks about the controversies contained in those chapters over dignity before turning to the authors making up this volume. Famously, Immanuel Kant argued that human beings have dignity in that as a matter of the ideal we are able to legislate for ourselves a moral law that has universal validity for all rational creatures. Dignity for Kant is that which is of "unconditioned and incomparable worth" as it stands as something beyond price.[2] But it is because humanity is capable of morality, and only because of such a capability, that humanity has dignity. Feminists have two worries about this Kantian conception of dignity. First, that Kant is talking about an ideal capability and that his definition might be used to exclude certain human beings from the reach of the ideal of humanity. Second, that everything we have learned from psychoanalysis and other forms of postmodern theory has argued that human beings are constituted at the core of our being by others and therefore the Kantian distinction between heteronomy and autonomy cannot hold. In what follows, I will try to trace out responses to these concerns in my own reformulation of both of these points. Ultimately, the question of dignity takes us back to the very heart of Kantian moral philosophy: the preservation of our humanity as an ideal of dignity beyond any measure in ontology. So, it is this question that will also take us along a careful reading of the debate between Levinas and Heidegger, as this dialogue is foundational to a number of the chapters making up this volume.

Turning now to the individual chapters, let me try to begin to clarify some misunderstandings of my understanding of dignity. In a thought-provoking essay Carolin Emcke writes: "Whereas Cornell writes that dignity 'precedes' the subject, that it cannot be taken away from the person, 'because it exists only in principle,' I would claim that dignity is always unlikely, against all odds, it is claimed when it is denounced, it shines only when it is violated. Dignity is only visible against a contrasting background of a humiliating, degrading, desperate situation." Although her thoughts are provocative, I am not sure that Emcke has captured my understanding of dignity. I do not believe that dignity is only visible against a "contrasting background of a humiliating, degrading, desperate situation," and yet, indeed, I do postulate dignity of the person as an ideal attribute that therefore in a sense precedes the subject. For me, the horrifying reality of the Holocaust, which Emcke so passionately describes, is perhaps one of the most terrifying examples in history of a people having their dignity systematically assaulted. It seems that Emcke reads me as tethering dignity to the actual ability of people to resist when they are under attack and actively claim their moral freedom. But what I have sought to do instead is to move beyond Kant in a certain sense and postulate dignity as inherent in us as an ideal, including in our own humanity, that is irreducible to any positive attribute, even the capacity to subject oneself to the moral law. Thus, I would not suggest a rational, moral will as the sole basis of dignity.

Human beings have their dignity violated all of the time, and in this sense I would suggest that we can pose a reading of Emcke implying that dignity remains as the trace in the face of the assaulted and tortured human being. It remains as a contrasting background that can not be destroyed. It remains no matter how the human being acts or does not act when confronted with heart-wrenching torture or brain-deadening pain. The trace of dignity within a person cannot die out even with the death of the human being. It is the dignity that remains even in the face of the dead piled up as corpses that calls us to witness to the full horror of what we have done to each other. It is because dignity remains that there is a call to all of us to reaffirm our own humanity and our responsibility before something as grand as the ideal of humanity itself. One of the most profound expressions of human dignity is in the ability to grieve, to recognize the horror of an event even against our inability to do anything about it.

But I take responsibility for Emcke misunderstanding because of a dilemma I confronted in a demand made on me to witness to the dignity of my mother's death, a demand made by my mother. This demand certainly took me into an in-depth exploration of both dignity and witnessing. Because my mother herself saw her exercise of the right to die as an expression of the moral will I was pulled in the direction of attempting to show why Kant was wrong about suicide and why his notion of the person needed to be enriched through psychoanalysis. In other words, I was witnessing to the dignity of my mother's claim of her own personhood during her demise as she saw her death, and let me quote her here, "I become my own person in the manner of my death."

In her thought-provoking essay Sara Murphy points out that in *Between Women and Generations* there is in fact a tension between some of the chapters in that in some I focus on the psychoanalytic reworking of autonomy, and in others I stress the pathos of the trace of dignity that calls us to, in all of its sublimity, a pathos that must be represented by the witness if it is to survive. The underlying question Murphy presents is: how can we reconcile *any* notion of Kantian autonomy with the psychoanalytic conception of each of us as dependent on others for psychic and physical survival? My ultimate point, however, is that these two different perspectives on dignity need not be contradictory.

To answer Murphy, let me just briefly rehearse my attempt to bring psychoanalysis to bear on a rewriting of a Kantian notion of autonomy that would take into account both our vulnerability as physical creatures and our constitutive psychic dependence on others. What I argued in simple terms is that Lacan's ultimate insight is that all children must confront the desire of the "mother other" and lose her as a fantasized object only for themselves. This loss of the mother as a fantasized object is what allows us to actually regain the mother as a whole person if we are able to confront the loss of her phantasmic form. This is what both allows us to have a relationship with her and free ourselves to gain an identity from our separate, enclosed relationship with this imaginary other.

What is often missed in Lacan is that this third term need not be phallic, and it certainly need not be an actual man; it can be a typewriter that the child identifies with the mother's work, it can be a love for another women, it can be a mother's basketball, which symbolizes her commitment to a sport. What is structurally necessary for the child to fend off the frightening *jouissance* of the other is that this other be symbolized so that the child can begin to separate its fantasy of being everything to the mother and yet find her again as a loving adult who actually supports the child in her efforts to be a separate person.

Symbolic castration in the work of the later Lacan is nothing other than the name for our destiny to be separate individuals who are not enthralled and imprisoned in a fantasized dyad. Rather than name the third term negatively as something like symbolic castration, which is still implying the needed threat to shatter the fantasy of this oneness with the mother, I named that law of psychic separation, "dignity." Dignity here would need to be understood affirmatively, not as symbolic castration with all of its negative overtones. As I wrote in *Between Women and Generations*: "A mother who stands up for her own desire, who claims it as her own, can split herself away from that fantasy Thing. By articulating her desire, by referencing it, she can pass down the one law that must be respected between mothers and daughters. It is the law of dignity that forbids incest, both literally and metaphorically. A child used by its parents, either in actual incest or in more subtle forms that encompass him or her as a 'thing' in the parents' lives, will be ensnared in the *jouissannce* of the big *Other*."[3]

The renaming of the law of psychic separation argued as a necessity in Lacanian psychoanalytic theory brings dignity into the purview of psychoanalysis and therefore reworks its meaning. It is, no doubt, not Kantian, but it is inspired by a Kantian aspiration to remain faithful to possibilities of freedom and transcendence. I followed Cornelius Castoriadis' redefinition of autonomy as the establishment of another relationship to the other and the subjects' own discourse, which allows that subject to slowly claim for itself decisions and choices that are figured as grounded in the subject. In following Castoriadis I accept that we can never draw a clean line between our conscious and unconscious investments, and therefore we can never do any more than igure our desires and choices as grounded in our self through a rational will because precise knowledge is never possible. However, in our struggle for individuation, and in our effort to claim our own person, which is always a process of reworking the way in which we imagine ourselves, we slowly claim our own person as that in which our own choices and decisions have indeed become ours. These founding fantasies through which we individuate ourselves always retain an imaginary dimension because there is no self without the basic organization of our primitive self by others. In a profound sense we can only know ourselves as already imagined by others. In this sense, the imaginary, by which I mean here the fundamental schemas given to us in our primordial self-images, lies at the very root of how we struggle to know ourselves. Self-knowledge then proceeds through an endless reworking of this basic material as the background we can never fully recapture, and yet which also facilitates our ability to reenvision who we are and how we might live.

The imaginary domain is the moral and legal right I named as the psychic space demanded by the principle of dignity. In this way we actually can rework the hypothetical fantasies we need to project as a story of ourselves in our attempt to make ourselves into a subject of our own desire. In principle, at the level of the ideal I argue that we must maintain this space as what recognizes in each one of us the possibility that we are the ones who give value to our world and to ourselves. It is this capacity in principle to give value to ourselves and to the world around us that I described as the practice of moral freedom and the self-responsibility that we must assume if we are to become individuated persons. As I also wrote, the psychoanalytic understanding of the process by which we assume responsibility for ourselves through claiming our own desire as a moral matter, moral in that it marks us as separate and responsible for who and how we desire, also could explain why we desire the freedom of others and not just negatively put up with it. Since we are dependent on others when we come into existence as subjects, and in my language as persons through the discourse of the big Other, our freedom is always social and relational. There is no better example of this dependence than that of the relationship of mothers and daughters. An unfree mother cut off from her own desire and correspondingly from the knowledge of her responsibility cannot pass on the value of freedom to her daughter. I then used this understanding of dignity to witness to my mother's exercise of her right to die as exactly that attempt to shape her own demise as one in which she sought to free herself from a kind of enthrallment to stereotypes of femininity, and by so doing claim her autonomy in a new relationship to the big Other that at the end of her life she saw as dominating her choices.

Kant famously argued against suicide because simply put it is an act in which we take our humanity as a means to promote our self-love and therefore paradoxically erase that ideal aspect of humanity when we extinguish ourselves. I suggested that once we understand that the concept of the person has an imaginary dimension to it, then we can make sense of how the shaping of one's own demise does not destroy the humanity of oneself understood as an ideal because we can, in the psychoanalytic sense I defined above, claim our autonomy by so doing. This imaginary dimension also allows us to project our dignity past the point of death through the image we leave behind for others. Strictly speaking, of course, Murphy is right that this is not Kant's understanding of autonomy, which is that as a rational agent we can exercise a will capable of determining itself by a moral law.[4] In Kant, of course, we can always do the wrong thing, and we often do, but it is our consciousness of the moral law, our ability to judge what we ought to do, that demands respect and constitutes our dignity.

The psychoanalytic reinterpretation of Kant is certainly consistent with more existential readings of Kant in which human beings are those who are the source of all value are beyond any valuational scheme that reduces them to a mere price.[5] I want to turn to Murphy's argument that dignity, as I am using it, involves not only a rewriting of Kantian autonomy but one that, to quote Murphy, "is able to sustain the ethical commitment to a form of alterity." As she rightfully notes, "In other words, what she often calls 'dignity' here has in some sense to do with autonomy—but it has more to do with a sort of autonomy that would rely for its meaning on a fundamentally heteronomous subjectivity, rather than, as is the case for Kant, reason." I actually have come to agree with Murphy that in *Between Women and Generations* I did not as successfully as I would have liked put together the two meanings of dignity that I offer—one more resonating with Kant, and the other more resonating with Levinas. I will seek to do so now, taking us back to the question I see as the heart of the matter in the debate over dignity: can we cherish our humanity as beyond any measure or valuation offered in ontology or any other description of our human nature?

In his defense of humanism Levinas locates our dignity in that before the face of the other we are uniquely called in our responsibility to him or her. In the recent film *Million Dollar Baby*, Frank has to face a classic Levinasian demand that is made by the other. After having coached a young woman to her million-dollar boxing match, Frank watches his prize fighter and now dear friend, Maggie, suffer terribly after an unexpected and dishonest punch left her paralyzed as a quadriplegic. Frank is the one who is to kill Maggie, at her request, in the name of her dignity because she wishes to die while the echoes of cheering crowds during her stellar and unfortunately tragically short career as a boxer still carry resonance. Frank, in anguish, seeks counsel from his local priest and is chided for even thinking of enacting such a cardinal sin. Such matters, according to the priest, are only fit for the judgment of God. Frustrated, Frank fills with anger and shouts to the priest that Maggie did not ask God to kill her, she asked him. Frank has become hostage to the other as there is no one else but Frank who can take on that responsibility. It is precisely in death, and our vulnerability to death, that often brings home in Levinas our responsibility to the other. This responsibility, of course, as portrayed in the movie *Million Dollar Baby* can often undo the subject in the deepest sense of the word. Yet, there is dignity in Levinas, in Kant's sense broadly construed, in that the human and its infinite worth must find a measure beyond ontology. This "beyond" in Levinas is the face of the other, beyond any substance or being itself. In *Million Dollar Baby* is Frank "free" to not decide once he is called? Is not Maggie's demand on him exactly a demand for a moral response? He can fail to respond, and he can fail to heed her desire to die, but once called he must decide. For my mother, there was no one else to witness to the dignity of her death but me. It had to be me, and, moreover, such witnessing demanded that I write of how my mother herself justified her right to die as crucial to the claiming of her own person and indeed as crucial to her exercise of freedom as a reimagined deleted hyphen narrative of her own decision to end her life in the way she chose.

We have one last problem that is raised by Murphy, and it has to do with why I defended dignity as an ideal attribute. It is ideal in Kant and Levinas because our dignity does not stem from our existence, but from some transcendence of it. And it is our ability to transcend necessity and make it our own that describes dignity as an ideal that marks the meaning of life that I am affirming here, while refusing to give a positive list of the attributes that make up that transcendence. It is a part of ideality that can never be fully reduced to the factual, and thereby to any set of positive attributes. Thus, inversely, no negative attributes can in fact undermine it. And so, I argued against Emecke that we do not lose our dignity even if we succumb to brutality.

So many of us—women, blacks, Chicanas, gays, lesbians, and the transgendered—have been thrown out of the ideal of humanity because we did not purportedly have the positive attributes associated with that ideal. I understand the criticisms of this ideal. My response is that the ideal of humanity demands vigilance to guard against the moment when it becomes an excuse for exclusion and degradation rather then a demand for respect.

CONTINUING THE DEBATE: LEVINAS, KANT, AND HEIDEGGER

As I wrote earlier Murphy asked the question of whether or not *dignity* is too weak of a word for the kind of responsibility that I adhere to in accepting the demand made on me by my mother to witness to the dignity of her death. She rightfully raises the question that this seems to be the acceptance of the other's demand on me as an absolute priority and for which I am responsible to heeding, and indeed submitting myself, as the hostage to that other. At the heart of Kant's Copernican Revolution, for Levinas, is the struggle to defend a vision of the human irreducible to the measure of ourselves as a psychological or natural being. So, although Levinas rejects the humanism that he understands as ultimately reducible to a kind of egoism of the self-sufficient "I," he remains close to Kant, as we will see in so many ways, in defending a different basis for humanism. This humanism of the other, for Levinas, saves humanism by relocating dignity in the individuation that is integral to the submission to responsibility. In submitting to this responsibility, to quote Levinas, "I am man holding up the universe full of things. Responsibility is saying prior to being and beings. Not saying itself in ontological categories."[6] It is humanity that introduces the idea of holiness into being, an idea of holiness that as an ideal must be lived up to for it can indeed, and tragically for Levinas, disappear.

This humanism of the other is fragile and can be extinguished. But, for Levinas, awakening means both to be vigilant and awake to the fragility of the ideal of holiness and to know in a deep sense it is up to us to keep this holiness in the world. Levinas, of course, is continually responding to Heidegger here. What I simply want to note here in my response to Murphy is that there is a greater connection between Levinasian holiness and Kantian dignity because they are both an attempt to preserve the transcendence of humanity. To explore this connection more thoroughly I now turn to Roger Berkowitz's chapter in this volume, which rightly notes that Heidegger is in a sense one of my main interlocutors and that I am ultimately on the side of Kant against Heidegger because of my continued adherence to the connection of transcendental imagination to ethics. But, as we will see, I also argue against Levinas in that the transcendental imagination cannot be excluded from an account of ethical receptivity. There is a deep sense in which I have been arguing against Heideggerian pessimism throughout my work. But there is a lesser known Heidegger who, beginning with his work in *Being and Time* attempts to think through the transcendence of humanity by rereading Kant's writing on the transcendental imagination in the *Critique of Pure Reason*. It is Berkowitz's contention, and I agree with him, that I remain close to the Kantian Heidegger. Let me now turn to Berkowitz's discussion of my relationship to Heidegger as this in turn will help us understand why I have felt the need to side with Levinas in his critique of Heidegger's later writings, even while arguing that Levinas cannot make sense of ethical receptivity to the other without the transcendental imagination.

Berkowitz rightly points out that in *Being and Time* Heidegger, through an original and controversial interpretation of Kant's notion of the transcendental imagination, connected finitude with transcendence and freedom in that the human being is fated to project himself or herself into the future. The early Heidegger always acknowledges his debt to Kant's theory of the transcendental imagination. His reinterpretation, if we dare to succinctly formulate it, is that Kant effectively undermines the traditional metaphysical notion of being as permanent presence by reading Kant to make "presence" a project of *Dasein's* being in time. It is the "I" of the transcendental apperception that abstracts, emphasizes and thus gives us the notion of an abiding presence.

All onto-theological definitions of being as eternal and permanent derive then, according to Heidegger's reading, from *Dasein's* fate of temporal projection. Heidegger justifies his reading by arguing that Kant himself privileges the *facultas praevidendi*, which anticipates images of the future and comports us to them over the other faculties of the imagination, which form either images of the present or the past. In this way, for Heidegger, it was Kant who disclosed both the finitude of thinking and the ontological character of *Dasein* as the being that temporalizes itself by pointing itself toward the future. Of course, there have been many criticisms of Heidegger's reading of Kant; my point is not to defend his reading in my short comments here. What is clear is that even in the second edition of the *Critique of Pure Reason* the deduction of the categories of understanding still originates in the synthesizing act of the productive imagination. I will return to the transcendental imagination in my own work shortly because, as Berkowitz points out, it is central to my own work, and is what I have relied upon to explain our receptivity before the suffering of others.

For now I want to return to Berkowitz's reading of Heidegger, which argues that by the 1930s Heidegger had distanced himself from the close connection he originally drew between *Dasein* and the transcendental imagination. For Berkowitz, Heidegger felt that his earlier work remained trapped in a subjectivist world view. Again, Berkowitz shows us that Heidegger's pessimism lies in our inability to escape by any will or action of our own from the technical worlding of our world, which is how "being reveals itself to man" in modernity. The more we try to escape our fate with action, will, or the two combined through the representation of ideals, the more we bury ourselves in the technical forgetfulness of being, which ultimately keeps ourselves from thinking. It is the thinking of our fate that is all that is left for us to do now. There are of course other interpretations on the relationship between Heidegger, *Being and Time*, and his later work. But Berkowitz is one of the most careful readers of Heidegger we have, and for our purposes here I will accept his position of how and why Heidegger distances himself from his earlier work.

Levinas' answer to Heidegger through the ideal of holiness is that the good imposed upon us as a responsibility to the other arises for us out of an anarchy that in a profound sense is prior to the constitution of the subject and, in fact, calls it into being. To return to Kant briefly, Kant famously argued against the notion of a traditional opposition of a permanent self and a so-called transient, temporal self by revealing that the transcendental ego only survives in time insofar as this imagination presupposes a horizon of identity and permanence. Why is this the case? Because this sense of abiding in time as an "I" is only accomplished through an already a priori synthesis that something can be experienced as the same through change. This is a highly original notion of how the self is self-constituting because it is constituted by something that is beyond itself, namely, the transcendental imagination, which gives it motion but cannot be known. Still, Levinas rejects this notion of the subject of the transcendental imagination in favor of a responsibility that arises prior to subjectivity, in a primordial confrontation of the face to face.

What is the face of Levinas? We need to look at this articulation of the face carefully because it has often been profoundly misunderstood. The face in Levinas is not reducible to the actual physical face of a human being. As he writes, "The face that looks at me affirms me. But face to face I can no longer deny the other. It is only the *noumenal* glory of the other that makes the face to face situation possible."[7] It is the respect in this sense that attaches to the noumenal face of the other that demands that I accept the commandment that I must do justice for him or her. As we will see, once the present of the third is there, and it is always already there for Levinas, this commandment that respect be attached to the other face is also a commandment that we seek to realize justice not just for this one other face but for all others. But I am getting ahead of myself here. I will return to Levinas' defense and critique of the Kantian social contract in the next section.

For now, I simply want to emphasize that the humanism of the other is not understandable without the noumenal glory of the face that calls to us in transcendence of ourselves by submitting to the responsibility that respect demands. Here we have Levinas' answer to Heidegger in a nutshell. It is the otherwise than being in the face to face that allows a nonsubjectivist notion of meaning to preserve the human and to open up a space for responsibility. This notion of responsibility is supposedly not captured by Heidegger's critique of the willing subject. As Murphy points out, however, this answer to Heidegger survives by making the face, or otherness, abstract from the very suffering human being that Levinas often figures as the face of the other: the widow, the homeless person, the stranger, or the tortured. Murphy here is echoing Luce Irigaray's critique of Levinas that even if this space in its noumenal glory is God, then it harbors a masculine face and one based in the father of monotheism. Thus, in a sense Levinas sacrifices his own notion of vulnerability of the actual physical suffering creature in order to preserve his answer to Heidegger that there is a preoriginary other before being. But we need to understand why Levinas was so determined to preserve the noumenal glory of the face in his response to Heidegger. For me, the ultimate problem is that he cannot explain a receptivity to others without the transcendental imagination. Before turning to Levinas and the transcendental imagination we need to understand why Levinas was so determined to preserve the glory of the face in his response to Heidegger.

Levinas attended the famous debate between Heidegger and the Kantian Ernst Cassirer in Davos in 1929. At that time Levinas considered himself to be on Heidegger's side of the debate. Of course, all this took place before the rise to power of Hitler and the Third Reich in Nazi Germany. Cassirer's heroism during the Nazi period is well known, and Levinas took himself to task for not grasping what is right in Cassirer's Kantianism: the preservation of humanism. For Levinas, however, Heidegger is right that meaning must be understood in terms of a greater transcendence than that allowed by an interpretation of the human bond to culture, to symbol formation, and, yes, to the imaginative production of the meaning of shared symbols. Levinas ultimately views the transcendence of meaning as beyond cultural determination but in a very specific sense. The transcendence of meaning, and correspondingly of human dignity, derives from the absolute moral priority of the other person that Levinas evokes in the telling phrase "the humanism of the other." *To be* for the other, otherwise than being, to serve the other morally, and to serve all others in justice is where Levinas "locates" the ultimate exigency of meaning and the dignity of all of us in the grandeur of humanity. Levinas deepens this sentiment in his own words:

> From a responsibility even more ancient than the conatus of substance, more ancient than the beginning and the principle, from the anarchic, the ego returned to self, responsible for Others, hostage of everyone, that is, substituted for everyone by its very non-interchangeability, hostage of all others who, precisely others, do not belong to the same genus as the ego because I am responsible for them without concerning myself about their responsibility for me because I am, in the last analysis and from the start, even responsible for that, the ego, I; I am man holding up the universe "full of things." Responsibility or saying prior to Being and beings, not saying itself in ontological categories. Modern anti-humanism may be wrong in not finding for man, lost in history and in order, the trace of this pre-historic an-archic saying.[8]

Thus, Levinas disagrees with Cassirer in that he rejects the idea that human freedom is rooted in the symbolic forms received and then reworked in self-consciousness. He rejects the notion of self-knowledge as the recognition and reimagination of the cultural products of consciousness as the transcendental source of meaning. But Levinas agrees with Cassirer that even if we must locate the basis of humanity differently than Cassirer does, we still must seek to protect the dignity of humanity. It is this protection of the dignity of humanity that ties Levinas to Cassirer in that Levinas, like Cassirer, also rejects Heidegger in his insistence—as Berkowitz rightly interprets the later Heidegger—on evoking a freedom that is not based in any attribute of the human but requires instead a resolute receptivity. This resolute receptivity is a careful disengagement from the human and more particularly all forms of conscious will because the fate of salvation must be given, never made. Heidegger suggests to us: "Through this determination of the essence of man the humanistic interpretations of man as *animal rational*, as 'person,' as spiritual-ensouled-bodily being, are not declared false and thrust aside. Rather, the sole implication is that the highest determinations of the essence of man in humanism still do not realize the proper dignity of man. To that extent the thinking in *Being and Time* is against humanism."[9] We must think our way through the forgetfulness of being and wait, as Heidegger famously tells us, for the gods to save us now. In his chapter in this volume Berkowitz reads the entire *ouvre* of my work as inspired by an ethical determination to show why and how we remain responsible for the world we make, and that indeed there is space for a nontechnical notion of freedom and dignity, and the justice they demand.

Berkowitz notes that even the later Heidegger may retain something like freedom. It is the happening of ownness in which man—and I am using this word deliberately–thinks the historically given. It is in this thinking that Heidegger suggests we have our highest destiny. Is this Pheng Cheah's vulnerable

freedom? I introduce Cheah's chapter at this point because Cheah is questioning my continuing commitment to the ideal of humanity as expressed in an
article with Sara Murphy titled "Antiracism, Multiculturalism, and the Ethics
of Identification." Of course, in his chapter in this book Cheah cannot be expected to offer us any detailed account of his own understanding of the relationship of the early Heidegger to the later Heidegger. It is the givenness of the
ownness that is our destiny that seems to be close to Cheah's vulnerable freedom.[10] A question to Cheah would be: "on which Heidegger" is his notion of
vulnerable freedom dependent? A further question would be: why does Cheah
locate the other than human as the inhuman and use the inhuman to refer
"to those forces that constitute and also exceed our ability to remake ourselves
that is a fundamental feature of our humanity"? In other words, the human is
never the source of meaning, even if as a complicated reworked source of
meaning, but is instead the fundamental feature that constitutes us in freedom. Ultimately, this line of questioning to Cheah is trying to understand
why he named this other "the inhuman"? It is important to note that Heidegger himself, at least in the "Letter on Humanism," wants to very carefully
distinguish his own complex position on humanism from any indication that
our acceptance of who we are as always already thrown from Being itself into
the truth of being should never be identified as inherently inhumane, let alone
inhuman. Heidegger confirms this when he suggests: "But in the claim upon
man, in the attempt to make man ready for this claim, is there not implied a
concern about man? Where else does 'care' tend but in the direction of bringing man back to his essence? What else does that in turn betoken but that
man (homo) become human (humanus)? Thus *humanitas* really does remain
the concern of such thinking. For this humanism: meditating and caring, that
man be human and not inhumane, 'inhuman,' that is outside his essence. But
in what does the humanity of man consist? It lies in his essence."[11] Is this simply a matter of rhetoric about how we define or name that which is outside of
the human and that which constitutes us? No one knows better then Cheah
how the rhetorical name is part of the constitution of what we express. So my
questions remain.

Cheah is right, however, that ultimately there may be a significant disagreement between us about both the role of the transcendental imagination
and the productive and reproductive imagination, or in the case of my coauthored essay with Sara Murphy among the three of us. If we were to follow the
Heidegger of *Being and Time* but take a slightly different turn, then we would
argue, and I have done so, that it is this projected future of possibility that affords us the chance of an imaginative, and of course actual, variation of who
we are as we project ourselves out into the future. So I am grateful to Cheah
for the word *affordance*, but I would keep it as a verb in that we are afforded
transformative possibilities by the transcendental imagination which gives us
to be toward a future horizon.

Ultimately, as I have already suggested, Cheah has raised one of the most telling and pressing questions, which is that of the status of the transcendental imagination as well as the status of the human. It is because of my continual worrying about what it might mean to forsake this category ethically that I hold on to it while at the same time recognizing the attending ethical dilemmas of any attachment to this ideal. Let me just return here to emphasize my own commitment to humanism by revisiting my discussion of Levinas as he tries to navigate in his own thought between Heidegger and Cassirer. To quote Levinas:

> The inner world is contested by Heidegger as by the social sciences. To think, after the end of metaphysics, is to reply to the silent language of the invitation, reply from the depth of listening to the peace that is the original language, marvel at this silence and this space. Simplicity and wonder that are also the endurance and the extreme attention of poets and artists it is, in the proper meaning of the term, keeping the silence, tending the silence. The poem or work of art tends the silence, *lets the essence of being be*, like the shepherd tends his flock. *Being needs man just as a fatherland or a soil needs natives.* The strangeness of man to the world, this stateless condition, would attest the last shudders of metaphysics and the humanism it upholds. By this denunciation of the 'inner world' Heidegger radicalizes Husserl's anti-psychologism. The end of subjectivity began with the twentieth century. The social sciences and Heidegger lead to the triumph of mathematical intelligibility, sending the subject, the individual, his unicity and his election back into ideology, or else rooting man in being, making him its messenger and poet.[12]

Obviously, Levinas has had a profound impact on my work. Although Levinas himself always sought to remain close to Kant, and we will see how important that is when we turn to the role of political theory, I remain more of a Kantian in that I wish to preserve the person, even if psychoanalytically tempered, as it is initially justified in the transcendental ego of the transcendental imagination. Indeed, instead I would provocatively suggest against Levinas that we cannot account for ethical receptivity without the transcendental imagination. As Berkowitz notes, the *Philosophy of the Limit* subscribes to the utopian powers of the transcendental imagination as both the power to envision the dissimilarity in the similar and the similarity in the dissimilar. It is the productive or transcendental imagination that produces the unity of our world as well as the specificity of objects as this or that. If there was no imagination to provide us with a sense of identity, even through temporal difference by synthesizing our horizons through common features that give *sense* to events and ourselves in events, then there would be no sense of a perduring "I," which could be "there" separate and receptive to the other. In other words, there has to be someone "there" to be receptive to the other as other. Levinas' ethics demands a certain kind of receptivity, and I am suggesting here that ultimately this receptivity is not explainable without the transcendental imagination. Said another way, my central point to Levinas is that in order to be produced by the ethical relationship we must obviously have been produced as an "I" that is other to the other and thus receptive to the other as other. This receptivity is what Richard Kearney has called the "empathetic aspect" of the transcendental imagination. To quote Kearney:

> Can we answer to and for the other if we cannot hear its call, if we cannot empathize? Since Kant we have recognized that imagination is the common root of both sensibility and understanding. While the role of imagination in understanding pertains to its productive and projective powers, its role in sensible intuition expresses its ability to remain open to what is given from beyond itself. Kant, at least as interpreted by Heidegger in *Kant and the Problem of Metaphysics*, identifies the intuitive dimension of imagination with its receptivity to the law, that is, its capacity for ethical *respect*. By extension, one could argue that the receptive power of imagination lies at the very root of our moral capacity to respect the otherness of the other person, to treat the other as an end rather then a means, to *empathize*. So that if we cannot be *free* without the projective capacity of imagination we cannot be *moral* without its receptive capacity.[13]

I accept the vulnerability and receptivity as that which opens us to otherness, including the otherness of our selves, and the larger physical world that can harm us or enhance us but on which we are inevitably dependant. Berkowitz speaks of my attempt to rework Levinas' notion of vulnerability to humility before the suffering of others rather than to awe before the moral law in our selves. I am willing to embrace the word *humility* because it conveys the sense I am seeking in that even if we can know what is right and wrong we can also know how hard it is to live up to that and how any one of us can crumble before overwhelming pain, certainly when it is imposed on our body as in torture.

But this receptivity to the suffering of others is for me ultimately rooted in an interpretation of the transcendental imagination. To defend this other subject is beyond my short response. In the end, however, I do not believe we can do without this other interpretation of the transcendental imagination in ethics and, indeed, in politics. I understand the consequences of this argument in the specific sense that it ultimately undermines Levinas' aspiration to protect humanism. Without falling prey to Heidegger's critique of modern subjectivity I am reintroducing a subject, if only a subject decentered. Precisely because this subject is constituted by the transcendental imagination it is beyond its grasp, at least its theoretical grasp. Still, this returns us to what Heidegger would have called a "philosophy of freedom and transcendental subjectivity rooted in modern subjectivity." Aware as I am of the consequences, I am also strongly arguing that there is no other choice for us if we are to preserve the ultimate ethical demand behind humanism.

In the Constitutional Court of South Africa there hangs a blue dress made up of plastic fragments. The artist made this blue dress to give to a dead woman, to lovingly clothe her with a covering that came too late. The artist was inspired—or perhaps in Levinasian language, called—to give this blue dress to a faceless dead woman because of a famous story that tells of a vulnerable woman who succumbed to death under torture. In the story, which seems to be true, there is nothing left of this woman's body so as to identify who she is. Her face was beaten beyond recognition. Her body was cut up beyond any possible identification. What was left of the violently dismembered body were the blue plastic underpants she made for herself out of fragments she found in the garbage of her prison. Purportedly, there was one telling feature about her, "[S]he was a brave one that one, she gave us nothing."

The blue dress is offered by the artist as her thanks, but also as we will see, nothing less than as an eternal reminder that the new South Africa has as one of its many difficult tasks the redemption of the dead from their senseless suffering. Emecke's earlier question to me is: what if she had not resisted? What if there was no notation that she was a brave one? Would we still attribute dignity to her and seek to address her as worthy of our respect rather then the defilement she underwent through torture and sexual violence? In her essay on my work Karin van Marle argues that my understanding of Kant's *sensus communis aestheticus*, as I explain it in *Between Women and Generations*, can be helpful in South Africa because the new South Africa is in a profound sense a people waiting to become everything the "new" represents. Throughout her work on constitutional interpretation van Marle insists that, in an obvious way, the constitutional court cannot look back to a history of precedent because the legal system of apartheid, even though much legislation still remains as law, can no longer be justified except by appealing to the projected aspirations of justice that frames the South African constitution itself. Thus, constitutional interpretation must remain explicitly toward the future of an "ought to be" and shared community, which is inseparable from the awe, and indeed horror, inspired by the sublimity of the apartheid past and what the blacks of South Africa were forced to endure. As van Marle writes: "The *sensus communis aestheticus* in Kant thus points toward an 'ought to be' of a shared community, and the enlarged mentality to which Kant refers does not refer to a given community but to the idea of humanity. So when we judge an object as sublime we include the 'should' of the universal, which is inseparable from an idealized humanity. The *sensus communis* thus demands a particular kind of public sense. Yet it is not that which we normally think of as a community. It is an imagined community where all the possible viewpoints of others are imagined."[14] It is the sublimity of ordinary people that is so often ignored by those who fail to see courage where it exists because they deny the humanity of those engaged in political struggles throughout the world.

The *sensus communis* is always fragile in that we can fail to heed the sublimity of the other. Of course, the woman in the blue dress, at least according to the one brief mention of her, seems to be a fine candidate for a Kantian moral heroine in that she stood against her torturers until the end. The blue dress is meant to cover the vulnerable body and the grandeur of the face of the woman in her unique humanity even as it is beaten beyond recognition. It is in only by imagining the trace of the face of the other, to imagine it when we are literally rendered faceless, that makes the respect for dignity, including the dignity of humanity, something that resists as a trace even when in our actual actions we were brought to our knees or destroyed. Through our vulnerability we know how easy it is for any one of us to be destroyed. The blue dress reminds us of our vulnerability as much as it reminds us of the dead woman's courage. That is what the ethical relationship demands of us, that we find the trace of the face even when it has been literally destroyed and insist on revering what has been defiled. As we do so we constitute the very fragile *sensus communis aestheticus* in which we can perhaps commune with one another in the overwhelming suffering and horror brought to actual human beings in the course of this daily, lived brutality that has come to so often define the "modern" world. To feel this horror in Kant's sense of the sublime can lead us not to collapse, but to imagine otherwise as we are pulled toward an ideal of humanity that is ultimately inseparable from the judgment we make that this kind of suffering is not only wrong but also senseless.

SEXUAL DIFFERENCE, GENDER, AND UTOPIA

Does the gift of the blue dress in any way minimize the faceless woman's suffering, the anguish of her last hours? Does it facilely try to restore what has been lost by insisting that her dignity be remembered? This danger of minimization is of course Emcke's worry about not recognizing in certain situations how our dignity is destroyed. Nothing will ever give that young woman back her life, or save her from that torture. By confronting her face, in Levinas' sense of the word, we open ourselves up to the full horror of what was done to her. In no way do we pretend that we can achieve a restoration that belies the reality of her terrible death. But in this moment we are called to what Walter Benjamin terms an *"anamnestic* solidarity" with the dead by refusing to turn away from the horror of what was done to her. The overwhelmingness of the suffering of which the blue dress is a reminder is a call not only to remember, but in Benjamin's sense of the word, to undertake the struggle for a different future that the dress pulls us toward in its demand that we allow ourselves to be pulled into the sublimity of her suffering. Benjamin suggests: "The past carries with it a temporal index by which it is referred to redemption. There is a secret agreement between past generations and the present one. Our coming was expected on earth. Like every generation that preceded us, we have been endowed with a weak Messianic power, a power to which the past has a claim. That claim cannot be settled cheaply."[15] But who were these men who scratched in their notebooks that "she was a brave one this one, she gave us nothing?" In his chapter in this volume on progress and evil, Martin Matuštik rightfully argues that I reject the idea that we can triumph over evil by taking away the human face of the evildoer. Indeed, the danger is that by dehumanizing the evildoer we fail to come to terms with evil itself. Immanuel Kant located evil in the *Willkur* (the will of our choosing self) and not in the *Wille*, or moral will. What Hannah Arendt called the "banality of evil" is close to this Kantian idea that evil is rooted in the pettiness of human beings as they seek what they want caught in the larger machinery of society without any kind of moral check or ethical limitation. Matuštik insightfully argues that there is a sense that Kant has it wrong and that evil might be rooted in, at least, the pretense of the good will. It is of course a question whether the pretense of the good will would more adequately fit under the *Willkur* rather then the *Wille*, but for now I want to review what I take to be the crucial insights of Matuštik's argument. He is suggesting that evil resides in a kind of naïve faith in our own goodness. This naïve faith becomes a kind of false reverence for what I take progress to be in that I elevate myself as the one who knows what is good for humanity and by so doing can name the other who threatens my knowledge of goodness as the evil other who sets himself against humanity because he sets himself against me.

As Matuštik rightly notes I associate cruelty with the draining of meaning and significance from the ideals that guide our action and that invoke such ideals only as code words for the self-righteousness that assures knowledge of what is good to those who think they are in pursuit of such good. Matustik is arguing that evil is a religious phenomenon in that it turns revelations into a form of self-assurance where belief becomes a form of knowledge justifying the commission of horribly cruel acts against the evil others seen as threats to the true progress of humanity. But Matuštik also reminds us that this drained world of meaning that leaves ideals as nothing but empty fetishes also may be the wellspring of this grasping on to the truth of what humanity demands at any given moment. Matuštik remarks: "Cruelty must be grasped as a religious phenomenon: I hold dear my naive innocence (this is evil's banality); then in offense I elevate immediate faith in my goodness into a moral idea of progress (this is radical moral evil that wants the regime change for the world); and at its most intense, in my despairing offence at the state of creation, I become a heroic yet cruel master praying to myself (this is the evil of spiritless religiosity, namely the diabolical)." (170, this volume) Offended despair shields itself in smugness and self-righteousness and guards itself in beating down the other; it is in this way that we fulfill the prophecy that the other is indeed evil.

Matuštik certainly calls us back to all of the worries about the ideal of humanity when they are deployed as justifications for some of the worst kinds of violence. Matuštik is right that I think the only answer to this dilemma is that the ideal of humanity should never be thought as ontologically immanent and therefore graspable by theoretical knowledge, and we must always understand that the visibility by which we configure any ideal carries with it an invisibility that is always being contested even as we try to bring to life and give form to these ideals aesthetically. There is always more to what it might mean to be human. As we envision women to be human beings, for example, the configuration of the ideal itself changes. And this means that all of the great ideals have a multiple ideality, to use Matuštík's phrase, in that they resist full comprehensibility even as they are configured and endlessly reworked through struggles over inclusion in the ideal of humanity itself.[16] Thus, the acceptance of human finitude, which relinquishes any notion that God's eyes are ours, does not mean that we have to relinquish ideals, but it does mean that we have to recognize the limits of any configuration before us in the world. Matuštík's warning of course is chilling because it reminds us just how often evildoers are absolutely convinced they are doing the right thing. In her extraordinary book, *Country of My Skull*, Antjie Krog tells of how the torturers of apartheid became completely disoriented, the vast majority of them good Christian men, by the fact that they were now being accused of wrong doing. In their acts of human cruelty they viewed themselves as the ones who had to suffer and endure the dirty work so that the good of a "civilized" white Africa could be preserved. In a deep and profound sense their disorientation, from which many never recovered, was due to the fact that their world crumbled and lost all meaning when the humanity they knew collapsed under what they could not see as possible—the inclusion of black South Africans in that ideal itself.

Heidegger would continue to dismiss this attempt to introduce finitude through recognition of the incomplete, and thus aesthetic nature, of all the great ideals. For Heidegger, any thematization or representation of ideals remains entrapped in theory at the very moment that it struggles over representation. From the beginning of my work I have strongly agreed with Levinas that we cannot forsake what Heidegger means by theory. As Levinas explains, we are never alone in the ethical relationship with the other. We are always with many others, or what Levinas calls the "third." To quote Levinas: "I must judge, where before I was to assume responsibilities. Here is the birth of the theoretical; here the concern for justice is born, which is the basis of the theoretical. But it is always starting out from the Face, from the responsibility for the other that justice appears, which calls for judgment and comparison, a comparison of what is in principle incomparable, for every being is unique; every other is unique. In that necessity of being concerned with justice that idea of equity appears, on which the idea of objectivity is based."[17]

In 1992 when I wrote the *Philosophy of the Limit* I was defending a place for theory in this Levinasian sense. And indeed, like Levinas, I felt that the starting place for the representation of a theory of justice was something like the Kantian social contract, which is why in both the *Imaginary Domain* and *At the Heart of Freedom* I worked to show that the imaginary domain could be understood as consistent with Kant's understanding of the social contract. This was not strategic, as Jay Bernstein suggests, but more specifically a kind of negotiation with what I felt was demanded by the requirement to represent justice and to defend ideals within that representative framework. At the time of *Philosophy of the Limit* many readers of Jacques Derrida's work had concluded that deconstruction had effectively undermined any place of the theoretical by showing that theoretical claims were always displaced in a representational schema that could never be fully comprehended. I was then, and am now, in complete agreement that no theory of justice can be self-completing and that this lack of completion is consistent with what I just said about the acceptance of our finitude and that the representation of frameworks for justice through hypothetical experiments in the imagination are ultimately hypothetical and representative. Yet, we are called by the ethical relationship to engage in those representations, to defend them, and, yes, to fight for them knowing all the while that they might be replaced and that their very finitude almost hopes for their very reconfiguration.

Levinas himself limits the liberal Kantian state by what he calls "charity." We are always reminded to do more as we seek peace not simply with the other man or woman, but for the other man or woman. Charity reminds us that the work of justice is always never done even if it is served by ideals and representations. I cannot emphasize this point enough. The *Philosophy of the Limit* sought to answer good conscience by endlessly insisting that what deconstruction shows us is that there is a limit on any claim through our theoretical knowledge of justice and that limit always points us to the "more" of what remains to be done and to a "beyond" of any of our current fields of representation. My purpose was to argue that Derrida radicalizes the notion of the "laying of the ground" in Kant's *Critique of Pure Reason* by showing us not only can the a priori of the transcendental aesthetic never be overcome by reason, allowing reason to come full circle and justify itself, but also the question of who is "man" cannot be said to work as another ground for pure practical reason. Most notably, I suggested that Derrida set deconstruction to work against all attempts to ontologize the meaning of man, including Heidegger's regardless of whether these ontologizations are optimistic or pessimistic. Therefore, my argument was that the deontological moment in Derrida was always done to show us that it is impossible to know definitively what is possible or what is impossible in terms of our dreams of how we might create a more just society. I read this understanding of the limit as a radicalization of Kant's insight, one that I have already suggested that Heidegger builds off from in his earlier writings in the sense that human reason is always seen as the reason of a finite creature, and the limits on how this finite creature thinks actually produces an openness to the future. This is the future of *Being and Time* that I earlier defended in which the transcendental imagination reinterpreted as *Dasein* is how we are *in time* always pointed to a future horizon that reconfigures our lived possibilities. I still hold to that sense of the future as a lived horizon of possibility combined with the Levinasian demand that we are commanded to not only represent this horizon for ourselves but to represent it as justice for all others.

This horizon, then, is always being envisioned and reenvisioned, and here I agree with Sheldon Wolin's earlier work of *Politics and Vision* in the claim that all political theory is somehow inscribed in some kind of vision of that ideal horizon and should acknowledge how any theoretical perspective is shaped by how that horizon is imagined. This first sense of the future is then connected to the second sense of the future in all of my work in that I argue that deconstruction shows us the limits of the knowable, and indeed of the imaginable, in the name of a future that might always yet arrive. In an introduction to a reissued version of my chapter in *Philosophy of Limit* on the violence of the masquerade I suggest:

> We can not know the future precisely; if something is the future, the other, then it is not in our system of calculable knowledge. Thus, the lighthouse, or lighthouses, can be read as giving us warnings. But of course it can also be read as giving us hope of redemption held out—to use Derrida's famous phrase—in the messianism without messiah. My interpretation, if you will, is more optimistic in that I read my own metaphor as giving us the glimmer of a good that is always beyond our immediate horizon of knowledge. The lighthouse, of course, could be read either way. Derrida is right that there is always a risk and a promise of redemption and the relentless protection of the "yet to come" as what might be different, as what might be other, and, yes, what might be a redeemed world. There is no promise of redemption without this risk. And yet, as Derrida himself always wrote, his own deconstruction was always in the spirit of Marxism in that he sought to delimit the realm of the possible in the name of the what might yet still be possible— the dream of a redeemed humanity that is inseparable from ideal of communism.[18]

Elizabeth Grosz rightly emphasizes the second sense of the future in the *Philosophy of the Limit* as pointing beyond any currently envisioned or represented field of reference. But Grosz also challenges me to rethink what she takes to be my continuing dualism in that I pit culture against nature. I think that she is right in that despite places where I always try to show the limits of subjective idealism, including the subjective idealism associated with Cassirer discussed earlier, I tend to put all meaningful notions on the side of culture which belies that nature itself is transformative. In a series of original works and articles, Grosz has shown us the radical implications of Darwin's theory of evolution. She is not alone in this work, but she is one of the most important thinkers about what this means for political theory and social philosophy. I accept her corrective. However, it is clear that my work has focused on transcendence and freedom, and that the ethical is in the end inseparable from these. Thus, while there should be a softening of the Kantian dualism in that nature has "spirit" and transformative powers, I would still wonder what is the full relevance of this insight for ethics.

My emphasis on transcendence and freedom depends very much on a commitment to the defense of ideals, and in this context I want to thank Ben Pryor for his important reminder of my relative silence about Nietzsche and the importance of Nietzsche for my work. Of course, it is well beyond the scope of my response to Pryor's excellent chapter to develop anything like a full engagement with Nietzsche's provocations to Kant's critical idealism. I do want to begin, however, by saying that I have no doubt that there is space for Nietzsche in the imaginary domain, and I do not read him as antithetical to my project as a whole, particularly in *Defending Ideals*. It is always important to remember that Nietzsche consistently distinguishes between the base ideals of our dying European culture and the honorable ideals of healthier moments that he imagines in the life of our species.

It is necessary to consider whether it is ideals themselves, or only unhealthy ideals such as the aesthetic ideal of slavish Christianity, at which Nietzsche aims his ire. I am, of course, in agreement with him so far as the need to take aim at a kind of aesthetic ideal based in resentment has never been more important for an ethics or politics hoping to muster strength for the challenges of our time. Thus, perhaps the real question is, can there be a healthy defense of ideals? Of course, I am arguing that there can be. Ben Pryor has succinctly defined my position: the meaning of ideals is, on this reading, in the imaginative task that we engage in when we defend ideals. It is also important to note that I share with Nietzsche his critique of a fetishistic sense of history, which inevitably institutionalizes itself as an ideology of capitulation. There is a kind of brute power—Nietzsche would use the word *macht*—of a blind appeal to the factual, which then becomes idealized, even idolized, in the affirmation of the status quo. We are surrounded by this idealization of the so-called power of the factual in so many of our political discussions today, which insist that we are left with nothing other than the endless grinding of the wheels of advanced capitalism. Indeed, Nietzsche often rails against these idols as gross attempts to break the resistance of young people who dare to imagine a world that is otherwise to this fetishized world of supposed facts. For it is Nietzsche who always reminds us that those facts are themselves fabrications, and it is in his relentless antipositivism that I have always found an ally in Nietzsche.

Pryor asks me the question, how does the Nietzschean critical movement, the discovery of the will to power and self-overcoming at the heart of our desire for justice, creep in and transform the presentation of the values on which we must insist, even as we question them? Following the lead of Elizabeth Grosz I have interpreted the will to power not as applied to persons, but rather to forces and points that are always pulling our world forward in a process of continual overcoming. In all of Grosz's work, both Nietzsche and Deleuze are understood to overcome mechanistic or theistic descriptions of the actions of forces. In a certain sense, the will to power can be interpreted as a disruptive and transformative *telos* of "life," which of course never reaches backward or forward into a final point of causation. On this reading, then, we cannot trace ideals back through any simple causal chain to an internalized, personalized notion of the will to power. I am not arguing that Pryor would necessarily disagree with the interpretation I am giving to Grosz's own engagement with Nietzsche and Deleuze, but I am arguing against any interpretation of Nietzsche that would suggest that ideals are, in a simplistic sense, debunked because they are rooted in the will to power. Perhaps more importantly, Nietzsche is one of our great thinkers of the imagination, and his antipositivism leads him to remind us again and again that even the best genealogy is an act of interpretation; it never insists on a final, objective causal chain behind human actions and ideals, because that would be the idolization of the factual that Nietzsche despises.

I do want to make one further comment, which is that while I accept that Pryor rightly defines the meaning I give to ideals, I am also calling for the advocacy of particular ideals, like the ideal of perpetual peace, even as I understand that these are only aesthetic ideas and can always be reconfigured as such. But we are situated in a time and place, and if we are to heed justice we are also called to advocate specific ideals like perpetual peace. When we advocate a configuration of a particular ideal, like perpetual peace or freedom, we also make judgments about how to define those ideals within a configuration. Meanwhile, we are called upon to develop critiques of the misuse of ideals, or their blatantly hypocritical deployment, as in the case of the Bush Administration's appeal to "freedom" to justify the war in Iraq. I would argue strongly against the position that attributes good faith to the Bush administration in their defense of the war in Iraq as justified by the ideal of freedom. Perhaps I am more of a Marxist than Pryor, but in place of the ideal of freedom for the justification of the war, I would put the crass material interest in oil and an ideological push for hegemonic control over the destiny of other nations.[19] My strong opposition to the war in Iraq and my critique of the notion that this war could ever be rooted in an ideal of freedom does not mean, of course, that I deny that there are competing configurations of what freedom means and that the contest over those definitions is politically and ethically important. Ultimately, I am in complete agreement with Pryor's reading of my work, to the effect that defending ideals is always an ongoing task that can never separate itself from "the historical conditions of that defense."

The significance of the two meanings of the future I have defended for theory can help us rethink some of the accusations against political theory, and more specifically against John Rawls that argue his entire theory is meant to guard us against politics. As I have defended hypothetical experiments in the imagination such as Rawls' veil of ignorance, they cannot determine principles of justice once and for all. The work they can do is more limited; they can help us imagine what it might mean if we did not allow our so-called natural fate to determine our place in social hierarchies. As Adam Thurschwell points out in this volume, my radical feminist liberalism, as he calls it, which seeks to reconcile the notion of the imaginary domain with Kant's idea of the social contract ultimately relies, at least in *At the Heart of Freedom*, on a reinterpretation of Hegel's philosophical narrative. This narrative is about how human beings come to claim their freedom from social hierarchies in a modern liberal society. Thurswell also rightly notes that I was dissatisfied with my initial Rawlsian defense of the imaginary domain. I defended the imaginary domain as a minimum condition of individuation; I did so under Rawls' claim that the conditions of self-respect would be recognized in a politically liberal society as an important common good. As Thurschwell argues there were two problems with this formulation that caused me to adjust my own position. The first problem was that this defense of the imaginary domain turned it into an empirical question, or at least one with an empirical base in that we were to ask whether the imaginary domain was necessary for minimum conditions of individuation and thus necessary for conditions of self-respect. I spent a great deal of the book trying to resolve the empirical answer to this question.

The second problem, as Thurschwell argues, was ultimately that it reduced my attempt to reconcile sameness and difference to Rawls' own notion of a ground of sameness that justice should be guaranteed if all citizens are to be able to participate in a liberal democratic society. Jay Bernstein, in his discussion of the *Imaginary Domain*, does not note that I no longer use Rawls in the same way as in *At the Heart of Freedom* where I move instead to a conception of somatic freedom. This type of somatic freedom can be reconciled with Kant's social contract but not commensurate upon it. Instead, as Thurschwell rightly notes my defense of somatic freedom follows from a move beyond Kant's own notion of subjective freedom that accepted certain natural inequalities as unmovable. Following Hegel, I argued that the liberation of the subject from naturalized, stratified differentiations that defined its role under feudalism could be extended to our sexuate being in that we are no more fated to have our sexuate being defined in terms of our current gender hierarchy then we are fated to live in predetermined social and economic roles associated with serfdom. There is a sense then that we are once again returned to the imagination in that the imaginary domain is meant to operate on two levels. First, it is meant to render visible sexual difference as something other then fate in the form of gender. Thus, it shows us the imaginary dimension of our sexuate being in the first place. Second, by providing the moral and legal space depended by the first move of the imagination, as it is relevant to sexuate being, we could re-inscribe into law the recognition that our fate as sexuate creatures need not find any natural constraint that would serve to justify continuing gender hierarchy or patriarchy.

There is a sense, then, that a law framed in this way can actually produce a new envisioning of our sexual difference by denying a certain phenomenality of the so-called reality of gender. In this way the imaginary domain defended as a right would not reproduce or reinscribe the subject in pregiven identities; it would instead reflect the imaginary element in sexuate identity itself.[20] But for all that I have said about the argument that I made in the *Philosophy of the Limit* that we are called to political theory, and more specifically its juridical variant, by an ethical command to do justice, we must not avoid the state or law as site of struggle. More important, despite my insistence on the facilitating force of the imagination, and yet at the same time the limits of the envisionable, I am only too well aware that politics as actual struggles on-the-ground often burst apart any preimagined scheme and even the ideals that purportedly guide those struggles.

In my first book, *Beyond Accommodation*, I sought to invert the political and ethical significance of Jacques Lacan's famous line "woman does not exist." My purpose was in a sense to show that through a deconstructive reading of Lacan the view of the feminine as what could not be symbolized adequately paradoxically holds open a place for a possible future beyond sexual difference that could not be captured by the realm of the intelligible. Judith Butler has beautifully described my use of the feminine in that first book:

> I find it very interesting when Drucilla says that she was persuaded by me, because I actually experienced myself as being persuaded by her to some degree. One of the things I was persuaded by was the use of the feminine as a category that does not describe something that already exists but actually inaugurates a certain kind of future within language and within intelligibility, inaugurating a future of intelligibility that is not yet fully known now. This utopian dimension actually led me to reconsider what it is that we've all been talking about under the rubric of essentialism when we use that term, and especially when we use it in relation to Irigaray.[21]

In that work I try to critically appropriate Irigaray's idea of *mimesis* in that we can, by playing with what remains beyond intelligibility, help to bring to the surface a mark of the feminine opening us to the future.

The feminine, in a sense, could expose the contingent nature of gender or any form of sexual difference. There was however a possible tension at play when I wrote of the need to open up and, as a result, symbolize and resymbolize the meaning of the feminine within sexual difference within any contested political or cultural arena. I distinguished this use of the feminine, however, as not best defined by Gayatri Spivak's strategic essentialism because there was no essentialism at risk here. Through my reading of Derrida I suggested that we can see how Jacques Lacan's rigorous distinctions among the imaginary, the symbolic, and the real, at least how he made those distinctions in his earlier work, could not hold. Thus the feminine could not be definitively pushed under to render any symbolization of the feminine impossible.

My hope was to show that there was not necessarily a tension between these two projects because the radical otherness of the feminine, if it cannot be neatly relegated to the unknowable realm of the real, can as a result be what can be played with to transform on a whole different level the symbolic meaning of feminine sexual difference. I emphasize this deconstructive reading, not so much of Lacan, but more important of the potential radical effect of the othering of the feminine in Lacan's work because I sought to suggest that in a profound sense this other feminine disrupted the realm of being and beings we associate with what both Irigaray and Derrida have called the "phallologocentric tradition" of Western philosophy.

In my later work, I instead choose to define this other place as beyond even the reach of the feminine as it was to be given meaning as that which disrupted precisely because it could not "be" within the phallologocentric terms of Western philosophy. It was in this use of the feminine as what was radically other and thus the "place" of a different future that could not yet fully be known, including a future of our sexual difference, that I found disagreement with Simone de Beauvoir.

In her debate with Irigaray de Beauvoir explicitly rejected what she saw as a utopianization of women's oppression. I hope to show that Irigaray, in a deep sense, had it right that we could invert the meaning of this radical otherness so as to challenge the order of being itself, which promised to ascertain the conceptual. Although I sided with Irigaray in her debate with de Beauvoir, at least at the time of *Beyond Accommodation*, I in no way wanted to do so in a disrespectful manner. I agree with Jay Bernstein that de Beauvoir's work has not been given the significant place it should have even in feminist philosophical circles. I indeed accept his gift and invitation to return to de Beauvoir and reread her seriously as an ally of the imaginary domain. But, having accepted with gratitude his gift I need also to note that he fundamentally misunderstands Lacan in that he attributes to him a defense of oedipal complimentarity.

Lacan's whole point, if one can dare to risk such an assertion, is that oedipal complimentarity is impossible because the feminine cannot exist within the symbolic order. Thus, there can be no sexual relationship. It is impossible to understand my earlier use of the feminine without first grasping the way in which Lacan completely breaks away with all psychoanalytic theories that seek to defend oedipal complimentarity. Bernstein suggests that we can extract from de Beauvoir what he calls the "mimetic preacquisition" of gender identity. I will not trace all of Bernstein's subtle steps here, but let me just say there is a difficulty in de Beauvoir's own text as to how we are going to put together the materialist history she provides us on the difference between the genders with the psychic reinscription of those identities in lived individuals. The argument suggests that the place of men, even in "primitive" societies, encourages them to develop a being for self because their place as hunters actually inspires risk taking that separates human beings from their natural environment. It has to be noted here that anthropologist after anthropologist has challenged any simple notion of gender identity in a "primitive" society, especially ones that can be rooted in the division between hunters and gatherers because in the end there is no necessary correlation between these activities and masculine privilege. But the deeper problem is even if there were: why and how would this history be passed down psychically? If one were to put it simply the whole role of psychoanalysis in left-wing theory has been to show us that whatever the material realities are of gender roles, there is no simple causal chain between those realities and how they are internalized.

In order to show the imperfection of all internalizations we need to have a complex theory of fantasy and symbolization, as these relate to the unconscious. And, as I have argued, in his most illuminating moments not only does Lacan show us how this internalization of gender identity will necessarily fail, but he does so by offering us a linguistic account of the unconscious that allows us to maintain a complex relationship between history and psychic reality. In Bernstein's account of mimetic preaquisition of gender identity boys and girls are differentiated from one another through the differential meaning of the status of *en-soi* in that little boys and little girls both seek to be what the other makes of him or her. Thus, during the *en-soi* period little boys are paradoxically forced to act like little men and, using Sartre's language, become ironically inauthentic by asserting a masculinized identity as the necessary source of authenticity.

The missing link in this theory of mimetic preaquisition of gender identity is how and why these roles are internalized and perpetuated. It is not enough to say that in history men and women have been "made up" to repeat certain forms of existence generation after generation, particularly after everything we have gained from reading Judith Butler and her work *Gender Trouble*, which shows how the performance of gender roles is as disruptive of gender categorization as it is of promoting their establishment. My question to Bernstein is: does not he risk the danger of all historicism in that the place for resistance through a complex process of internalization is rendered incoherent? The real question then becomes: does Bernstein believe there is a need for psychoanalytic theory to explain resistance to as well as capitulation to gender hierarchy?

The utopian aspiration of *Beyond Accommodation* remains in all of my work. Part of the utopian aspiration is indeed what Thurschwell points to, or the idea that we are not fated to be gendered (at least not in any form we recognize now). Feminism is then, in a deep sense, an aspiration to somatic freedom, as Thurschwell defines it. I have suggested that in 1995 when I wrote the *Imaginary Domain*, and even in 1998 when I wrote *At the Heart of Freedom*, that we needed to justify a very specific form of Kantian liberalism as the way in which we could theorize the social bond. But I have since come to question whether Kantian social theory is the only necessary theoretical undertaking, at least when we attempt to defend something like the imaginary domain as a legal or moral right.

Like so many other people of my generation the victorious struggle against apartheid in South Africa was a source of hope and inspiration. I was led to South Africa initially to simply try to learn how and why the struggle was possible such that it led to victory and not simply degenerate into senseless violence and civil war. Of course, I was also concerned with critiques of imperial academic scholarship that have taught us that other cultures and traditions not only can justify ideals such as human rights but even be more able to foundationally support them, than perhaps their supposedly superior Western counterparts. Of course, since 1989 I have become increasingly concerned that my attempt to reconcile radical liberal feminism with socialism seemed to run afoul with triumphal neoliberal notions that had very little attachment to the Kantian social contract. The question began to haunt me: how can we begin to think about the social bond so as to reconcile what is best in a moral understanding of liberalism with the aspiration to socialism? It was too evident that this had been asked and continues to be asked in South Africa. I wanted to learn from a country in which questions of social injustice are very much alive and on the political and social agenda.

In 2003, I began a project called the Ubuntu Project in South Africa. The project is still underway, and I am even more aware about how much I need to learn about *ubuntu*. But what is clear so far is that *ubuntu* allows us to understand the inadequacy of conceiving a social bond through any notion of the social contract and with it the idea of reciprocal simultaneity. These do not yield a rich enough understanding of how we are bonded together so as to justify the kind of obligations that we have to undertake to fully realize the Bill of Rights of the South African Constitution. Indeed, for all that I have written about the significance of dignity in a 2004 debate with Judge Albie Sachs I argued against dignity as the sole ideal through which the constitution was to be interpreted. I suggested instead that *ubuntu* could give us a more far-reaching explanation of the kind of obligations the citizens of South Africa would have to undertake if they were to realize second- and third-generation rights, which include not only social and economic rights but the right of generations to come to inherit an intact planet.

Indeed, as this project has developed we are lead all the way back to Heidegger in that the meaning of *ubuntu* is inseparable from the question of whether African jurisprudence actually gives us a different enough notion of law capable of escaping from Heidegger's accusation that all notions of law, including Kant's moral understanding of the social contract, will fall prey to technological thinking. Thus, the Ubuntu Project has led me back to some of the deepest inspirations in my work and to most pressing issues: how is the radical transformation of how we are human together possible? And so, we wonder if the critique of eurocentrism is searing enough and different enough from Western conceptions that it can offer a challenge to the so-called economic mandates of neoliberalism, and ultimately to Heidegger's pessimism to actively attempt to change the world. Is there a beyond to the Heideggarian nightmare in which man is eaten up by his own accomplishments? Perhaps all of my work has been devoted to writing against Heidegger that we ultimately cannot know whether there is this beyond once and for all and absolutely. The very mention of this beyond is itself a trace that confirms its presence and gives us a simple intervention into such Heideggerian pessimism: the possibility for something better.

NOTES

1. As so often in the past I am indebted to the careful reading and loving support of my dear friends Maureen MacGrogan and Sally Ruddick. Of course, I am also indebted to my two editors Ben Pryor and Renee Heberle for all of the work they put in to make this volume possible.

2. Immanuel Kant, *Groundwork on the Metaphysics of Morals*, trans. H. J. Paton trans. (New York: Harper Torchbooks, 1964), 103.

3. Drucilla Cornell, *Between Women and Generations: Legacies of Dignity*, second edition (New York: Rowman and Littlefield, 2005), 56–57.

4. See for example Henry Allison's excellent discussion of the difference between the *Groundwork* and the *Critique of Practical Reason* in that Kant seemingly breaks with the *Groundwork*, which attempts to negatively show our freedom and access to the intelligible realm of moral ends to his position in the *Critique of Practical Reason* that such negative freedom is in fact a deduction from the fact of reason understood as our consciousness of the moral law, which in turn shapes in principle our knowledge to differentiate between right and wrong. In Kant of course it is not that we actually do the right thing; it is that we would have the consciousness of what is the right thing for us to do. In Henry Allison, *Kant's Theory of Freedom* (Cambridge, England: Cambridge University Press, 1990), 242.

5. Christine M. Korsgaard, *Creating the Kingdom of Ends* (Cambridge, England: Cambridge University Press, 1996).

6. Emmanuel Levinas, *Humanism and the Other*, trans. Nidra Poller (Chicago: University of Illinois Press, 2003), 57.

7. Emmanuel Levinas, *Entre Nous: Thinking of the Other*, trans. Michael Smith and Barbara Harshav (New York: Columbia University Press, 1998), 34, emphasis added.

8. Emmanuel Levinas, *Humanism and the Other*, trans. Nidra Poller (Chicago: University of Illinois Press, 2003), 57.

9. Martin Heidegger, "Letter on Humanism," in *Martin Heidegger: Basic Writings*, David Krell ed. (New York: Harper & Row, 1977), 210.

10. However, he writes from the standpoint of the Heidegger of *Being and Time* who undoubtedly can be interpreted as moving from Kant's transcendental self to *Dasein*. To quote Richard Kearney: "Thus understood, imagination becomes another name for *Dasein* in that its 'aesthetic' function of time, as the 'formal a priori condition of all experience', makes it essentially receptive to experience, and therefore temporally situated. And it is productive like *Dasein* in its free and spontaneous activity of

projecting like *Dasein* in its free and spontaneous activity of projecting (*entwerfen*) and understanding (*verstehen*) its existential possibilities. In this receptive/productive role of *poiesis*, imagination reveals itself to be the forerunner of *Dasein*." In the Heidegger of *Being and Time*, *Dasein*, or the transcendental imagination, still projects its own freedom and takes responsibility for it. Freedom is no longer an attribute of the human personality in a positive sense but it still works through the third of Kant's imaginative faculties, the anticipation and pre-formation of the future horizons of possibilities.

11. Martin Heidegger, "Letter on Humanism," in *Martin Heidegger: Basic Writings*, 199–200.

12. Emmanuel Levinas, *Humanism and the Other*, trans. Nidra Poller (Chicago: University of Illinois Press, 2003), 61.

13. Richard Kearney, *Poetics of Imagination: Modern to Post-modern* (New York: Fordham University Press, 1998), 232.

14. Karin Van Marle, "The Capabilities Approach, The Imaginary Domain, and Asymmetrical Reciprocity: Feminist Perspectives on Equality and Justice," *Feminist Legal Studies* 11 (2003), 263.

15. Walter Benjamin, *Illuminations: Essays and Reflections*, trans. Harry Zohn (New York: Shocken Books, 1968), 254.

16. In this way of thinking about the visible and invisible I am reinterpreting the profound work of Merleau-Ponty where he suggests that every visible dimension of being is connected to an imaginary dimension because no aspect of being including a shared symbolic world of language can ever be fully visualized by one perspectival field. See generally, Maurice Merleau-Ponty, *The Visible and the Invisible* (Evanston: Northwestern University Press, 1969).

17. Emmanuel Levinas, *Entre Nous: Thinking of the Other*, trans. Michael Smith and Barbara Harshav (New York: Columbia University Press, 1998), 104.

18. Cornell, "The Thinker of the Future" Identities: Journal for Politics, Gender, and Culture Issue 7 (2004), 29.

19. See Noam Chomsky, *Hegemony or Survival: America's Quest for Global Dominance* (New York: Metropolitan Books, 2003), as well as Greg Palast, "Secret U.S. Plans for Iraq's Oil," BBC News, http://news.bbc.co.uk/1/hi/programmes/newsnight/4354269.stm, March 17, 2005. Accessed April 11, 2007.

20. See for example, as someone who worries about the way in which rights reinscribe victim identity, Wendy Brown, *States of Injury* (Princeton: Princeton University Press, 1995).

21. Pheng Cheah and Elizabeth Grosz, "The Future of Sexual Difference: An Interview with Judith Butler and Drucilla Cornell," *Diacritics* 28, (1998), 21.

List of Contributors

ROGER BERKOWITZ, Bard College. Roger Berkowitz's academic interests meld philosophy with the law; he writes and lectures on political theory, legal history, and jurisprudence. He is the author of *The Gift of Science: Leibnitz and the Modern Legal Tradition.* His many honors include the American Jurisprudence Award and three Max-Planck Institute fellowships.

J. M. BERNSTEIN, The New School for Social Research. J. M. Bernstein's interests include American pragmatism, social and political philosophy, critical theory, and Anglo-American philosophy. His publications include *Against Voluptuous Bodies: Adorno's Late Modernism and the Meaning of Painting* (forthcoming), *Classical and Romantic German Aesthetics* (editor), *Adorno: Disenchantment and Ethics, Recovering Ethical Life: Jürgen Habermas and the Future of Critical Theory,* and *The Fate of Art.*

PHENG CHEAH, University of California, Berkeley. Pheng Cheah's interests include eighteenth to twentieth century continental philosophy and critical theory, postcolonial theory and anglophone postcolonial literatures, theories of globalization, philosophy and literature, legal philosophy, social and political thought, and feminist theory. Among Pheng Cheah's publications are *Inhuman Conditions: Cosomopolitanism and Human Rights, Spectral Nationality: Passages of Freedom from Kant to Postcolonial Literatures of Liberation, Cosmopolitics—Thinking and Feeling Beyond the Nation* (edited with Bruce Robbins), and *Thinking Through the Body of the Law* (edited with David Fraser and Judith Grbich).

DRUCILLA CORNELL, Rutgers University. Drucilla Cornell is professor of political science, women's studies, and comparative literature at Rutgers University, currently visiting at the University of Stellenbosch in South Africa.

Prior to beginning her life as an academic, Cornell was a union organizer for a number of years. Other academic appointments include visiting distinguished professor of philosophy at Warwick University, UK; visiting professor of philosophy at SUNY Stonybrook; professor at the National Endowment of the Humanities Summer Institute. A very limited list of her publication includes: *Beyond Accomodation: Ethical Feminism, Deconstruction and the Law*, *The Philosophy of the Limit*, *Transformations: Recollective Imagination and Sexual Difference*, *The Imaginary Domain: Abortion, Pornography, and Sexual Harrassment*, *At the Heart of Freedom: Feminism, Sex, and Equality*, *Just Cause: Freedom, Identity, and Rights*, and *Between Women and Generations: Legacies of Dignity*. Her work has been translated into French, German, Japanese, Serbo-Croation, Portuguese, and Spanish. She lectures widely and has recently given papers and conducted seminars in South Africa, Japan, Serbia, and Macedonia. A produced playwright, productions of her plays "The Dream Cure," "Background Interference," and "Lifeline" have been performed in California, New York, Florida, and Ohio. Her dramatization of James Joyce's *Finnegan's Wake* runs every year in Dublin, Ireland.

CAROLIN EMCKE, Yale University. Carolin Emcke is a journalist and philosopher who studied philosophy, history, and political science in London, Frankfurt/M, and Harvard. Dr. Emcke is a staff writer for the German News Magazine *Der Spiegel*, covering human rights violations and wars. Her publications include: *Echoes of Violence: Letters from a War Reporter* (previously published as *Landschaften der Gewalt—Briefe)*, and *Kollektive Identitäten: Socialphilozophische Grundlagen*.

ELIZABETH GROSZ, Rutgers University. Elizabeth Grosz taught in the Department of Philosophy at the University of Sydney, in the Centre for Critical Theory and Cultural Studies at Monash University, and in the Departments of Comparative Literature and English at SUNY Buffalo before coming to Rutgers. Her areas of research are contemporary French philosophy, feminist theory, and theories of space and time. A few of her many publications include: *The Nick of Time: Politics, Evolution, and the Untimely*, *Volatile Bodies: Toward a Corporeal Feminism*, *Becomings: Exploration in Time, Memory and Future*.

RENÉE J. HEBERLE, University of Toledo. Renee Heberle teaches in the Department of Political Science, the Department of Women's and Gender Studies, and in Law and Social Thought at UT. She is the editor of and contributor to *Feminist Interpretations of Theodor Adorno*, co-editor with Victoria Grace and contributor to *Theorizing Sexual Violence* (forthcoming), and author of "Disciplining Gender, Or: Are Women Getting Away with Murder?" (*Studies in Law, Politics and Society*), and "Deconstructive Strategies and the Movement Against Sexual Violence" (*Hypatia*).

MARTIN J. BECK MATUŠTÍK, Purdue University. Martin J. Beck Matuštík received his Ph.D. in from Fordham University. A student signatory to *"Charta 77"* in Czechoslovakia, Matuštík's work engages with globalization and the challenge of radical evil. He is the author of six single author books, two edited collections, and a co-editor with Patricia Huntington of New Critical Theory, a series at Rowman and Littlefield Publishers. Among his books are *Jurgen Habermas: A Philosophical-Political Profile, Postnational Identity: Critical Theory and Existential Philosophy in Habermas, Kierkegaard, and Havel,* and, most recently, *Radical Evil and the Scarcity of Hope: Postsecular Meditations* (the work in his chapter here is expanded upon in *Radical Evil*). His areas of research are critical theory, social and political philosophy, nineteenth and twentieth century continental philosophy and continental philosophy of religion.

SARA MURPHY, Gallatin School for Individualized Study, NYU. Sara Murphy's research interests include nineteenth-century literary cultures, autobiography and memoir, critical theory and feminist theory, psychoanalysis, literature and liberalism, and visual culture. Her recent articles and presentations have focused on women's writing, psychoanalysis, autobiography, and multiculturalism.

BENJAMIN PRYOR, University of Toledo. Benjamin Pryor is an Associate Professor and Chair of Philosophy and the Co-Director of the Program in Law and Social Thought at the University of Toledo. His research interests include continental philosophy and its relation to legal studies, particularly in the thought of Michel Foucault and Jean-Luc Nancy. He is the author of "Giving Way to Freedom: A Note on Schelling and Nancy" (*Schelling Now*), "Law in Abandon: Nancy and the Critical Study of Law" (*Law and Critique*), and "Counter-Remembering the Enlightenment" (*Philosophy Today*).

ADAM THURSCHWELL, Cleveland Marshall College of Law, Case Western University. Adam Thurschwell is currently a visiting professor in the American University College of Law. He has represented defendants in capital prosecutions, including Terry Nichols, one of the two individuals charged in the federal Oklahoma City bombing case. Recent publications include: *Capital Punishment* (forthcoming), "Specters and Scholars: Derrida and the Tragedy of Political Thought" (*German Law Journal*).

KARIN VAN MARLE, University of Pretoria. Karin van Marle is an associate professor of law in the Department of Legal History, Comparative Law and Jurisprudence. She is author of "The Multiplicity of Transition" in the *Comparative and International Law Journal of South Africa,* "In Support of a Revival of Utopian Thinking, the Imaginary Domain and Ethical Interpretation" in the *Journal of South African Law,* and "Laughter, Refusal, Friendship: Thoughts on a 'Jurisprudence of Generosity'" in *Stellenbosch Law Review.*

Index

301.092
LOR. I
#524278